Americanizing the Movies
and "Movie-Mad" Audiences,
1910–1914

The publisher gratefully acknowledges the generous contribution to this book provided by Eric Papenfuse and Catherine Lawrence.

Americanizing the Movies and "Movie-Mad" Audiences, 1910–1914

Richard Abel

UNIVERSITY OF CALIFORNIA PRESS
Berkeley   Los Angeles   London

University of California Press, one of the most distinguished university presses in the United States, enriches lives around the world by advancing scholarship in the humanities, social sciences, and natural sciences. Its activities are supported by the UC Press Foundation and by philanthropic contributions from individuals and institutions. For more information, visit www.ucpress.edu.

University of California Press
Berkeley and Los Angeles, California

University of California Press, Ltd.
London, England

Several chapters and entr'actes are revised and expanded versions of earlier essays, which are listed in the acknowledgments on pages xvi–xvii. The A. A. Milne epigraph is from *Winnie-the-Pooh* (New York: E. P. Dutton, 1926), 70.

Library of Congress Cataloging-in-Publication Data

Abel, Richard, 1941–
    Americanizing the movies and "movie-mad" audiences, 1910–1914 / Richard Abel.
        p. cm.
    Includes bibliographical references and index.
    ISBN-13, 978-0-520-24742-0 (cloth: alk. paper)
    ISBN-10, 0-520-24742-6 (cloth : alk. paper)
    ISBN-13, 978-0-520-24743-7 (pbk.: alk. paper)
    ISBN-10, 0-520-24743-4 (pbk. : alk. paper)
        1. Motion pictures—United States—History.   2. Motion pictures—Social aspects—United States.   3. Nationalism—United States.   I. Title: Americanizing the movies and "movie-mad" audiences, 1910–1914.   II. Title.
    PN1993.5.U6A67 2006
    791.430973—dc22   2005025769

Manufactured in the United States of America

15 14 13 12 11 10 09 08 07 06
10 9 8 7 6 5 4 3 2 1

This book is printed on New Leaf EcoBook 50, a 100% recycled fiber of which 50% is de-inked post-consumer waste, processed chlorine-free. EcoBook 50 is acid-free and meets the minimum requirements of ANSI/ASTM D5634–01 (*Permanence of Paper*).

Writing, not an automatic, but a problematic History.

LUCIEN FEBVRE
Combats pour l'histoire

It would be sheer fantasy to imagine that for each historical problem there is a unique type of document with a specific sort of use. On the contrary, the deeper the research, the more the light of evidence must converge from sources of different kinds.

MARC BLOCH
The Historian's Craft

History can work for you, you know how to use it.

ELMORE LEONARD
Tishomingo Blues

è🍂

[Eeyore] turned and walked slowly down the stream for twenty yards, splashed across it, and walked slowly back on the other side. Then he looked at himself in the water again.
"As I thought," he said. "No better from *this* side."

A. A. MILNE
Winnie-the-Pooh

CONTENTS

ILLUSTRATIONS

ACKNOWLEDGMENTS

Several institutions provided crucial support for the research and writing of this book. Generous funding came from a number of sources: a 2000–2001 National Endowment for the Humanities Fellowship, a sabbatical leave from Drake University, a Faculty Research Grant from Drake University, a Research Grant from the Center for the Humanities at Drake University, research funds from the College of Literature, Sciences, and the Arts at the University of Michigan, and a timely research grant from Vetenskapsradet/Swedish Research Council awarded to an international research team for acquiring source material. The research also benefited greatly from Cowles Library's Inter-Library Loan Services at Drake University and the Periodical Department of the Hatcher Graduate Library at the University of Michigan.

I am greatly indebted to the readers of a draft manuscript for the University of California Press: Lea Jacobs offered invaluable ideas for reorganizing and completing the manuscript and, later, for making several further revisions; an anonymous reader also prodded me to make my own position more clear in the introduction, pointed me to several productive sources, and flagged my more speculative claims. During the lengthy period of writing (continually delayed by the task of editing the Routledge *Encyclopedia of Early Cinema*), a host of colleagues and friends offered encouragement, created forums for debate and discussion, helped to locate sources, raised crucial questions, posed counterarguments, and pushed me to develop further several lines of analysis. They include Robert C. Allen, Rick Altman, Constance Balides, Jennifer Bean, Giorgio Bertellini, Robert Birchard, Mats Björkin, Ivo Blom, Eileen Bowser, Paolo Cherchi Usai, Scott Curtis, Marina Dahlquist, Nico de Klerk, John Fullerton, Douglas Gomery, Tom Gunning, Daan Hertog, Steven Higgins, Catherine Jurca, Charlie Keil, Antonia Lant, James

Latham, Patrick Loughney, Terry McDonald, Richard Maltby, Madeline Matz, Paul Moore, Jan Olsson, Shawn Shimpach, Charles Silver, Ben Singer, Janet Staiger, Shelley Stamp, Melvyn Stokes, Gaylyn Studler, Judith Thissen, William Uricchio, Nanna Verhoeff, Gregory Waller, and Kristen Whissel. My parents (Owen and Ruth Abel), brother (Ted Abel), and sister-in-law (Deb Abel) graciously put up with me on a research trip to northeastern Ohio.

I am grateful to the facilities and generous staff of the following libraries and archives: the Academy of Motion Picture Arts and Sciences: Margaret Herrick Library (especially Barbara Hall); Cleveland Public Library (especially Evelyn Ward); Boston Public Library; George Eastman House: Film Department; Huntington Library; Lawrence Public Library; Lowell Public Library; Lynn Public Library; Marnan Collection, Minneapolis (Margaret and Nancy Bergh); Minnesota Historical Society Library; Museum of Modern Art: Film Department; National Film/Television Archive, London; Nederlands Filmmuseum, Amsterdam; Pawtucket History Research Center (Elizabeth Johnson); Pawtucket Public Library; Rhode Island Historical Society Library; Rochester Public Library; Stark County District Library; State Historical Society of Iowa Library; Toledo Public Library; University of Iowa Library: Special Collections; U.S. Library of Congress: Motion Picture and Sound Recording Division, Manuscript Room, and Periodicals Room; and Youngstown Public Library.

At the University of California Press, Mary Francis consistently conveyed her enthusiastic support for the project, patiently accepted the delays in writing, and with Kalicia Pivirotto, deftly shepherded the manuscript through several stages of evaluation. Rachel Berchten managed the tough task of overseeing the multiple phases of editing and production with grace, and Susan Ecklund expertly handled the copyediting.

Encore une fois, I pay tribute to my partner, best reader, and collaborator, Barbara Hodgdon, an acclaimed scholar in her own right, an exceptional writer, and a mesmerizing performer, especially in the field of Shakespeare in performance.

Several chapters and entr'actes are revised and expanded versions of earlier essays:

"The 'Culture War' of Sensational Melodrama, 1910–1914," in Yvonne Tasker, ed., *Action and Adventure Cinema* (Routledge, 2004), 31–51.

"The Passing (Picture) Show in the Industrial Heartland: The Early 1910s," in John Fullerton and Jan Olsson, eds., *Allegories of Communication* (John Libbey, 2004), 321–32.

"The 'Imagined Community' of the Western, 1910–1913," in Charlie Keil and Shelley Stamp, eds., *American Cinema's Transitional Era: Audiences, Institutions, Practices* (University of California Press, 2004), 131–70.

"Finding the French on American Screens, 1910–1914," in John Fullerton, ed., *Screen Culture: History and Textuality* (John Libbey, 2004), 137–57.

"Reframing the Vaudeville/Moving Pictures Debate, with Illustrated Songs," in Leonardo Quaresima and Laura Vichi, eds., *The Tenth Muse: Cinema and Other Arts* (Forum, 2001), 473–90.

"A Marriage of Ephemeral Discourses: Newspapers and Moving Pictures, 1910–1914," *Cinema et Cie* 1 (Fall 2001), 59–83.

"Early Nonfiction Now and Then: 'Phantom' Viewing in the Archives," *Aura* 2.3 (1996), 4–11.

L'Envoi of Moving Pictures

When the last photo-play has been written,
And in the city and village has been tried;
When films, reels, and screens are forgotten,
And all pantomime actors have died.
We shan't rest, for why should we need be
Unamused for a season or two?
There'll be sure to be some one at work on
Amusement schemes vital and new.

He who likes naval things shall be happy;
He shall sit in his upholstered chair,
And drink in such joys of the future
As will make him sit straight up and stare;
He shall have many wonders to choose from.
Both from earth and the planets around,
Yet many will long for the pictures
With which the earth used to abound.

And many a graybeard shall praise them—
"Ah, they were the things!" they'll exclaim.
And the new generation will wonder
At their enduring hold upon fame.
So some manager wiser than others,
Will hunt up the films of to-day,
And have a most brilliant revival
Down the whole of the Great Milky Way!

HARVEY PEAKE,
Motion Picture Story Magazine
(June 1912)

Introduction

Are you an imitation American?
HERBERT KAUFMAN,
Cleveland Leader (20 August 1911), C2

This book can be read as a companion to *The Red Rooster Scare: Making Cinema American, 1900–1910* (University of California Press, 1999), since it takes up some of the latter's claims and arguments and extends them into the early 1910s. It argues, for instance, that the Americanization process—specifically, the concerns about constructing a distinctive American national identity—continued to frame early cinema's institutionalization as a popular mass entertainment, particularly if certain categories of spectators formed its core audience—namely, recent working-class immigrants, women (especially young working women), and children. It also argues that early cinema, as a mass entertainment, has to be conceived in terms that reach beyond the production of film texts and their promotion in the trade press to focus on distribution and exhibition practices, as well as regional or even local discursive traces of their promotion and reception.

Yet this book differs from the earlier one in that its analyses are shaped by several related theoretical constructs. The initial impetus came from Benedict Anderson's notion of a new kind of "imagined community," the *nation,* that emerged through "the interaction between a system of production and productive relations (capitalism), a technology of communication (print), and . . . a general condition of irremediable linguistic diversity."[1] Specifically, Anderson focuses on "the novel and the newspaper" as forms of "print capitalism" that fostered a national consciousness in the nineteenth century by creating "unified fields of exchange and communication," giving "a new fixity to language," and, in turn, giving certain languages—for instance, English—more power.[2] As a corollary to his provocative framework, this book focuses on moving pictures as a new technology of communication, one that epitomizes the general transformation at the turn of the last century that produced a more or less unified arena of exchange and communication in-

3

creasingly dominated by visual culture rather than by print culture. My own interest in the role that moving pictures played in this process is twofold. One is how the diverse audiences attracted to moving pictures, much like Anderson's network of people joined together as readers, constituted—or were represented as constituting (or not)—an "imagined community of nationality." Yet another goes beyond Anderson to analyze how the films themselves, or certain kinds of films, and the stars that performed in them may have represented an "imagined community of nationality" on the screen.

Anderson's "imagined community of nationality" seems strikingly relevant for a creole society like the United States in the early twentieth century, when a more or less homogeneous "white nation" was "imagined" in the context of extreme, even violent, social fractures—class, race, and ethnicity being the principal fault lines.[3] Or, as Eric Hobsbawm so succinctly puts it, describing the United States' "problem" of how to assimilate a "heterogeneous mass" of immigrants: "Americans had to be made."[4] Consequently, my analyses also are shaped by a more complicated notion of "Americanization," the most widespread of the terms used by those concerned with the issue of national identity at the time—others included "the melting pot" and "cultural pluralism."[5] The late nineteenth century, Matthew Jacobson and others argue, saw "a fundamental revision of whiteness itself" as the basis of national identity.[6] In the earlier part of the century, the "salient feature of whiteness" had been its contrast to "nonwhiteness," or, as Alexander Saxton bluntly writes, "white citizens" were given "equal opportunities. . . through the enslavement of African Americans, the extermination of Indians, and territorial expansion at the expense of Indians and Mexicans."[7] Now, its internal divisions—"the shifting perception of racial difference *among* 'free white persons'. . . took on a new and pressing significance."[8] This was especially noticeable in "the discourse of immigration restriction," which, under the influence of Anglo-Saxonism and eugenics, "favored a scheme of hierarchically ordered white races."[9] Yet this discourse, Jacobson adds, had its ironic "compensations": if the Irish, Italians, Jews, and Slavs became "less and less white in debates over who should be allowed to embark for American shores," they also became "whiter and whiter in the debates over who should be granted the full rights of citizenship" (in contrast to Asians and American "Negroes").[10] It was this further distinction, or emphasis, that divided those who sought "to protect the national character from the dangers posed by the immense immigration of the times" and those who sought "to assist the immigrants in adjusting to the strange and often harsh conditions of life they encountered."[11]

These concepts frame the book's exploration of how US cinema was inextricably bound up with Americanization and the process of imagining a national identity during the early 1910s. In one sense, my aim is to complicate and make more specific Miriam Hansen's recent claim that the later classical Hollywood cinema partly owed its success abroad to the way that moving pictures and moviegoing "at the domestic level" forged an American "mass public out of an ethnically and culturally heterogeneous society."[12] In another sense, my aim is to reintroduce gender—drawing on and sometimes modifying the work of Hansen, Judith Mayne, Janet Staiger, Kathryn Fuller, Lauren Rabinovitz, Shelley Stamp, Jennifer Bean, and others on early cinema[13]—as a significant category in the analysis of imagining a national identity, especially in terms of how women could be represented on screen and addressed as an assumed audience. Attempting to fulfill either aim in a limited space, of course, demands choices. Accordingly, the book takes up several related topoi that reveal the different ways in which the shifting principles of exclusion and inclusion so characteristic of Americanization played out.

One of the more useful is the sensational melodrama and what Shelley Streeby calls its surrounding "culture of sensation," which "racialized bodies" as more or less "alien."[14] Sensational melodrama, as Ben Singer has shown,[15] would have been long familiar to moviegoers in a variety of forms—from the fast-paced action in the dime novels or story papers of the 1880s,[16] to the "blood-and-thunder sensationalism" of the popular 10–20–30 stage melodramas in the 1890s and 1900s.[17] The latter retained the basic elements of earlier melodrama—"moral opposition, pathos, extreme emotion, and structural incoherence"—but their crucial attraction was "graphic action and intense spectacles of danger," particularly as worked out in "sensation scenes." By 1907–8, these stage melodramas were undergoing what would turn into a precipitous decline as their audience of working-class and white-collar amusement seekers suddenly abandoned them en masse for moving picture shows. Singer is wonderfully insightful in analyzing these forerunners to the serial-queen melodrama of the middle and late 1910s. However, he barely glances at the period of the early 1910s and at probably the most consistently popular sensational melodramas at the time: the western film (the cowboy, cowboy girl, and Indian picture) and its rival, the Civil War film (especially the "girl spy" pictures), whose production and circulation coincided with the Golden Jubilee commemorations of the war's major battles. Nor does he consider two seemingly disparate forms of sensational melodrama—the detective film and animal picture—that seem nearly as important: not only did they, along with the western, lead to popular series and serials (often starring women), but they were produced by European companies as well, and the French crime thrillers in particular came to be seen as quite different from their American counterpart—and *foreign*. This distinction between what was validated as *American* in contrast to what was perceived as *foreign* or *alien* also played out in two other ways: the uneven development of the distribution systems for both variety film programs and feature films, as well as the swift emergence of a highly publicized movie star system.

A parallel, equally useful topos encompasses exhibition practices, programming formats, audiences, and moviegoing patterns. Given the size and diversity of such a country as the United States, choices here are perhaps even more difficult. In contrast to the usual focus on metropolises such as New York or Chicago or to the recent claims for researching rural areas, especially in the South,[18] I have selected three regions of the country that proved crucial, although not often acknowledged, to the emergence of nickelodeons and then picture theaters (the Warner brothers, for instance, originated in Youngstown, Ohio; Louis B. Mayer, in Haverhill and Lawrence, Massachusetts), not only because of their relatively high population density but also because of the extensive railway transportation system that bound their major urban areas together and linked all three along the country's northern corridor. Those three selected regions—part of New England (eastern Massachusetts and Rhode Island), northern Ohio, and the upper Midwest (from Missouri through Iowa to Minnesota)—also were marked by differences in settlement history, industrial base, and immigrant population. That, in turn, means that they offer a unique opportunity to examine, with some degree of specificity, how moving pictures could both foster a more or less homogeneous *American* mass public and serve to reinforce an "ethnically and culturally heterogeneous society." Moreover, city newspapers in all three regions generally looked with considerable favor on moving pictures: in fact, W. Stephen Bush, addressing the New York Woman's Press Club in early 1913, praised "the dailies of the Middle West," alluding specifically to the *Cleveland Leader,* for first having "begun to take the motion picture seriously."[19] As a consequence, the book's arguments about "imagining community" in US cinema during this period are grounded not only in surviving archive film prints and an extensive trade press discourse but also in still largely unexamined newspaper ads, stories, and columns.

This book focuses on the historical period of 1910–14 for several reasons. By 1910, according to *Nickelodeon,* the "moving picture revolution" had succeeded in creating "an absolutely new form of popular amusement" in the United States.[20] Moreover, as *The Red Rooster Scare* demonstrates, the new amusement was sufficiently Americanized, now that the challenge posed by Pathé-Frères, whose French films once dominated the nickelodeon era, had been overcome. Still, that Americanization had to be sustained through what is often called the "era of transition" and particularly during the years prior to the outbreak of World War I (in August 1914), after which "foreign" films nearly were eliminated from the American market. Yet setting the book's boundary at 1914 has to do with more than the war. By then, the "Independents" had succeeded in their struggle with the "Trust," and the groundwork was laid for the emergence of the Hollywood studio system. Developing steadily from 1910–11 on, multiple-reel and then feature-length films (nonfiction as well as fiction) radically changed distribution and exhibition practices, including the musical component of programs: orchestras and organs, and their "fine music," for instance, replaced illustrated songs and/or vaude-

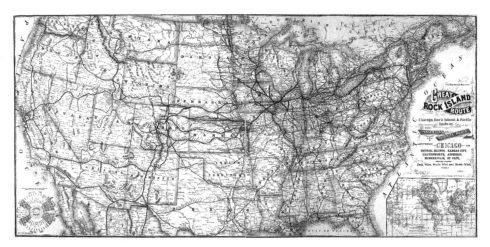

FIG. 1. Rock Island Railroad map, 1893.

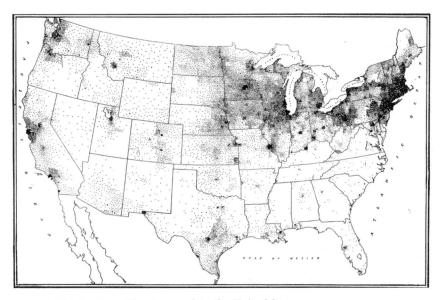

FIG. 2. Distribution of foreign stock in the United States, 1910.

ville acts as popular attractions. As a kind of culmination of this change, new picture palaces such as the Strand in New York, managed by S. L. "Roxy" Rothapfel, were opening by early 1914.[21] Along with these features, as well as the parallel development of series and then serials of "connected stories,"[22] both of which served to regularize the variety program format in ex-

FIG. 3. Clyde Wolfe (seated left) and the Odeon Theater orchestra, Canton, ca. 1913.

hibition, a system of publicity developed predicated on "picture personalities" that, by 1914, already was proving a major attraction for "picture fans."[23] Finally, as *Moving Picture World* noted, again in 1914, public interest by now had led many newspapers to publish a weekly page devoted to moving pictures, and some were even printing daily syndicated material on star players as well as picture brands, all of which was "eagerly gobbled up by the reader who [was] interested in the 'movies.' "[24]

Because of its dual concern for moving pictures and moviegoing, this book is structured, somewhat in the manner of *The Red Rooster Scare,* along two parallel trajectories. The primary trajectory begins with a chapter on the Americanization of film distribution (including both variety and feature programs), encompasses four chapters on the development of American sensational melodramas—westerns (in two parts), Civil War films, detective films and animal pictures, specifically in contrast to French crime thrillers—and ends with a sixth chapter on American movie stars. A second trajectory of "entr'actes" moves through a series of relevant (yet little-known) transformations that characterized exhibition and reception: the development of different venues, program practices, and audiences (again, in two parts); the place and function of illustrated songs as a particularly American attraction on variety programs; the place and function of nonfiction, from short subjects and newsreels to feature-length documentaries; and the emergence of a mutually beneficial, promotional relationship, ultimately focused on women, between newspapers and moving pictures. Throughout, these chapters and entr'actes alternate so as to highlight as well as raise questions about the "imagined community of nationality" created by the intersection of moving pictures, their publicity, and their audiences. In addition, each chapter and entr'acte is accompanied by selected documents or texts and illustrations from the period. Ellipses in the documents and texts from the period indicate omitted text.

Much like *The Red Rooster Scare*, this book too has a personal resonance. Recently I discovered that my mother's father, Clyde Wolfe (a coal miner's son), not only began his career as a clothing store window designer in Canton (Ohio) during the early 1910s (he eventually would become the "dean of Canton's display specialists"),[25] but also played the clarinet in small orchestras that accompanied the moving pictures at two theaters in the city: the Grand Opera, which switched from vaudeville to moving pictures in early 1913, and the Odeon, one of the first picture theaters in the city. He grew up on the city's southwest side in a neighborhood not far from that of his future wife, Lillie Melcheor, an illegitimate child in a family of German ancestry— photos still survive of her grandfather (whom she remembered raising strawberries), who, along with his brother, served in the Thirty-eighth Ohio Battalion during the Civil War. Although they knew each other from attending the same public school and church, I like to imagine Clyde and Lillie meeting, around 1913, on one of the trolleys (an uncle of hers was a conductor) that bisected their neighborhoods on its hourly journey to the downtown amusement district or perhaps in the Grand Opera or the Odeon, where my grandfather played sweet music below the screen and my grandmother sat entranced in the audience. This book is dedicated to their memory.

Signs of the Times

By HARRY LEWY

I may as well begin, and tell
    Exactly who I am,
For a line or two will soon show you
    I'm a Moving Picture Fan.

When I feel blue, as I often do,
    I look for a comedy "Indian Head,"
Or I may, perchance, see one from France,
    That bears the mark of the "Rooster" Red.

Then again I may, the very same day,
    Enjoy a film with the Monogram "E,"
And I always feel that I cant miss a reel
    That follows the sign of the "Wingéd V."

A tale of the West, often seen at its best,
    By the orange "Diamond S" I can tell.
And for bushels of pleasure (that is, in a measure),
    I'll search for the "Liberty Bell."

When things go bad, and I feel sad,
    The "Turning Sun" soon cheers me;
And I must say this, I never will miss
    One that ends with the Circled "A. B."

Motion Picture Story Magazine (February 1912), 158.

Chapter 1

American Variety
and/or Foreign Features

The Throes of Film Distribution

Imagine that you are a young woman who has decided to join one of your store clerk or stenographer friends going to the movies after work in downtown Des Moines, Iowa, in the spring of 1913. On Sunday, May 4, you read the *Des Moines News* and know what programs will be playing in at least four moving picture theaters that next week.[1] On Tuesday, for instance, what are your choices? At the Casino (just opened in December) is *Pathé's Weekly* (a newsreel), Essanay's *The Crazy Prospector,* and Vitagraph's *Cinders.* At the Family, Bison-101's two-reel *The Indian's Secret* and *Billy's First Quarrel.* At the Unique, Majestic's two-reel *Children of St. Anne* and *Her Sister's Secret.* The Colonial has a special feature (running all week), the five-reel *Satan* or "The Drama of Humanity . . . from Creation to the present time."[2] Which theater you and your friend choose could depend on several factors, but, as a frequent moviegoer, you could count on familiarity and the relative quality of the variety programs at three of these theaters, each changed daily and supplied by a different film service or distributor: the Casino (General Film), the Family (Universal), and the Unique (Mutual). You also could be attracted, however, by *Satan's* promotion as a sensational historical epic or by its novelty as a special feature (from Europe, no less), since the only previous film of four reels or more to play in the city was *Queen Elizabeth,* with Sarah Bernhardt, the previous September.[3] And you could not see that film, either when it was booked at a legitimate theater, the Berchel, because the tickets cost twenty-five to fifty cents (those to *Satan* cost just ten cents), or when it returned in early February by special request to a neighborhood theater, Namur's University Place, because you could not make time to take the trolley after work on Wednesday, the only day it was screened.[4]

This snapshot of a fictional moment in the everyday life of an "ordinary" moviegoer can serve to introduce an important, highly contested arena for this study of the "imagined communities" of US cinema during the transition era of the early 1910s. That arena is film distribution, or what Ivo Blom recently described as a "missing link" in histories of early cinema.[5] Indeed, how were moving pictures packaged for distribution to exhibitors? What strategies of packaging were dominant between 1910 and 1914, what changes occurred in packaging, and what companies were involved in either promoting those changes or sustaining already profitable strategies of distribution? Previous studies—most notably by Janet Staiger, Robert Anderson, Eileen Bowser, and Michael Quinn[6]—have provided invaluable research information and analyses of these turbulent years in which the distribution model of a variety program of short films was increasingly challenged by several alternative models that featured a long film of three or more reels. They have tended to focus, however, on the effect of economic and legal practices in creating an industrial structure of distribution (Staiger), on the Motion Picture Patents Company (MPPC) and its distribution arm, General Film (Anderson), or on attempts to create a viable model of distributing feature films (Bowser, Quinn). While this chapter obviously relies on that research, particularly that of Bowser and Quinn, it aims (1) to draw a rather differently contoured map of how distribution models worked at the local or regional level, and at different moments, by examining newspaper ads in selected cities chiefly from the Northeast to the upper Midwest,[7] in conjunction with trade press ads and articles; and (2), looking forward to later chapters, to situate those models and their changing modes of operation within the broad framework of Americanization, its assumptions of more or less distinct national identities, and its conflicted principles of assimilation and exclusion, especially because so many of the initial attempts to distribute features involved imported European films from Italy, France, Denmark, and Germany.

Standardizing the American Variety Program

Officially announced in early 1909 (although incorporated in September 1908), the MPPC sought to rationalize the US film industry by pooling the patents of the Edison and Biograph companies in order to regularize (and monopolize) film production and exhibition. Seven other US companies besides Edison and Biograph—Vitagraph, Selig, Lubin, Essanay, Kalem, George Kleine, and Star Film (Gaston Méliès)—along with the largest producer of all, Pathé-Frères, joined the new combination as members licensed to manufacture and/or sell moving pictures and equipment in the United States. Once established, the MPPC also moved to control distribution by licensing many of the country's more than 100 rental exchanges so as to force exhibitors to show only its films. As Staiger and others have argued, the MPPC's later claim that it helped to stabilize the industry and improve service to exhibitors was largely correct. Prints circulated more efficiently and in greater numbers based on set weekly fees; new titles became more attractive because used prints were recalled after a certain length of time; affordable fire insurance was made available to licensed exhibitors. Yet "the Trust," as it was soon dubbed, excluded several important European manufacturers (Great Northern/Nordisk, most Italian firms) and a significant number of rental exchanges, especially in Chicago. Moreover, its two-dollar weekly licensing fee angered exhibitors, which soon provoked major exchanges run by Carl Laemmle, William Swanson, and others to withdraw.[8] Strong market demand also encouraged nonlicensed manufacturers to emerge: New York Motion Picture (NYMP), Laemmle's own Independent Motion Picture (IMP), Powers, and Thanhouser. Despite difficulties in creating a stable distribution system, their gradual success in competing with the MPPC is evident in one of the first weekly columns devoted to moving pictures, in the *St. Louis Times*.[9] Two months after first mentioning "independent" films, in early January 1910, the column gave "top billing" in consecutive weeks to a NYMP "Bison" brand western and an IMP sensational melodrama.[10] Further evidence can be found in a *New York Morning Telegraph* report on the accomplishments of the "independents," also in early January, or be gleaned from the opening of more and more "independent" picture theaters such as the Jewel in downtown Lowell, Massachusetts, in late March 1910.[11]

When the combined strategy of licensing and lawsuit threats failed to squelch the so-called Independents, in April 1910, the MPPC formed the General Film Company, which purchased controlling interest in nearly all licensed exchanges in order to create a coordinated national distribution network for its films. By guaranteeing licensed exhibitors a "complete service," General Film rationalized the industry around a variety program of single-reel and split-reel films that could be "freshened" daily. It also instituted a system of standing orders for weekly programs and another of run-clearance zoning that classified theaters so that a limited number had exclusive rights to "first-run" pictures in their area. Through General Film, the MPPC used a proven industrial logic to market a variety package of standardized commodities (indistinguishable except in brand name), equating cans of film with any other kind of canned goods. Within a month of General Film's founding, IMP and NYMP set up their own distribution arm, the Motion Picture Distributing and Sales Company (Sales), which adopted many policies and practices advanced by their competitors, especially the variety package of films that could be changed daily and give priority to "first-run" films.[12] This time the column of "Moving Pictures and Vaudeville" ads in the daily *St. Louis Times* suggested both General Film's initial advantage and Sales's growing market niche, abetted by IMP's publicity stunt about the "death and resurrection" of its star, Florence Lawrence (see chapter 6).[13] Almost all the major theaters, especially those downtown like the Grand Central, Casino, and New Bijou, as well as others in secondary commercial districts, were supplied by General Film. Yet, beginning with the Clinton in north St. Louis and the 600-seat New Theater in south St. Louis, more and more theaters contracted with Sales, most notably the 1,000-seat Vandora, which opened downtown on April 27 to show "the celebrated IMP pictures" (including those of Lawrence) and others on the first day of their release.[14] By the end of May, at least a half dozen theaters explicitly were advertising "independent" films, and one even got away with calling itself the Imp.[15]

Over the course of the next few months, Sales enlarged its portion of the market considerably, largely due to the strenuous efforts, so *Billboard* claimed, of Laemmle.[16] At the beginning of July, Sales could distribute just two titles per day, Monday through Saturday, to little more than thirty exchanges, including those of Laemmle (Chicago, Minneapolis, Omaha), Swanson (Chicago, St. Louis), William Steiner (New York), W. E. Greene (Boston), and Miles Brothers (San Francisco).[17] That month consolidation with two other Independent factions, however, more than doubled the number of titles on its programs to four or five per day, and those now offered two titles each from IMP, Bison, Powers, and Thanhouser, as well as one each from a half dozen European manufacturers—Great Northern, Éclair, Lux, Cines, Itala, and Ambroiso.[18] By September, Sales was funneling its weekly programs to fifty exchanges throughout the country, with important additions in Ohio—Victor Film (Cleveland) and Toledo Film (Toledo).[19] That fall and winter, major downtown picture theaters in a wide range of cities could depend on a regular supply of Sales's films. In Massachusetts, they included newly constructed theaters such as Louis B. Mayer's 1,800-seat Broadway in Lawrence and the 1,500-seat Central Square in Lynn.[20] Elsewhere in the state, the Jewel was joined by the Scenic and Star in Lowell.[21] In Ohio, three of the earliest downtown theaters to advertise in the *Toledo News-Bee* featured Sales's films: the Isis, Hart, and Crown.[22] Farther west, in Des Moines, Sales' programs were restricted to the Family and Unique until a remodeled Elite opened on the city's east side, in May 1911, and repeatedly advertised its "famous IMP films."[23] By then, Sales had a near monopoly on Independent film distribution, having added American, Reliance, Solax, and Rex product to its programs, funneled through even more exchanges such as Lake Shore (Cleveland) and Western Film (New York, Milwaukee, Kansas City, and Seattle).[24] Within just one year, the company had gained control of close to one-third of the market.[25] If, in cities from Washington to Toledo to Des Moines, licensed films remained dominant, in others, such as Cleveland, the vast majority of downtown "photoplay" theaters presented "Independent shows."[26]

By the spring of 1911, consequently, film distribution seemed a "closed market." All but a handful of European manufacturers were excluded from circulating their films, and Pathé had been cajoled into limiting its imports of French films and, at a new studio in Jersey City, producing what manager

FIG. 4. Motion Picture Distributing & Sales Co. ad, *Moving Picture World* (5 August 1911), 260.

Jacques Berst called "American films" for "the national tastes of America."[27] Indeed, even US entrepreneurs wanting to invest in new firms found it difficult to gain a foothold in a market so tightly controlled by the two combines. General Film and Sales could supply their exchanges regular weekly shipments of films, a daily mix of dramas, comedies, and "educational" films averaging four to five reels, which in turn could be shipped on just as regularly to their contracted exhibitors.[28] In Cleveland, the General Film office could stock first-run licensed theaters, for instance, with Biograph, Pathé, Selig, and Lubin films on Mondays and Vitagraph, Kalem, Pathé, and Edison films on Fridays. At the same time, Lake Shore and Victor could stock first-run Independent theaters with a selection of American, IMP, Éclair, Yankee, and Champion films on Mondays and Bison, Thanhouser, Solax, and Lux films on Fridays. Indeed, the dominance of these two combines is strikingly evident in the unusual ads that General Film, Victor, and Lake Shore all placed, in December 1911, on the first Sunday moving picture pages of the *Cleveland Leader*.[29] However, enough films—from small US manufacturers and especially European firms (e.g., Messter, Deutsches Biograph, Film d'Art, Hepworth, Aquila, and Comerio)— remained available beyond the reach of either General Film or Sales and enough new theaters were opening that a second Independent company, National Film Distributing, attempted to package a competing weekly program of at least three titles per day.[30] Although it never accumulated enough customers ultimately to survive beyond early 1912, National Film Distributing certainly publicized its presence—for instance, matching the full-page Sales ad with one of its own, in the *Morning Telegraph*'s special Christmas issue.[31]

Success, however, did not safeguard either Sales or General Film from internal dissensions and disputes, and Sales proved the more vulnerable, at least in the short run. In October 1911, the company's general manager, Herbert Miles, resigned to head a new production firm, Republic Film.[32] Three months later, when Gaumont voided its contract with Kleine, it chose not to join Sales but to sell its films without affiliation to either distribution faction.[33] Moreover, a proposed plan to combine all of Sales' contracted exchanges into one, similar to that of General Film, so sharply divided members that half threatened to bolt the organization.[34] A further sign of the split was Sales' refusal to admit another new company, Gem Films (financed by Swanson, one of its own founders), to its membership, which pitted those who wanted to maintain the current system against those who believed that a more open market would raise the level of film product.[35] In early February, the disquiet became public in a *Billboard* article, "Is the Open Market Inevitable?"; by late March, despite its insistence that "everybody's doing it . . . the independent trot [and to its very own beat]," Sales was breaking up.[36] The precipitant, Staiger and Bowser suggest, probably was Harry Aitken, the successful owner of Western Film Exchange, who took over both Majestic and Reliance in late 1911.[37] In March, with the support of Wall Street bankers, he established Mutual Film as a rival Independent faction, supported by an arrangement with his exchanges to distribute the films of the companies he controlled (he also had interests in American and NYMP).[38] The objective of Mutual, according to the *New York Dramatic Mirror,* was "to buy out exchanges and consolidate them along the line of the General Film Company."[39] By May, Sales was little more than a shell, with the majority of its remaining members reorganized as Universal Film Manufacturing and the others joined together with Mutual Film and Western Film Exchange in a second combination, Film Supply.[40]

Initially, Universal seemed to be in a stronger position to distribute its variety package of weekly programs. It boasted of more than forty exchanges across the country, but concentrated along the eastern seaboard and in the upper Midwest, all contracted to rent twenty-one reels a week.[41] Its IMP, Bison, and Rex films especially were reputable and popular; moreover, Éclair, which also now was producing American films at its Fort Lee facilities, joined Universal after a brief month or two with Film Supply.[42] The latter company also distributed twenty-one reels weekly through thirty exchanges, concentrated at first in the Midwest and South, with its most popular American brands coming from Thanhouser, American, Reliance, and Majestic.[43] In the *Cleveland Leader,* Lake Shore Film made a point of promoting its alliance with Mutual and, thereafter, advertising its "exclusive service" from Film Supply, "the cream of the world's independent films."[44] Tellingly, both companies, much like General Film, offered American films for the most part and a very limited number of European films: Universal's weekly programs included only one reel each from Éclair, Itala, and Ambrosio; Film Supply had slightly more, with Gaumont (whose director, Herbert Blaché, played a leading role in organizing the company) providing at least two reels and Lux and Great Northern one each.[45] Not long after it added Éclair to its ranks, however, Universal went through a bitter, protracted struggle (allegedly marked by raids and gunfights) with NYMP, which announced its own withdrawal from the company in late June.[46] Although Universal eventually gained control of its Bison brand, NYMP negotiated a deal with Mutual by August to distribute its reorganized and enhanced production of Kay-Bee, Broncho, and Keystone films.[47] The deal helped Mutual quickly raise its number of purchased exchanges to twenty-six, from New York and Boston through Cleveland, Toledo, Des Moines, and beyond.[48] That fall its "invasion" of the Northeast was especially impressive as more and more theaters—for example, the Star and Washington in Boston, the Scenic in Lowell, the Star in Pawtucket—contracted with its weekly service.[49] In November, the 4,000-seat National Theater in Boston (perhaps the largest in the country) switched to Mutual films, as did the 1,500-seat Central Square in Lynn.[50] By December, Mutual's affiliation with Film Supply was no longer needed, and it acquired exclusive rights to distribute as well the core of its former partner's programs—Thanhouser, American, Reliance, and Majestic.[51]

UNIVERSAL PROGRAM

MONDAY JUNE 24	IMP—"The Dividing Line" NESTOR—"The Dawn of Netta" CHAMPION—"Sisters"
TUESDAY JUNE 25	GEM—"The Reason" BISON—"His Message" ECLAIR—"Romance in Old Kentucky"
WEDNESDAY JUNE 26	POWERS—"Helping Hands" NESTOR—"Reaping the Whirlwind" ANIMATED WEEKLY
THURSDAY JUNE 27	REX—"The Weight of a Feather" IMP—"A Child's Influence" ECLAIR—"Three Men and a Girl"
FRIDAY JUNE 28	POWERS—"A Jealous Wife" NESTOR—"Young Wild West" AMBROSIO—"The Actor's Test," "Sacred City"
SATURDAY JUNE 29	BISON—"The Colonel's Peril" IMP—"Portuguese Joe," "His Other Self" ITALA—"The Great Bank Failure"
SUNDAY JUNE 30	REX—"Looking Backward" PARIS ECLAIR—"Willy Wants a Free Lunch," "Picturesque Portugal," "Women's Work in Oporto"

UNIVERSAL EXCHANGES

Empire Film Exchange, New York City.
Peerless Film Exchange, New York City.
Great Eastern Film Exchange, New York City.
Metropolitan Film Exchange, New York City.
Swanson Film Exchange, Denver, Colo.
Swanson Film Exchange, Salt Lake City, Utah.
Laemmle Film Service, Minneapolis, Minn.
Laemmle Film Service, Omaha, Neb.
Laemmle Film Service, Chicago, Ill.
Laemmle Film Service, Des Moines, Ia.
Victor Film Service, Buffalo, N. Y.
Victor Film Service, Cleveland, O.
Rex Film Exchange, Albany, N. Y.
Toledo Film Exchange, Toledo, O.
California Film Exchange, San Francisco, Cal.
California Film Exchange, Los Angeles, Cal.
Central Film Service, Indianapolis, Ind.
Miles Bros., San Francisco, Cal.
Miles Bros., Los Angeles, Cal.
Eagle Film Exchange, Philadelphia, Pa.
Exhibitors Film Service, Wilkesbarre, Pa.
Philadelphia Film Exchange, Philadelphia, Pa.
Philadelphia Projection Co., Philadelphia, Pa.
Independent Film Exchange, Pittsburgh, Pa.
Pittsburgh Photoplay Co., Pittsburgh, Pa.
Swaab Film Service, Philadelphia, Pa.
W. E. Greene, Boston, Mass.
Consolidated Film & S. Co., Atlanta, Ga.
Consolidated F. & S. Co., New Orleans, La.
J. W. Morgan, Kansas City, Mo.
Independent Western F. Ex., Portland, Ore.
Pacific Film Exchange, Seattle, Wash.
Canadian Film Exchange, Calgary, Alberta.
Canadian Film Exchange, Toronto, Can.
Gaumont Co., Toronto, Can.
Gaumont Co., Montreal, Can.
Gaumont Co., Winnipeg, Can.
Gaumont Co., Vancouver, B. C.
Washington Film Exchange, Washington, D. C.
Standard Film Exchange, Chicago, Ill.
Wichita Film & S. Co., Wichita, Kan.
Boston Film Rental Co., Boston, Mass.
Baltimore Film Exchange, Baltimore, Md.
Pacific Film Exchange, Butte, Montana.
United Motion Picture Co., Oklahoma City, Okla.
Cincinnati-Buckeye F. Ex., Cincinnati, O.
Texas Film Exchange, Dallas, Tex.
St. Louis Film & S. Co., St. Louis, Mo.

UNIVERSAL FILM MFG. CO.

FIG. 5. Universal Film Mfg. ad, *Motion Picture News* (22 June 1912), 40.

By early 1913, consequently, General Film, Universal, and Mutual once again had created something like a "closed market" for distributing a variety package of constantly changing films. That did not halt efforts, of course, to crack open the system. Ousted from Universal as the result of ongoing internal disputes, Pat Powers announced the formation of another rival, Indepen-

FIG. 6. Lake Shore Film & Supply Co. ad, *Cleveland Leader* (15 December 1912), S5.

dent Exchange, but this turned out to be little more than a promotional gimmick.[52] Blaché succeeded in reorganizing what remained of Film Supply into Exclusive Supply, but its releases from Gaumont, Great Northern, Solax, and several other minor firms hardly amounted to a full weekly program—a further indication of how weak was the position of foreign imports, at least as the potential core of a variety package for distribution.[53] One sign of the relative degree of stability that the three companies achieved, at least for US manufacturers, was the even more prominent ads for General Film, Victor, and Lake Shore that ran in the *Cleveland Leader* in December 1912.[54] Another in the same newspaper was a weekly report on upcoming films in early February: they would be appearing in first-run theaters already "branded" as Universal, Mutual, and General Film houses.[55] Similarly, in Pawtucket, each brand had its own picture theater: General Film, the Music Hall; Mutual, the Star; Universal, the Globe; and Film Supply, the Pastime.[56] Signs of the Independents' strength were even more evident. In late January, Mutual took out a joint half-page ad with the Unique Theatre in the *Des Moines News*, celebrating not only their reciprocally profitable alliance but also its own status as a "synonym for progressiveness" in the industry.[57] Three months later, both Mutual and Universal ran special ads on a new weekly moving picture page in the *Minneapolis Journal.*[58] Simultaneously, and just as my imagined young woman was deciding on what movie theater to attend, the two distributors began running strip ads in the *Des Moines Register and Leader* that simply circulated the brand names of their regular programs.[59] Although General Film did not itself run similar ads there, one of its members, Essanay, did, promoting its "five-a-week" programs of "pure photoplays."[60] These dueling strip ads, which also included those of one Independent manufacturer, Reliance, ran each Sunday from late April until late July.[61]

In September 1913, *Motography* claimed that "the single-reel subject" remained "the backbone of the business," strongly implying that the variety program of daily or frequently changed short films would continue to attract audiences throughout the coming season.[62] That claim gained some credence from Mutual's campaign for its regular programs, in late 1913 and early 1914, with exceptionally prominent ads in such newspapers as the *Minneapolis Journal* and the *Chicago Tribune.*[63] Indeed, the variety package that any exchange sent to its customers was not unlike a daily newspaper or a constantly updated popular magazine that moviegoers could browse at will in the continuous programs that many theaters still offered.[64]

Opening the Market with European Specials

Those in the trade press who opposed a "closed market," whatever its efficiency and profitability, had long argued for an "open market" (more common in Europe, especially Great Britain and Germany) that would not only encourage new manufacturers and distributors to invest in the business but also produce more expensive, higher-quality films that could have a much longer "shelf life," as well as reach the "better classes."[65] One strategy that both *Moving Picture World* and *Billboard* promoted to create a more open market was the production and distribution of "specials" or "features," usually (but not always) longer films.[66] Their prime example was Pathé's four-reel *Passion Play* (1907), which still was in circulation, usually for religious holidays, four years after its initial release. Yet this and other examples—for example, sports films such as the Gans-Nelson wrestling championship or the Jeffries-Johnson boxing championship, Wild West entertainments such as *Buffalo Bill Wild West and Pawnee Bill Far East*—were singular subjects and not susceptible to standardized production. Among MPPC manufacturers, Vitagraph had produced a few multiple-reel films such as *The Life of Moses* (1910) and *A Tale of Two Cities* (1911), but General Film distributed them as single reels within the usual weekly variety program, respectively, in consecutive weeks or on consecutive days. It was special European imports that gradually would break open the market and eventually challenge the variety model, with the assistance of none other than Sales.[67]

An initial breach came with Sales's distribution of Itala's two-reel *The Fall of Troy* in the spring of 1911. One month in advance of its release, the *Morning Telegraph* urged Independent exhibitors to "strive valiantly to secure" this "spectacular" production, and the *Dramatic Mirror* printed a glowing review, praising its "vast, stupendous beauty."[68] In Youngstown, Ohio, the "special and exclusive . . . $30,000 Motion Picture Spectacle" was the featured attraction at the Park (a vaudeville house) on Easter Sunday, and the local newspaper printed a half page of still photos from the film.[69] In Lowell, the Jewel ran a rare ad in *L'Etoile,* the local French-language newspaper, for a four-day showing, also over the Easter weekend; two weeks later, the Scenic Theatre did likewise, in the *Sunday Telegram,* for its own three-day showing of "this mammoth feature."[70] At the Janet Theatre in Chicago, a *World* reporter had trouble gaining admission to the film one evening because "a mass of waiting people filled the lobby and extended out into the street."[71] A writer for *Motion Picture Story Magazine* was enthralled at the end: "By moonlight the Grecians, hidden within the great wooden horse, climbed out, and with

FIG. 7. Mall ad, *Cleveland Leader* (17 September 1911), N4.

torches, flaming yellow, fired the city. A last glimpse showed the doomed lovers looking thru the marble pillars of the palace at the red destruction."[72] "Seen as far and wide" as the lavish review in the *Morning Telegraph* predicted,[73] *The Fall of Troy* led to other imports that summer: two more Italian epics, Cines's four-reel *The Crusaders, or Jerusalem Delivered,* and Milano's five-reel *Dante's Inferno,* as well as a sensational melodrama, Great Northern's three-reel *Temptations of a Great City.* In July, all three were advertised as distributed by either Sales or Pliny P. Craft (producer and distributor of *Buffalo Bill Wild West and Pawnee Bill Far East*), who shared a Union Square address in New York.[74] Yet within weeks, not only were the latter two films now distributed exclusively by Monopol Film (with Craft as general manager), with an uptown address near Times Square, but *Dante's Inferno* also had been licensed by General Film.[75] Although these moves remain murky, Monopol's handling of the latter film initiated two new distribution strategies that would differentiate "features" from variety programs.

The first strategy, the road show, came from the legitimate theater: a distributor took a film "on the road," renting individual theaters on a percentage-of-the-gross basis. Monopol pioneered this strategy with *Dante's Inferno* by advertising the film as "the successor to the Passion Play" and booking it for at least one-week runs in the prestigious Shubert theater circuit, beginning with two shows daily (ticket prices were fifteen to seventy-five cents) at the Auditorium Theatre in Baltimore, on 14 August 1911.[76] Business reportedly was brisk, and the film was rebooked for a second week, a phenomenon repeated at Klaw & Erlanger's Grand Opera House in Cincinnati. In late August and early September, just prior to the opening of the fall theatrical season, *Dante's Inferno* played for a week or more at other Shubert theaters in such cities as Montreal, Chicago, St. Louis, Brooklyn, and Washington. At the Belasco Theatre in the latter city, accompanied by a "lecture and appropriate music," it "scored a tremendous success" and was held over an extra week.[77] The second strategy was a "state rights" system of distribution in which a person or firm purchased the right to license a film's exhibition in a particular territory—at legitimate, vaudeville, and/or picture theaters. Although it had been used irregularly for previous "specials," Monopol showed the system off to real advantage with *Dante's Inferno*.[78] The earliest state rights bookings came in mid-September: in Lawrence, surprisingly, where the film played for a full week at the Grand Opera, and in Cleveland, also for a full week at a downtown picture theater, the Mall (and at the regular price of ten cents).[79] During the next three months, the film ran anywhere from three days to a week or even two weeks (sometimes with an increase in price), in chronological order, at the Opera House in Providence, the Opera House in Lowell (with special sound effects), the Palace in Youngstown, the Grand Opera in Boston (with a lecture performed by W. Stephen Bush),[80] the Colonial in Rochester, the Mazda in Minneapolis, the Colonial in Des Moines, and the Manhattan in New York.[81] And it continued to reappear throughout the following year—for example, in February, at the Star in Pawtucket and the Elite in Des Moines; in mid-May, at the Rex in Youngstown for a full week; and in July, at the Empress in Toledo, where "so vast were the crowds" that it was booked an extra day.[82]

If *Dante's Inferno* demonstrated the viability of the road show and state rights systems of distribution for longer films, it remained a singular subject, much like the *Passion Play*, best promoted as a "special event." Moreover, its visual spectacle was validated by cultural and/or religious respectability. So too were *The Crusaders*, if to a lesser extent (since it was adapted from a less familiar Italian epic), and another Monopol import, Milano's three-reel *Homer's Odyssey*.[83] The initial licensees for *The Crusaders* apparently were World's Best Films of Chicago and Feature & Educational Films (F & E) of Cleveland. In September 1911, World's Best boasted that it had sold rights to eight states in the Midwest and Northwest;[84] at the same time, F & E booked engagements in northern Ohio: one Sunday at the Elysium (a legitimate theater) in Cleveland and, to "great interest," the "first four days of Aviation Week" at the Auditorium in Canton.[85] Another two months passed before the film was featured one Sunday at the Park in Youngstown. Only in December and January did its circulation widen farther into New England, for three-day or full-week runs—at the Palace in Boston, the Jewel in Lowell, and the Victoria in Lawrence.[86] The response to *The Crusaders* in Boston was conflicted, to say the least: although it "drew big crowds to the Palace [and] was viewed by many school children," the state police refused to allow screenings on Sundays, allegedly because one scene "revealed two warriors in a terrific duel."[87] By March, other licensees were booking it at the Star in Pawtucket (where it did only moderate business) and the Isis in Minneapolis; that summer, the film finally played at major theaters in Lynn, Toledo, and Des Moines.[88] Monopol first broached news of *Homer's Odyssey* in October 1911 but did not advertise it until four months later, then lined up licensees with assists from Jake Wells's purchase of "ten southern states rights" and a two-page promotion in the *New York Sunday American*.[89] One of the film's initial bookings turned out to be a full-week run in April at the Auditorium in Minneapolis, and it returned in early June at the Metropolitan.[90] The following fall, the film could be found at picture theaters from the Columbia in Cedar Rapids, Iowa, to the Jewel in Lowell, and in November it still could be booked for a full week at the Colonial in Des Moines.[91]

In May 1912, W. Stephen Bush singled out these "three great features," all "clean and classic subjects," as a portent of the future, for so unexpectedly finding "favor with the American public."[92] The French-American Film Company set out to duplicate Monopol's success, but with two multiple-reel French films, Film d'Art's *Camille* and *Mme Sans-Gene*, that it combined in a five-reel package that could be exhibited either as one or in consecutive programs.[93] The attraction here, of course, was the stars, Bernhardt and Réjane, respectively, who had agreed to reprise two of their more famous stage roles in moving pictures. After the company mounted an extensive ad campaign in the *Morning Telegraph*, the films won a lengthy adulatory review from Bush in the *World* and convinced the *Dramatic Mirror* to inaugurate a new weekly column, "Reviews of Feature Subjects."[94] Initial bookings were widely distributed in legitimate theaters or vaudeville houses: *Camille* alone at the Valentine in Toledo one weekend in March; and both films together at the Lyceum in Rochester also in March, at the Majestic in Brooklyn in May, where they were "admired by big audiences," and at the Lasalle Opera House in Chicago, where the pair ran for a record ten weeks, by far the longest yet for a moving picture.[95] In Cleveland, the films shifted from road show to state rights performances, playing for two weeks at the Alhambra in April, another week at the Princess, then one week more at the Mall in May.[96] At the same time, the films were being leased as a special package elsewhere in Ohio, for instance, to vaudeville houses in Canton and Youngstown,[97] and throughout the summer in regular picture theaters in the upper Midwest and the Northeast. Indeed, one or both films remained in circulation in New England well into the fall, finally showing up in early November at the Dreamland in Lynn, where each film, consecutively, enjoyed a two-day run.[98]

Although the trade press consistently advocated the production and distribution of "special" films or "features," it recognized the difficulty of countering the industry's dependence on the "popular cry" for "first-runs" in variety programs.[99] Rather than a few scattered "special event" films that took six months or a year to circulate widely, argued the *Dramatic Mirror*, there had to be "a reasonably dependable supply of new and appealing productions of sufficient strength" and number for the state rights system not only to demonstrate, as Epes Winthrop Sargent put it, that "a photoplay" could be much more than "a daily newspaper" but also to be profitable more quickly and assuredly.[100] Sargent also was well aware that features required more time, energy, and money to market and demanded of both distributors and exhibitors "a radical departure in [the] usual styles of advertising," promoting each title's unique attraction and targeting its most likely audience, especially through local newspapers.[101] Here again, F & E may have served as a model, even if its experience licensing *Temptations of a Great City* is difficult to assess. The film had several Sunday engagements early on: at the Auditorium in Canton in October 1911 and at the Lyric in Youngstown in December.[102] After that, there are few traces of its appearance: at the Star in Pawtucket in February 1912, at the Orpheum in Toledo in June, and at the Alpha Theater in the black ghetto of Cleveland in early September.[103] Yet, unlike the previous films, this sensational story of a wealthy young man tempted by "wine, women, and song and reduced to poverty" enjoyed little press coverage other than to dismiss its "cheaper melodramatic character."[104] If the strong box office garnered at the Pawtucket Star is any indication,[105] however, the film must have prompted F & E to risk acquiring rights to the other multiple-reel sensational melodramas being released with increasing regularity by Éclair and Great Northern's new affiliate in charge of "special features."[106] For several months in the winter of 1911–12, F & E mounted a big publicity campaign not only in the trade press but also in the *Cleveland Leader*, most notably for Éclair's three-reel crime thriller, *Zigomar*.[107] The unexpected success of this film and the relative failure of later French thrillers will be analyzed in some detail in chapter 5, but, for now, it is worth noting that *Zigomar*, along with other imports such as Éclair's *Land of Darkness* and Great Northern's *A Victim of the Mormons*, allowed F & E to expand its Cleveland office, as well as establish branches in new territories—in Indianapolis, Detroit, Chicago, and Milwaukee.[108]

Now that "feature films," in the words of *Billboard*, had to be considered "an important branch of the moving picture business" by early 1912, the market broke wide open, as an increasing number of "outsiders" not aligned with Sales hastily organized to rent exclusively to Independent exhibitors.[109] Most followed F & E's lead by securing rights within a given territory to distribute a group of two- and three-reel films (chiefly sensational melodramas and historical dramas) by at least one European company.[110] From its headquarters in Chicago, Feature Film offered a selection of French titles from Pathé, including *The Siege of Calais, Notre Dame de Paris,* and *Victims of Alcohol*.[111] Apparently, the company did well enough to open branch offices from Columbus and Toledo to St. Paul and New Orleans.[112] New York Film offered some of the same films in the Northeast.[113] In Springfield, Massachusetts, Century Film gained the rights to handle Éclair features, beginning with *The Land of Darkness,* for much of New England.[114] And Warner's Features got its start by selling the rights to another Éclair film, *Redemption,* through offices from New York to California.[115] In the wake of the *Titanic* disaster, World's Best

Films seized on the sensational elements of Great Northern's *The Wreck of the Aurora*.[116] In Toledo, Tournament Film secured the rights to distribute Deutsche Biograph's German features starring Asta Nielsen, beginning with *Gypsy Blood* and *The Traitress*.[117] A good number of these state rights firms succeeded, at least in the short term. Between March and May, either F & E or Feature Film supplied the Park and/or Orpheum in Youngstown with weekly Sunday shows that included *A Victim of Mormons, Siege of Calais,* and *The Land of Darkness*.[118] In April and May, World's Best Films shipped *The Wreck of the Aurora* to theaters from Toledo to Des Moines.[119] And, from April through July, Tournament booked its Asta Nielsen features into the Hart and Empress in Toledo, the Park and Orpheum in Youngstown, and perhaps even the Central Square in Lynn.[120]

However much controversy these sensational melodramas from Europe later provoked, together with other Italian and French "specials" they did have an impact on both General Film and Sales. In October 1911, shortly after *Dante's Inferno* began its lengthy run, General Film modified its weekly variety package to include two- and three-reel specials (eschewing any hint of sensational melodrama), beginning with Selig's *Two Orphans* and Kalem's *Colleen Bawn*. Although these specials had no regular release pattern, they did seem aimed at first-run picture theaters that changed their programs two or three times a week rather than daily so that reels could be shown one after the other on a program or separately on consecutive days.[121] The Lyric in Minneapolis showcased this strategy, presenting three-day runs of *Two Orphans* (early October), *Colleen Bawn* (late October), Kalem's second Irish drama, *Arrah-Na-Pogue* (early December), Selig's *Cinderella* (early January), and Vitagraph's *Vanity Fair* (late January).[122] The *Cleveland Leader* reveals how General Film circulated a popular feature like *Cinderella*, starring Mabel Taliaferro,[123] through its hierarchy of theaters: in early January, the film played at the downtown Avenue on Monday and Tuesday, then at the Cameraphone the following Sunday; two weeks later it was at the Home for a special Thursday showing; in February, it played first at the Cozy and then at the Superior, both on a Monday and Tuesday.[124] Yet not all first-run theaters in other cities specialized in General Film "features," even when they did not change programs daily; instead, the Comique and Olympia in Lynn, the Voyons in Lowell, and the Odeon in Canton all remained more committed to the variety program of single reels. In late 1911, Sales also experimented with distributing multiple-reel films such as Thanhouser's *Romeo and Juliet* and *David Copperfield* and occasional foreign imports such as Ambrosio's *The Golden Wedding*, which reportedly "made a great hit" at Chicago's Janet Theater.[125] Yet the company experienced difficulties (best taken up in chapter 2) in trying to distribute Bison-101 multiple-reel westerns on a more regular basis in the spring of 1912, which may well have contributed to its dissolution.

Selig's three-reel *The Coming of Columbus* inaugurated a further change in

General Film's distribution policy. Shot before and during a Columbus Day pageant organized in Chicago in October 1911, perhaps in an attempt to create an American "national epic" to rival the Italian features, the film's release was delayed until May 1912, for reasons that remain unclear.[126] Whatever the case, General Film used the film to begin releasing multiple-reel "specials" on a regular basis.[127] Benefiting from unusual coverage in the trade press, as well as Selig's own extensive ad campaign that reached out to local newspapers,[128] *The Coming of Columbus* played often and widely. For a full week in early May, once again the Lyric in Minneapolis showcased its presentation, demonstrating, in the words of the *Minneapolis Journal*, "the undeniable value of moving pictures as a means of visualizing past historical events for their keener comprehension by both grownups and children of today."[129] Later that month, in Los Angeles, Clune's Main Street Theater kept it for "a full week instead of the usual three or four days" and still turned people away at the last performance.[130] In Des Moines, the Colonial reproduced Selig's publicity illustration for its four-day run, adding this caveat: it was "endorsed by educators, press, pulpit, historians, and public."[131] In Canton, in order to kick off its summer schedule of pictures, the Orpheum picked up on another Selig promotional idea—an essay contest on the subject of the film for schoolchildren—and gave them a special morning matinee two weeks before its scheduled weekend run.[132] For parents, the *Canton News-Democrat* published a full-page article on the film's making, with ten accompanying photos, both probably supplied by Selig.[133] Yet not all bookings were successful: a Salt Lake City exhibitor lost money by deciding to show the film not at his own 1,000-seat venue but at a larger legitimate theater.[134] The unusual attention to *The Coming of Columbus* in Canton (and perhaps similar cities) highlights the controversy over how "aliens" could be "Americanized" during this period, and how moving pictures might be used for such ends. In this case, concerns over the recent influx of Italian immigrants into the area and the desirability of their assimilation may have prompted these strategies;[135] yet such a hypothesis has to account for the absence of any reference to the film being shown in nearby Youngstown, where a larger Italian immigrant population had five small picture theaters catering specifically to them.[136]

Throughout the summer and into the fall of 1912, General Film stuck to a release schedule of one two- or three-reel "special feature" each week. Initially the films were as likely to be imported as "made in the USA"—for example, Pathé's *The Orleans Coach* (June) and *Fire at Sea* (August) or Cines's *Rameses King of Egypt* (August) and *Daughter of the Spy* (September)—but increasingly American titles predominated, as US manufacturers stepped up their production.[137] The success of these "special features," or at least the demand for them from exhibitors, convinced General Film to announce that, beginning in November, it would "offer its customers two multiple-reel sub-

FIG. 8. General Film Co. ad, *Moving Picture World* (13 November 1912), back cover.

jects each week."[138] By then, however, all three competing Independent distributors also were offering multiple-reel subjects, most of them also American products, as an integral part of their weekly programs. Film Supply
alone included foreign imports, specializing in at least one Gaumont historical drama or sensational melodrama per week, along with one or more
titles from Solax, Majestic, or American. Universal handled one or more
Bison-101 westerns, plus another one or two titles from IMP and/or Rex. Mutual offered at least one western or Civil War film each from Kay-Bee and
Broncho. Whereas Universal and Mutual "features" became an increasingly
stable, profitable component of the moving picture business (in contrast to
Film Supply's), those of General Film met with some resistance. While the
company's "special features" service added to exhibitors' costs (but so did
that of the Independents), Quinn argues, the films rarely received special
treatment: "no extensive, long-term advertising, no long-term announcement of their release, no extended runs, and no higher admission prices."[139]
General Film was indeed slow to address these complaints, even after the
number of its "specials" increased to four per week—as evident in the persistent ads for nothing more than its "established service" in the *Cleveland
Leader* through early March 1913—which forced first-run exhibitors, Quinn
concludes, to differentiate themselves according to the level of commitment
they made to them.[140] And the lack of a speedy response did not bode well

FIG. 9. General Film Co. ad, *Motion Picture News* (26 April 1913), 5.

for the company, as lengthy features from Europe made further inroads into the US market.

Standardizing the Features Market with American Films

In September 1912, a *Billboard* writer claimed that "novelty foreign pictures are exceedingly popular," and nothing perhaps demonstrates that more clearly than *Queen Elizabeth*.[141] Prompted in part by the success of *Camille*, exhibitor Adolph Zukor and Broadway producer Daniel Frohman founded Famous Players Film in New York expressly for the US distribution of this second Bernhardt vehicle, a three-reel French-British adaptation of another of the actress's stage roles (in a Victorien Sardou play), whose initial ads displayed a morbid fascination with "MURDER" and Elizabeth's climactic death scene, which was turned into "Sarah Bernhardt Is Going to Die!"[142] After previewing the film in New York for "a large and enthusiastic gathering of newspaper men and critics," Famous Players adopted a combined road show and state rights strategy of distribution for this "artistically tinted and toned" historical drama (with a special musical score composed by Joseph Carl Breil), modeled partly on what had worked so well for *Dante's Inferno* the year before.[143] According to Frohman, Zukor even got him to persuade the MPPC to license their film, to ensure wider distribution.[144] On August 12, *Queen Elizabeth* opened at the Powers Theater in Chicago, for a five-week run (tickets cost twenty-five cents to one dollar); by early September, through an arrangement between Zukor and Marcus Loew (former business partners), it was playing in Loew's seventeen theaters throughout New York City—which, on average, drew "$200 a day more" than usual.[145] For the next several months, on the added strength of excellent reviews and a front-cover illustration for *Photoplay* (September 1912), Famous Players booked the film for road show engagements, usually for a week, at a range of legitimate theaters: the Berchel in Des Moines in mid-September, the Colonial in Cleveland in October, and the Valentine in Toledo in December.[146] At the same time, however, through state rights licensees, it also played in major picture theaters, either for a week—at the Opera House in Lowell or the Colonial in Lawrence in October (where tickets cost ten to fifty cents), the Olympia in Boston (lectured by Geoffrey Whelan), and the Casino in Washington, "surrounded by a bill of refined vaudeville specialities"—or even for one- or two-day runs (at regular prices)—at the Rex in Youngstown in November, the Hippodrome in Rochester in December, or the Grand in Canton in February.[147] In Cleveland, probably as in other large cities, *Queen Elizabeth* also processed through regular picture theaters, including a new suburban theater, the Quincy, in December.[148]

Although Famous Players announced ambitious plans for a series of feature-length American films, the company encountered difficulties in

FIG. 10. *Queen Elizabeth*
(production still), *Photoplay
Magazine* front cover
(September 1912).

both production and distribution and "flirted with bankruptcy throughout early 1913."[149] Meanwhile, other US companies sought to duplicate the success of a singular film like *Queen Elizabeth*. Masko Film set out to exploit an American stage actress, Blanche Walsh, who re-created a well-known role in a three-reel adaptation of Tolstoy's *Resurrection*.[150] After initial screenings in regular picture theaters in New York City and Lawrence in July 1912, the film's bookings seem to have been few and far between: the Garden in Washington in September, the Premier in Lowell in October, the Colonial in Rochester in December, and the Colonial in Des Moines, six months later.[151] United States Film challenged Famous Players by casting Helen Gardner as Cleopatra, in a five-reel adaptation of another Sardou play. Much like a theatrical show, *Cleopatra* was "given a try-out . . . at a large picture house a few miles outside New York City" in mid-November 1912 and then heavily promoted not only in the *Dramatic Mirror* but also in the *Cleveland Leader,* in a full page of publicity stills of Gardner as the "Sorceress of the Nile."[152] At first, its bookings seemed propitious: two weeks at the Duchess in Cleveland through Christmas and New Years, one week at the Garden in Washington in March, a special engagement at the new Gordon Theater in Rochester also in March, another at the Boston Symphony Hall in late April.[153] Thereafter, it worked its way around the country ever so slowly and usually for short runs: three days at the Crystal in Minneapolis in May, two days at the Alhambra in Toledo in August, two days at the Palace in Cedar Rapids in September, and a full week at the Star in Des Moines, promoted by an unusual half-page newspaper ad, but not until May 1914.[154] In Quebec, it was even censored as "too voluptuous for the general public."[155] Gardner at least had the financial clout to produce other features, beginning with *A Princess of Bagdad* (1913); the Dudley Company offered a more feeble challenge with its five-reel version of *Richard III,* starring the Shakespearean actor Fredrick Warde.[156] The recent rediscovery and restoration of a surviving print of the latter film probably has received more attention than the original ever did.

Other new or established companies sought to exploit religious subjects on the order of *Dante's Inferno,* but with mixed success. Neither Crown Feature, with Milano's three-reel *St. George and the Dragon,* nor World's Best Films, with Ambrosio's four-reel *Pilgrim's Progress,* could muster significant circulation.[157] New York Film must have thought it had the goods with a four-reel adaptation of Max Reinhardt's *The Miracle,*[158] but the owner of a stage production that had "played in London for more than a year" sued, delaying its release, and its distribution also suffered.[159] Even General Film experimented with a state rights licensing of Kalem's five-reel *From the Manger to the Cross.*[160] Previewed "for church people in the fall of 1912," this American "Passion Play" (shot on location in Palestine and Egypt) was praised by some but condemned by others, which compromised its distribution.[161] Supposedly "a decided hit in Boston" the following spring, it had rare bookings elsewhere: a single Saturday at the Coliseum in Des Moines, a single Wednesday at the Voyons in Lowell, two days at the Crystal in Cedar Rapids.[162] Still, it featured prominently for three days in April (and again in May) at the Lyric in Minneapolis, where special stage settings, an augmented orchestra, and a chorus framed the screen.[163] The only film that came close to matching *Dante's Inferno* was the four-reel *Satan,* sold directly to state right licensees by Ambrosio's US agency, which promoted it as "suitable for schools, churches, and theatres."[164] Reviews described as "impressive," even "brilliant," its handling of sin's powerful sweep through four ages: Satan's "plans to conquer the earth" after his expulsion from heaven, his taunting (as a Pharisee) of Christ, his temptation of a medieval alchemist, and his melodramatic involvement in a modern clash of class and romantic interests.[165] Most bookings of the film were for heavily advertised full-week runs: the Mall in Cleveland (February), the new Gordon

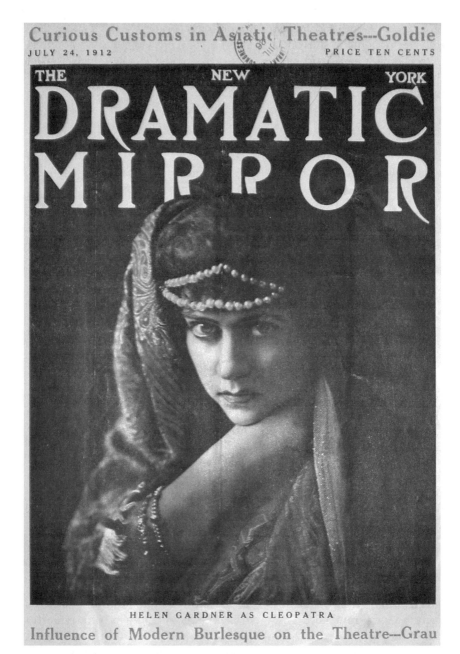

Curious Customs in Asiatic Theatres—Goldie

JULY 24, 1912   PRICE TEN CENTS

THE NEW YORK
DRAMATIC
MIRROR

HELEN GARDNER AS CLEOPATRA

Influence of Modern Burlesque on the Theatre—Grau

FIG. 11. Helen Gardner, *New York Dramatic Mirror* cover (24 July 1912).

in Rochester (March), the Empress in Toledo (March), and the Colonial in Des Moines (May), where "10,000 saw this magnificent photoplay."[166] But *Satan* also swept through other theaters (the Alhambra, Globe, and Olympia) in Cleveland in March, was rebooked at the Colonial in Des Moines in June, and played twice in Canton (at the Auditorium in March, then at the Orpheum in June). In Ohio alone, "more than 200 days' bookings [had] been secured" by May, and 15,000 people reportedly attended the High Street Theater in Columbus during an eight-day run.[167]

If *Satan* can be seen as a little-recognized model for Griffith's more complex treatment of a similar subject in *Intolerance* (1916), it more immediately set a precedent for George Kleine's distribution of Cines's eight-reel *Quo Vadis?* After Gaumont ended its contract in early 1912, Kleine had acquired exclusive rights to distribute Cines films within General Film's weekly programs, but he had not previously sought to import any production as big as this adaptation of Joseph Sienkiewicz's best-selling novel of spectacular degradation (and Christian suffering) in Nero's Rome. On 21 April 1913, Kleine boldly premiered *Quo Vadis?*, much like a Broadway play, at the Astor Theatre in New York City (tickets for the twice-daily show cost 25¢ to $1.50).[168] Reviews were ecstatic, and Kleine reprinted a half dozen each from New York and Chicago in full-page advertisements in much of the trade press.[169] He also used his branch offices to set up fifteen touring companies to road show the film, beginning in early May, at McVicker's Theatre in Chicago, the Garrick in Philadelphia, the Academy of Music in Baltimore (where 20 percent of the population saw the film), and Teller's Broadway Theatre in Brooklyn.[170] In late June, *Quo Vadis?* opened at the Tremont in Boston (admission was twenty-five to fifty cents), where it ran for three months; in July, it began a four-week run at the Hippodrome in Cleveland (also accompanied by a full page of publicity stills in the *Cleveland Leader*), after which it played another week at the suburban Alhambra.[171] By August, it was running almost simultaneously in cities across the country (again, at ticket prices of twenty-five to fifty cents): two weeks at the Auditorium and then three weeks at Mason's Opera House in Los Angeles, three weeks at the Columbia in San Francisco, two weeks at the Opera House in Providence, one week at the Berchel in Des Moines, three days at the Alhambra in Toledo.[172] That fall, Kleine continued to book the film for weeklong runs: at the Lyceum in Rochester, the Metropolitan theaters in both Minneapolis and St. Paul, the Opera House in Lawrence, and the Star in Pawtucket.[173] By December and January, it was returning to cities from Rochester and Toledo to St. Paul and San Francisco; in New York, it was rebooked for a week at a new palace cinema, the Regent.[174] Publicity stills stressed the film's reproduction of famous nineteenth-century paintings, attesting to its status as art, but, more important, local ads tended to "Americanize" the production, attributing it to Kleine and sometimes erasing any reference to its Italian origins.

Long before Griffith's *Birth of a Nation* (1915), *Quo Vadis?* thus established "the dollar photoplay attraction in . . . regular theaters,"[175] and Kleine made plans not only to secure other spectacular Italian features such as Ambrosio's *The Last Days of Pompeii* but also to invest in a studio of his own for their production in Italy.[176] Simultaneously, World Special Films gained exclusive rights to distribute Pasquali's version of the same title, forcing the two films to compete for theaters that fall and winter.[177] In cities such as Des Moines and Canton, audiences could even see both films in the same week at different downtown theaters. The only other European feature that almost measured up to *Quo Vadis?*, however, was Pathé's four-part *Les Misérables*. Unable to release its French films of more than three reels through General Film, Pathé had supported K. W. Linn (the former manager of its Chicago office) in founding a separate distribution firm, Eclectic, in New York City in late 1912.[178] Although Eclectic handled other films such as *The Mysteries of Paris*, the company's primary title clearly was *Les Misérables*.[179] Despite impressive reviews in April 1913, Eclectic had difficulty selling states rights for the original twelve-reel version, and Linn was forced to reduce the US print to eight or nine reels.[180] That film seems to have premiered at the New Grand Central in downtown St. Louis in early July and, much like *Quo Vadis?*, then played legitimate theaters from San Francisco to Boston in August and September.[181] Bookings thereafter included large picture theaters such as the Knickerbocker in Cleveland (held over for a second week in late September) and legitimate theaters such as Orchestra Hall in Chicago (for most of October) and the Grand Circus Theater in Detroit and the Shubert Masonic Theater in Louisville (at least through November).[182] Its greatest success undoubtedly came at the Tremont Temple in Boston, where it ran for nearly three months straight, through late November; by contrast, the film did not appear in New York until January 1914, at the Carnegie Lyceum (where tickets cost twenty-five cents to one dollar).[183] Although not quite the smash hit that *Quo Vadis?* was, *Les Misérables* did "have legs" (when it finally appeared in certain "unsold" regions): in April 1914, it was booked for a week at the Berchel in Des Moines, as well as for four days at the Palace in Cedar Rapids (at both theaters, tickets were twenty-five cents); the Palace even took the unusual step of running a full-page ad for the film in the local newspaper.[184]

Perhaps provoked by the success of many of these (mostly foreign) blockbusters, in the summer of 1913 two US firms, seeking to avoid the problems faced by a film such as *Cleopatra*, set out to regularize feature film distribution.[185] One of these has been largely ignored: Warner's Features. The previous summer, Warner's had begun distributing multiple-reel films, initially sensational melodramas of one kind or another, through nine offices located in the Northeast and Midwest.[186] In late 1912, the company gained a measure of respectability by contracting to release the films of Gene Gauntier Feature Players, directed by Sidney Olcott.[187] The following spring, soon after more offices were opened from Los Angeles to Washington, Abe Warner issued this claim—"American features, made in America by American actors and actresses, now have the call over those made abroad"—and exhorted manufacturers to respond to the "the future demand for features."[188] In August, the company was reorganized, as Pat Powers became president, and geared up to begin offering "an exclusive and permanent weekly service of three incomparable three and four reel features," all bought on the "open market" from eighteen independent producers (among them, besides Gauntier, were Helen Gardner Picture Players and Marion Leonard Features) and distributed through some two dozen offices.[189] The Warner brothers' long familiarity with northeastern Ohio may have led the company to use its Cleveland office to inaugurate this service: while newspaper ads stressed the company's "variety of features," in language ("Boys, We've Got the Goods") reminiscent of "straight-talking" Carl Laemmle several years earlier, the downtown Princess began to feature Warner's films exclusively.[190] Other picture theaters soon followed: in New England, the Boston office signed up exhibitors like the Bijou in Pawtucket and the Opera House in Lowell; in the upper Midwest, the Des Moines Colonial abandoned its mixed schedule of American and foreign features for Warner's service.[191] By November, one of Rochester's more "progressive exhibitors," Fitzbaugh Hall, also was showing Warner's Features.[192] The company was successful enough to run one-page bulletins in the *World* through March 1914, supply one of Toledo's principal downtown theaters, the Alhambra, well into the summer, and sustain its advertising campaign in the *Cleveland Leader*.[193] Yet there were signs that its films (perhaps stigmatized as sensational melodramas, more suitable for working-class audiences) eventually could not compete with longer, more "respectable" features: the Des Moines Colonial dropped Warner's Features in December 1913, and the Lowell Opera House and Pawtucket Bijou switched to Famous Players' service in early 1914.[194]

Although it took more than a year for Famous Players to put its ambitious 1912 plans into full operation, the company probably was more responsible than Warner's for regulating and standardizing feature film distribution and programming. In the summer of 1913, Quinn argues, Famous Players concluded that the current state rights system was proving unworkable and moved quickly to establish five affiliated companies (in Boston, New York, Pittsburgh, Minneapolis, and Chattanooga) that would not only distribute but also participate in financing the company's films.[195] In addition, distribution contracts were issued to a half dozen other established exchanges (in New York, Detroit, St. Louis, Kansas City, San Antonio, and San Francisco) to handle what ads proclaimed would come to "30 Famous Features a Year."[196] The initial films released in early September exemplified the company's policy, in contrast to Warner's, of headlining renowned stage actors in film adaptations of major authors and playwrights: Minnie Maddern Fiske in *Tess of the*

Another Pleasing Surprise for the New England Exhibitors

IN addition to our contracts already signed for New England on all of the FAMOUS PLAYERS FEATURE PRODUCTIONS, we have closed contracts with the ALL STAR FILM CORPORATION for New England on all of their productions this season.

First release, "*Arizona*," Sept. 15th. Produced by Augustus Thomas. Is this not a wonderful combination?

Mrs. Fiske in "*Tess d'Urbervilles*" and Mary Pickford in the "*Bishop's Carriage*" have already made a wonderful success, just as we said they would.

The FAMOUS PLAYERS and ALL STAR Circuit of Theatres are forming fast. Below is a list of theatres that have signed exclusive contracts for their city or town.

GORDON'S OLYMPIA	Boston, Mass.	EMPIRE THEATER	Bridgeport, Conn.
KEITH'S BIJOU DREAM	Boston Mass.	KEANEY'S THEATER	New Britain, Conn.
OLYMPIA THEATER	Chelsea, Mass.	POLI'S THEATER	Waterbury, Conn.
WALTHAM THEATER	Waltham, Mass.	POLI'S THEATER	Meriden, Conn.
DORCHESTER THEATER	Dorchester, Mass.	LYCEUM THEATER	Stamford, Conn.
PARK THEATER	Worcester, Mass.	DAVIS THEATER	Norwich, Conn.
CRESCENT THEATER	Revere, Mass.	EMPIRE THEATER	Hartford, Conn.
MAJESTIC THEATER	Fitchburg, Mass.	CASINO THEATER	Providence, R. I.
ACADEMY OF MUSIC	Lowell, Mass.	STAR THEATER	Pawtucket, R. I.
PARK THEATER	Taunton, Mass.	OPERA HOUSE	Newport, R. I.
VICTORIA THEATER	Lawrence, Mass.	NEW PORTLAND THEATRE	Portland, Me.
ORPHEUM THEATER	Haverhill, Mass.	GRAPHIC THEATER	Bangor, Me.
PALACE THEATER	Fall River, Mass.	MYSTIC THEATER	Lewiston, Me.
GLOBE THEATER	Brockton, Mass.	ROCKLAND THEATER	Rockland, Me.
NATIONAL THEATER	Winchendon, Mass.	GREY AND McDONNOUGH	Augusta, Me.
STAR THEATER	Manchester, N. H.	DREAMLAND THEATER	Bath, Me.
WHITE'S OPERA HOUSE	Concord, Mass.	NICKLE THEATER	Portland, Me.
GREY AND McDONNOUGH	Portsmouth, N. H.	JOHNSON OPERA HOUSE	Gardiner, Me.
OLYMPIA THEATER	Lynn, Mass.	MAJESTIC THEATER	Burlington, Vt.

Is your House, Mr. Exhibitor, listed above? If not, we advise you to Hurry. You have no time to lose. We can only sign up a limited number of exhibitors in New England. Remember, we have in stock, in addition to the FAMOUS PLAYERS and ALL STAR Feature Productions, "200" other big features at your disposal. A line will secure for you all the information you desire.

Famous Players Film Co. of New England

HARRY ASHER, General Manager

100 Boylston Street *Telephone, Oxford 2580* BOSTON, MASS.

FIG. 12. Famous Players Film Co. ad, *Boston Journal* (13 September 1913), 5.

D'Urbervilles and Mary Pickford in *In the Bishop's Carriage.*[197] Distributed widely around the country, beginning with full-week runs at the Knickerbocker in Cleveland, these two films served as a lure to entice major exhibitors to sign up for the regular schedule instituted later that month.[198] The tactic seems to have worked, as flagship cinemas from Gordon's Olympia in Boston, Gordon's in Rochester, and Saxe's Lyric in Minneapolis to Tally's Broadway in Los Angeles and Grauman's Imperial in San Francisco elected to become exclusive venues for Famous Players films.[199] Within another month or two, they were joined by other "first-class houses," from the Olympia in Lynn and the Star in Pawtucket to the Orpheum in Canton and the New Majestic in St. Paul.[200] Bolstered by a contractual arrangement to also distribute All-Star features, along with selected foreign features such as Pasquali's *The Last Days of Pompeii* in certain regions, by November Famous Players increased its schedule of releases from three features per month to three or four per week.[201] Although certain titles—especially All-Star productions such as *Chelsea 7750* and *Checkers,* with prominent stage actors—did not measure up to the high quality promised by the company and did rather poorly at the box office,[202] overall the Famous Players features proved successful, due in no small part to stars like Pickford in *Caprice* (1913), *A Good Little Devil* (1914), and *Tess of the Storm Country* (1914) and Dustin Farnum in *Soldiers of Fortune* (1914). Perhaps there is no more typical example of the company's success than this: when the first palace cinema, the Garden, opened in Des Moines in early May 1914, a special newspaper supplement promoted it as the city's first exclusive venue for Famous Players features, which likely would have delighted the fictional young women of my opening.[203]

Open or Closed, It's Got to Be American

In September 1913, a *Morning Telegraph* writer—using a phrase previously reserved for the legitimate theater—described what to look for in the "coming season" of motion pictures.[204] So profound was the impact of "big films" or features that, in the year-end reports on the industry, the US trade press almost unanimously agreed that, yes, 1913 "was peculiarly the year of the feature."[205] The term included specials of five reels or more, typically foreign features, irregularly distributed either through a system of road shows or through state rights licensing. Yet, by the spring of 1914, it also included the regular weekly program of up to a half dozen releases of four reels or more, nearly all of them American, a standardized program whose viable *seriality* Warner's and Famous Players had now demonstrated, but in slightly different ways.[206] Whereas Warner's built up a brand name based on the variety and novelty of its sensational melodramas (and thus remained closer to the variety model established by the major distributors), Famous Players secured its brand with adaptations of "classic" literary texts and especially stage and screen stars. Building on the latter model, for the 1914–15 season, Paramount promised to institutionalize the standardized feature program even more securely, by introducing a form of block booking, for an even greater number of features.[207]

This is not to say that the familiar variety program of shorter films (also largely American) distributed by General Film, Mutual, and Universal (and which still could be changed daily) was about to disappear.[208] Indeed, at least two innovations served to sustain the format in the face of feature films. One was General Film's grudging acceptance of a modified "open market," advocated initially by Universal and Mutual, which allowed exhibitors to show "independent features in conjunction with licensed pictures."[209] If this "open market" seemed to offer distributors a potentially larger market share, it also exacerbated competition and kept either Warner's or Famous Players from dominating the distribution of features. Still, General Film hedged its bets by adopting an exclusive service for selected "first-class houses," which guaranteed that no other licensed theaters in their area could show the same weekly programs of new films.[210] The other innovation was the introduction of sensational melodramas in serial form, typically released in weekly or biweekly episodes (of one or two reels each) over the course of three or more months—a distribution format designed to compel moviegoers to return again and again to their favorite theaters. Beginning with Selig's *Adventures of Kathlyn* (1913–14), most of these made women characters (and American female stars) the central attraction of their stories (see chapters 5 and 6). Even though they may have acknowledged that features had their place on the US market, many trade press writers (and even manufacturers), well into 1914, firmly agreed with the following assessment by the *Dramatic Mirror*'s "Film Man": "From my own contact with photoplay fans . . . , it is the varied programme [of short films] that has produced the best results."[211]

Document
"The Backbone of the Business," *Motography* (20 September 1913), 191–92

While split reels, as an American institution, have not entirely disappeared, lingering still in the old combination of comedy and scenic, they have lost their importance to the manufacturer. The tabulation of current releases from week to week shows a slowly but constantly increasing number of two-reel subjects, with an occasional three-reel to show the modern trend.

There is no argument against multiple reel subjects. On the contrary, there is no question that the future of motography as an entertainment is calculated to fill comfortably the gap between dinner time and bed time—with, of course, sufficient allowance for the conveniences of dressing, conveyance, etc. This gives, as a maximum, about three hours, and a minimum of say two hours. This space of time may be filled in with a number of short subjects, constituting a sort of motographic vaudeville, or with one long subject, the "motographic legitimate." That the latter course is successful is proven by the popularity of "Quo Vadis" and "Les Miserables," for example.

The future of the multiple-reel subject is among the most interesting speculations of the motion-picture business. The tremendous themes that may be encompassed in several thousand feet of film, the practically unlimited field of exploration among the classics of literature as well as the adaptation of modern sources of fiction, render the long motion picture an object of extraordinary interest for its artistic as well as its remunerative value. The competition of the film with the staged drama, always potential, is made dynamic by the picture of equivalent scope and length. So the multiple-reel subject is unquestionably worthy of our keenest effort and most careful study.

Nevertheless, while concentrating our best effort for the development of the future on the multiple-reel "feature," we must not overlook the present demand of the pleasure-seeking public.

The backbone of the motion-picture industry is now, as it has been for several years, the single-reel subject.

The metropolitan theater, a visit to which entails considerable preparation and some transportation, provides only a minor proportion of the enjoyment of today's picture fan. The neighborhood theater is, after all, still the great boon to mankind that the motion picture first made it. And there is no question that the neighborhood theater depends for its popularity on the short, diversified program; generally three reels and a song—an hour's show. The boundaries between one show and the next, though definite, are not important, and the visitor may drop in at any time, whenever he and his family get ready or get the notion, and remain until the return of the scene which was showing when he entered. The diversity of subjects presented in the one program is largely responsible for his interest, for he is reasonably sure of finding at least one theme of interest.

The down-town theater which caters particularly to the transient day trade, the after lunch and few-minutes-to-spare patronage, is in the same category. The program may run for an hour or more; but a considerable portion of the patronage never remains for the whole show, but departs after a reel or two. This particular clientele regards its nickel well spent, even for one reel, since the time was pleasantly "killed" until the important business or social moment had arrived.

In each of these places the multiple reel subject is inappropriate and out of harmony. Attendance at the show is not an important matter, perhaps; it is merely pleasant occupation of the otherwise idle time. The big subject requires in such cases too much application, too long attendance.

Yet these people of brief attendance are by no means ignorant of dramatic usage, nor are they satisfied with mere slapstick entertainment. Perhaps they are the very ones to appreciate the "features" in their place: but they do not want features every night, nor at noon. What they insist upon having is single reels of all possible strength and excellence, features cut short.

What we are trying to emphasize by all this argument is that the long feature show answers an entirely different demand from that for the regulation mixed program and cannot be a substitute for it. The same people attend both, to be sure, but they go under different circumstances. All the feature shows in the world, welcome as they are, will not lessen the continued demand for the program of single reel, and perhaps split reel, subjects.

The point is that it will not do to make the single reel production suffer for the multiple reels. If the producer this year can make a better feature than he could last year, he should also be able to make a better single reel. The danger is that the enthusiasm for bigger things may overshadow the real importance of the smaller, and that the production of the plebian single reel, become commonplace, may be unconsciously neglected. It is so easy to slur over the finer points when production becomes an old story to the manufacturer, and he is turning out so many a week in standing orders.

Develop the multiple-reel feature as fast as the market will stand it; but do not forget the value and importance of the single, nor the fact that it, too, may be further developed and improved.

The Power of a Nickel

I'm only a nickel, and where shall I take you?
The very best place that a nickel will go,
Where bullets wont harm you and Nature wont fake you;
Why, straight thru the doors of the first Picture Show.
    . . .

L. M. THORNTON,
Motion Picture Story Magazine
(March 1912), 131

Entr'acte 1

Mapping the Local Terrain
of Exhibition

Come on, girls, let's go to the show. You get the tickets, Gertie.
Of course, it's Dutch treat, you know.
W. W. WINTERS, *Nickelodeon*, 1 September 1910

In May 1911, the drama critic of the *Cleveland Leader*, William Sage, felt compelled to write a special column on "moving-picture theaters."[1] He not only acknowledged that "the public [was] talking about the picture-plays it sees just as it talks of the flesh-and-blood ones"—and a much "bigger section" of the public at that—but also admitted that he himself found them "vastly entertaining." Three months later, in a second column, Sage amplified his remarks on this "personal side" of moviegoing and added a frank warning to "regular playhouses": "Cleveland has one hundred and twenty [picture houses] and the weekly attendance . . . is half a million. If it came only from those who do not go to the regulation theaters there would be no need of apprehension, but it attracts the class of theatergoers who patronize the high-priced houses."[2] Other papers in northern Ohio, a crucial section of the country's industrial "heartland,"[3] shared the *Leader*'s interest, if not its concern. In October 1910, in the *Youngstown Vindicator*, for instance, staff writer Roy Stafford wondered why so many people in this steel-producing city (fifty miles southeast of Cleveland) "visit[ed] the local picture shows," why "no other institution in the city quite fill[ed] the place" of its moving picture theaters.[4] The answer came in several anecdotes claiming to demonstrate that "shoppers find them a convenient place to rest, appointments are kept in them, acquaintances are made there, [and] romances often have their beginnings within their doors."

The shared yet divergent interests of these newspaper stories (others will be found throughout this book) make a promising point of entry for mapping the terrain of what at the time often were called simply "picture shows." The term spans a range of developments in exhibition that occurred in the "little noticed . . . period of the early 1910s that bridge[d] the nickelodeon and the palace," to quote an architectural historian,[5] when

45

small storefront theaters, by early 1910, were increasingly giving way, in words of the *New York Morning Telegraph,* to "modern moving picture theaters."[6] Our sense of these chiefly has come from a limited range of sources: reports in the trade press devoted to moving pictures, summary articles in monthly or weekly magazines,[7] and recreational surveys conducted by moral reform groups in cities from New York and Chicago to Waltham, Massachusetts, Kansas City, Missouri, and Portland, Oregon.[8] Yet one source has gone largely unexamined: daily newspapers. The reason is obvious enough for the nickelodeon period: exhibitors initially had little need of them for advertising purposes—and, with some exceptions, the papers reciprocated by giving moving picture shows little notice. From 1910 on, however, as exhibitors in some cities began to buy advertising space on a regular basis, local papers, in turn, began to devote stories, columns, and even pages to various phases of the ever more popular "photoplays" or "movies" (see entr'acte 5).[9] In conjunction with city directories and other documents, professional manuals, and, of course, trade press reports, this newspaper material proves invaluable for mapping more specifically the venues of exhibition for moving pictures in particular cities and their changes over time: especially the moves to standardize as well as "elevate" or "uplift" exhibition, moves that at the same time allowed for degrees of differentiation. This material also facilitates any effort to describe and understand the range of program formats in specific venues (and their changes over time), as well as the promotional frameworks within which moving pictures circulated—and what "imagined community" of spectators that programming and publicity assumed.

As suggested in the introduction, my own research on newspapers and moving pictures, supported by indications in the trade press, has led me to focus on three regions of the United States—other than metropolises such as New York, Philadelphia, and Chicago—all of which proved crucial to the emergence of nickelodeons and then picture theaters, not only because of their relatively high population density but because of the extensive railway transportation system that bound their major urban areas together. Those three—New England (especially northeastern Massachusetts and Rhode Island), northern Ohio, and the upper Midwest—also were marked by differences in their settlement history, industrial base, and immigrant population. Although what follows can hardly exclude other sources and areas of the country,[10] my effort to revise the history of moving picture exhibition in the early 1910s depends greatly, as does that of the next entr'acte, on information gathered from local newspapers in selected cities in these three regions. In short, what choices, however restricted, were available to what audiences in those cities, and especially to the growing numbers of regular moviegoers, some of whom, as in Canton (which could have included my grandparents), were described by one local newspaper as "motion picture mad"?[11]

In early 1910, a writer in *Nickelodeon* imagined three classes of picture theaters in the near future.[12] The "first class" would resemble the best "dramatic and vaudeville houses," show only the "highest type" of pictures, and include "appropriate . . . musical features." The second would "use a less costly grade of pictures and lower-salaried vocalists" (some might even include "cheap vaudeville") and would charge less for admittance. The third (namely, nickelodeons), with "a minimum of operating expense," would appeal "to a certain patronage chiefly because it is cheap." It would take several years for those imagined first-class picture theaters to become numerous, but trade press writers persisted in appraising conditions and revising their perceptions accordingly. In 1911, David Hulfish classified picture theaters by location as well as size, status, and admission price. He distinguished the "elaborate" from the ordinary "storefront city" theater, then noted the development of two other kinds: the large "combination" house of vaudeville and moving pictures that catered to a residential area, and the "large exclusive picture house" located in an urban shopping district.[13] Two years later, Frank Woods reiterated the three kinds of theaters first foreseen by *Nickelodeon,* but with a twist: (1) "the five-cent houses, with pictures that appeal only to the least cultivated persons"; (2) "the ten to twenty cent theaters, that cater to the great middle class"; and (3) "the regular theater . . . commencing to divide its time between stage productions and . . . greater-features."[14] Six months later, Epes Winthrop Sargent saw a simple dichotomy emerging: one house ran "longer subjects and the other the short lengths," with the latter still relying on "drop in" patronage.[15] In May 1914, W. Stephen Bush focused on size, quality of service, and the length of films shown.[16] His "first-class motion picture theater" possessed a large seating capacity, tended to run pictures of five reels in length or more, and provided "the highest degree of comfort with safety." The second, which often operated as part of a circuit or chain, tended to show "shorter features with a suitable admixture of single reels." The third had "a smaller seating capacity" and "depend[ed] on variety and a short program," but it could compare favorably with the others in terms of quality of service.

However well they mark certain changes in exhibition venues, the trade press classifications remained approximate as well as inconsistent. Moreover, they all were captive to a Progressive discourse of "uplift," strongly inflected by distinctions of socioeconomic class. They ignored, for instance, the licensing system innovated by General Film—and then followed by Universal and Mutual—that classified theaters into those within a certain zone that were contracted to show first-run films and those within other zones that showed second-run, third-run, or even "commercial" films, after a period of "clearance."[17] They also ignored building codes and city licensing fees, which differed from place to place. In one of the earliest appraisals of such codes, in February 1911, William Braun found that New York, Chicago, and San Francisco all classed theaters according to their seating capacity: in the first two metropolises, "all theaters seating over 300 persons must conform throughout in construction to the same laws which govern regular theaters"; in the latter, the figure was 400.[18] In New York, the code also meant that larger houses paid a licensing fee of $500 per year, whereas smaller houses (in which "songs and recitations [were] not rendered on a stage") paid only $25 per year.[19] In Youngstown, Ohio, such a two-tier system of licensing was similarly draconian—the lower fees pertained to moving picture theaters with a capacity of 299 persons or less—but some theaters also offered standing room for up to 200 more.[20] St. Louis, by contrast, classed all picture theaters as one but sharply distinguished them from legitimate theaters and vaudeville houses by forbidding "the placing of any stage, platform or scenery in any motion picture exhibition room."[21] Under pressure from theater owners, the New York code was rewritten in July 1913 to raise the seating capacity breaking point to 600 persons.[22] By then, major architectural firms such as Thomas Lamb (New York), Stearns & Castor (Philadelphia), M. M. Gleichman (Cleveland), and Aroner & Somers (Chicago) also were designing large, elegant first-class picture theaters that would soon earn the reputation of "palace cinemas."[23]

A closer look at individual cities introduces other factors that not only affected the gradation of picture theaters but also produced anomalies in their standardization and differentiation. In Cleveland, the largest city in northern Ohio, with a population of 560,000, according to the 1910 census (double that of 1890), the picture theaters that advertised regularly in the Sunday *Leader* were located in nearly a dozen commercial districts.[24] Some of the more important theaters were located downtown—the Mall, Avenue, Bijou Dream, Cameraphone, Oxford, Corona, Princess, Orpheum, Bronx, and a former legitimate theater, the Duchess (1,400 seats)—but not all of these were large: the Mission-style Dreamland seated just 262.[25] Almost as many were either near a working-class district on the city's northeast edge—the Superior (660 seats), New Colonial, Norwood, and Gordon Park—or near a mixed-class suburb farther out—the Doan, Home (600 seats), and Manhattan.[26] Others were clustered in contiguous shopping districts just south of that area—among them, the U.S. Theater (1,600 seats), Penn Square (950 seats), National (700), and Delmar—or in a middle-class suburb farther east—the Alhambra (1,200 seats), Knickerbocker (1,200 seats), Monarch (1,000 seats), and Quincy—which, in another ten years, would become the city's "second downtown."[27] At least two, the Tabor and Broadway, helped an-

FIG. 13. Penn Square Theater, Cleveland, *Moving Picture World* (23 December 1911), 998.

chor another shopping district along Broadway on the city's southeast edge. Another dozen—among them the Park National, Fairyland, Pearl, Clark, Cozy, Fulton, and Gordon—occupied two nearby areas in the southwest. Finally, the Lakewood, Madison, and Gordon Square (1,200 seats) anchored a mixed-class suburb on the city's western edge. These theaters constituted one-third of the city's total number, which came to 120 in 1911; most of the rest, according to city directories, were residential theaters, catering to a range of local districts usually differentiated by class and ethnicity.[28] Still, several downtown theaters—the Princess (one of the first to adopt Warner's Features service), Orpheum, and Bronx—clearly appealed to working-class audiences, for they also advertised in the labor weekly, the *Cleveland Citizen*.[29] The only major theater with an all-black clientele, the Alpha, located on the city's near east side, advertised solely in the African American weekly, the *Cleveland Gazette*.[30]

Cleveland can be taken as a model of picture theater status, size, and geographic distribution for many large to medium-sized cities at the time. That is the case for cities from Minneapolis (300,000 population),[31] to Toledo (170,000 population)[32], both of which had more than forty picture theaters by 1911.[33] In Minneapolis, downtown there were at least four classed as regular theaters, seating more than the building code limit of 350—the Crystal (which opened in 1909, with 575 seats), Isis, Seville, and Lyric (1,700 seats) along with a host of others—including the Mazda, Scenic, Novelty, Orient, and Gem.[34] Once a legitimate theater, the Lyric turned into the city's largest "exclusive picture theater" in September 1911; there S. L. Rothapfel soon gained fame as a model manager with his selection of music and moving picture programs.[35] Smaller theaters also emerged in either secondary shopping districts or ethnic neighborhoods.[36] The Cozy (opened in 1910) was one of the first to anchor the "east side" across the river from downtown.[37] The People's (opened in 1909) and Third Ward catered to an older German immigrant community on the "north side." Even more theaters—among them, the Southern (also opened in 1909), Iola, Ione, Olympic, and New Park—were concentrated in several "south side" shopping areas that drew on nearby Swedish, Norwegian, and Jewish immigrant communities. By 1911, others such as the American, Elite, Harriet, Lake, and Melba finally began to locate in the middle-class residential "lake" district on the "west side." In the summer of 1913, all these were joined by several more large downtown theaters: the Alhambra, Hippodrome, and a former vaudeville house, the Princess (800 seats). In nearby St. Paul, also by 1911, picture theaters similarly were reported in "practically every section of the city."[38]

In Toledo, the downtown picture theaters also ranged from larger houses such as the Empress (next to a major department store), the Columbia, which ran vaudeville and moving pictures until it was renovated and renamed the Princess (870 seats) in early 1913, and the Colonial (1,000 seats), which opened in early 1912 exclusively for moving pictures, to smaller ones such as the Royal (300 seats), Hart, and Crown.[39] Small theaters also appeared quite early in secondary commercial districts: in 1908, the Majestic near the Dorr-Detroit area on the southwest side; in 1910, the Orpheum in the Lagrange-Manhattan area on the north side.[40] Others clustered near industrial areas: the Crescent and People's in East Toledo (home of a Hungarian immigrant community); the Auburn and Temple on the city's western edge. Even more theaters catered to residential areas: the Jewell (in 1909), Diamond, Crescent, and Air Line in the rapidly growing area of South Toledo; the Circle (also 1909) and Wanda along Nebraska Avenue (one of two Polish immigrant communities); the Yale (500 seats) on the near north side; and the Laurel (650 seats), "Toledo's . . . Prettiest Neighbor Theater" (on the corner of Dorr and Detroit), which had a much-publicized grand opening in August 1913.[41] As in Cleveland, several downtown theaters—most notably the Hart but also the Princess, Royal, and Crown—appealed specifically to working-class audiences by advertising in the labor weekly, the *Toledo Union Leader*. And the Hart proselytized *Union Leader* readers in particular to "get in the habit of dropping in . . . when you are downtown."[42]

The Cleveland model also holds for a smaller city such as Des Moines (86,000 population), where picture theaters initially were sited in two prin-

FIG. 14. Crystal Theater,
Minneapolis: exterior
and interior, ca. 1910,
Minnesota Historical
Society.

cipal areas.[43] Most important was the downtown shopping district, the hub
for a network of streetcar lines stretching into the city's residential areas. The
Colonial (opposite a major department store) and Family (within a block of
three legitimate theaters) were especially prominent.[44] A second, smaller district lay just below the state capitol building on the city's east side, where the
Elite catered to chiefly white-collar and working-class audiences. By late
1911, new picture theaters began to open in residential districts, all adjacent
to streetcar stations. Charles Namur, owner of the Colonial,[45] initiated this
development with the Idle Hour/University Place on the prosperous northwest side (near Drake University), the Highland Park in a northern middle-
class suburb, and a third theater in the predominantly Italian working-class
area on the near south side.[46] Within two years, up to ten small theaters in all
were clustered near University Place and in the east side areas surrounding
the capitol (largely Scandinavian and Jewish communities).[47] Downtown,

during that time, the Unique (700 seats) and Majestic (1,100 seats) shifted to moving pictures; the Star and Family (1,000 seats) were renovated extensively; and still others were newly constructed—the Casino (550 seats), Royal, Palace (1,100 seats), and Black Cat.[48] By early 1914, more than twenty picture theaters were operating throughout the city.[49] That spring A. H. Blank, owner of the Star and Casino, announced the downtown opening of the "picture palace" Garden Theater with a special supplement in the *Register and Leader*.[50]

Yet not all cities of a similar size to Des Moines followed this model. In the medium-sized industrial cities of Massachusetts and Rhode Island, moving picture theaters tended to be located exclusively in the downtown commercial districts, drawing on a large pool of skilled and unskilled workers, the majority of them recent immigrants packed into nearby tenements.[51] In Lowell, for instance, "foreign-born whites" made up more than 40 percent of the city's 105,000 population, with those from Poland, Russia (Jewish), Greece, and Portugal (concentrated mostly in "ethnic islands") nearly equal in number to those who had arrived earlier from Ireland and French Canada.[52] By 1910, they had a half dozen downtown picture theaters, along with four vaudeville houses, to choose from, with many—the Colonial, Jewel, Merrimack Square, and Premier—seating 1,000 or more.[53] In nearby Lawrence, where "foreign-born whites" made up no less than 50 percent of the city's 85,000 population, the picture theaters were fewer (and suffered during the bitter six-week strike of early 1912, and its aftermath) but also often larger: the Broadway (1,800 seats), New Nickel (1,700 seats), and Victoria (900 seats).[54] Wedged among other cities just north of Boston, where "foreign-born whites" constituted 30 percent of its 90,000 population, the "shoe city" of Lynn had no more than a half dozen downtown theaters.[55] Yet again, several were quite large—the Olympia (3,200 seats) and Central Square (1,500 seats).[56] Finally, in Pawtucket, on the outskirts of Providence, where "foreign-born whites" constituted 35 percent of the city's 50,000 population, all the moving picture theaters were located downtown—the Bijou (1,200 seats), Star (900 seats), Pastime (500 seats), Music Hall, Globe, and Scenic—and the Star and Pastime were closest to the Polish, Jewish, and Italian immigrant neighborhoods, partly within Central Falls (just north of the city), precisely where one of two new theaters opened in 1913–14. [57]

Similar patterns developed in smaller industrial cities outside Cleveland in northeastern Ohio. In the "bold, vulgar" steel-producing city of Youngstown, where new Slovak, Czech, and Italian immigrants made up 25 percent of the 80,000 population, the big theaters were all vaudeville houses fronting the central square: the Grand Opera (1,600 seats), Park (1,600 seats), and Princess (800 seats).[58] Licensing laws kept the picture theaters small: by 1911, fifteen (including the Rex, built by Harry Warner) stretched along one street for several blocks on either side of the square, with five (on

FIG. 15. Central Square
Theatre, Lynn, Mass.,
ca. 1912.

the east side) catering largely to Italians and other recent immigrants.[59] A "Ministerial Association" investigation implicitly condemned those five, arguing for the construction of a "model picture theater" in that "congested foreign district."[60] Before 1914, no more than two theaters, at any one time (none lasted very long), were located beyond the downtown center.[61] Moreover, no large picture theater appeared until late 1912, when C. W. Deibel could afford to risk paying a higher licensing fee and completely rebuilt the Dome (1,000 seats), next to the city's largest department store.[62] In the nearby steel town of Canton, where Hungarians, Italians, and Russian Jewish immigrants constituted 20 percent of its 55,000 population, a half dozen vaudeville houses and picture theaters, including the Grand Opera and Odeon (where my grandfather performed), similarly surrounded a downtown public square. Yet as early as late 1911, neighborhood theaters such as the Happy Hour, a former skating rink, began to appear and even advertise occasionally in local newspapers; by 1913, such theaters reportedly were "being built in all sections of the city," much as they were in Cleveland, Toledo, Minneapolis, St. Paul, or Des Moines.[63]

   In many of these cities, one can see a move toward standardization that, within another decade, would lead to regional and even national cinema chains or circuits. As Douglas Gomery has shown, such chains participated in the "revolution in mass selling" created by grocery stores (A & P, Krogers) and variety stores (Woolworth's, Kresge) at the turn of the last century; the most important developed in metropolises such as New York (Marcus Loew's circuit of "small time vaudeville" houses), Philadelphia (the Mastbaum brothers' chain of picture theaters), or Milwaukee (the Saxe brothers' chain).[64] But this move to standardize took various forms, depending on local conditions. In Cleveland, Edward Kohl and C. M. Christensen, together or separately, controlled up to fifteen picture theaters, including the National, Broadway, Dreamland, and Bronx.[65] Through Atlas Amusement, "Manny" Mandelbaum owned several more (including the Knickerbocker), whose profits he poured into rental exchanges (Feature & Educational Films, Lake Shore Film) and eventually multiple-reel film production.[66] Nearby, the Warner brothers built up a circuit of theaters, in conjunction with their rental exchange in Pittsburgh, Duquesne Amusement & Supply; by 1912, they too began to invest in producing and distributing multiple-reel films. In Des Moines, Namur's four picture theaters were superseded by another chain that included the downtown Casino, Star, and Garden, which Blank would build into a major circuit across the state.[67] In Toledo, there was no one dominant chain; instead, by 1913, William Bettis controlled a "family of theaters," anchored by the Colonial and Alhambra, and the Empress's owners constructed two large residential theaters, the Laurel and National.[68] In New England, different patterns emerged. Some theater chains radiated out from Boston: Gordon Amusement (owners of Dreamland in Lynn),[69] Scenic Temple (owners of the Merrimack Square in Lowell),[70] Olympia (also in Lynn), or Theatre Comique (again, in Lynn). Others remained local: in Lawrence, at least for a short time, one company ran the Broadway, New Nickel, and Premier, while a second ran the Victoria and Pastime; in Pawtucket, Star Amusement controlled the biggest theaters, the Star and the Bijou, by late 1913.[71]

If there was a general consensus in the trade press that, by early 1914, the era of nickelodeon was "on the wane" and that of the palace cinema was about to begin,[72] there was far less agreement on the range of picture theaters that now dominated the urban landscape. For theaters in specific cities—at least within New England, northern Ohio, and the upper Midwest—could differ greatly in the relative size and status of their downtown and residential locations. Still, one can hazard several generalizations. Smaller cities that depended heavily on a single industry tended to have picture theaters located exclusively in a centralized commercial district, supporting the *Dramatic Mirror*'s claim, in October 1912, that "a motion picture audience . . . [was] drawn from the population living within walking distance of the theater."[73] Such theaters could be few and large, as in Lynn, Lowell, and Pawtucket, or they could be small and more numerous, as in Youngstown—despite the fact that all had a large pool of "foreign-born white" skilled and unskilled workers. Yet in more diversified cities of widely varying size, from Cleveland or Toledo to Minneapolis or Des Moines, the picture theaters tended to be distributed among several commercial centers as well as a range of neighborhoods differentiated by class and ethnicity or race.[74] And the specific combinations often confounded the classifications offered by trade press writers such as Woods and Bush. Whatever the differences, however, the moviegoing experience was not necessarily more homogeneous in one kind of city and more heterogeneous in another—as the next entr'acte will show.

Document
A. L. Barrett, "Moving Pictures and Their Audiences,"
Motion Picture News (16 September 1911), 8–9

The five million people who comprise the daily moving picture audience of the United States are drawn from every age, rank, and condition, notwithstanding the favorite and very common sneer made by those unacquainted with very evident facts that they can only satisfy the ignorant and poorer classes because of their extreme simplicity and cheapness of admission. If these sneerers would take the trouble to observe for ten minutes the persons entering a moving picture house in any neighborhood, they would find sufficient evidence to refute such a statement, for although, fortunately, thousands of the very poorest and ignorant people can and do attend them, yet they possess an almost equal attraction for those more fortunately circumstanced, and near the large theaters where picture plays are presented will be found lines of carriages and automobiles, the occupants being women and men well known in the religious, educational, and social world, who represent both the wealth and brains of the nation, and to whom neither cheapness nor mediocrity could possibly appeal. Such audiences do not find this once depressed "poor man's amusement" beneath them, in fact, they can better appreciate the scientific research that originated the amusement as well as the picture plays themselves, particularly the educational films or travelogues representing scenes with which many of them are already familiar. With the advent of kinemacolor, this pleasure will be greatly enhanced and those who have traveled abroad will again be able to see the favorite spots in England, France, Italy, Switzerland, Germany, and other countries which they remember so well, not merely in a book of colored views only or on a black and white moving picture, but in actual vivid colors or neutral tints that have been wrought by time.

Picture plays as at present conducted are attracting favorable comment on all sides and in the audiences are found clergymen, members of college faculties, students, philosophers, lawyers—men and women—the brains of the nation. In the minds of the wealthy, there is always an unthinking prejudice against that which is patronized largely by the poorer classes, and if the leaders of the moving picture industry had been satisfied with mediocrity in their production, they would have had a corresponding quality in their audience, but the strenuous insistence for the best has been rewarded by a steady improvement in the audience, until now people are willing to pay as much as seventy-five cents for a good seat at the best moving picture plays, and the patrons are drawn from the highest ranks. . . .

To drop from royal favor and seventy-five-cent seats to the five-cent open air shows in a vacant lot where the films are but second-rate, we see even here whatever refinement and culture a neighborhood possesses as well as the poorer people. There will be seen the local physicians and trades people taking an hour's amusement when the opportunity offers, the tired mother who at last has an hour she can call her own, and although attended by a couple of her numerous brood, can enter heartily into the troubles of a cruelly persecuted pair of lovers, and when no one is looking, can enjoy a comfortable weep over the "Schoolmaster's Overcoat," can laugh the next minute at the adventures of Mutt and Jeff, and then, as she came in during the middle of a set of pictures, can enjoy a chat while one of the touchingly beautiful illustrated songs is being rendered by some local Scotti or Bispham endowed with lungs warranted to last under the strongest pressure, and when this performance is over, is ready for one of the beautiful travelogues, or a pictorial description of railroad building in the West. The moving picture show is also a favorite rendezvous for groups of young people where they can remain in the open air, and thousands of boys seem to find more pleasure and profit in investing five cents for one of the performances than the same amount in a drink at the saloon with the privilege of kicking their heels on the sidewalk when their nickel is gone. It is a favorite place for the workingmen also, who like the open air performances, where they can usually enjoy a quiet smoke, and there is no necessity, moreover—so distasteful to a tired man—of specially dressing for an hour or so's entertainment.

At the majority of performances, the rate of admission is the same for all seats, and every occupation, class and condition will be found represented, yet we rarely hear of friction. The physician may frequently find himself next to a laborer, the college student in close proximity to what would elsewhere be termed a "gallery god," but all, the last mentioned included, conduct themselves quietly. In the picture play performance there is the same excitement, the same crucial moments, the same recognition of some favorate [sic] actor to be found in the ordinary theater, but—there is not the same noise or disturbance that the gallery always evidences, to the annoyance of the rest of the audience. The picture play audiences are generally speaking, a quiet, orderly crowd in which women and children mingle without fear of annoyance, except on very rare occasions, now becoming rarer every day. This was not always the case, it must be admitted; there have been many instances where some well-known objectionable characters in a neighborhood have deliberately set out to annoy or insult persons frequenting moving pictures, and have succeeded admirable until caught.

. . . With the exceptions that prove the rule, a moving picture audience will be found to be orderly, quiet and composed of both the brain and brawn of the nation. It is a perfectly respectable, innocent form of amusement where mothers and daughters can go unattended, parents can take their children, and working persons can go to spend a pleasant couple of hours without the necessity of an entire change of apparel, or expending at least thirty-five cents for a very poor seat, with the knowledge that they are looked on as the poor part of an audience; and besides this, they return home at a reasonable hour and are fit for their work the next morning. Since the managers have manifested greater interest in the care of their audiences as well as the films presented, parents have placed more confidence in them and we now frequently see groups of carefully brought up young girls going unescorted to the picture plays, and comparatively few people have the slightest fear in allowing their older children to go there unattended. This managerial watchfulness should continue unabated as the plays often appeal to young people particularly and convey such wholesome morals that they make the best teachers, besides infusing, as they do so frequently, some bit of information, suggesting some historical epoch, showing some industry or exemplifying some religious truth.

. . .

My Picture Girl

There's a girl who stays in the Golden West
That I never shall see or know;
She's the Picture Girl that I like the best—
But I never shall tell her so.
She has wistful eyes that shine like stars,
And hair like velvet night,
And I might as well wish for the Moon, or Mars,
But I love her, that's honor bright.

For she's always thinking of me, you see,
In her far away, sunny land,
Thinking and planning, just to please me;
And working to beat the band.
But never for her the applauding throng
That backs the footlights' glare,
Her only "lime" is the noonday sun—
No paint or powder there!

She can ride her horse like a cattleman,
She can handle a rope or gun,
And my heart beats now in a rat-a-plan
When I think of the risks she's run.
I have seen her leap from an engine cab
And roll in the sand below,
Risking her life for one thrill's quick stab
To the people who watch the show.

But you needn't think that a cowgirl's part
Is all my film girl knows
(She can swing her train with a grande dame's art,
And her love is as sweet as a rose),
But the best of it is that she's always near,
No matter how far I go;
She never has guessed that I hold her dear—
And I never shall tell her so.

JOHN SUMNER,
Motion Picture Story Magazine
(June 1912), 112

Chapter 2

The "Usable Past" of Westerns

Cowboy, Cowboy Girl, and Indian Pictures,
Part 1

In April and May 1911, *Motion Picture News* ran a page titled "Film Charts" in which the Independent films released weekly in New York City were categorized into four "tracks."[1] Two of those, *dramatic* and *comedy,* had long been used by the new industry to broadly distinguish certain types of film product; a third, *educational,* was a more recent invention, born out of the general effort to "uplift" moving pictures, and included both fiction and nonfiction films. The fourth track, *western,* was the most specific and, in the handicapping metaphor of the charts, had entries that ran "the fastest kind of a race." They "abound," as the *News* put it, "in the life, snap, and vigor that mean so much to M. P. audiences." This is a vivid yet far from anomalous indication of just how important westerns were not only to the Independents but also to the US moving picture industry as a whole. Just two months earlier, for instance, an exhibitor in Zanesville, Ohio, who also toured a "floating theater seating 1000" on the Ohio and Mississippi rivers, reported that wherever he showed films his audiences wanted "Wild West pictures."[2] At the same time, thousands of miles away in England, the trade weekly *Bioscope* published a feature article about Essanay's "cowboy pictures," not only to express its own enthusiasm but to satisfy the alleged demands of its readers because the company's "Western subjects . . . [had] become so popular" there.[3] Indeed, "so numerous" were westerns both here and abroad, *Billboard* noted, in reviewing Selig's *The Outbreak* (March 1911), that it now took "extraordinary strong situations" as well as marvelous scenery and "fine horsemanship" to make them interesting.[4]

These wide-ranging yet complementary texts offer a point of entry for reassessing the western at a crucial juncture in its development as a production and marketing strategy and as an "American product" highly suitable for internal consumption as well as export, especially to Europe.[5] Specifically, this chapter and the next focus on the volatile years of 1910–13, when westerns proliferated despite repeated criticism in the trade press, when the competition between the MPPC and Independents became particularly fierce, and when changes began to occur—for instance, the distribution and exhibition of multiple-reel and then feature films, as well as the emergence of movie personalities or stars (see chapter 6)—that would transform the industry, in short, the moment when, as Rick Altman puts it, a range of possibilities for the genre was being "explored, sifted, and codified."[6] This chapter sketches out several important stages of that exploration and codification, drawing on certain manufacturers' production strategies, commentary on those strategies as well as specific films in the trade press, and an analysis of extant archive prints. Then, after highlighting the 1912 crisis in production and distribution, the next chapter uses the popularity of westerns abroad as well as at home to frame several perspectives for analyzing variations on the emerging genre's "imagined community of nationality." It also glances at the "constellated communities" (the term is Altman's) that the westerns' "usable past" may well have served—what, in Herbert Blau's prescient words, was "commonly remembered and adhered to, or thought of as better forgotten," and what was not.[7] Finally, it reconsiders the western's alleged decline in 1913–14. The overall aim in both chapters is to argue for the unique significance of the western—a crucial instance of what Miriam Hansen has called, yet without naming this "genre-in-the-making," the "new sensibility" of "action" that so characterized American modernity or modern "Americanism"[8]—to a discussion of the intersection of those long-contested cultural artifacts of historical consciousness—*genre* and *nation*—in US cinema of the early 1910s.

Attack/Counterattack

The "life, snap, and vigor" cited by the *News* had been associated with westerns as "quintessential American subjects" at least since 1909, and particularly those that *Moving Picture World* dubbed the "school of action" westerns allegedly aimed at the "masses."[9] It was this kind of "wild and wooly" picture in which Selig and Essanay specialized and which Independents like New York Motion Picture exploited with its Bison films to secure a niche on the US market. The trade press generally was not adverse to them. The *World* noted that, when Selig made a cowboy picture "full of action" such as *The Cowboy's Stratagem* (August 1910), "it [made] a good one"; even the *New York Dramatic Mirror* could agree, in praising the "exciting chase" and "daredevil riding performed by real cowboys and real Indians" in Kalem's *The Cowpuncher's Sweetheart* (September 1910).[10] Perhaps the best surviving example is Essanay's *Under Western Skies* (August 1910), which G. M. Anderson shot for the company in and around Morrison, Colorado.[11] The plot of this one-reel film is full of twists and turns: drunken cowboys make a woman the stake in a poker game, and, after a gun battle, the survivor forces her to marry him; her fiancé (who has been away on a trip east) tracks them down and gets her to flee with him, but abandons her when they lose their way in the desert; found by her husband (now a respectable miner), the woman pledges herself to him anew and persuades him not to shoot the coward she once promised to marry. Given this action-packed story and its "good badman" hero, the *World* was struck by how the acting and particularly the graphic portrayal of "the desert and the environments of Western life" made it "seem more plausible or real."[12] In short, this was but one of an increasing number of films that began to exploit the iconographic tradition of Wild West landscapes already widespread in American popular culture and, in Alan Trachtenberg's apt phrase, its myth of "unimaginable natural wealth."[13] Through its unique integration of landscape and narrative, the western, as Nanna Verhoeff so concisely puts it, was becoming the "genre of [a promised] future, narrating the past."[14]

Just as often, however, the "school of action" westerns were dismissed as no better than dime novels. The *Mirror* was especially harsh in criticizing Independent films for being inauthentic and having badly constructed stories and/or poor acting.[15] More pointedly, the *World* chastised Pathé's *The Gambler's End* (November 1910) for trading on a "yellow back type of story" that had "too much bloodshed" and too many "crude . . . repulsive scenes."[16] For its part, *Variety* often damned "wooly western" films such as Selig's *Girls on the Range* (February 1910) with sarcasm: this single reel of "hundreds of gun plays, abductions, and d-e-a-t-h" was just the sort of thing to lure "women who drop into a picture show after a shopping trip."[17] By late 1910, this attitude culminated in a spirited attack published in the *World* as "The Indian and the Cowboy (By One Who Does Not Like Them)."[18] Not content simply to argue that "there [were] far, far too many of these pictures," the author countered the claim from exchanges and exhibitors that "children demand them"— one that *Film Index* sanctioned, citing a New York Child Welfare Committee survey, by asserting that "three-fourths of the boys" questioned liked "Cowboys and Indians" best.[19] Instead, this author imagined an "intelligent . . . small boy" who (much like himself) knew better: "Indians and Cowboys [were] nasty, dirty, uncomfortable, unpleasant people." At best, he argued, kids looked on "these . . . stupid . . . Indian and Cowboy subjects with a mixture of amusement and toleration." Soon after, *Nickelodeon* claimed: "The Western photoplay [had] outrun its course of usefulness and [was] slated for an early demise."[20] Why? "Film makers went West" not to portray "real Western conditions" but simply "to find a stamping ground for melodrama, [and] western melodramas [had now] lost their ability to create suspense. . . . the old thrills [were] exhausted." As a kind of tongue-in-cheek support, one month later *Nickelodeon* printed a full-page caricature sketch in which half of the character stereotypes film producers supposedly could not do without came from Indian and cowboy pictures.[21]

That these charges were fired off to provoke better film product may be inferred from their disappearance (for the most part) from the trade press throughout 1911.[22] One obvious reason was that, despite the criticism, westerns continued to be popular, for their "authentic" landscapes as well as for thrilling action, and with a wide audience—Indians themselves sometimes excepted.[23] In April, for instance, several theater managers in Canton listed westerns as one of two or three kinds of films that their clientele favored; similarly, two major downtown theaters in Lynn often used westerns in competing for customers.[24] Given their popularity, as well as the critical favor shown its own "Indian-cowboy fight pictures" such as *The Rustlers* (January 1911) and *The Outbreak* (March 1911),[25] Selig announced in June that one of the three reels it now released every Tuesday would be "A WESTERN" because the company was "humbly acced[ing]" to public demand.[26] A month later, the *News* cited several Essanay westerns (in which girls outwitted or outran Indians) as examples of what the "average audience" liked in its films.[27] By summer's end, the *News* was making this typical claim: a cowboy picture, a good comedy, and a good educational film were all that was needed to compose an ideal program—especially if a cowboy could perform "the most daring feats of horsemanship," as did rodeo rider Tom Mix in Selig's *Saved by the Pony Express* (July 1911).[28] Not only does Mix leap from one galloping horse to another in that film, but he quickly has to rope and break a bronco in order to deliver a letter that exonerates a friend on trial.[29] This claim especially held true, the *News* asserted, "in small towns and cities [where] the cowboy and Indian [were] as popular as when they first appeared."[30] Another exhibitor just outside New York City, writing to the *World,* agreed: based on his own experience of seeing "an average of twenty reels of licensed film a week for three years. . . cowboys and real comedy [were] popular everywhere and always."[31] Even Vitagraph, which at that time made very few westerns, played on their popularity in at least one ad by representing its audience as a posse of rootin', shootin' cowpunchers.[32]

The Indian pictures in which Pathé, Biograph, Kalem, Bison, and Powers specialized were equally popular but not always critically favored.[33] Powers films such as *The White Chief* (September 1911) were roundly condemned as unintentionally hilarious for casting "un-Indian-like white men" as Indians.[34] Bison films sometimes were faulted, as in *A Redskin's Bravery* (May 1911) or *The Red Man's Penalty* (October 1911), for their trite stories and carelessly staged action and acting.[35] Yet most Indian pictures won praise, even those like Bison's that exploited the "school of action" formula but had "real Indians" playing all the roles, such as the warring Sioux and Pawnees in *A Warrior's Squaw* (February 1911) or the heroic protagonists in *Starlight the Squaw* (March 1911).[36] In Bison's *A Squaw's Retribution* (June 1911), one of many films that drew on Edwin Milton Royle's famous play, *The Squaw Man* (1905), Mona Darkfeather began to gain recognition for her "very good work" as a woman (with child) who, abandoned by her white lover, now that he has ac-

FIG. 16. Mona Darkfeather (Kalem),
Motion Picture Story Magazine
(March 1914), 13.

quired a fortune, takes revenge by drowning the white woman with whom he has taken up.[37] In the same company's *Little Dove's Romance* (September 1911), which so impressed the *World* with its "imaginative quality," white trappers have to rescue Little Dove (played by Darkfeather) from their treacherous half-breed cook; but it is a young man from her own tribal village who pursues and kills the half-breed and then gently persuades her that she is better off with him than with the departing trapper with whom she has fallen in love.[38] Unexpected examples of such Indian pictures even came from Vitagraph. Highly praised by the *Mirror* (which also noticed its director, Rollin S. Sturgeon), *The Halfbreed's Daughter* (November 1911) countered the usual stereotype of the half-breed with a revenge story in which an Indian actor named Eagle Eye, "with excellent effect," plays the father who has to avenge the death of his young daughter, whom a white prospector had "lured away" from their cabin and then abandoned.[39]

The "more artistic" Indian pictures, in the words of the *World*, assumed a position closely aligned with contemporary efforts by white Americans not only to preserve the images, cultural artifacts, and rituals of a people they had pushed to the edge of extinction but, perhaps most notably in Edward S. Curtis's famous twenty-volume photographic project (1907–30), to "exalt the Indian [and] depict the noble traits of his character."[40] Cloaked in the rhetoric of authenticity, such pictures served up the Indian as a no-longer-threatening Other for (white) consumption. The *Mirror* had joined the *World* in praising this impulse for "preservation" in earlier films, from Kalem's *The White Captive of the Sioux* (July 1910) to Biograph's *The Broken Doll* (October 1910) or *The Song of the Wildwood Flute* (November 1910), the latter of which allegedly depicted a harvest dance ritual.[41] An unusual variation on the first film occurs in Kalem's *Her Indian Mother* (December 1910), in which the daughter of an Indian and a Hudson Bay Company representative decides to remain in her mother's village rather than return with her father to Montreal.[42] Not surprisingly, the "preservationist" attitude was especially evident in those Pathé films that involved Indian characters exclusively and were directed by James Young Deer, a Winnebago Indian who had come to head the company's western unit after long experience in Wild West shows and earlier western films.[43] For the *Mirror, Old Indian Days* (June 1911) succeeded as "a poetical picture" in its depiction of a couple torn by conflicting codes of honor; likewise, for the *World, The Cheyenne Bride* (August 1911) aptly celebrated the bravery, honor, and strategically deceptive tactics of rival Sioux and Cheyenne tribes.[44] Perhaps the most acclaimed of these Pathé Indian pictures, *The Legend of Lake Desolation* (August 1911), made its central character not the white girl who is raised by Indians and then convinced that she should return to her original family but the old chief whose heart is broken and who, with the coming of winter drifts out onto a lake, in a final tableau, and sets his canoe afire.[45]

If Essanay, Selig, Kalem, and Pathé all continued to make westerns a significant part of their weekly releases, at least three Independent companies made cowboy pictures nearly the exclusive province of their production, with Bison alternating between Indian and cowboy pictures. By April, the American Film Company was releasing "Two 'Flying A' Cowboy Films" a week, an output equal to that of Bison and Champion and double that of Nestor.[46] For several weeks in May and June, *Billboard* promoted the titles of all three major companies for their good stories, acting, scenic effects, photography, and horsemanship.[47] But the *World* also began to pay more attention to the Independents' cowboy pictures, for instance, reprinting exhibitors' letters praising "Flying A" films and accepting American's own contention that it was "recording into film classics the romantic stories of the West."[48] One possible reason for this approval was that Allan Dwan had signed on as chief writer-director for American's western unit that spring, for the *World* heralded one of his early films, *The Ranchman's Nerve* (July 1911), as the most "notable film" of the week.[49] With titles like this, American began sporting a new logo to advertise its "Cowboy Films,"[50] and it boldly proclaimed its El Cajon Valley location in Southern California as "the last West" left.[51] Soon Nestor joined in touting the authenticity of its one-reelers. Each week, with its western unit also now located in California, Nestor released three films suffused with a "genuine western atmosphere," while American promised

FIG. 17. American Film Co. ad, *Moving Picture World* (16 September 1911), 770.

the "highest possible grade of western pictures" with "real cowboys" and "backgrounds of surpassing beauty."[52] In early 1912, American even experimented with a unique publicity ploy, publishing stories of the "Flying A" pictures, in advance of their release as films, in dozens of newspapers across the country.[53]

Initially, it may seem surprising that attacks on westerns cropped up again in late 1911 and early 1912. Now it was the *News* that led the charge, in November, citing the great number of letters from moviegoers who were "utterly sick and tired . . . of Wild West pictures."[54] Specifically, the *News* called on the Independents either to stop making "such foolish pictures" or to "produce Western subjects . . . with an elevating, uplifting story." A month later, the *World* took up the cry, claiming that the "perfect riot of these 'Wild West' things" had "gone far enough": did the manufacturers really "imagine that two-thirds of the population [were] dime-novel-reading boys between the ages of ten and sixteen?"[55] Yet this criticism coincided with changes already under way in the industry—witness, for instance, the efforts at American— that would transform the western precisely in ways advocated by the trade press. The best evidence, however, came in late 1911, with an announcement by NYMP, perhaps inspired by the new level of spectacle and the "three-dimensional aspect" that D. W. Griffith had achieved in mounting battle scenes in *Fighting Blood* (June 1911) and *The Last Drop of Water* (July 1911), the first of which, at the Voyons in Lowell, was promoted as "the greatest western picture ever made" and, at the Lyric (Minneapolis), "held the audience spellbound and at its termination always evoked applause."[56] NYMP would abandon the "regular style of [Bison] Indian and cowboy pictures" (which it admitted too often were "travesties of Western life"), reorganize its production, and make "nothing but sensational, spectacular Western subjects, with enormous casts," drawn from the riders, horses, and stock of the Miller Brothers 101 Ranch Wild West Show.[57] Moreover, unlike Griffith's films, these would be two-reel special features, directed by the former IMP director Thomas Ince.[58]

"Elevating" the Western

That all this criticism evaporated, perhaps as expected, can be attributed to several new production and marketing strategies in the industry. Although identified primarily with a different company, each confirmed the *World's* conclusion, in reviewing *The Last Drop of Water*, that "To Americans pioneer stories must always be welcome, for not only have these humble heroes opened up a new and wonderful land, but they have transmitted to later and present generations the endurance and contempt or danger, which are to this day a heritage of the American character."[59]

One such strategy, of course, was distinctive to Essanay. As early as Octo-

FIG. 18. Essanay ad, *Moving Picture World* (21 October 1911), 226.

ber 1911, probably in a move to challenge the "Flying A" films, Essanay began running weekly strip ads in the trade press that staked its claim as the "indisputable originators of Cowboy Films."[60] To support that claim there is a surviving print of *The Sheriff's Chum* (April 1911), the main attraction, according to a rare newspaper ad, at the Dome Theater in Youngstown one Sunday that spring.[61] Here, Anderson not only pursues and captures an escapee from a town jail but discovers that his visiting "best friend" from the East has tried to seduce his wife and then bests him in a rousing fight that the *New York Morning Telegraph* found "as dramatic and well worked up as any heretofore seen in motion picture plays."[62] At the same time, there was the testimony of an experienced cowhand who, in a letter to the *Mirror*, described Anderson as by far "the best cowboy character delineator of any film concern."[63] By November, Essanay was promoting Anderson, its western leading man and director, as the "most photographed man" in the business.[64] The timing made Anderson one of the first recognized movie personalities or stars, for it coincided with Majestic Pictures' attempt to exploit Mary Pickford's departure from Biograph and promote "Little Mary" as its own.[65] Anderson's appeal was unmistakable in several unique newspaper stories that circulated weeks before Essanay announced its promotional campaign, specifically in several northeastern Ohio steel towns, first in the *Youngstown Vindicator* and then in the *Canton News-Democrat*.[66] There, picture fans took to calling Anderson "Bullets," a nickname that theater managers frequently used in their ads to promote "Essanay's Great Western Thrillers" well into the summer of 1912.[67]

By early 1912, Essanay itself was singling out Anderson's "inimitable character of Broncho Billy" and deploying it like a trademark or brand name to sell some of the one-reel westerns in which he appeared.[68] As Broncho Billy, Anderson was often a "good badman," an outlaw with enough conscience to finally turn away from crime and lead an honorable life. An early surviving example would be *A Pal's Oath* (October 1911), in which a "pal" promises to keep Anderson's secret—that he has stolen some money to pay a doctor for tending the friend's injuries—but then arranges his arrest in order to court and marry the woman Anderson loves.[69] Released from jail several years later, Anderson plans his revenge, only to peer through a cabin window and see the "pal" embrace his wife and young daughter—and find that he cannot fire his revolver. This redemptive character often had the benefit of strong stories, as in *The Stage Driver's Daughter* (October 1911),[70] and most notably in *Broncho Billy's Christmas Dinner* (December 1911). Expecting to rob a stagecoach, Broncho Billy has to save its passengers when the horses are spooked by drunken cowboys; a young woman on the stage then invites him home for dinner, and, when she turns out to be the sheriff's daughter, he confesses, is given immunity, and is accepted at the table. The *Mirror* found the "thrilling ride on [the] stage coach . . . as exciting and realistic as anything of its character ever shown in pictures"; the *Morning Telegraph* agreed, describing it as "a real hour of unalloyed thrill—for it will hold you as if it did last that length of time."[71] Indeed, a surviving film print reveals some deft framing and editing, including an unusual high-angle midshot/long shot taken from a camera mounted on the stagecoach behind Broncho Billy as he struggles with the horses' reins.[72] The *Mirror* was impressed as well by the acting "in the quieter moments," as when a pensive Broncho Billy is washing up in the foreground space of a small room, while the family and other guests cluster around the Christmas dinner table visible through a background doorway.

A second strategy emerged with the Bison-101 plan to make two-reel westerns. Special multiple-reel westerns, of course, had circulated before—for example, Selig's *Ranch Life in the Great Southwest* (1910), *Buffalo Bill's Wild West and Pawnee Bill's Far East* (1910), and Atlas's three-reel *The James Boys in Missouri* (1911)—and the latter, although vilified in the trade press, certainly had been a hit at such theaters as the Star in Pawtucket.[73] But this was the first attempt, noted by *Billboard* at the time, to produce fictional "features" on a regular, weekly or biweekly basis.[74] The company itself promoted the first of these, *War on the Plains* (February 1912), as marking a "new era in western pictures"; in a full page devoted to its release, the *World* compared it favorably to the latest historical spectacular from Italy, Ambrosio's *The Golden Wedding*.[75] *Battle of the Red Men* (March 1912) similarly was called as "epical" as Itala's earlier *The Fall of Troy*.[76] This strongly suggests that the Bison-101 westerns were perceived not only as noteworthy rivals of the Italian imports that were transforming film distribution and exhibition but also as far more successful than single specials such as Selig's much-delayed *The Coming of Columbus* in establishing the basis for an American "national epic."

By the time that *The Indian Massacre* (March 1912) and *Blazing the Trail* (April 1912) were released, the trade press was absolutely taken with the Bison-101 westerns.[77] In an unprecedented four pages in the *World*, Louis Reeves Harrison told the story of *The Indian Massacre*, in which the struggle between an Indian tribe and white settlers is driven by parallel desires.[78] One involves food and escalates into an attack on a white settlement and the retaliatory massacre of an Indian village; the other involves offspring and leads to a white child being seized during the initial massacre to replace a dead

FIG. 19. *Broncho Billy's Christmas Dinner,* 1911 (production still).

FIG. 20. Bison-101, *War on the Plains,* 1912 (production still), *Moving Picture World* (27 January 1912), 298.

Indian baby. Just before the retaliatory massacre, however, the Indian mother returns the white child and, in a final long shot tableau, stands silhouetted on a bare hilltop before the platform bearing her own dead child.[79] As for *Blazing the Trail*, the *Mirror* extolled the "magnitude of [its] backgrounds" and Ince's astute "management of the exceedingly large number of players" that bestowed "an air of reality" on an otherwise familiar narrative of white settlers threatened while crossing the plains.[80] Especially striking, even now in a surviving archival print, are scenes that exploit reciprocal foreground-background contrasts: the Indians looking down from a hilltop on the wagon train far below; the white men later looking down on the Indian encampment and then riding up out of a foreground gully to attack the camp and rescue a white woman and the young man who had tried to save her.[81] The *Mirror* also lauded the craft and artistry of *The Deserter* (March 1912), noting especially its final long shot tableau in which an army deserter (Francis Ford), having exonerated himself by saving a wagon train from an Indian attack, is honored with a formal military burial, presented in graphic detail, in the empty desert.[82] The *Sunday Telegraph* added that "the toning . . . used consistently throughout" *The Deserter* was especially "appropriate and most effective."[83]

The Bison-101 productions had a huge impact in exhibition and served not only to promote the Independents as a whole but also to further establish the western as a serious historical subject. One sign of that impact was a photo of the entrance to the Savoy Theatre in Seattle, "showing the splendid advertising and featuring of Bison films" such as *War on the Plains*.[84] Other signs were even more telling. In Cleveland, *War on the Plains*—"a combination of military, western, cowboy and Indian that suits everybody"—along with *The Crisis*, received special attention in the *Cleveland Leader*: the one in a review that noted "the crowds waiting for seats" at the downtown Mall theater, the other in a photo story that also included Sarah Bernhardt's *Camille* and Biograph's *The Girl and Her Trust*.[85] A third title, *Battle of the Red Men*, circulated through at least three leading theaters, including the newly built Park National—and on a lucrative weekend program.[86] In Boston, *The Indian Massacre* was given a special advance screening for exhibitors (and pronounced " 'big' in every sense of the word"); in nearby Lynn, all the Bison-101 westerns played exclusively at the Central Square over a four-month period and were the sole feature attractions all week in late May and early June.[87] The *Lynn Daily Item* even praised *The Lieutenant's Last Fight* (June 1912) not only for its "thrills" but also because "it is educational in its scenic reproduction of American history now closed."[88] In Toledo, in late March, "the big spectacular photo-play" *The Deserter* was given the largest newspaper ad in the city to date for its two-day screening at the downtown Colonial.[89] Most of the Bison-101 westerns, however, were shown at the nearby Crown, and by April that theater was promising a "new, fresh, and entertaining 101

FIG. 21. Bison-101, *Indian Massacre*, 1912 (production still), *Moving Picture World* (9 March 1912), 857.

Ranch Bison every Saturday."[90] Similarly, in Minneapolis, from late February through June, these "thrilling headliners" played first at the Crystal (usually in four-day runs) and then at the Isis (on weekends), where the *Lieutenant's Last Fight* "arouse[d] the most hardened of moving picture 'fans' " with its depiction of "war in all its realism."[91] That spring, in Des Moines, the Family Theatre also placed a rare ad for *Blazing Trail*—the latest of the "famous Bison '101' Ranch Wild West, Two Reel Indian and Cowboy Features"—in both of the city's leading newspapers.[92]

A third strategy, somewhat surprisingly, was associated with Vitagraph. As I have argued previously, cowboy girl westerns (from Selig, Essanay, and Bison) already were numerous by 1910, and they were no less so two years later.[93] Many of these were "school of action" westerns of one sort or another. In Vitagraph's *A Girl of the West* (January 1912), the plucky sister of the hero's sweetheart does her own horseback riding to single-handedly foil a rustlers' plot.[94] In Alice Guy Blaché's *Two Little Rangers* for Solax (August 1912), a postmaster is robbed and a cowboy falsely accused of the crime until the postmaster's two daughters track down the real criminal and, unable to get him to surrender, set fire to his shack (with him inside).[95] Reviewing Essanay's *Broncho Billy's Narrow Escape* (July 1912), the *Morning Telegraph* cited the "novel turn" in which a ranchman's daughter "makes a hard ride" to prevent the lynching of a ranch hand falsely accused of stealing her father's horse.[96]

And, in a tribute to the "Kalem beauties" who performed in the company's westerns—from Alice Joyce to Ruth Roland, whose *The Girl Deputy* (February 1912) pleased a New York "audience very much"—the *Mirror* praised their daring, expert skills as horseback riders, even if specific films like *The Ranch Girls on the Rampage* (May 1912) upset one of its reviewers when those "beauties" played characters no better than "hoodlums."[97]

Although not known as a producer of westerns, Vitagraph released a good number of films in the genre from late 1911 through the first half of 1912, most of them rather different from *A Girl of the West*. Their chief characteristics were these: they exhibited the "quality" of the company's more familiar historical films and literary adaptations, they were directed by Sturgeon, and they often told unconventional stories.[98] A good example is *How States Are Made* (February 1912), which, as the *World* put it, "deals with a well-known phase of Western life that everybody seems to have overlooked in the mad scramble to supply the demand for 'Western stuff' ": the Oklahoma land rush of 1893.[99] The *Mirror* not only praised the feat of depicting hundreds of settlers lined up to dash across the Cherokee Strip but also found the "events leading up to the exciting ride" so convincing "that the whole story seems like history instead of acted fiction."[100] A year later, the *Mirror* cited this film specifically in demonstrating that Sturgeon was a major filmmaker.[101] Another is *The Greater Love* (May 1912), which, the *Mirror* argued, made "an exceptionally virile and decidedly new version of this rather timeworn situation": an outlaw and a sheriff are rivals for the same woman.[102] In short, the story was "cleverly devised," delaying knowledge of the outlaw Kansas Kid's identity until after he has been found injured by the sheriff, cared for by Nell, confessed his love for her, and taunted his rival before riding off into the hills; after the requisite gunfight, he takes the wounded sheriff back to Nell and lets himself be arrested.[103] *The Craven* (April 1912) is perhaps the most unusual of all: in the *Mirror*'s words, a "significant example of the peculiarly strong type of Vitagraph Western picture."[104] Here a woman discovers the man she has married is really a coward, even though his boastfulness has led to his election as sheriff. When a man sought for murder shows up near town, it is she who goes out and kills him with a well-aimed rifle shot and then has her husband collect the body and take credit for the deed. Yet in advertising the film, Vitagraph deflected its "peculiarity" with a quip: "Only goes to show that the wife is sometimes the 'better man' of the two."[105]

A Crisis Leads to Competing Western War Spectacles

Despite their critical success and popular appeal, Bison-101 westerns suffered because the industry's distribution system, pegged to one-reel and split-reel films, could not easily accommodate their regular release. According to the *Mirror*, these "really high-class" features were too expensive to be profitable "at the prevailing rate of 10 cents per foot paid by the exchanges," and many of the latter refused to pay a higher price.[106] The Sales Company tried to solve this problem by setting up a special department to handle the Bison-101 features (and others) by licensing those exchanges and newly formed state right companies willing to pay fifteen cents per foot for rental prints.[107] Perhaps this solution would have worked well enough for NYMP, but it never had a chance because of growing divisions among the Independents that finally led to Sales's breakup in May 1912.[108] Initially, NYMP entered into a contractual agreement with one faction, Universal, but relations quickly soured between the company and Carl Laemmle, who headed IMP and eventually would become the leading figure at Universal.[109] An acrimonious court case—and alleged gun battles around the Bison-101 locations near Los Angeles—delayed the release of further western features throughout the summer and led some writers to predict that the "latest fashion" for western and Indian films was "disappearing."[110] Yet even after NYMP switched its allegiance that August to the other faction, Mutual/Film Supply, it lost any claim on the Bison brand to Universal (Swanson now was engaged in producing its westerns) and had to reorganize its production under the new brand names of Broncho (with Ford now as director) and Kay-Bee (with Ince).[111] As a result, no new features with either the new Bison (Universal) or the Broncho logo appeared until September, and none with the Kay-Bee logo, until November.[112] This was especially detrimental to Ince's three-reel *Custer's Last Fight,* which, although reviewed enthusiastically by Harrison in June and ready for release in July, did not reach theaters until October.[113]

The consequences of this crisis initially were mixed. For several months, nearly all the westerns in circulation were one-reelers.[114] However popular, as Essanay's *Broncho Billy* series in particular continued to be, these were promoted not as "special attractions" but as regular weekly releases—in Cleveland, the downtown Orpheum scheduled Essanay westerns on Sundays, specifically for a clientele of working men and their families.[115] Important exceptions were the two-reel Indian pictures made by Dwan at American, beginning with *The Fall of Black Hawk* (July 1912) and *Geronimo's Raid* (September 1912), and Warner's three-reel *Peril of the Plains* (September 1912), which marked both companies' initial moves into "feature" production.[116] Moreover, imported two-reel French "westerns" such as Gaumont's *Their Lives for Gold* (July 1912) and Eclipse's *The Red Man's Honor,* starring Joë Hamman (December 1912), now found a welcome market.[117] Although the *Mirror* castigated *Their Lives for Gold* for being inauthentic and overly "crammed full of exciting captures, struggles, and escapes," the film seems to have been quite successful in exhibition: in Toledo, it was featured at the Empress one weekend in August and then rebooked one week later.[118] In a similar vein, the crisis opened up the growing market for multiple-reel films to other sensational melodramas that relied heavily on thrilling action—namely, jungle or animal pictures and especially Civil War films (these are the subject, respectively, of chapters 5 and 4). Whereas Selig and Gaumont specialized in the one, Kalem took the lead in the other, beginning with titles such as *The Siege of Petersburg* (July 1912). That summer, the two factions struggling over the Bison brand also decided that "the Civil War [could] be exploited in the same careful manner," especially for subjects that demanded spectacular battle scenes.[119]

When the Bison, Broncho, and Kay-Bee westerns finally did appear in the fall of 1912, however, the trade press seemed eager to embrace them. Both the *World* and the *Mirror* found much to like in Universal-Bison's *The Massacre of the Santa Fe Trail* (September 1912), "a big feature Indian story" that was "crammed full of action."[120] By contrast, *A White Indian* (September 1912), the *World* claimed, would "attract attention" chiefly because Mona Darkfeather played the main character.[121] For the next six months, Universal committed to releasing, on average, one multiple-reel Bison western per week, and Darkfeather proved a crucial attraction in a series of Indian pictures, directed by Frank Montgomery, from *Star Eyes' Strategy* (October 1912) to *Mona of the Modocs* (February 1913).[122] So successful were many of these films that, in May 1913, she and Montgomery formed their own company; when the venture soon collapsed, she began appearing that summer in one-reel Nestor Indian pictures.[123] Some of the other Bison westerns won praise from both the *World* and the *Mirror*, either for the clarity of their storytelling, as in *Early Days in the West* (October 1912), or for the novelty of staging an ambush, as in *The Massacre of the Fourth Cavalry* (November 1912).[124] Yet far more came in for repeated criticism, especially for their slight stories, illogical construction, or less than adequate acting. Both the *Mirror* and the *World*, for instance, castigated *The Flaming Arrow* (March 1913), the first of a promised series written by melodrama playwright Lincoln J. Carter, for being full of "trite," "well-worn" action.[125] The surviving print bears this out to some extent, in a story that aligns White Eagle (an orphaned, college-educated halfbreed) and a colonel's daughter against a revengeful white rival, a disreputable Mexican, and marauding drunken Indians.[126] Yet the film is efficiently told, skillfully combining spectacular battle scenes with close shots, as in the cut-in close-up of White Eagle discovering muddy evidence of the rival's deception and the concluding shot of the reunited couple coming forward into medium close-up.

The trade press consistently found much more to commend in the westerns released by NYMP, beginning with Broncho's *A Frontier Child* (September 1912) and *For the Honor of the 7th* (October 1912).[127] The long-delayed *Custer's Last Fight*, for instance, the *Mirror* lauded for achieving "the most realistic battle . . . ever witnessed" in moving pictures; the *Morning Tele-*

graph agreed, claiming it as one of the "most masterly offerings of the entire year."[128] Also highly praised in the *Mirror*, *The Sergeant's Boy* and *The Vengeance of Fate* (both October 1912) risked telling stories that ended as ironically or grimly as did the company's earlier films. In the first, a boy raised by an army sergeant enlists after he is told to renounce his love for a colonel's daughter; he dies heroically in an Indian attack, and the girl stands "silently by and watche[s] the body of the man she loved carried to the grave," murmuring, "And he never knew."[129] In the other, a traitorous rival is shot in an Indian attack (from which the hero saves his wife and child) and then "left in the woods for the hungry wolves to feed upon."[130] One of the first films released under the Kay-Bee label, the three-reel *The Invaders* (November 1912), struck Harrison in the *World* as "an absorbing picture of dramatic conflict . . . the top of its kind, from an artistic point of view"; the cinematography impressed him as comparable "to the best photography as applied to still life, with far greater emotional effects."[131] Kay-Bee's *The Altar of Death* (November 1912) confirmed, for the *Mirror*, that Ince's production teams were "masters" in making such films.[132] The *Morning Telegraph* added: "Secure this Kay-Bee and then watch for others. If like this, they will all be winners."[133] That mastery continued in westerns that, unlike the Bison films, began to turn away from focusing on Indian stories. In Broncho's *A Shadow of the Past* (January 1913), a thief, long thought dead but now a white renegade leading an Indian attack, spares his former wife (who has remarried) and her child, only to flee and be "killed by the officer whose family he protected."[134] Kay-Bee's three-reel *The Wheels of Destiny* (February 1913), by contrast, was enhanced by "the delightful and convincing playing of [a] charming young actress," especially in a moving recognition scene between a father and daughter.[135]

The impact of the Broncho and Kay-Bee westerns in exhibition confirmed the *Morning Telegraph*'s admiration, in reviewing *The Army Surgeon* (November 1912), for their "wonder of stage direction and bigness," as well as the *Mirror*'s claim that Ince, along with G. M. Anderson (but in a quite different way), had caught "the true vitality of the Western drama."[136] In Lynn, the first Kay-Bee and Broncho titles were said to rival the earlier "famous Bison '101' westerns."[137] Central Square promoted them as a weekly "special attraction," beginning in late November; Dreamland did the same with the Universal-Bison westerns.[138] In Baltimore, between January and March 1913, westerns of all three brands each week figured prominently in downtown theater ads.[139] In the second week of February, there were no less than six, including *Mona of the Modocs* and *A Shadow of the Past;* a good number circulated on a regular basis from one theater to another, one night to the next, especially on Thursdays, Fridays, and Saturdays; and several Bison features returned after a month's "clearance" of their initial screening. In Cleveland, where

FIG. 22. New York Motion
Picture Company ad,
Motion Picture News,
(21 September 1912),
back cover.

Lake Shore Film heavily promoted its Broncho and Kay-Bee westerns and where *Custer's Last Fight* served as the inaugural feature at the downtown Oxford Theatre in October, the Doan complemented its ad for *The Law of the West* with this claim: "There is no more popular film before the public today than the Kay-Bee western war pictures."[140] In Des Moines, the Unique promoted its contract with Mutual by taking out an unusual half-page newspaper ad that included a weekly schedule highlighted by "the celebrated Kay-Bee western features" each Friday.[141] In Toledo, where Bison westerns were a weekly attraction throughout the fall, a unique weekend listing of moving pictures at residential theaters in every section of the city, starting in January 1913, included a disproportionate number of Kay-Bee, Broncho, and Bison westerns.[142] By April, one of those, the Wanda (near a Polish immigrant community) was designating Saturday a "WESTERN NIGHT."[143] Finally, some NYMP titles such as *Custer's Last Fight, A Shadow of the Past,* and *The Wheels of Destiny* achieved an unusually long "shelf life," returning to major downtown theaters from Pawtucket and Lynn to Des Moines as much as six to eight months after their initial release.[144]

From Westerns to Famous Players

Given this range of evidence, westerns played an unusually important role in regularizing and Americanizing the distribution and exhibition of moving pictures in the United States. At theaters contracted with General Film, each week throughout 1911 audiences could count on seeing one or more cowboy, Indian, and/or cowboy girl pictures from Essanay, Selig, and Pathé (as well as others less regularly from Kalem, Vitagraph, Biograph, and Lubin), and usually on the same day of the week. At those contracted with Sales, they could count on even more such pictures from NYMP, American, Nestor, Champion, and Powers, also often on the same day of week. In 1912–13, the western spectaculars produced by Ince and Ford for NYMP and later by Montgomery and others for Universal then proved crucial in establishing multiple-reel films as a regular feature of Film Supply/Mutual and Universal's weekly programs. One significant measure of the popularity and profitability of Kay-Bee and Broncho films, for instance, was the doubling and sometimes tripling of box office receipts at the Star Theatre in Pawtucket, when it contracted with Mutual in October 1912.[145] Equally, if not more, important was the fact that the Bison-101, Kay-Bee, Broncho, and Bison (Universal) westerns constituted regularly renewed, critically acclaimed American subjects that could compete favorably with the increasing number of European feature imports available through road show and state rights systems of distribution. Arguably, their regularized distribution, along with that of multiple-reel Civil War films (see chapter 4), anticipated the system that Warner's Features and Famous Players would establish for American features during the 1913–14 season.

Document
Louis Reeves Harrison, "The 'Bison-101' Headliners,"
Moving Picture World (27 April 1912), 320–22

The New York Motion Picture Company is certainly engaged in blazing the trail of artistic achievement so far as depicting battled scenes is concerned, as I have never seen action more vivid and realistic than was shown in advance releases privately exhibited a week ago. Many of the foreground struggles between the primitive red man and the all-conquering white race would furnish themes for intense figure compositions, and the larger ensembles are marvelously clear. Vastness in them does not involve vagueness, but comprehensiveness of exterior detail.

The elimination of the wandering tribes hunting over this continent and so continually fighting among themselves that evolution had become improbable and decadence set in has been the subject of many written stories and almost as many pictured ones, not so much from interest in the dissolving races themselves as from the tragic action characterizing the continuous warfare for supremacy between representatives of progress and those of degeneration or arrested development.

The pictures are introduced by the moving portrait of a buffalo admirably centered, who gives the impression, in a grave sort of way, that he is something of a wag, but the story of his kind has been that of the Indian by whom he was being annihilated long before the white man came. This food animal of the continent formerly existed as far east as the Atlantic and as far north as Newfoundland. These animals were nearly extinct east of the Mississippi, and they were in the process of extermination in their native wilds when the white flood began to sweep over the country.

There were probably less than a million Indians scattered over that part of the continent now known as the United States, subject to the ravages of relentless killing and torture—cruel, crafty and predatory—with no universal language, or marks of gradual enlightenment, and incapable of contributing anything of value to human evolution when European races began to fight their way from ocean to ocean under all sorts of difficulties, including methods of fighting that it was a difficult matter to kill a redskin, whereas the whites were constantly exposed by their peaceful occupations to indiscriminate slaughter.

There is no discovery of rights and wrongs involved in the Bison productions. Conditions alone are presented, especially those which existed after the government attempted to regulate and control the various tribes, according them privileges still unenjoyed by white citizens, and punishing with severity acts of outrageous cruelty by the natives, and less severely acts of oppression by responsible whites. Race hatred was unavoidable and it is only modified today. The average descendant of colonial families has little use for the red man, regards him with distrust and, with a few poetic exceptions, considers him hopelessly beyond the pale of social contact.

The Indian, however, remains one of the most interesting and picturesque elements in our national history. He is almost typical of the fighting male, a restless, dominating, ever-struggling human creature, principally engaged in works of destruction, but representative of the ancestral strain that conquered all the other creatures delivered from the fertile womb of Mother Earth. He was essentially a man of physical action, using only that part of his brain which enabled him to be crafty in the hunt for food, though he had vague poetic ideals and nebulous dreams of barbaric splendor. Mentally he was far below the Egyptian of 6,000 years ago, but he was the physical superior of any man on earth except the strong-armed European who cultivated brain along with brawn.

The United States Government first tried to lead the tribes into civilized pursuits, but Mr. Redman was not strong of arm nor strong of purpose. He took to drink on small provocation and had a drunkard's lack of ambition, was satisfied with enough to keep him going and oppressed by an ingrowing distaste for work of any kind. Many Americans of high intelligence exhibited a genuine friendship for the Indians; the establishment of schools and colleges for them shows that. On the other hand, a lot of heartless scoundrels like those now preying on white people robbed the red man by much the same methods, and constant "uprisings" ensued as a consequence.

These uprisings became a habit with the tribes as they are also with the New York Motion Picture Company directors. If the plain truth be told, we know in advance that the Indians are going to have a war dance and attack the settlers, that some hero or heroine will go through all sorts of perils to reach the military post, and that the troops will arrive in the nick of time. This pounding on the tom-tom of one idea indicates that the plays are made on the spot, and the sameness is only relieved by one strong outreach for sympathy. That occurs in "The Crisis"—it might better have been called "The Weakling."

In "The Crisis" there is a bid for interest in the central figure, a parson's son, that is effective. We are all mortal and most of us realize that there is an element of good in the victim of bad habits. We like to see him redeem himself. That is more manly than simply being good when there was no chance to be otherwise. In consequence, the weakling, the parson's son, reaches out beyond the screen and strums human sympathy. The types are good in this play so far as the men are concerned.

One woman sweeps on the screen like a whirlwind. She is Anna Little, a corking rider, full of vim in action, and one of the best actresses in her role I have ever seen. She is a find and only needs wider opportunity in plays of clearer character conceptions. It is a pleasure to see a heroine who can do something more than smile, roll her eyes, and embrace. The American girl is best typified by those of energy, never by the chalk-faces who stand at street corners on the Rialto.

If I may be accorded opportunity for a little suggestive criticism, and no man of ability resents this, I think there is the right material in this company for some spirited historical plays of high value. The average photodrama pretending to depict episodes in our development as a nation deals principally with the stale and insipid love affairs of a young lady we do not know with a young man we care nothing about. All that we are profoundly affected by— the sufferings and struggles of American pioneers—are often presented as side issues of minor importance.

Such plays are more than silly and they are far from entertaining. The Father of Our Country is the usual victim and is shown as anything but the noble, dignified and splendid leader that he was. I would like to see a portrayal of Washington during his earlier fights, those with Indians, and how about Tippecanoe? Our great leaders must be shown in their reverses, in their bitter disappointments, with hard earned victories instead of an unimportant young man hugging and mugging his girl. Such plays would tell our story abroad, be educational at home, and could be made as replete with thrilling incident as those of no purpose.

I noticed in the Ranch 101 headliners that the directors gave careful attention to nearly all minor details—they obtained superior ensemble effects by skilled handling of individual features, and I have reason to think that they could bring out historical plays of thrilling interest such as would go straight to the hearts of American people with accuracy of detail. These would be all the more interesting because of the larger bodies of men handled and would not belittle episodes we have all been taught to reverence.

I strongly approve their presentation of foreground action. In most hand-to-hand battles of the stage, the supers fall dead like stiffs and never move. In real life, while the fighting male is mad with fury, he rises and goes at it as long as he has a breath and a heart beat left. Man never gives up the ghost without a last determined struggle. If anything these small-scope actions could be intensified. The audience is the same in primitive instincts as that which watched the gladiatorial contests in Rome.

. . .

The New York Motion Picture Company has not gone to extremes one way or the other in revealing the characteristics of the American Indian. There has been a lot of slush written and voiced on this subject, but there is a middle course that is nicely balanced. One of the Indians of the company— he enacts the part of a chief—is a star actor. His gestures and movements are a source of perpetual study. The directors have apparently let Lo play his own role and he does it to perfection. The chief is quite good in comedy as in tragedy—a delight in one and impressive in the other.

I must take off my hat to the directors for showing the pioneer as he was, one of the hardest fighters in the world, pitted against a barbarian who would have swept the barbarians of Europe from the face of the earth. The early settler was a man, every inch of him, and the iron in his blood has descended to those who promulgated the Monroe doctrine. From him came the soldiers who freed the country from British rule and fought every war for liberty since then, who took under their protection the unhappy children of all nations, and at least tried to give them opportunity to enjoy life, liberty, and the pursuit of happiness.

Bein' Usher in a Motion Picture Show

There's lots o' things I like to do; go swimming, shoot, and camp,
And ride a horse, and row a boat, and play football, and tramp.
But of all the fun a-goin', more than anything I know,
I'd like to be an usher in a Motion Picture Show.

To wear a uniform of blue, and walk on up the aisle,
And show the people to their seats, and boss the crowd in style,
And look around as if I owned the whole blame thing, you know.
Gee! I wish I was an usher in a Motion Picture show.

But best of all about it is to see each Photoplay,
And never miss a single one, but see them every day.
The cowboys riding round like mad, the soldiers, Indians—oh,
I'd give a lot to usher in a Motion Picture show.

And think of all the things I'd learn; the lots of history,
Geography, and such—O my, the foreign lands I'd see!
I'd learn more than I do at school of all such things, I know,
All just by bein' usher in a Motion Picture show.

Fred White, he says, when he's growed up, he'll be a millionaire.
And Tom says his ambition is to fill the Pres'dent's chair.
I've got one wish, beside it any other would seem slow—
I want to be an usher in a Motion Picture show.

MARY CAROLYN DAVIES,
Motion Picture Story Magazine
(June 1912), 102

Entr'acte 2

Moviegoing Habits and Everyday Life

"Mrs. Jones, Let's take in this here show. Never been in one? Well, come on in now. I'll pay, and I've got some candy that I promised Johnnie I would get him, but he'll never know if we eat some, come on." Exit Mrs. Jones and her talkative friend through the entrance of one of the five-cent theaters.

w. w. WINTERS, "With the Picture Fans," *Nickelodeon*
(1 September 1910)

Certain practices first established by nickelodeons may have carried over into the early 1910s, even as moving picture theaters increased in size and status: lengthy hours of operation, relatively cheap admission costs, and more or less short variety programs that often changed daily. Yet new patterns of standardization and differentiation emerged to modify those practices (as chapter 1 has shown) and sometimes alter the habits of moviegoers, some of whom had grown up with the pictures, as kids attending nickelodeons, while others had been enjoying them for ten years or more. This entr'acte, consequently, addresses what Gregory Waller recently has called some of the "most basic issues in film history"[1]—the relation of screening sites to programming and their relation, in turn, to moviegoing practices—again, largely within the regional framework of New England (especially northeastern Massachusetts and Rhode Island), northern Ohio, and the upper Midwest. It also explores how different the "imagined community" of moviegoers could look, depending on the source of that imagining, either in words or pictures.

By now, it is hardly surprising to read that, during the early 1910s, the temporal conditions of moviegoing were not always the same from one city to another or even within one urban center. But the range of differences could be significant. In most cities, downtown picture theaters tended to be open every day of the week. In those such as Youngstown and Canton, where "blue laws" forbade live entertainment on Sundays, vaudeville theaters and "opera houses" also turned into picture theaters on Sunday afternoons and evenings.[2] In New England industrial cities such as Lowell or Lynn, where similar laws were in effect, "Sunday concerts" of moving pictures were restricted to evening hours; yet in others such as Pawtucket, there were no Sunday moving picture programs at all. Daily opening and closing hours also varied widely. Some downtown picture theaters opened their doors in the morning and ran until late at night. Typical were those that began their programs at 10:00 or 11:00 A.M.: the Grand Photoplay (Rochester), the New Dome (Youngstown), the Hart (Toledo), or the Colonial (Des Moines).[3] Among those with the longest hours were the Cameraphone (Cleveland), which opened at 8:30 A.M., and the Empress (Toledo), which opened at 9:30 A.M. (but 10:00 A.M. on Sundays). Yet, in a surprising number of cities, downtown theaters were open only in the afternoons and evenings. In Lowell, for instance, all the theaters opened at 1:00 P.M. and closed at 10:30 P.M., Monday through Saturday. The same was true of Lynn and Canton, for vaudeville houses and picture theaters, as well as Minneapolis, where the Seville opened at noon, the Crystal at 1:00, and the Lyric at 2:00. In Pawtucket, the Bijou, Star, and Pastime had similar hours, but their doors were closed between 5:00 or 5:30 and 7:00 or 7:30 P.M. (dinner hours), except on Saturdays. Ticket prices were standardized at five cents for a range of theaters—for instance, nearly all those in Des Moines, the small theaters (including the Rex) in Youngstown, or the less prestigious (such as the Empress and Hart) in Toledo—and at ten cents for the larger or more luxurious theaters (from the New Dome in Youngstown and Alhambra in Toledo to the Colonial in Des Moines and Lyric in Minneapolis) and for any of those in Lowell, Lynn, or Pawtucket (matinees were an exception).

Neighborhood picture theaters, already numerous by the early 1910s, also seem to have had varied hours of operation yet quite standardized admission costs, at least within a single city. In Cleveland, for instance, an elegant new suburban theater such as the Knickerbocker (ten cents) ran only two programs in the evenings, at 7:00 and 8:30, with an added Saturday matinee, but similar hours could be found at smaller, more ordinary theaters such as the Ezella, which also had a Sunday afternoon and evening show.[4] In Toledo, a similar pattern emerged, with theaters running evening shows on weekdays and added matinees on the weekend. The Laurel was open from 6:30 to 10:30 and, additionally, from 2:30 to 4:30 on weekends, yet the south side Diamond advertised continuous weekend shows, from 1:30 to 9:30. Most theaters, including the Laurel, seem to have charged five cents on weeknights but raised that to ten cents on the weekends (except for children at matinees), and that was true of theaters that drew quite different audiences— from the Orpheum, in a west side shopping district, to the Crescent, in an east side industrial area.[5] In Des Moines, Namur's residential theaters also raised their ticket price from five to ten cents for the weekend, but they were open every afternoon, from 2:00 to 5:00, and again every evening, from 7:00

to 10:00.[6] Although the evidence is scanty, Boston's residential picture theaters also seem to have had similar hours, with slight variations in the afternoon and evening show times (they opened anywhere from 1:45 to 2:30 in
the afternoon and from 6:30 to 7:15 in the evening), but most charged from
ten to fifteen cents (even on weekdays), perhaps because "vaudeville and
songs" were part of the program.[7]

Other factors besides operating hours also affected when, where, and how
often people went to the movies. A surprising number of picture theaters
across these regions, even as late as 1913–14, still changed their programs
daily, a practice supported by the major licensed and Independent distributors (detailed in chapter 1). This was the case with many downtown and even
some neighborhood theaters. In New York, for instance, where hardly any
picture theaters advertised, the Keith circuit showed different sets of two first-
run licensed films daily at the Union Square and Harlem Opera House, after
which each set circulated through Keith's other four picture theaters.[8]
Adolph Zukor's Comedy Theatre (on Union Square), by contrast, featured
at least one new independent release daily, during fifteen hours of screening,
from 8:00 A.M. to 11:00 P.M.; later Ganes' Manhattan Theatre, according to
the *Dramatic Mirror,* would run three new licensed films each day.[9] In Cleveland, the Avenue, Cameraphone, and Penn Square advertised a daily schedule of licensed films, while the Mall, Tabor, and Clark did the same for their
Independent films. In downtown Toledo, at least through the end of 1913,
the Colonial and Princess were presenting, respectively, four and three reels
of different first-run MPPC films daily, while the newly opened Hippodrome
(which ran continuous shows from 10:00 A.M. to 10:30 P.M., for five cents admission) each day offered three reels of first-run Universal films. In Des
Moines, the Casino presented three reels of first-run MPPC films each day
well into 1914, while the Unique did likewise with first-run Mutual films. For
several months in early 1914, one theater, the Black Cat, even experimented
with daily-changed programs of second-run feature films, for just five cents
a ticket.

Yet as many, if not more, theaters changed their programs less often and
timed those changes to their competitive advantage, whether they showed licensed or Independent films.[10] In Lowell, the Voyons changed its licensed
films on Monday and Thursday, with an added special program on Sunday,
whereas the Jewel changed its Independent films on Monday, Wednesday, Friday, and Sunday. In Pawtucket, the Star changed its programs (first from General Film, then from Mutual) on Monday and Thursday; the Pastime, on Monday, Wednesday, and Friday. In Canton, the Odeon also offered four weekly
changes of licensed films: Monday, Wednesday, and Friday, with another new
program on Sunday. In Minneapolis, the Seville changed its Independent
films on Sunday, Tuesday, and Thursday; the Crystal did likewise, except its
third change came on Friday. In Des Moines, the Family and Golden, both In-

FIG. 23. "The Movies," *Des Moines News*
(12 October 1913).

dependent theaters, changed their films three times a week but on alternate days. Whatever the frequency of changes, however, most ran "continuous shows," which continued to encourage the kind of "drop-in" clientele familiar from the nickelodeon period. Only a few picture theaters initially sought to present programs more characteristic of "legitimate" theaters, beginning and ending at set times. One was Keith's Bijou (Boston), where Josephine Clement ran five daily shows of two hours each (changed twice a week), with licensed films, a one-act play, classical music, and a short lecture.[11] Rarely did "at least three of those five shows not call for the 'standing room only' notice outside." Another was the Lyric (Minneapolis), where S. L. "Roxy" Rothapfel initially ran four daily shows of an hour and half each (also changed twice a week), with licensed films and special musical arrangements.[12] As more venues like the Lyric or Knickerbocker (Cleveland) emerged by 1912–13, they and certain other downtown theaters whose programs changed only twice or thrice a week proved well positioned to accommodate and exploit the growing number of multiple-reel films and features.

Still, the constantly changing variety package, however frequently changed and of whatever length, seems to have remained a major means of

attracting many, if not most, moviegoers. The regularity of the variety program allowed exhibitors to promote their more popular films in consistent
ways: the Orpheum (Cleveland) had its "good Essanay" (usually a western)
every Sunday; the New Grand (Minneapolis), "Monday's Biograph release";
the Alhambra (St. Paul), a new *Pathé Weekly* every Monday; and the Cozy (also
Cleveland), its "Vitagraph night" every Thursday.[13] This kind of promotion
continued when multiple-reel films were introduced in 1912 and 1913: the
Crystal (Minneapolis), for instance, presented its celebrated Kay-Bee Indian
pictures and Civil War films every Sunday through Tuesday, whereas the
Unique (Des Moines) featured them on Friday and Saturday. On the one
hand, in many cities (certainly downtown, but even in some neighborhoods), the variety program could draw a quite heterogeneous audience
over the course of a week or even a day, and give impetus to what *Nickelodeon*,
in 1910, was perhaps first to call "picture fans."[14] On the other, the routine
patterns of attendance that it fostered also could differentiate those fans according to their "taste" for a particular brand of film or for a "personality"
such as Essanay's Broncho Billy Anderson or Vitagraph's Florence Turner
(see chapter 6). By contrast, in seeking to "elevate" the variety program or
multiple-reel feature, respectively, the Keith Bijou (Boston) and Lyric (Minneapolis) deliberately set out to attract a more exclusively middle-class clientele. Here, as in the Saxe brothers' theater chain (which acquired the Lyric
in 1912), the ambience of the theater served to lure "regular patrons."[15] For
their "comfort and convenience," the Bijou offered "well-appointed reception room[s] . . . with checking facilities, writing desk and telephone service," maid service, a "men's smoking room," and young women as ushers "in
uniforms of gray nun's veiling, caps, kerchiefs, and aprons."[16] Among its
amenities, the Lyric had "a playground for the children [presumably the very
young] with all kinds of toys" and a "rest room . . . for shoppers where hot tea
and cocoa [were] served by colored matrons after the matinee free."[17]

Specific traces of moviegoers' daily or weekly habits during this period,
as most researchers know, are difficult to puzzle out. The trade press, settlement studies, and recreation surveys showed great interest in who attended
picture theaters and what kinds of pictures they preferred but paid less attention to where they went and when. Moreover, they continued to circulate
stereotypes and clichés. In late 1911, for instance, an anonymous report in
the *Morning Telegraph* described certain kinds of audience members this way:
whereas "the man on your right . . . shows his feelings only by the brightness
of his eyes and the tenseness of his face," "a woman near you will be all a-
quiver" or another nearby, "chewing gum," belatedly will realize the danger
posed by a villain and cry out to the hero.[18] Several years later, F. H. Richardson claimed that men predominated at downtown theaters (at least in New
York and Chicago), and a 1913 San Francisco recreation survey complemented his observations by noting that women and children frequented

FIG. 24. Cartoon,
Cleveland Leader
(21 May 1911), M8.

neighborhood theaters, especially on weekends.[19] But Richardson's "downtown sections," unlike those in most cities, excluded "shopping districts," where women, he admitted, were the primary audience.

Yet tantalizing observations did crop up, especially about women and children. In the special February 1912 issue of *Billboard,* Jos. F. Hennegan noted that, in downtown districts, "clerks, stenographers, etc., employ their noon hour in seeing moving pictures" almost daily.[20] More specifically, in Champaign, Illinois, a downtown exhibitor was surprised to find how important "the gentler sex" was to the moving picture business: "The same women come day after day with their children to the afternoon matinee."[21] Similarly, in Detroit, a feature writer was surprised one Monday morning to find so many "women and girls" waiting for "the box office of a moving picture theater to open."[22] The close relationship between shopping and moviegoing persisted, as it did in the story cited earlier in Youngstown, but notice the reported impact of a 1912 change in the Illinois labor law for women, which closed the state's stores at 9:00 P.M. on Saturdays: people used to go to the picture shows first and then do their shopping, now they shop and then go to the pictures—"from 9 to 11 P.M. is a busy time."[23] A 1913 survey of Waltham, a small factory town on the western outskirts of Boston, showed that single working women living in boarding rooms or lodging houses were more likely than men to attend the downtown Boston picture theaters, and regularly, at least once a week.[24] About the same time, in Worcester, an industrial city farther west, a reporter complained that women used picture theaters as lunchrooms: at noon, "half of the women patrons [are] nibbling lunch biscuits, cakes, or sweet meals of some kind."[25] Several studies of young working women in New York all noted that moving pictures were second only to dance halls as a preferred amusement, although the theaters the women frequented may have been in their own neighborhoods.[26] Indeed, a 1913 survey in Chicago found that one of the first things the relatives of a Jewish immigrant girl did was perform this ritual of "Americanization": after buying her some "American clothes," they would next "take her to the nickel-show."[27] In *The Art of the Photoplay* (1913), Eustace Hale Ball concluded more generally that "the moving picture show . . . [had] now become a standard amuse-

FIG. 25. People leaving a motion picture show, *World's Work* (February 1911), 14024.

ment at which wives, mothers, sisters and daughters of the best classes in America [were] the most devoted patrons."[28]

This interest in, and sometimes concern over, women as moviegoers was based, at least in part, on the recognition that the increasing leisure time so characteristic of the early twentieth-century United States "had come to women" in particular and that much of that leisure was spent in commercial establishments.[29] As legislation raised the minimum working age for children, they too enjoyed its benefits but also came under greater scrutiny, especially from middle-class reformers.[30] Much of our information on children's attendance at moving picture shows, in fact, derives from recreation surveys of cities and towns across the country: although sometimes surprising, it also was generally positive. In the small industrial town of Ipswich, Massachusetts, for instance, 80 percent of all high school students went to the moving pictures once or more a week; the figure was slightly lower for those in grades 5 through 8: 70 percent for boys and 55 percent for girls.[31] In the larger city of Springfield, Illinois, 60 percent of the boys and nearly 55 percent of the girls attended once a week, while 40 percent of the boys and 30 percent of the girls went twice weekly.[32] In the even larger city of Portland, Oregon, where moving pictures were accepted as an "educational device" and residential theaters were said to serve as "social centers," the figures were even higher: 90 percent of young people under the age of fourteen attended picture theaters at least once a week, and 75 percent went at night.[33] Perhaps it is not surprising that 65 percent of the girls this age (7,564 in all) attended at night (if they went with family members to neighborhood theaters), but "a considerable number of boys and girls under eighteen years of age" (especially girls aged sixteen to eighteen) went "unaccompanied by adults." Indeed, an even greater number—more than two-thirds—were found "unaccompanied" at night in Cleveland.[34] Yet no one seemed unduly alarmed because generally "young people [were] well cared for while in the theaters."[35] Dorothy Donnell even celebrated the picture theater as a "school": "Everywhere the white-and-gold exteriors of the Motion Picture theaters unite the children. They hurry, ragged-shoed and out-at-the-knee, with their playmates with starched waists, from the schools, tugging at grown-up hands, scuffling into their places with eager feet."[36]

Picture theater ads in city newspapers supported some, if not all, of these findings and observations. The placement of ads could be telling. Perhaps not unexpectedly, picture theater ads in the single-industry cities of Lynn, Lowell, Youngstown, and Canton, with their large working-class populations, appeared early on alongside those for vaudeville houses. Yet this was not the case in Toledo or Des Moines, where they were kept separate from vaudeville houses and especially legitimate theaters until 1913. In the *Cleveland Leader*, by contrast, they not only remained separate but made up much of a Sunday page that, for two years, shifted among various sections of the Sunday edition before settling, in late 1913, in the society section, aimed primarily at middle-class women. The way that ads addressed potential moviegoers and fans also could be revealing. No longer did theaters tend to make the explicit appeals to women and children that once served to legitimate the "cheap amusement" during the nickelodeon period; instead, most now assumed both to be part of their regular audience. Still, certain theaters in Lowell and Lynn continued to polish their image as "educational" venues for children (and use them as promoters): in the summer of 1911, the Voyons hosted 300 playground children one Saturday afternoon; the following year, the Central Square manager one day invited "a thousand children of the vacation schools as his guests."[37] Yet so did the Princess, in Peoria, Illinois, which paid special attention to unattended schoolchildren who came to afternoon screenings.[38] In 1913, the transformed Princess in Toledo took what seemed an anomalous position, highlighting its "special attention shown LADIES and CHILDREN," along with its "free telephone service . . . individual sanitary towels and drinking cups [and] private retiring rooms for LADIES AND GENTLEMEN."[39] Yet it probably was assuring working-class patrons that they enjoyed the same quality of service that was available in more elegant theaters, from the Boston Bijou to the Saxe brothers' circuit in the upper Midwest.[40]

In their own ads, companies circulated particular images of moviegoing or of an "imagined community" of moviegoers. In September 1912, for in-

The moving picture show is as important to the development of the generation as the other surrounding factors

FIG. 26. "The Moving Picture Show," *Motion Picture Story Magazine* (September 1912). The cartoon's caption reads, "The moving picture show is as important to the development of the generation as the other surrounding factors."

stance, *Motion Picture Story Magazine* printed a striking cartoon that made the urban moving picture show not only the equal of other social institutions but also implicitly middle-class—close by the store, office, church, school, and factory (the least important, graphically)—and equally accessible by foot, trolley, or other vehicle.[41] Less than a year later, in the *Morning Telegraph,* General Film launched a series of ads modeled on those for fashionable clothes and accessories in mass magazines such as the *Saturday Evening Post.*[42] Most depicted a half dozen people posed at a particular moment of attending a picture theater: lined up to purchase a ticket at the box office, showing the ticket to a uniformed male usher, seated (and seen from behind) watching the screen (in this case, a western) or (seen from the front) smiling and laughing in their seats. While all were obviously "clean," well-dressed whites, from little children to elderly grandparents, most were young adults, sometimes grouped in a family (with only one child) but more often as couples, same-sex friends, or single figures absorbed into a happy crowd. And their clothing was suggestive of white-collar workers or either working-class or rural people "out on the town." Several months later, Mutual placed several unusually large ads in Sunday newspapers like the *Saint Paul Daily News.*[43] One of these also depicted numerous people lined up at the box office (in a far more opulent lobby), including a pair of young women, an elderly couple, several young children, and at least one single man. That the children may not have been chaperoned was suggested by a second ad that showed a mother sending her excited children off to see "Mutual Movies" because "you can safely let the children go *alone.*" Mutual's imagined audience also was "clean," well-dressed, and white, the clothing suggestive of middle-class patrons as well as white-collar workers and rural

FIG. 27. Mutual Movies ad, *St. Paul News* (30 November 1913), 12.

people, as an extensive list of Mutual theaters in Minnesota and the surrounding region attested.

Newspaper stories seemed to confirm such ads at times, but they also could complicate matters even more.[44] If Youngstown picture theaters supposedly attracted shoppers, acquaintances, and young couples, for instance, those in nearby Canton were said to "appeal most strongly [to] the working man and his family."[45] Yet rarely did ads in either city make even implicit appeals to women. In Des Moines, everyone supposedly was a moviegoer, "from the coal miner north of the city who walks a mile or more to attend the picture show in Highland Park to the rich man who stops his automobile in front of the show in University Place."[46] Yet a 1913 civil suit pressed by an out-of-town pastor revealed that blacks were legally restricted to balcony seating (when they were admitted to moving picture theaters at all) in most northern cities and not only in Des Moines.[47] Revealing in a different way was a contest sponsored by the *Toledo Blade*, in early 1911, in which readers were asked to submit short pieces of moving picture criticism for weekly cash prizes.[48] Initial announcements assumed a generic reader, but several indicated that men were expected to be the chief contestants.[49] Yet, when young women won two of the first three prizes, the *Blade* addressed its next announcement to them as well.[50] As a group, as many young men as women won the second and third weekly prizes, but all the fourth (and last) week's "prizes [were] won by girls."[51] What pictures the young women (apparently all unmarried) saw and where also did not fit expectations. Some attended neighborhood theaters such as the west side Temple, the south side Circle (near one Polish immigrant community), or the Diamond in South Toledo, but others saw their films at the downtown Princess (an earlier small house, rather than the renamed Columbia) or the Empress. This suggests that downtown Toledo picture theaters appealed to young women as well as the working men hailed by the Hart in the city's labor weekly. Moreover, three chose to write about westerns, and not simply cowboy girl pictures. This further suggests that surveys in which adolescents and children still preferred Wild West pictures as late as 1913 may not have been off the mark, and that many girls or young women shared those preferences.[52]

Undoubtedly the most unusual evidence for moviegoers' habits comes from the 1912–13 accounts book for the Star Theater in Pawtucket.[53] That is, *some* moviegoers' habits, especially if one assumes, as did the Civic Theatre programs of 1913–14, that much of the Star's audience came from the nearby neighborhoods of Polish, Jewish, Italian, and other (largely working-class) immigrants.[54] Covering three different periods of programming—state rights specials and MPPC films (December 1911 to September 1912), Mutual programs (October 1912 to August 1913), and Famous Players features (September and October 1913)[55]—this rare document, week after week, meticulously notes each day's receipts, from which one can draw a number of conclusions.[56] First of all, the Star's audiences flocked to the Mutual programs (receipts increased dramatically in October–November 1912 and were sustained through the next eight or nine months), which regularly presented Kay-Bee and Broncho westerns and Civil War films, Keystone comedies, and occasional French or Italian crime films. In other words, they were particularly attracted to sensational melodramas, an attraction already prefigured by the success of earlier state rights specials such as *The James Boys in Missouri* and *Temptations of a Great City*.[57] Second, audiences attended the Star in the highest numbers on Saturdays (hardly surprising) and in the next-highest numbers on Mondays or Thursdays (the lowest almost always was on Fridays). Because the Star's programs changed each Monday and Thursday, one can presume that regulars were such fans of Kay-Bee, Broncho, Keystone, and/or French and Italian crime films that they were eager to attend the opening day of their three-day runs. Indeed, the weekly routine of attending the Star on Mondays, Thursdays, and/or Saturdays was so ingrained that it persisted during the initial months that the Star booked Famous Players features (which changed on Mondays, Wednesdays, and Fridays). Third, receipts dropped just enough with the switch from Mutual films to Famous Players features that the managers changed the venue for the latter to the larger and more centrally located Bijou, whose audiences probably were more diverse but also more middle-class than immigrant working-class. Although one can make too much of how suggestive this may be of the class and ethnic "tastes" of different audiences by 1913–14, there is further evidence of the Star's usual clientele's preference for sensational melodramas, when the theater switched to Universal programs in March 1914, kicked off by a full-week run of *Traffic in Souls*.[58]

Indeed, the *when, where,* and *why* of moviegoing could be answered in a variety of ways in the early 1910s. To paraphrase and redirect the focus of Miriam Hansen's recent intervention, audiences experienced moving pictures "in locally quite specific, and [unevenly] developed, contexts and conditions of *reception*."[59] Whatever the "imagined community," whatever the particular venue or city, the "regularities" of an audience's perceived weekly routine, even when drawn from evidence as detailed as that of the Pawtucket Star's accounts book, still can present the historian with a host of unaddressed questions: When were wage earners (of whatever class) generally paid; what were the shopping hours for most businesses; did specific ethnic groups attend particular picture theaters on particular days; when did children most frequently attend, and when did adults; when did women most frequently attend, and when did men; how did religious practices (Pawtucket and adjacent Central Falls, for instance, were predominantly Roman Catholic) affect moviegoing; how did attendance patterns differ from one picture theater to another? Yet whatever answers to these questions one might hazard, in Pawtucket or elsewhere, they probably would not contradict at least one surprising conclusion: the eagerness of the Star's fans, by late 1912, to see Mutual's first-run multiple-reels films on the very first day of their release. If so, their eagerness would be an equally telling testament to the hold moving pictures now had on working people's weekly habits of planning and spending their leisure time as the rare settlement finding, in May 1912, that "the moving picture show allowance [was] as much a part of the expense for necessities as . . . the rent and the grocery bill."[60]

Document
Mary Heaton Vorse, "Some Picture Show Audiences,"
Outlook (24 June 1911), 441–47

. . .

We talk a good deal about censorship of picture shows, and pass city ordinances to keep the young from being corrupted by them; and this is all very

well, because a great amusement of the people ought to be kept clean and
sweet; but at the same time this discussion has left a sort of feeling in the
minds of people who do not need to go to the picture show that it is a doubtful sort of a place, where young girls and men scrape undesirable acquaintances, and where the prowler lies in wait for the unwary, and where suggestive films of crime and passion are invariably displayed. But I think that this
is an unjust idea, and that any one who will take the trouble to amuse himself with the picture show audiences for an afternoon or two will see why it is
that the making of films has become a great industry, why it is that the picture show has driven out vaudeville and the melodrama.

You cannot go to any one of the picture shows in New York without having a series of touching little adventures with the people who sit near you,
without overhearing chance words of a *naïveté* and appreciation that make
you bless the living picture book that has brought so much in the lives of the
people who work.

Houston Street, on the East Side, of an afternoon is always more crowded
than Broadway. Push-carts line the street. The faces that you see are almost
all Jewish—Jews of many different types; swarthy little men, most of them,
looking undersized according to the Anglo-Saxon standard. Here and there
a deep-chested mother of Israel sails along, majestic in *shietel* and shawl.
These are the toilers—garment-makers, a great many of them—people who
work "by pants," as they say. A long and terrible work-day they have to keep
body and soul together. Their distractions are the streets, and the bargaining
off the push-carts, and the show. For a continual trickle of people detaches
itself from the crowded streets and goes into the good-sized hall; and around
the entrance, too, wait little boys—eager-eyed little boys—with their tickets
in their hands, trying to decoy those who enter into taking them in with them
as guardians, because the city ordinances do not allow a child under sixteen
to go in unaccompanied by an older person.

In the half-light the faces of the audience detach themselves into little pal-
lid ovals, and, as you will always find in the city, it is an audience largely of
men.

Behind us sat a woman with her escort. So rapt and entranced was she with
what was happening on the stage that her voice accompanied all that happened—a little unconscious and lilting *obligato*. It was the voice of a person
unconscious that she spoke—speaking from the depths of emotion; a low
voice, but perfectly clear, and the unconsciously spoken words dropped with
the sweetness of running water. She spoke in German. One would judge her
to be from some part of Austria. She herself was lovely in person, and young,
level-browed and clear-eyed, deep-chested; a beneficent and lovely woman
one guessed her to be. And she had never seen Indians before; perhaps never
heard of them.

The drama being enacted was the rescue from the bear pit of Yellow Wing, the lovely Indian maid, by Dick the Trapper; his capture by the tribe, his escape with the connivance of Yellow Wing, who goes to warn him in his log house, their siege by the Indians, and the final rescue by a splendid charge of the United States cavalry; these one saw riding with splendid abandon over hill and dale, and the marriage then and there of Yellow Wing and Dick by the gallant chaplain. A guileless and sentimental dime novel, most ingeniously performed; a work of art; beautiful, too, because one had glimpses of stately forests, sunlight shifting through leaves, wild, dancing forms of Indians, the beautiful swift rushing of horses. One must have had a heart of stone not to follow the adventures of Yellow Wing and Dick the Trapper with passionate interest.

But to the woman behind it was reality at its highest. She was there in a fabled country full of painted savages. The rapidly unfolding drama was to her no make-believe arrangement ingeniously fitted together by actors and picture-makers. It had happened; it was happening for her now.

"Oh!" she murmured. "That wild and terrible people! Oh, boy, take care, take care! Those wild and awful people will get you!" *"Das wildes und grausames Volk,"* she called them. "Now—now—she comes to save her beloved!" This as Yellow Wing hears the chief plotting an attack on Dick the Trapper, and then flies fleet-foot through the forest. "Surely, surely, she will save her beloved!" It was almost a prayer; in the woman's simple mind there was no foregone conclusion of a happy ending. She saw no step ahead, since she lived the present moment so intensely.

When Yellow Wing and Dick were besieged within and Dick's hand was wounded—

"The poor child! How can she bear it? To see the *gliebte* wounded before one's very eyes!"

And when the cavalry thundered through the forest—

"God give that they arrive swiftly—to be in time they must arrive swiftly!" she exclaimed to herself.

Outside the iron city roared; before the door of the show the push-cart vendors bargained and trafficked with customers. Who in that audience remembered it? They had found the door of escape. For the moment they were in the depths of the forest following the loves of Yellow Wing and Dick. The woman's voice, so like the voice of a spirit talking to itself, unconscious of time and place, was their voice. There they were, a strange company of aliens—Jews, almost all; haggard and battered and bearded men, young girls with their beaus, spruce and dapper youngsters beginning to make their way. In that humble playhouse one ran the gamut of the East Side. The American-born sat next to the emigrant who arrived but a week before. A strange and romantic people cast into the welter of the terrible city of New York, each of them with the overwhelming problem of battling with strange conditions and an alien civilization. And for the moment they were permitted to drink deep of oblivion of all the trouble in the world. Life holds some compensation, after all. The keener the intellectual capacity, the higher your artistic sensibilities are developed, just so much more difficult it is to find this total forgetfulness—a thing that for the spirit is as life-giving as sleep.

And all through the afternoon and evening this company of tired workers, overburdened men and women, fills the little halls scattered throughout the city and throughout the land.

There are motion-picture shows in New York that are as intensely local to the audience as to the audience of a Tuscan hill town. Down on Bleecker Street is the Church of Our Lady of Pompeii. Here women, on their way to work or to do their brief marketing, drop in to say their prayers before their favorite saints in exactly the same fashion as though it were a little church in their own parish. Towards evening women with their brood of children go in; the children frolic and play subdued tag in the aisles, for church with them is an every-day affair, not a starched-up matter of Sunday only. Then, prayers finished, you may see a mother sorting out her own babies and moving on serenely to the picture show down the road—prayers first and amusement afterwards, after the good old Latin fashion.

It is on Saturday nights down here that the picture show reaches its high moment. The whole neighborhood seems to be waiting for a chance to go in. Every woman has a baby in her arms and at least two children clinging to her skirts. Indeed, so universal is this custom that a woman who goes there unaccompanied by a baby feels out of place, as if she were not properly dressed. A baby seems as much a matter-of-course adjunct to one's toilet on Bleecker Street as a picture hat would be on Broadway.

Every one seems to know every one else. As a new woman joins the throng other women cry out to her gaily:

"Ah, good-evening, Concetta. How is Giuseppi's tooth?"

"Through at last," she answers. "And where are your twins?"

The first woman makes a gesture indicating that they are somewhere swallowed up in the crowd.

This talk all goes on in good North Italian, for the people on Bleecker Street are the Tuscan colony. There are many from Venice also, and from Milan and Genoa. The South Italian lives on the East Side.

Then, as the crowd becomes denser, as the moment for the show approaches, they sway together, pushed on by those on the outskirts of the crowd. And yet every one is good-tempered. It is—

"Not so hard there, boy!"

"Mind for the baby!"

"Look out!"

Though indeed it doesn't seem any place for a baby at all, and much less so for the youngsters who aren't in their mothers' arms but are perilously engulfed in the swaying mass of people. But the situation is saved by Latin good temper and the fact that every one is out for a holiday.

By the time one has stood in this crowd twenty minutes and talked with the women and the babies, one has made friends, given an account of one's self, told how it was one happened to speak a little Italian, and where it was in Italy one had lived, for all the world as one gives an account of one's self when traveling through Italian hamlets. One answers the questions that Italian women love to ask:

"Are you married?"

"Have you children?"

"Then why aren't they at the picture show with you?"

This audience was an amused and an amusing audience; ready to laugh, ready to applaud. The young man next to me had an ethical point of view. He was a serious, dark-haired fellow, and took his moving pictures seriously. He and his companion argued the case of the cowboy who stole because of his sick wife.

"He shouldn't have done it," he maintained.

"His wife was dying, *poveretta*," his companion defended.

"His wife was a nice girl," said the serious young man. "You saw for yourself how nice a girl. One has but to look at her to see how good she is." He spoke as though of a real person he had met. "She would rather have died than have her husband disgrace himself."

"It turned out happily; through the theft she found her father again. He wasn't even arrested."

"It makes no difference," said the serious youth; "he had luck, that is all. He shouldn't have stolen. When she knows about it, it will break her heart."

Ethics were his strong point, evidently. He had something to say again about the old man who, in the Franco-Prussian War, shot a soldier and allowed a young man to suffer the death penalty in his stead. It was true that the old man's son had been shot and that there was no one else to care for the little grandson, and, while the critic admitted that that made a difference, he didn't like the idea. The dramas appealed to him from a philosophical standpoint; one gathered that he and his companion might pass an evening discussing whether, when a man is a soldier, and therefore pledged to fight for his country, he has a right to give up his life to save that of an old man, even though he is the guardian of a child.

Throughout the whole show, throughout the discussion going on beside me, there was one face that I turned to again and again. It was of an eager little girl of ten or eleven, whose lovely profile stood out in violent relief from the dingy wall. So rapt was she, so spellbound, that she couldn't laugh, couldn't clap her hands with the others. She was in a state of emotion beyond any outward manifestation of it.

In the Bowery you get a different kind of audience. None of your neighborhood spirit here. Even in what is called the "dago show"—that is, the show where the occasional vaudeville numbers are Italian singers—the people seem chance met; the audience is almost entirely composed of men, only an occasional woman.

It was here that I met the moving-picture show expert, the connoisseur, for he told me that he went to a moving-picture show every night. It was the best way that he knew of spending your evenings in New York, and one gathered that he had tried many different ways. He was in his early twenties, with a tough and honest countenance, and he spoke the dialect of the city of New York with greater richness than I have ever heard it spoken. He was ashamed of being caught by a compatriot in a "dago show."

"Say," he said, "dis is a bum joint. I don't know how I come to toin in here. You don't un'erstan' what that skoit's singin', do you? You betcher I don't!"

Not for worlds would he have understood a word of the inferior Italian tongue.

"I don't never come to dago moving picter-shows," he hastened to assure me. "Say, if youse wanter see a real show, beat it down to Grand Street. Dat's de real t'ing. Dese dago shows ain't got no good films. You hardly ever see a travel film; w'en I goes to a show, I likes to see the woild. I'd like travellin' if I could afford it, but I can't; that's why I like a good travel film. A good comic's all right, but a good travel film or an a'rioplane race or a battle-ship review—dat's de real t'ing! You don't get none here," he repeated. He was sincerely displeased with himself at being caught in a place that had no class, and the only way he could defend himself was by showing his fine scorn of the inferior race.

You see what it means to them; it means Opportunity—a chance to glimpse the beautiful and strange things in the world that you haven't in your life; the gratification of the higher side of your nature; opportunity which, except for the big moving picture book, would be forever closed to you. You understand still more how much it means opportunity if you happen to live in a little country place where the whole town goes to every change of films and where the new films are gravely discussed. Down here it is that you find the people who agree with my friend of the Bowery—that "travel film is de real t'ing." For those people who would like to travel they make films of pilgrims going to Mecca; films of the great religious processions in the holy city of Jerusalem; of walrus fights in the far North. It has even gone so far that in Melilla there was an order for the troops to start out; they sprang to their places, trumpets blew, and the men fell into line and marched off—all for the moving-picture show. They were angry—the troops—but the people in Spain saw how their armies acted.

In all the countries of the earth—in Sicily, and out in the desert of Arizona, and in the deep woods of America, and on the olive terraces of Italy—they are making more films, inventing new dramas with new and beautiful backgrounds, for the poor man's theater. In his own little town, in some far-off fishing village, he can sit and see the coronation, and the burial of a king, or the great pageant of the Roman Church.

It is no wonder that it is a great business with a capitalization of millions of dollars, since it gives to the people who need it most laughter and drama and beauty and a chance for once to look at the strange places of the earth.

The Motion Picture Cowboy

I have rode upon the prairie,
      An' the hills so bright and green,
But those days would all be hist'ry
      Only for the picture screen.
For I kin live them wild days over,
      As when we, on Ol' Percell,
Was together punchin' cattle
      Down along the Musselshell.

   . . .

And I, too, am on a picture ranch,
      Where old cowboys all should be,
Killin' redskins for a picture
      That the public loves to see;
An' in years to come you'll find me
      Where I'll make my farewell stand,
Punchin' cows upon the canvas
      In this new-born, Western land.

   . . .

HARRY E. WEBB,
Motion Picture Story Magazine
(August 1912), 136

Chapter 3

The "Usable Past" of Westerns

Cowboy, Cowboy Girl, and Indian Pictures,
Part 2

"America" for Export

It was during this period that American companies first realized that they could successfully export films to Europe—and westerns turned out to be their most popular product. Perhaps this should not have come as such a surprise, given the extent to which images of the American West had long been familiar to Europeans, from the exhibitions of George Catlin in the 1840s to the initial tour of Buffalo Bill's Wild West in the late 1880s and early 1890s.[1] Jacques Portes, for instance, has explored French conceptions of American Indians as "the last remnants of a primitive humanity" and of the cowboy as a new hero of such typically American qualities as simplicity, energy, and self-confidence.[2] More specifically, Francis Lacassin has traced the rise of the Eichler publishing house, in France and Germany, which began in 1907 with translations and adaptations of the *Buffalo Bill* dime novels, following close on the second European tour of Buffalo Bill's Wild West in Paris and other cities.[3] So popular was *Buffalo Bill,* along with others based on the detective Nick Carter, that Eichler was releasing a new series every six months, from *Riffle Bill* or *Texas Jack the Scourge of the Indians* to *Sitting Bull the Last of the Sioux,* whose heroes followed "the trails of the American West, already blazed by Buffalo Bill."[4] As a mythic space symbolizing America, the Far West also had been glimpsed in early Pathé-Frères films such as *Indians and Cowboys* (1904) or *A Detective's Tour of the World* (1906), where, in one of the latter film's scenes, the hero has to be rescued from "red skins" by the banker-embezzler he is pursuing.[5] Such globe-trotting adventure films, writes Deniz Göktürk, would crop up repeatedly among French and especially German feature films before World War I, often mapped according to the contours of European colonialism.[6] At least one episode in these adventure films usually was set in the Far West, an "uncivilized" world in which one or more Europeans could be tested and validated.

But what of the American westerns in Europe? In Great Britain, the trade weekly *Bioscope* already was taking note of their popularity as early as the summer of 1910. An August editorial, for instance, reported that any observer making the rounds of picture theaters in London or the provinces would be convinced that "undoubtedly Western films are the favorites of an audience."[7] It did not matter whether they were "Indian stories, cowboy subjects, or Western dramas," as long as they had "the true coloring and atmosphere of the great silent West." The films of Selig and Essanay were frequently cited—from *The Range Riders* (with Tom Mix) or *Ranch Life in the Great Southwest* to *A Cowboy's Vindication*[8]—and, in its ads, Essanay pointedly distinguished the films " 'Made in the West' by Westerners" from its other releases.[9] They were joined by the Independents in early 1911, when American Film began releasing one and then two "cowboy pictures" a week through Western Import, followed soon after by Bison, through Tyler Film.[10] Not until then did the American trade press as a whole begin to take note of what the British were calling a "welcome . . . invasion," with *Nickelodeon* singling out the success of Essanay's "wild west dramas" in London, evidenced by the expensive advertising at the Empire Theatre for *The Girl on the Triple X*.[11] In May, the *News* finally reported that Flying A westerns, along with those of Bison and Champion, were hits not only in London but in the provinces.[12] Shortly thereafter, *Motography* repeated what by then was well known: throughout England, "phases of cowboy and Indian life are the most popular subjects for American films."[13] If *Bioscope* now gave feature stories to films such as Selig's *Range Pals* or Flying A's *The Ranchman's Vengeance* and *The Poisoned Flume*, Essanay illustrated, in one of its ads, the kinds of posters the company circulated, two of which boldly promoted "cowboy photoplays."[14] *Motography*'s report was even reprinted in the *New York Times* (which rarely gave any attention to moving pictures), under a headline that perfectly sums up the commercial and ideological function of westerns: "Exporting an Imaginary America to Make Money."[15]

As Kristin Thompson has established, by 1911, London was the "selling center" for American film product in Europe and beyond, so it is not surprising that westerns now began showing up in other countries—but their distribution was not uniform.[16] That summer, for instance, American films began to appear frequently on rental exchange lists in Paris, with the westerns of Selig, Kalem, Pathé, and Bison especially prominent. By the winter of 1911–12, they were joined by Nestor and Flying A westerns, as well as Vitagraph's "drames du Far West."[17] At the same time, according to censorship records, Selig, Kalem, Pathé, and Flying A westerns all circulated widely in Sweden; and based on Pathé archival records, many of its westerns were sold, later in 1911, to Finland.[18] In fact, the Swedish trade monthly *Nordisk Filmtid-*

ning already was printing ads for the "latest Indian films" as early as January 1910.[19] Moreover, surviving cinema programs in Stockholm and elsewhere often highlighted "Wild West," "Indian," and "Cowboy" films.[20] By contrast, Essanay initially focused its attention on Germany, opening a sales office in Berlin in the summer of 1911; within less than a year, according to censorship records found and analyzed by Göktürk, the company's *Broncho Billy* films were being distributed widely throughout the region.[21] Seizing on all this activity, in August 1911, *Motography* was quick to extol the "American film" as a major, profitable product for export throughout the globe.[22] Despite any earlier trade press misgivings, the fictitious Wild West of the cowboy and Indian films was crystallizing into the American subject par excellence—the one "doing most," as even the *Cleveland Leader* reported, "to make the American moving picture film popular abroad."[23] Now, according to *Daily Consular Reports,* which collated information gathered overseas, the industry could confirm that audiences "eagerly watched the highly colored dramas of the prairies and the mountains" not only throughout Europe but also in South Africa, South America, and Australia.[24]

The "Imagined Community" of "The Great West": Cowboy Pictures

"Do you know The Great West as it was and is?"[25] Although this question may have been just one of several rhetorical ploys to advertise Flying A westerns in Great Britain in early 1912, it also concisely points to the West as a deeply embedded concept in American history, from "the screen upon which [Thomas] Jefferson projected his vision of a nation both democratic and enterprising . . . replete with accessible images" to the *frontier,* "an area of free land, its continuous recession, and the advance of American settlement" that, for Frederick Jackson Turner, "explain[ed] American development."[26] What indeed was the "Great West" that was "known" and represented in American westerns, however diverse? In what ways did westerns map this fluid border territory of spatial and temporal negotiation?[27] What "imagined community of nationality" did they tend to produce? Moreover, who were the audiences invited to share this knowing, and in what ways did they constitute (or not) a more or less "constellated community"? Americans of various kinds may have been attracted to the "authentic" geographic landscapes of the West and the action-packed stories of "western life," but what those meant for specific audiences was not always the same. That "empty land," even when arid and inhospitable, could have different mythological or ideological functions,[28] as could the recurring "larger-than-life" characters of the stories, whose values and practices contributed to an emerging sense of nationality or nationhood that was far from inclusive. Although the reception of westerns in Europe is well worth further study for its own sake, here their popularity abroad prompts a reexamination of what American companies imagined they were putting on show, and for whom, at home. More specifically, it suggests a closer look at certain films, as well as the discourse surrounding them at the time, not only in the trade press but also in local newspapers.

So, what comes of looking again at Essanay's "cowboy pictures" starring G. M. Anderson? Although Anderson was well known in the United States as *the* "photoplay cowboy," either as "Bullets" or as "Broncho Billy," it was in Great Britain and Germany that his films first seem to have coalesced into the "famous *Broncho Billy* series."[29] The company did not open a branch office in Paris until early 1912,[30] so it took six months for the *Broncho Billy* series not only to take its place among a host of dramatic and comic series in France (a format initially more characteristic of that country than of the United States) but also to rival or displace "imitations" such as the westerns of Joë Hamman. Although some reviews and columns in the United States began to refer to "Broncho Billy pictures" by the spring and summer of 1912, just as Anderson was establishing a permanent studio in Niles, California, the series label did not become widespread until later that year.[31] First of all, then, the increasingly regular series in which Anderson's cowboy character appeared now can be seen as one of several efforts in the US industry to emulate the production and marketing strategies of repetition and variation found not only in French films, for instance, but in serialized magazine stories and juvenile pulp fiction. Among them were Essanay's own comic western series, *Alkali Ike*, beginning in 1911; Nestor's forgotten attempt, in 1912, to exploit the popular juvenile series, *Wild West Weekly*, with regular releases of one-reel films; American's equally neglected 1913 comic western series, *Calamity Anne*, starring Louise Lester;[32] Edison's more familiar *What Happened to Mary* (starring Mary Fuller), released in conjunction with monthly stories published in *Ladies World*, in 1912–1913;[33] and a slew of detective series throughout 1913 and into 1914 (see chapter 5). Essanay's *Broncho Billy* series simply proved the most successful of the lot.[34]

More important, Anderson's phenomenal appeal—what the English called the "irresistible charm of personality and the breezy, easy, infectious humour . . . of [this] magnetic man"—gave credence to Essanay's boast, furthered by certain newspapers, that Broncho Billy was the first American "world famous character-creation."[35] And, in the United States, that appeal ranged widely, at least according to the *World*, taking in the masses in the "gallery," young boys, and, in New York City, "the ladies."[36] Seeking to explain this, Andrew Brodie Smith argues (persuasively, I think) that, in contrast to Bison-101's spectacular westerns, for instance, Anderson developed Broncho Billy as a heroic figure along the lines worked out in films such as *Broncho Billy's Christmas Dinner.*[37] That is, he often first appeared on screen as either an outlaw or Hobsbawmian "social bandit,"[38] or else as a cowboy between jobs and almost never as a rancher, entrepreneur, or any kind of property owner.

FIG. 28. G. M. Anderson as Broncho Billy, *Motion Picture Story Magazine* (October 1913), 3.

If this characterization sustained his appeal to working-class audiences and boys, other attributes attracted a middle-class audience. For Broncho Billy usually underwent a transformation, through "moral and psychological conflict," into a respectable "ethical role model."[39] By incorporating Christian themes of moral uplift, self-sacrifice, and redemption, the films—examples include *Broncho Billy's Bible* (June 1912) and *Broncho Billy's Last Hold Up* (August 1912)—often evoked the ideals of evangelical Protestantism.[40] Although never strictly a parent, his character sometimes served as a surrogate father, as in *Broncho Billy's Heart* (November 1912) and *Broncho Billy's Ward* (February 1913), making him an appealing figure to mothers as well as children.[41] Even the character's name, at least according to Anderson, came from a story written by Peter B. Kyne and published for middle-class readers in the *Saturday Evening Post*.[42] In short, the *Broncho Billy* series became incredibly popular by hewing to "traditional, middle-class ideals of morality, manhood, and character," without totally eliminating the figure's initial appearance as "a stoic, isolated male"—and immigrant boys like Harry Golden later admitted that, indeed, Broncho Billy taught them "New World" attitudes and instilled in them their "first ideals of American manhood."[43]

FIG. 29. Essanay, *Broncho Billy's Gratitude*, 1913 (production still).

This recurring story of redemption, however, always assumed that Broncho Billy was white, as was the emergent social order into which he was accepted. The series, consequently, either repressed or displaced other figures and stories, not unlike the way Anderson himself, after 1911, abandoned playing nonwhite roles. Moreover, that he had to rename himself, masking his own ethnicity, his Jewishness, in the industry gave a sharply ironic twist to the series character's assimilation.[44] *Bioscope's* special reviews of two Flying A westerns in 1911 highlight this repression/displacement, and in different ways. *The Ranchman's Vengeance* (May 1911) offers a striking contrast to the films Dwan would shoot for the company shortly thereafter.[45] Although conventional in mise-en-scène, framing, and editing, the film tells an unconventional story: the ranchman hero is a Mexican American, Lorenz Pedro, and his revenge is directed at a white interloper, Tom Flint, whom he has rescued from the California desert and who then steals away his wife and little daughter, only to abuse them and finally kill the woman. After a struggle, Pedro throws Flint off a cliff into the sea; then, at her mother's gravesite, the girl stops the despairing man from shooting himself. Although Mexicans or Mexican Americans were the subject of a good number of earlier westerns, they commonly played villains—as in *Broncho Billy's Mexican Wife* (November 1912)[46]—victims, or those grateful either to be rescued by or to sacrifice themselves for whites. *The Ranchman's Vengeance,* then, is a revealing anomaly in having a hero usually seen as "racially inferior" and marginalized in the "imagined community" of the West—although Romaine Fielding's later westerns for Lubin will offer an anomaly of a different sort.[47] The general absence of US trade press reviews is suggestive, especially in contrast to its acceptance in England as a "clean . . . popular" film with a strong plot and "excellent acting." For one, the film's ending is more characteristic of European than American films—at least until the Bison-101 two-reelers of the following year—and this may partly account for its popularity there. For another, the lack of reviews, *Billboard's* excepted, which identifies only the "ranchman's servant" as Mexican,[48] could mean either that its circulation was limited to marginal areas of the United States—specifically in Southwest venues catering to Mexican Americans—or that the names in its intertitles had to be expunged from any ads elsewhere.

The other Flying A western was one of the earliest surviving films shot by Dwan, *The Poisoned Flume* (August 1911). A widow, Mrs. Napier, fears for her ranch's survival, and a neighbor named Martinez tries to gain control of the ranch by marrying her daughter. Rebuffed, he poisons the flume carrying water to the ranch but is discovered by the widow's new foreman, who is wounded and then, with his fellow cowboys, kills Martinez in a gunfight. This story is accentuated by unusual choices in framing—for instance, high-angle shots of the flume curving off into the distance, others that stage foreground action at the flume against expansive backgrounds—and by a dramatic climax in which Martinez vainly tries to escape on the trestle carrying the flume over the valley.[49] The final image also is unusual but apt: his body falls into the flume and drifts slowly off in its current. Although this film clearly offers "extraordinary strong situations," as demanded by *Billboard,*[50] it does so in such a way as to both evoke and mask a significant factor in the West's development. For the flume carrying water to the Napier ranch was part of a vast system of irrigation that only recently had transformed California into what Donald Worster has called, with some ambivalence, a model of the "modern hydraulic society."[51] The unusually arid environment of the American West, he argues, was developed chiefly by an intensive, efficient, large-scale manipulation of scarce water resources. What is intriguing here is that, by the early 1900s, an alliance of private and government capital and engineering expertise had become necessary for this development to reach, as Worster puts it, a critical stage of *florescence.*[52] Yet what gets represented in a western such as *The Poisoned Flume* derives from an earlier period of *incipience,* in which individuals (including a good number of independent women) and small communities living in relative isolation took the first steps toward what Worster has dubbed the "redemption of California."[53] In other words, in its depiction of the flume as both visual attraction and dramatic prop and of the cowboy hero who "gets the girl in the end," the film asserts the frontier myth of socioeconomic individualism and mobility that would become a staple of the genre throughout the rest of the century.[54]

Several other surviving cowboy pictures exhibit an even more explicit interest in the Wild West's relation to—and crucial significance for—the modern world. Kalem's *The Driver of the Deadwood Stage* (December 1912) could not have a more conventional story: an outlaw hides in a trunk put on top of a stagecoach in order to secretly rob a $60,000 gold shipment, and the stage driver is arrested and charged with the theft.[55] Yet the resolution comes from an unusual variation on the boy reader besotted by dime novels: the driver's young son proves his father's innocence by means of a Brownie camera.[56] As the boy stands on a hilltop overlooking the road where the stagecoach passes, he snaps a photo and waves to his father—but he does not see what the spectator does: the outlaw rising halfway out of the trunk. Only when he develops the filmstrip and examines the negative (in close-up) does he really see, and realize the "truth." This film not only conflates past and present (its world is both "western" and "modern") but also refigures the cowboy hero as a kind of young "picture fan" who shoots images (rather than bullets), discerns the meaning of those images, and shares them with others.[57] In staging a reenactment of the western in still/moving images, it also demonstrates the genre's moral and social value. Selig's two-reel *Cowboy Millionaire* (February 1913), a remake of its popular 1909 film, refigures the cowboy hero quite differently: he inherits a fortune and is transported to Chicago, where he acquires a wife and mansion. When his cowboy buddies visit, he initially thinks about returning with them, but their rowdy, "uncivilized" behavior convinces him to remain in the city. With a good deal of snap, this film maps the historical subject of the western: a passage in space—from West to East (or Midwest)—and in time—from one century to another. It also recycles some of the images and stories out of which the western emerged—a lengthy opening *actualité* of rodeo stunts, a train ride, a melodrama stage production, and a large painting that recalls Remington's *Cowboy on Horseback*.[58] Moreover, the hero shifts from participating in the "Wild West" to being a spectator, much like the film's own audience, "shocked" at the increasingly comic antics of his buddies. His final gesture, turning the painting to the wall, may erase the heroic cowboy from his own story—but hardly from film history.

The "Imagined Community" of the "Great West": Indian Pictures

A different trajectory of analysis results from looking again at the Bison-101 westerns, whose reception in Great Britain and France was no less enthusiastic than in the United States. Bison's reorganization and alliance with 101 Ranch Wild West had been reported in the French trade press as early as December 1911,[59] and within a month of their release in the United States, beginning in March 1912, the company's first two-reel titles began to appear almost simultaneously in both countries.[60] In Great Britain, according to *Bioscope*, these films were "a revelation—even to picture men . . . unequalled in the entire annuals of Cinematography."[61] They were not only "beautiful from a scenic point of view" but "exceedingly well constructed" stories, consistently well acted by an ensemble of players (rather than relying on a star like Anderson), and often achieved a finish that was "dignified," "moving," and uniquely realistic—as in *Blazing the Trail*, where the young woman, her lover, and her brother are silhouetted on the horizon after leaving the foreground crosses marking their parents' graves, or in *The Deserter*, where the hero's military funeral ends at a "lonely grave on the edge of the boundless prairie," with his comrades silhouetted against the sinking sun.[62] Other films' stories told of weaklings, cowards, or "bad men" who, through their experiences in the West, underwent testing and transformation. One of the more intriguing—unfortunately, it seems not to survive—is Broncho's *The Man They Scorned* (November 1912), which the *Mirror* described as "well-written, well-acted . . . and worthy of praise," and not only for its "wonderful battle scene."[63] Here the hero, a "tenderfoot" recruit sent to a western fort, is an anomaly, a "much-despised Jew," who quietly bears the taunts of his fellow soldiers and the unjust reprimands of the fort's colonel. By the end, he has rescued the colonel from an Indian ambush, held off the attackers with a single rifle until reinforcements can arrive, and, recovering in a hospital, been cheered by "the soldiers that had so recently mocked him." *The Man They Scorned* may be no more unusual than the earlier *Ranchman's Vengeance*, but it is far less ambiguous in representing Jewish (in contrast to Mexican) assimilation into an American social order—and not in an eastern city, but on the western frontier.[64]

Most of the Bison-101 films, however, were Indian pictures, which sometimes seemed clearer to the British and French than to Americans. For *Bioscope*, for instance, they presented "the Redskin drama par excellence"; for the *World*, even if the Indian was recognized, in a lengthy article on Bison-101 films, as "one of the most interesting and picturesque of elements in our national history," the films remained primarily stories of "the pioneer as he was, one of the hardest fighters in the world."[65] So, what happens when we reconsider them as prime subjects for an analysis of the place and function of the "Indian" in the "imagined community" of the West?[66] Among the films mentioned earlier, *The Lieutenant's Last Fight*, which received special promotion in France, is especially worthy of note.[67] US trade press ads described this film as a "military drama," in which "a troop of cavalry [is] entirely wiped out by Indians" and "the Lieutenant meets a heroic death" in a "heart-gripping, soul-stirring finale."[68] Yet as extensive reports in the *News* and the *World* attest, as does a surviving print,[69] the film's hero is actually a Sioux chief's son, Great Bear, who is commissioned as a US Army officer at

Fort Reno, scorned by all but a colonel's daughter, unfairly accused in a fight, court-martialed, and sent back to his tribe in dishonor. Angered by his disgrace, the Sioux declare war and attack a cavalry escort for the women leaving Fort Reno, but now Great Bear dons his lieutenant's uniform in order to save the white woman who trusted him. The ensuing battle favors the Sioux until he reaches a hillside above the encircled whites and begins shooting; the tide turns as he sounds a bugle call to halt the attack, and a rescue party of cavalry arrives—but not before he is killed by a retreating Sioux warrior. Unlike *The Deserter,* this film ends in a tableau of Great Bear's fallen body at twilight, " 'unwept, unhonored, unsung,' his heroism unknown even to the girl for whom he gave his life."[70] Out of place and time in the worlds of both the Sioux and the whites, Great Bear has only one option: self-sacrifice, not for what is defined as the "Indian recent past" but for a "white imminent future."[71]

A variation on this story occurred six months later in Kay-Bee's *The Invaders,* but here the hero is the daughter of a Sioux chief, a Pocahontas figure named Sky Star (Anna Little).[72] Two interrelated story lines drive this narrative. In one, Sky Star rejects a suitor her father has accepted and then is attracted to a white man in a railroad survey crew. In the other, the Sioux protest to the colonel at a nearby fort that the surveyors are violating a recently signed treaty (an intertitle actually names the railroad crew as the "invaders") and then persuade the Cheyenne to join in an uprising. In alternating sequences, Sky Star is injured in a fall, riding to warn the whites, but recovers just enough to reach the fort, while the Sioux attack and kill the survey crew.[73] From then on, the combined Indian forces ambush a cavalry detachment and lay siege to the fort;[74] after the post telegrapher fails to signal another fort (the Indians cut the lines), a lieutenant proves himself worthy to the colonel (and his daughter) by escaping and returning with more troops—to rout the Indians. In the surviving print, *The Invaders'* battle scenes remain impressive—"with comprehensive views of near and far distance characteristic of these productions"[75]—that is, marked by reverse-angle full shot/extreme long shots, some taken from a high-angle position. Yet even more striking is the film's relative evenhandedness in depicting whites and Indians—the surveyor's point-of-view shot of Sky Star through his scope is matched by shots of the Indian suitor viewing their exchange from a distance—and its refusal to celebrate one at the expense of the other—just as the killings of both whites and Indians resonated equally in the title of the earlier *Indian Massacre.*[76] Focusing on the white characters' regretful respect for Sky Star, who has died of her injuries shortly before the siege is broken, the final tableau "meditates" on the figure of the "vanishing Indian." In the long shot of a darkened room, lit only by shafts of moonlight falling through a background window and an open door (frame right), the colonel's daughter kneels and weeps by her bed (frame left) then returns to the downcast

FIG. 30. Kay-Bee, *The Invaders*, 1912 (production still), *Moving Picture World* (9 November 1912), 542.

lieutenant (who closes the door), and the colonel himself pauses over the barely visible body and then closes the window shutters.

In both Great Britain and France, the Bison-101 Indian pictures were among the earliest imported American films that ran more than one reel, and they were far more regularly released than those of any other US company.[77] That put them in the same category as all the French, Italian, Danish, and German multiple-reel films then coming into vogue on the European market. And that, in turn, enhanced their status not only as an American product but also as a potential national epic, in which the conquest of the West offered a foundational story of national identity, a mythic narrative of origins.[78] Yet it was the Indian rather than the cowboy or horse soldier that seemed the more significant figure for Europeans. The US industry, according to *Motography*, considered "scenes of cowboys and Indians . . . [an export] commodity of genuine commercial importance" because they were "picturesque," that is, "bizarre, exciting, and unusual in American life."[79] For the British, by contrast, what appealed was the portrayal of "primeval man, with all his passions" confronting "the savage forces of Nature" and having to rely on his own resources—which even made the settlement of the New World an extension of a British-style civilization.[80] The attraction was similar for the French, who were even more fascinated by Indians, for it confirmed their conception of America as a new mythic space of the primitive and the barbaric.[81] For both Americans and Europeans, then, the "vanishing American" was an especially salient figure of what Renato Rosaldo has called the "imperialist nostalgia" for the defeated heroic Other.[82] Yet, if in Europe the "Redskin drama" symbolized a form of barbarism that might revitalize their older civilizations,[83] in the United States the Indian more often served as a figure of exclusion from or assimilation into—and, either way, justified—a new "imperial" nation.[84] Indeed, perhaps even more than the historical pageants so popular at the time (and which at least one company sought to reproduce in moving pictures),[85] Indian pictures enacted an ongoing ritual performance of "innovative nostalgia" that, in the new medium of moving pictures, "placed nostalgic imagery in a dynamic, future-oriented . . . context."[86]

In other words, the multiple-reel Indian pictures may have been particularly effective in binding disparate audiences in the United States into an "imagined community of nationality," whether within a single theater or across a variety of theaters, within a single city or across the country.[87] Here, in conjunction with the respectful attitude of most films, the shape-shifting Indian, more mythic figure than historical subject (especially since their numbers had dwindled so drastically in the late nineteenth century), would have been crucial. For, unlike the more fixed identity of the Mexican (at least prior to Fielding's westerns) or the African American in Civil War films—and more like the latter films' Southern soldier whose sense of honor and sacrifice made him (or her, in the case of a "girl spy") suitable for assimilation— the "in-between" figure of the Indian was open to multiple reading and interpretation. The specifics of that reading would have depended, at least in part, on an interested spectator's race/ethnicity, class, and/or gender; yet however different, it could have aided in elucidating and confirming that spectator's social position within the "nation."[88] Could a French-Canadian woman assembling shoes in Lynn, a Polish shopgirl in Toledo, and a Swedish or Jewish stenographer in Des Moines have read an Indian such as Sky Star or one of Mona Darkfeather's heroines more or less similarly, that is, as a worthy figure of their own assimilation? Could a Slovak steelworker in Youngstown and a Hungarian glass factory worker in Toledo have taken an Indian such as Great Bear (especially in contrast to the more unusual White Eagle in *The Flaming Arrow*), however differently, as a figure of doubt or warning in relation to their own assimilation? By contrast, could a second-generation German businessman in Cleveland or my own grandfather in Canton (who probably would have agreed with Louis Reeves Harrison's overt racism) have interpreted that same figure as reason for finding one or even both of the others unfit for assimilation? Although written earlier, Mary Heaton Vorse's 1911 description of a Jewish immigrant audience in a Lower East Side theater, even if fictionalized, offers an even more specific model of reading.[89] There, enthralled by a one-reel Indian picture, a young woman anxiously projected herself into the figure of Yellow Wing and her love for Dick the Trapper, murmuring out loud from time to time: "Surely, surely, she will save her beloved!" and "The poor child! how can she bear it? To see the *geliebte* wounded before one's very eyes!"

Indian pictures, consequently, were especially well suited to resolve what, as early as 1910, was seen as a problem for the industry: how to address the heterogeneity of such a vast country and its diverse audiences' social positionings. "Nominally American," *Moving Picture World* editorialized in 1910, "the United States is without doubt the most cosmopolitan country in the world. Here you have, besides native Americans, enormous numbers of other peoples in the process of Americanization: French, Germans, Italians, Russians, Swedes, Austrians, and other European nationalities in large numbers."[90] In other words, Indian pictures may well have worked to forge, in Hansen's words, an *American* "mass public out of an ethnically and culturally heterogeneous society," yet one in which some degree of separation still marked their "constellated communities" or audiences.[91] In March 1913, the *Cleveland Leader* concisely summed up the ideological or "educational" function of such films: "Bison, Broncho and Kay-Bee . . . are producing historic subjects that are worthy of exhibition in every school in the country."[92]

The "Imagined Community" of the "Great West": "Cowboy Girl" Pictures

Finally, a passing remark in Emilie Altenloh's 1914 dissertation on moving picture audiences in Germany—that women often were "at the center of the action" in American westerns—prompts a closer look at the numerous "cowboy girl" westerns of the period.[93] Many of these were "school of action" westerns of one sort or another whose affinity with "girl spy films" will become apparent in chapter 4. And they continued to be made well into 1913, as evidenced in Selig's *Sallie's Sure Shot* (July 1913), where, in a quickly edited sequence of close shots, the heroine (Kathlyn Williams) not only keeps two thieves at bay with a rifle but spins and fires, cutting the fuse on a stick of dynamite set to blow up her father's cabin.[94] A few cowboy girl films involved cross-dressing, as in Pathé's *The Sheriff's Daughter* (1911), where the heroine dresses like her outlaw boyfriend and, on horseback, misleads his pursuers (headed up by her own father), allowing him to escape. A more unusual surviving example is Bison's *A Range Romance* (December 1911), in which a man leaves his wife back east in order to forge a new life on a western ranch and takes his young daughter, disguised as a boy.[95] After twelve years, the wife goes in search of him, finding work as a cook on the same ranch; at the same time, the ranch foreman discovers that the young cowboy he has befriended is the now-grown daughter (still in disguise), which sets up a final scene of recognition and reconciliation around the dinner table—with two generations of couples. Cross-dressing, as Verhoeff notes, literalized the mobility granted the "wild women" of such films—in physical movement, narrative action, and gender-bending.[96] For, in taking on the roles "normally" assigned to men, they not only transgressed stereotypical boundaries but also revealed the instability of social categories.

Yet not all cowboy girl westerns could be branded "school of action" westerns, nor did their gender-bending require cross-dressing.[97] Vitagraph's *The Craven*, for instance, can be read as a character study, a "quality" film with strong social implications. Not only does it focus on the sheriff's wife (Anne Schaeffer) as a perceptive and skillful frontier woman, but it ends with a close shot of her alone, dejected, revealing that her sacrificial heroism—not unlike that of Great Bear—goes unrecognized, because never publicly voiced by her coward of a husband.[98] Vitagraph may have cut back on its production of westerns after the summer of 1912, but one of these, *Una of the Sierras* (November 1912), offers a "character study" of a different kind.[99] The story sends an orphaned gold miner's daughter, unexpectedly left "enough gold to pay the national debt," to her aunt's city mansion, where the young woman rapidly, and with zest, learns the ways of modern society—and ultimately saves her suitor's company from a rival's plot to corner its stock. Much like Selig's *Cowboy Millionaire*, *Una of the Sierras* plays as a comedy or satire, in which the behavior of an "uncivilized" character upsets all kinds of social norms: riding in a car for the first time, she leaps from the back seat to the front and then sits on the hood; later, on the beach, she frightens away a suitor by taking off her shoes and socks, hiking up her skirt, and dashing into the surf. Yet its role reversals are far from frivolous, especially when the young woman outdoes the men as a sharper financier: at the climax, she takes control of a stockholders' meeting—dominating the foreground space, with her back to the camera. Moreover, although the film barely hints at this, through her name and an intertitle describing her as "a child of nature," Una clearly can be read as part Indian.[100] Indeed, her spontaneity, spunk, and "native" intelligence are made so appealing that this "half-breed" figure puts a provocative spin on then-current representations of the "New Woman."

Whether they wore the brand of "action" or "quality," cowboy girl westerns were far from anomalies at the time. Important contexts for their circulation include juvenile series for girls such as *The Ranch Girls*, which began publication in 1911,[101] and the commanding presence of women in Buffalo Bill's Wild West and especially the Miller Brothers' 101 Ranch Wild West. Edith Tantlinger and Lucille Mulhall starred in the earliest 101 Ranch Wild West shows—one as a sharpshooter, the other as a champion steer roper who much impressed Teddy Roosevelt[102]—and Lucille Parr and Bessie Herberg both appeared as "poster girls" for the 1912 tour of 101 Ranch Wild West.[103] Newspapers were quick to exploit the popularity of such figures. Beginning in late 1912, Gertrude Price's many syndicated stories in Scripps-McRae papers promoted western stars such as Mona Darkfeather (Bison and Universal-Bison), Ruth Roland (Kalem), and Louise Lester and Pauline Garfield Bush (both Flying A).[104] If these and other cowboy girls deserve a closer, more serious look, it is not just because they constitute a "missing

FIG. 31. Alice Joyce, *Motion Picture Story Magazine* cover (September 1913).

link" to later serial queens such as Kathlyn Williams, whose own early pre-serial promotional stories often highlighted her adventurous roles.[105] It is because, as working women characters and actors (some of whom, like the 101 Ranch Wild West riders, were suffragettes),[106] they embodied a healthy, active, even strenuous, often single way of life that had enormous appeal for young women who, as will be discussed in a later chapter and entr'acte, even then were forming the core of an emerging "picture fan" culture. Whatever the brand of cowboy girl western, Athenloh's remark from distant Germany is telling and contrasts sharply with what the *World* thought Europeans were learning about American women from the movies: that here they were treated with "delicate courtesy" and a "universal chivalrous spirit."[107] Instead, what a good number of the westerns so popular here and abroad in the early 1910s had at their center was a vigorously active heroine, a "Western species" of what the Europeans perceived as a distinctly *American* New Woman.[108]

A Vanishing Market for the Western?

According to some sources, the western was fading in importance by the summer of 1913. The *Mirror,* for instance, interviewed J. J. Raymond of Gordon Amusement, a major New England exhibitor, who reported that "the Western picture has grown stale."[109] In cartoons and reviews, the *World* now tended to dismiss Anderson's cowboy hero, for instance, as fit chiefly for "youthful admirers."[110] Fewer cowboy girl westerns appeared in circulation, coinciding with a general movement that increasingly delinked working women from suffrage, after the failure that spring to win the right to vote for women, and more closely aligned them with mass consumption. Perhaps more important, as Kay-Bee, Broncho, and Bison expanded their production of multiple-reel films to include the Civil War and the Spanish-American War, to exploit the spectacle of large-scale battle scenes and masculine heroics, those war films soon outnumbered western subjects. Moreover, none of these companies opted to make westerns of more than three reels during the emergence of the feature-length film as a regular production and marketing strategy in 1913. Finally, according to Consulate Reports released by the Department of Commerce in early 1914, "the cowboy picture had run its course in foreign lands," and "European picture goers" in particular were "growing tired [of] the cowboys and Indian fighters of Western America."[111] As W. Stephen Bush concluded, the western, once "thought to be the foundation and hope of the motion picture," had come to its "destined end" of the trail.[112]

Yet news of the western's demise seemed much exaggerated. Despite reports to the contrary, Essanay's *Broncho Billy* series remained popular, and Anderson was "easily the favorite screen actor playing in western subjects."[113] Indeed, *Broncho Billy's Mistake* (September 1913) received admiring trade press notices, and with *Broncho Billy Gets Square* (October 1913), the series began to experiment with multiple-reel production.[114] Moreover, Essanay westerns such as *An Episode at Cloudy Canyon* (August 1913), as a *Mirror* reviewer noted, "depart[ed] from the ordinary owing to the absence of sub-titles."[115] Selig also increasingly featured the "skill, verve, and nerve" of Tom Mix in multiple-reel cowboy pictures, beginning with *The Law and the Outlaw* (June 1913) and *The Escape of Jim Dolan* (November 1913), and his westerns were hardly among those that European audiences had "grown tired of," at least in Paris.[116] Even if Kay-Bee was producing fewer westerns, they too were said to still have "great sales . . . abroad."[117] Encouraged by favorable trade press notices, Kalem made Indian pictures (now often starring Darkfeather) a staple of its production, which, with *The Big Horn Massacre* (December 1913), soon became regular multiple-reel releases.[118] The most intriguing (and least examined) westerns, however, came from Romaine Fielding, who had become head of Lubin's nomadic southwestern unit in the summer of 1912.[119] Initially one-reelers, these westerns (with Fielding as writer, director,

PARK FAMILY THEATER

FEATURED EVERY WEDNESDAY THURSDAY

BRONCHO BILLY

WHEN A FELLER NEEDS A FRIEND

FIG. 32. "When a Feller Needs a Friend," *Moving Picture World* (5 April 1913), 40.

and star) either featured Mexican or Mexican American heroes in "Mexican border plays" or else told grim, violent stories whose endings could be even more troubling than those of Bison-101 or Kay-Bee.[120] Fielding's skill at embedding disturbing psychological character studies within isolated, pitiless landscapes, writes Linda Kowall Woal, reached new heights with the two-reel *The Toll of Fear* (April 1913), where, in a tour de force star turn (see chapter 6), he himself played two brothers, the only two characters.[121] In tracking outlaws into the mountains, one brother goes mad with fear and, in a delirium, shoots himself; after finding his body, the other brother suffers a similar fate, holing up in a deserted mission and shooting at the walls, until they collapse on him. This film much impressed the *Morning Telegraph:* "If unpleasant it is striking in every sense."[122] *The Rattlesnake—A Psychical Species* (November 1913), by contrast, has a vaquero suffer rejection by his lover (who then marries a white surveyor) and slowly take on the reptile's characteristics, exiled in a desert cave; later he jealously looses a rattlesnake to strike the woman's husband but has to kill it instead when it threatens the couple's daughter— and he regains his sanity and humanity.[123]

When feature-length westerns eventually did begin to appear in early 1914, they did not follow the "tradition" established by Bison-101, Kay-Bee, Broncho, and Bison (Universal) Indian pictures, which offered leading roles to actual Indians;[124] instead, they turned back to adapt famous stage plays with white heroes from a decade earlier, such as Jesse Lasky's *The Squaw Man*

(March 1914), directed by Cecil B. DeMille and starring Dustin Farnum.[125]
One of these, Selig's nine-reel *The Spoilers* (March 1914), directed by Colin
Campbell and starring William Farnum, even featured on the inaugural program of the "picture palace" Strand in New York.[126] Whatever its ebbs and
flows, the continuing popularity of westerns eventually would reach new
heights several years later—in the cowboy features of William S. Hart (for Tri-
angle/Artcraft), Tom Mix (for Fox), and Francis Ford's brother Jack, better
known later as John (for Universal).[127]

The Western and American Modernity

Even if the western did suffer a momentary fading or "vanishing," that does
not diminish the significance of all those cowboy, Indian, and cowboy girl pictures that were so popular in the early 1910s. As I have argued in *The Red
Rooster Scare,* we can learn a great deal about how early cinema in the United
States became an increasingly Americanized phenomenon just prior to
1910 by reexamining the emergence of the western in relation to the then-
dominant foreign films of Pathé and others. But we can learn just as much,
as I argue here, about that Americanization process and the contingent development of a "New World" national identity by reexamining the shifting
figures of inclusion and exclusion in the "imagined community" of westerns
in the early 1910s, in part by following the trails left by "Old World" as well
as "New World" critics and audiences and taking seriously their fascination
with all those films that have gone unrecognized or even misrecognized for
so long. If the cowboy (and cowboy girl) registered as *the* figure of *American*
modernity in early moving pictures—"the first living and breathing thing of
modernity that was photographed in motion," wrote Harrison with such pre-
science, in January 1914, remarkably anticipating Hansen[128]—the long van-
quished and now vanishing Indian, more fictional than historical, played his
(or her) ideological counterpart, either as the most noble foe and foil of that
modernity or as its most inclusive, most assimilable figure of "otherness."

Document
"Latest Snapshots Local and Worldwide," *Cleveland Leader* (2 March 1913), M11

. . .

A Cleveland minister, speaking from his pulpit recently, said that three-
fourths of all the pictures he had witnessed in the local theatres were simply
"animated dime novels." The good man didn't say how many pictures he had
seen and his criticism, therefore, has little weight. There are forty-two manufacturers who regularly release films. The total output is about 100 picture
subjects a week. Only four manufacturers make exclusively Western or Indian

subjects. A half dozen others make occasional pictures of that type. Twenty per cent of the output is comedy. An average of more than fifteen subjects a week are scenic or topical and of the highest educational value. A classifying of the past month's releases shows 62 per cent of the pictures to be domestic dramas in no sense similar to dime novel stories. The minister must have selected his subjects with the greatest pains to find three out of four of them cheap, sensational stories. The day of the story with the low appeal is practically gone. Bison, Broncho, and Kay-Bee, three of the companies making Western, Indian and war pictures, are producing historic subjects that are worthy of exhibition in every school in the country. They are thrillers, to be sure, and a romance runs through them all, but as examples of real warfare with its attending patriotism and daring and bravery they are lessons no youngster ever can forget. They teach love for the country's flag, respect and admiration for the living heroes and veterans. Each one is a lesson in discipline. Not one-tenth of the entire product of the regular film makers deserves to be classed with dime novel literature.

In a Minor Chord

Percy sings in the Nickelo,
Picture songs with first-run show;
Steps to the front, quite debonair,
Hums for a moment the latest air.
Pianist, absently, fingers her "rat,"
Gives side-combs a friendly pat;
Dimpled fingers then strike the key;
It's a gladsome time for gay Percy!
His pretty girl is in parquet row—
Who wouldn't sing at a first-run show?

Percy sings in the Nickelo.
Picture slides the lanterns throw;
Describes pale Luna, with plaintive cry,
Warbles of forests, fields and sky,
Sings of the maiden, all forlorn,
Of dear, old mother, pale and worn;
Pitches his ballad in key of E.
It's a pleasant time for bold Percy!
A certain lass enjoys it, so—
Who wouldn't sing at a first-run show?

Percy sings in the Nickelo.
Sometimes high, sometimes low.
Pictures red, and white and blue
Flash on the screen, in front of you.
Scenes are oft-times flecked with "rain,"
But to the songster it's all the same.
He sings of wealth and poverty,
Time of his life for staunch Percy!
Smiles at his "steady" in parquet row—
Who wouldn't sing in a picture show?

WILLIAM LORD WRIGHT,
Motion Picture News
(25 November 1911), 25

Entr'acte 3

A "Forgotten" Part of the Program

Illustrated Songs

Several years ago, in the pages of *Cinema Journal,* Ben Singer and Bobby Allen engaged in a spirited debate over the relationship between vaudeville and moving pictures during the transition from nickelodeons to larger moving picture theaters.[1] Sometimes, "Singer and Allen" even sounded like "dueling cavaliers" in a knockabout music hall routine. Each had a different take on the pros and cons, articulated in the trade press and elsewhere at the time, of mixing the two kinds of amusement within a range of New York City venues during the period 1908–12. Yet lost in their either-or debate was any sense that, if moving picture exhibition nearly always occurred within some kind of "combination show," often the dominant combination (especially outside New York City) paired the pictures not with vaudeville but with illustrated songs, as well as other musical arrangements.[2] Typically, it is worth recalling, the illustrated song involved a vocalist and pianist performing a popular song, backed by a projected set of twelve to sixteen colored glass slides that, in sequence, "illustrated" the lyrics.[3] "Behind the scenes," in the projection booth, the act also had to have either a stereopticon mounted alongside one or two projectors or a machine that combined showing slides and moving pictures (with the requisite number of operators).[4] It is this "forgotten" part of the program in the early 1910s that I want to recover in this entr'acte, for, surprisingly, illustrated songs still could be as much of an attraction to audiences as the pictures: first, by exploring the discourse on illustrated songs in the trade press and by mapping their promotion in the newspaper ads for various venues (once again, chiefly in New England, northern Ohio, and the upper Midwest), at least through 1913; then by speculating on the function and significance of the songs and singers as both a programming practice unique to the United States and the only part of the program that always was distinctly American—and the reasons for their decline and disappearance after 1913.

Rereading the trade press discourse on which Singer and Allen consistently draw in their debate, one is struck by how vaudeville and illustrated songs, evaluated within a familiar framework of moral discourse, were treated as separate, and different. The trade press position on whether or not vaudeville was a worthy complement to moving pictures was hardly unanimous.[5] As an advocate of live performance, *Variety* consistently promoted the "small-time" or "pop" vaudeville format developed by Marcus Loew, William Fox, and others.[6] In a column written for *Motion Picture News*, Robert Grau also praised Loew for making a success of his "favorite policy of 'pop' vaudeville" in no less than fifteen theaters in Greater New York.[7] In *Moving Picture World*, a late 1910 report on theaters "in the Northeast in general and in Boston in particular" noted that most had booked vaudeville in conjunction with pictures for "over two years," with "beneficial" results.[8] Yet this praise always referred to the larger and/or prestigious theaters that could afford to book quality acts.[9] Beyond the limited circuit of such theaters, the trade press usually saw the "added attraction" of vaudeville as folly or worse because it too often was "base and vulgar." In early 1910, *Nickelodeon* condemned the "cheap vaudeville" that smaller houses were attempting to exploit and cited its failure in cities such as Philadelphia, Chicago, and St. Louis.[10] That summer, in *Film Index*, Epes Winthrop Sargent claimed that 80 percent of moving picture audiences looked unfavorably on vaudeville simply because most theaters could afford only the "cheapest class" of acts.[11] Shortly thereafter, John Bradlet contended that the *World* had "fought against cheap vaudeville" long and hard, and the fight was beginning to have results.[12] By early 1911, attacks on cheap vaudeville could be found everywhere in the trade press.[13] In short, within the then prevailing reformist discourse of "uplift," condemning cheap vaudeville as vulgar and offensive served to mark moving pictures in general as a far more beneficial entertainment or "social force" for the "masses."

A similar campaign against illustrated songs was mounted at the time, but it was less virulent and relatively short-lived. For the most part, these attacks targeted the singers and songs that, much like cheap vaudeville performers, vulgarized the picture show.[14] H. H. Buckwalter praised one prominent manager in Denver for "cutting out . . . illustrated songs" and, with them, "the undesirable portion of the audience," thereby increasing his receipts; the *World* once even resorted to the scare tactic of naming two singers who had been sent to the slammer.[15] Josephine Clement proved to be the most reputable foe of illustrated songs: in selecting good music for her programs at the Boston Bijou, she stated flatly that illustrated songs were "out of place."[16] But the Boston Bijou aspired to be something like a "conservatory of music," whereas most picture theaters were places, as the *News* put it, "where people can go to hear the latest popular songs."[17] With at least one exception, the colored glass slides accompanying the songs not only were exempt from criticism but also generally won praise.[18] Indeed, from December 1909 through June 1911, *Film Index* actively promoted them with its weekly "Song Slide Department" column, which gave synopses of the most recent releases from the major manufacturers: Scott & Van Altena, DeWitt C. Wheeler, Henry Ingram, Alfred Simpson, Levi, and others.[19] By 1911, the trade press as a whole was praising song slide manufacturers for keeping pace with filmmakers in improving their product.[20] *Film Index* perhaps best summed up the prevailing opinion: song slides had developed into "a fine art," and DeWitt C. Wheeler and Scott & Van Altena now regularly produced "slides that ten years ago would have been regarded with amazement."[21] When Essanay announced its contest, in 1910, to find "a word which [would] lucidly describe the entertainment given in a moving picture theater," the *World* simply assumed that the term would have to include "pictures, illustrated songs, and music."[22] Similarly, in his *Cyclopedia of Motion-Picture Work* (1911), David Hulfish calculated the expenses for song slides and one or more singers in constructing model budgets for every type of picture theater, including the "large exclusive picture house."[23]

For the most part, these assumptions about the prevalence of illustrated songs can be substantiated by a close examination of local programming. Take the unusual daily block ads for picture theaters in the *Saint Louis Times,* for instance, in the first months of 1910.[24] In January, more than half of the theaters presented pictures and illustrated songs, with the downtown Grand Central and residential Casino and Grand-Arsenal holding to the standard format of two songs—such as "Daisies Won't Tell" or "Beautiful Eyes"—for every three reels of film.[25] Only a quarter of the theaters offered vaudeville acts as part of their programs, and all but one of those included songs as well. The ads for the rest were so cryptic that it is difficult to ascertain what they may have shown besides moving pictures. By May, the number of venues listed had reached more than fifty: a half dozen of those were airdomes or roof gardens (recently opened for the summer), but another twenty new ones were permanent theaters.[26] Vaudeville could be found in more than one-third of these venues, including downtown theaters such as the New Imperial and the renovated New Bijou, but the higher figure also came partly from the airdomes, which all featured live acts. Yet, half of the theaters (twenty-five in all), from the downtown St. Charles and Broadway to the residential Knickerbocker and Washington, continued to offer exclusive programs of pictures and illustrated songs. Moreover, many still identified their singers (Audrey Abbott at the Grand Central, Tom Turner at the Ideal), and a few even continued to name the songs—Leo Dale, at the Shenandoah, singing "What's the Matter with Father" and "Give My Regards to Mabel."[27] This ratio of programming formats again was as characteristic of theaters renting Independent films as it was of those using licensed films: whereas the Delmar alternated "high-class vaudeville" and the "latest motion pictures," the Clinton explicitly advertised, "No souvenirs, stamps, or vaudeville given. It is not necessary. Just [licensed] pictures and songs."[28]

The presence of illustrated songs was no less prominent elsewhere, and not only in "neighborhood theaters," where *Nickelodeon* claimed it was "well nigh a necessity,"[29] but just as often in larger theaters where, allegedly, the songs could be dispensed with—in downtown shopping and entertainment districts. In Boston, for instance, where a unique state law mandated an interval of three to five minutes between one projected reel of film and another (to minimize eye strain), both the Comique (Tremont Row) and Jolliette (Bowdoin Square) played Independent films and illustrated songs exclusively.[30] In Springfield, Illinois, the *World* reported that, whether a theater showed Independent pictures (as did the Royal) or licensed subjects (as did the Grand), its programs always featured illustrated songs but never vaudeville.[31] Similar programs could be found at small theaters like the 262-seat Majestic, in Sioux City, Iowa, and the York or Forest (the one north, the other south of downtown Chicago), where illustrated songs alternated with several reels of licensed films.[32] In downtown Milwaukee, new theaters such as the 900-seat Princess (the first Saxe brothers theater) and the 1,500-seat Butterfly also were "devoted to moving pictures, illustrated lectures, organ recitals, [and] illustrated songs."[33] According to clippings books in the Keith-Albee Collection, in Providence, Rhode Island, the Nickel Theatre consistently promoted its singers and songs as much as its three reels of pictures.[34] In early May 1910, for instance, the advertised songs were "Dinah from Carolina" (sung by the Nickel Quartet) and "All That I Ask of You Is Love" (sung by a Miss Shannon). In late January 1911, the following songs appeared in sharp contrast to Biograph's *His Trust Fulfilled:* "Where the Desert Meets the Nile," "Don't You Wish It Was Summer," and "Columbia the Gem of the Ocean." In late December that same year, the variety program may have produced an overarching narrative, from "When You Kiss an Italian Girl" to Essanay's *Broncho Billy's Christmas Dinner* and then on to "Lord, Have Mercy on a Married Man."

If, in many cities and towns, illustrated songs continued to attract audiences beyond 1910–11, in others the surviving evidence is less clear. In Cleveland, Canton, and Youngstown, for instance, where the picture theaters advertised relatively extensively and most had small orchestras (witness my grandfather and his clarinet), there is almost no trace of illustrated songs during the early 1910s. That also is the case in Des Moines, although songs and singers had been a major attraction at several downtown theaters just a few years earlier.[35] In Providence, by contrast, the Nickel told its clientele that it was dropping illustrated songs from its programs in June 1912, and then chose not to revive them.[36] Yet, in nearby Lynn and Lowell, the downtown picture theaters seem not to have considered such a move. In Lowell, both the Pastime and the new Star alternated their licensed or Independent reels, respectively, with songs; as late as September 1913, the Opera House was advertising the "latest pictures and best illustrated songs."[37] In Lynn, the Central Square switched from vaudeville and pictures to pictures and songs in March 1912, a practice that lasted at least through November.[38] When the Olympia, also in Lynn, hired the "spellbinding" Geoffrey Whalen to lecture its pictures in late 1912, the Comique met this competition, in early 1913, with the added attraction of "lifelike effects" to accompany its pictures, plus illustrated songs.[39] Meanwhile, across the country, that spring and summer, in Cedar Rapids, the downtown Crystal heavily promoted Ray W. Fay performing illustrated songs—and just as it began booking special multiple-reel films.[40] Later that year, in describing "prosperous" houses between New York and Chicago, the *News* cited the Pitt (apparently in or near Pittsburgh) as a model of "refined advertising"—one-quarter of its display poster was allotted to the singer.[41] Even in Des Moines, in a brief attempt to run daily changes of second-run multiple-reel films, in early 1914 the Black Cat featured "Orlena Anelro, contralto, in beautifully illustrated songs," with new slides provided daily by Chicago Song Slide Exchange.[42]

In a series of articles titled "Motion Picture Making and Exhibiting," *Motography* certainly still considered illustrated songs a valuable asset to moving picture programs through the summer of 1913.[43] Moreover, the *World* continued its "Song Slides" column, along with ads from Scott & Van Altena and others, at least through that spring, and the *News* carried Chicago Song Slide ads well into the fall.[44] Yet the most telling evidence comes from several widely dispersed major cities in 1913. In Baltimore, as many as four downtown picture theaters gave special attention to their singers and/or songs. In January, for instance, the Picture Garden promoted the Trevett Quartette, "those singing boys from Chicago," on a par with its program of Universal films; the New Pickwick, the "home of Vitagraph," headlined Billy Frisch doing "clever song novelties"; and the Blue Mouse had the "splendid tenor" Leonard Chick performing "new song novelties."[45] By late April, Nat Hilt had joined Chick in moving to the Picture Garden; Alfred Armond now performed new songs like "Some Boy" at the Blue Mouse; Archie Lloyd, "the singer who has 'made good' with the Baltimore public," was at the New Pickwick; and Dick Queen could be heard "in spotlight singing" at the Lexington.[46] In Minneapolis that spring, the downtown Crystal, Isis, and Orient all advertised "special singing numbers" along with their multiple-reel films.[47] But so did several picture theaters in secondary shopping districts or residential areas of the city, such as the Elite and New Park.[48] Moreover, the

FIG. 33. Scott & Van Altena, "Butterflies" (1912), Marnan Collection.

Seville still was listing its singer, Howard Dawson, as late as November, and the Crystal had "three singers to interpret popular songs between reels" as late as December.[49] Finally, in Toledo, all three theaters in the Empress Company circuit (the Empress, Laurel, and National) advertised singers and songs up to January 1914.[50] And the downtown Princess made "music a feature" of its General Film Exclusive Service programs with the "Ionic Male Quartette every evening" at least through April 1914.[51]

There are different ways of explaining how and why illustrated songs remained a popular act in picture theaters during the early 1910s. Projection booths usually already had a stereopticon for making announcements, promoting upcoming films, and advertising local businesses—not unlike the current practice in multiplex cinemas.[52] Theater payrolls also usually already included a pianist and stereopticon operator. The only major added expense then came from hiring one or more singers, but their salaries were considerably lower than those of even "cheap vaudeville" performers. Illustrated songs also perfectly suited the variety program format of many picture theaters. Indeed, "the bright dashes of color in [the] slides," as the *World* put it, "furnish a pleasing contrast to the monochromatic picture plays, and the softer vocal music of the song relieves the orchestral stress of the accompaniments played to the motion pictures."[53] Surviving song slide sets confirm this vivid sense of color: for instance, in DeWitt C. Wheeler's "Pansy Mine" (1911) or Scott & Van Altena's "Butterflies" (1912).[54] But they also reveal surprising effects: in Scott & Van Altena's "Just to Live the Old Days Over" (1909), a memory image of a young woman appears in a close-up of a hand-

FIG. 34. Scott & Van Altena, "Just to Live the Old Times Over" (1909), Marnan Collection.

held mirror; in Wheeler's "What a Funny Little World This Is" (1911), a man "sits upon the moon and smilingly regards a beaming globe," surrounded by clouds and stars.[55] And theaters like the Nickel could combine the pictures and songs into unexpected narratives. As for the music, it was not uncommon during the nickelodeon era for Tin Pan Alley publishers to pay professional singers to tour a circuit of theaters so as to popularize their tunes by performing illustrated songs.[56] Although this practice largely disappeared in the early 1910s, music publishers such as Jerome Remick recognized how picture theaters still could turn a recent song like "Oceana Roll" into a "big hit."[57] In fact, *Billboard* claimed that picture theaters had been "a most potent agency in bringing before the public numerous new ragtime and sentimental ballads," which they then could purchase in local music stores or department stores.[58]

Yet whatever their popularity, illustrated songs began to lose much of their allure by 1913–14, and for multiple reasons. Song slide manufacturers never reached a level of industrialization, and economic clout, even close to that of the motion picture industry by the early 1910s. Whereas they were lucky to turn out perhaps a dozen new sets of song slides per week, by 1913 the latter released nearly ten times that number of reels of new film. Besides, the weekly charge for renting a song slide set rarely came to more than two dollars, whereas that for renting first-run films could run more than fifty dollars. Undoubtedly, as they gained an increasing hold on the market, feature-length films also had an impact. For features not only transformed the program format of many picture theaters, bringing it closer to that of the "legitimate" theater; they also changed theaters themselves from places where some people went to learn the latest songs to "refined" spaces where they now went to hear orchestras "toning the picture,"[59] and to listen to interludes of special orchestral arrangements, the kind of music first developed by Rothapfel and others. Finally, as a form of popular culture increasingly de-

FIG. 35. Scott & Van Altena, "That Swaying Harmony" (1912), Marnan Collection.

pendent on local musical talent, illustrated songs were a casualty of theater managers' growing loss of control over exhibition. Their control had begun to erode with the emergence of the General Film Company and then Universal and Mutual, all of which "sold" a weekly packaged film service to those exhibitors who continued to run variety programs. It eroded further with the emergence of Warner's Features and Famous Players, which also "sold" a weekly packaged film service to those who now chose to run features. Paralleling and complementing this development of a national system of distribution were a growing number of regional circuits of picture theaters, whose programming could be planned and managed from a central office.

The heyday of illustrated songs may have lasted no more than a decade, but that does not diminish their role in early twentieth-century audiovisual culture. For one thing, illustrated songs made picture theaters a unique mix of national mass culture and local popular culture. Much like moving pictures, they were cultural commodities that could circulate throughout the country, almost simultaneously; yet both songs and slides, even more than the pictures, became "finished products" only in performance. In short, they helped immeasurably to sustain the notion, first established in the earlier nickelodeons, that picture theaters could serve as "social centers" in many communities. As long as managers retained a degree of local control, their theaters were public places where groups of people, from downtown shopgirls, stenographers, and shoppers to factory workers, from schoolchildren to families from a variety of neighborhoods, could regularly gather and make "their own." For another thing, although just what songs were performed and by whom could differ from theater to theater, several general patterns seemed to emerge during this period.[60] Whereas women often performed the illustrated songs up to 1910 or 1911, as was the case at the Nickel in Providence, men usually did the singing after that, as was the case in either Baltimore or Minneapolis. Did this shift strengthen the close ties illustrated songs already had with a largely female clientele, and thus make them even more attractive? Or did it tend to make their attraction too exclusive, and so begin to marginalize illustrated songs on picture theater programs?

Another pattern that becomes particularly noticeable in the context of westerns and Civil War films is the "innovative nostalgia" that so many of the songs evoke, with their sentimental, romantic, or patriotic lyrics set to the new rhythm of ragtime. The figures in the slides support this sense of nostalgia, for many—apparently "lower-middle-class" whites—seem to exist in a "world in between," particularly marked by their tendency not to sport the current fashions advertised in such mass magazines as the *Saturday Evening Post* or *Ladies' Home Journal* but to dress slightly behind the times, more like the figures in amusement park post cards of the period.[61] Not yet successful or comfortably well-off, they seem drawn not so much to the future—unlike the amusement park figures attracted to the technologies of modernity—as to a past simpler life, whether that of the "old country" (Ireland was a particular favorite, but others such as Italy were not) or that of a rural area or small town.[62] Indeed, the songs and slides arguably create a more or less homogeneous story of migration and assimilation to modern America that stressed rootedness in a relatively restricted sense of the past, in what might be called a variation on the Anglo-Saxon "myth of origins." As a cultural form perhaps even less inclusive than westerns or Civil War films, consequently, illustrated songs would have "educated" migrants (from inside and outside the country's borders) in quite different ways to actively, grudgingly, or at least ambivalently participate in the process of "Americanization."

Document
"Unique Effects in Song Slides," *Film Index*
(6 May 1911), 12–13

It doesn't seem so very long ago that the writer used to make Meyer Cohen sad by suggesting that he sang so loudly because he was afraid of the dark, but that was about the time that the illustrated song came into its own for the second time.

Of course you must have heard Meyer sing to appreciate the remark but then most persons have heard him sing to the slides in the days before he became the business brains of Charles K. Harris. He was one of the first, if not the first to connect the songs and the lantern slides although Tony Pastor used to make a hit just fifty years ago with patriotic airs and lantern slides to

match. The difference was that Mr. Pastor used any slide that came handy
while in the new dispensation some effort was made to match the subject and
the slide although even then the "stock" slide was painfully in evidence and
at least one singer used to start the Holy City with the usual startling statement that last night he slept and to prove it the lantern man threw upon the
screen the more or less humorous portrait of a fat person with a red nose
that to the old timer suggested the trick effect in which the sleeper swallowed
innumerable rats. It was the same slide, but with the rat left out; yet anything
went in those times and the idea of spending several hundred dollars upon
a set of special illustrations would have startled. Indeed when Harris sent a
company to Shenandoah Valley to illustrate "The Green Fields of Virginia"
it was a seven weeks wonder. Now as much money is spent on some songs as
would have sufficed to run a studio a month ten years ago.

Five years ago it was enough of a novelty that the pictures fitted the situation but to-day the audiences have been led to expect more than that and it
is the tricked slide that brings the most applause.

From a purely altruistic point of view it is to be questioned whether a picture of a bird on its nest truly illustrates a line to the effect that the hero will
return when the birdies nest again, but usually the slide gets a hand, the
women murmur "Ain't it sweet" and the slide maker makes some more of the
same sort because he is in business to fill a demand, not to furnish an art education with each set of slides.

But at the same time the successful song illustrator of to-day is a power for
good in leading the taste of the vaudeville and photoplay audiences to better things. Not alone are the purely descriptive pictures more illustrative of
the line of the song, but the effect slides are constantly being improved in
artistic value and novelty of idea. Firms like the veteran De Witt C. Wheeler
and more recent entrants like Scott and Van Altena produce slides that ten
years ago would have been regarded with amazement and twenty years ago
with awe. There were fine slides in those days but they were mostly of natural scenery or art reproductions. To-day the brush and the camera are
united to gain the best results and the artist and the photographer are
equally important.

Perhaps some of the credit should go to Blakely Hall for it was on The
Standard while it was under his direction that the touched up photograph
was brought to full development. The process was in use by photo-engravers
before then but it was on The Standard that the idea was brought to its then
highest point.

But the slide maker has improved upon the methods and between paint
work and trick photography the product becomes notable. It is interesting
to the old timer to take some of the recent product and compare it with the
slides that once were considered to be in the highest manner of art.

Scott and Van Altena submit some notably good specimens, in "Blanket

Bay," for instance, they offer a combination of cloud effect pictures with a studio posed trundle bed ship in which the lighting of the interior print is apparently done by the painted moon in the cloud study and there is no hint of pasting and joining so well has the work been done. It is a bedstead boat sailing a sea of billowy clouds and the touching up only serves to heighten the realism instead of betraying the trickery.

Much the same care in detail is shown in a scene of "Yiddle on the Middle of Your Fiddle" in which the gas is lighted in an interior supposed to be seen at night. Think a little thing like that would have been looked after two decades ago? Hardly, and yet it is just one instance of the care that must be shown these days. Another example is found in a slide for "The Heidelberg Glide" where two Dutch dancers in miniature pose on the sabots of two larger figures. They make the pose exactly, the photographs being made to fit before taking. Time was when "about" was as good as "exact."

There seems to be no limit to the things that may be done and they are being better done all the time. The insertion of a face in a flower harks back to the days when the calcium was used and no show was considered complete without the dissolving effects from "Rock of Ages" to the black-berries that became small Negro babies, but the old-time operator who has been taking a Rip Van Winkle sleep would rub his eyes hard could he see a slide in "I'll Be With You When the Southern Roses Are in Bloom." The face fits the flower. The girl might have grown into the heart of the rose for all the photograph shows to the contrary.

Pretty frame effects are planned with skill and prove a welcome break to plain poses and the frames run all the way from wall paper and burlap to seascapes with the figure cunningly inset, and floral or modeled designs.

Wheeler offers some novelties in comedy pictures, a department in which he seems particularly happy. In "Jimmy Valentine" he shows that hero making off with an actual horse and cart in his arms to illustrate the statement that "he would steal a horse and cart" and in "My What a Funny Little World This Is" the singer sits upon the moon and smilingly regards a beaming globe, a fine effect with painted clouds that seem real. "In Old New York He Found Her" shows the statue of Liberty as the exact spot where the discovery was made, for she stands upon the pedestal beside the bronze goddess and he is climbing up, a novelty idea that gets a laugh and even a "hand" all to itself. A sprinkling cart that sprinkles is used in a song about the water wagon and there is a real monster for "That Boog-aboo Man" that will strike terror into the heart of any six-year-old. But the Wheeler studio is good at the more serious style and a dainty conceit in "Sweet Red Roses" shows the lover listening to the whispers of his inamorita who peers at him from a bouquet as large as himself.

It takes a lot of thinking to get something new these days when most of the obvious ideas have been worked out, but the slide maker cannot keep on doing the same thing over and over again and the novelty must come. One good idea from the Wheeler studio is a spoon in light and shade that is thrown over the figures of a colored couple. It is simple and effective but it is novel, too, and that is what counts.

And methods change with the improvement in the quality. Once upon a time the photographer or the song publisher would coax some friends to take a Sunday off and help out. They might, or might not, prove good subjects but it was more or less Hobson's choice. There were professional models to be had but models cost money and costs had to be counted then. Once in a while someone would get reckless and hire an "army" of a dozen or more people for some military song but Decoration Day parades and State Camp sham battles had to serve for most of the military scenes and the State Camp pictures were easy to obtain in the days when the focal plane shutter and reflex cameras were still wearing long clothes and taking kindly to the milk bottle. Today the slides offer the work of regular models who are trained to camera work and a wider range of general subjects to draw from. Instead of being rushed through in a couple of days with such properties as may be handy the same care is taken with their preparation as is used in the preliminary work on a photoplay and the pictures are worth while looking at.

Every now and then the statement gets into print that the illustrated song is doomed but like the man who has heart disease and yet lives to a green old age the picture song seems to wax and grow prosperous upon dire predictions for the slide makers are more than keeping abreast of the times. They have passed far enough ahead to lead popular taste and the work of some of the best makers is an art education in palatable form.

A Dixie Mother

Its appeal is manifold and universal.
Its interest is intensely human.
It runs the gamut of every emotion.
It solves the difficult problem of rousing patriotism
    without kindling animosity.
It portrays love in its purest aspect, heroism without bravado,
    and sentiment without sentimentality.
Its moral quality is true, sweet, and nobly uplifting.
It is the embodiment of ideal Americanism.

REBECCA MIDDLETON SAMSON,
Rockville Center, N.Y.,
Motion Picture Story Magazine
(July 1911)

Chapter 4

The "Usable Past"
of Civil War Films

The Years of the "Golden Jubilee"

On 21 April 1911, most US newspapers carried stories commemorating the beginning of "America's Great Civil War" fifty years earlier. The editorial page of the *Des Moines News,* for instance, not only gave its readers a fact sheet of statistics on the men and money involved in the war but also excerpted accounts of the bombardment of Fort Sumter: one by a "northern wartime historian," the other by the southern author of *The Lost Cause* (1867).[1] These were but the first of countless stories and other forms of commemoration that could be found in newspapers throughout what was called the "Golden Jubilee" years of 1911–15. Some recounted famous battles on the anniversary of their fighting; others told of the experiences of surviving local veterans. In April 1912, the *Cleveland Leader* even offered an exclusive edition of Benson J. Lossing's *A History of the Civil War* (1866–68), specially illustrated with "Brady war photographs" and a "great battlefield series in full color."[2] Coinciding with all these were Civil War reenactments, most of them encampments linked to specific battles. Originally staged by veterans, especially those of the Grand Army of the Republic, they increasingly included survivors of both sides of the conflict, their descendants, and others in "living history" communities (exclusively male, and white) of reconciliation.[3] The largest of these was planned as a spectacular "Peace Jubilee" to be held at Gettysburg on 1–4 July 1913, and its "enormous tent city . . . of Blue-Gray fraternalism"—superbly analyzed by David Blight—created, for an allegedly white nation, a strong sense of "national harmony and patriotism."[4] Local historical pageants during this period also often included Civil War episodes, according to David Glassberg, with most of them "displaying a similar pattern of departure, reported sacrifice, and return," long familiar, David Mayer would add, from Civil War stage melodramas.[5] Essentially "domestic scenes," these episodes, Glassberg concludes, "emphasized the sacrifices common to both sides of the conflict" rather than the divisive issues that had provoked the war.

In the "twilight zone" between "living memory and written history," as C. Vann Woodward described the years just prior to the Golden Jubilee,[6] this culture of reunion involved forgetting perhaps even more than remembering, transforming the nightmare of the war into a more palatable dreamscape. For the South, that forgetting was epitomized in the myth of the "Lost Cause," where, in the words of Nina Silber, the old South became "a land of idyllic plantation settings, heroic men, and elegant women . . . [and] the system of slavery . . . a happy and mutually beneficial arrangement."[7] For the North, by the turn of the century, that forgetting had turned into ambivalence toward the war, a greater acceptance of the South, and an erasure of slavery as a chief cause—and a flagrant disregard for the lynchings of blacks, largely in the South. Stemming from the influential work of James Ford Rhodes, the then-dominant "nationalist" tradition of historiography assumed now that the South's secession was as honorable as the Union's preservation was necessary, and that both sides were blameworthy—the one before, the other after the war.[8] That tradition accepted the myth of the "Lost Cause," whose effect was to grant a nostalgic dignity to the suffering and sacrifices of white Southerners during the war, on which a "new South" might emerge, but also, after the premature ending of Reconstruction, to turn freed blacks into a "social problem," a kind of "white man's burden."[9] Although generally convinced of the rightness of the Union victory, Northerners shared the South's nostalgia for a vanishing way of life, especially in the face of the social conflicts produced by urbanization and industrial progress. Reunion culture, which flourished in numerous novels and plays between 1880 and 1900—from John DeForest's *The Bloody Chasm* (1881) and the fiction of Thomas Nelson Page to Charles Townsend's *The Pride of Virginia* (1901)— and was unusually popular in the North, thus offered a means of holding in concert the opposing appeals of "a modern and premodern world."[10]

As a popular subject, at least for most audiences, the Golden Jubilee celebrations built on this reunion culture, providing a crucial impulse and context for the production and marketing of so many Civil War films between 1911 and 1914. Indeed, such films undoubtedly were made in far greater numbers than they would have been otherwise, especially during the shift to multiple-reel films and features in 1912–13. Initially, they tended either to follow the "school of action" formula or, much like local historical pageants and stage melodramas, to tell domestic or family-oriented stories. Perhaps inspired by the reenactments and their attraction for spectators, manufacturers soon realized that Civil War battles could be exploited for their visual spectacle.[11] Bison-101's decision, in the summer of 1912, to begin making Civil War films inextricably linked them with westerns, particularly spectacular Indian pictures, as uniquely American sensational melodramas focused on war.[12] Yet unlike westerns, they were made exclusively by a few American companies and marketed primarily in the United States. Accordingly, this chapter takes up several interrelated shifts that characterize the Civil War films: first, the shift from action melodramas and domestic subjects to those focused on spectacular battle scenes, a shift that more or less coincided with the emergence of multiple-reel films; second, the shift from film stories that consistently created empathy for the South—perhaps more prominent in moving pictures than in other cultural forms and practices at the time—to those that, overall, created empathy for both sides in the spirit of reconciliation. The aim here, as in the two chapters on westerns, is to analyze the "imagined community of nationality" represented in Civil War films and the "constellated communities" for whom the "usable past" of their stories may have had meaning. In short, how did these films contribute to Dudley Miles's claim, in his famous essay, "The Civil War as a Unifier" (January 1913), that "the war deepened and spread the sense of nationality," as it was transformed over time, until the United States became "one people in fact as well as in name"?[13]

Girl Spies, Dutiful "Darkies," and Cowardly Men

Before 1910, Eileen Bowser writes, the few popular films that depicted actual or fictional incidents in the Civil War, with Kalem's *Escape from Andersonville* (1909) a notorious example, seem to have favored the North.[14] In a review of Kalem's *The Girl Spy* (May 1909), *Moving Picture World* noted that such films, "as a rule, had emphasized the heroism of the North."[15] A year later, the *World* was agreeing with letters from southern exhibitors, such as one in Charleston, West Virginia, complaining that "all civil war films have the Northern army come out ahead."[16] The *World's* explanation for this supposed phenomenon was simple, if incomplete: the market for moving pictures south of Pennsylvania and west of the Mississippi or Missouri rivers (excepting the Pacific Coast) was undercapitalized.[17] In other words, manufacturers did not have to cater to audiences in the South. Yet, for nearly two years (from late 1910 through much of 1912), companies such as Kalem and Biograph, which tended to specialize in Civil War films, mostly chose to tell stories with Confederate heroes or heroines. Reviewing Vitagraph's *A Little Lad in Dixie* (March 1911), even the *New York Morning Telegraph* noticed this "present trend toward telling the story of 'the war' from 'the other side.' "[18] Clearly, the companies were adhering to a general pattern in so many previous Civil War novels and plays, and counting on the popularity of such stories far beyond the South. But they also often seem to have been drawing on a more specific storytelling tradition, tales of "confidence women" or "girl spies," many of them written by women.

As early as 1879, a British writer had claimed: "The Civil War in America was more productive of female warriors than almost any conflict since the days of the Amazons."[19] The claim was not without foundation, as Elizabeth Leonard discovered, in using government documents, memoirs, and works of fiction to recount the lives of Southerners such as Belle Boyd and Rose O'Neal Greenhow or Northerners such as Elizabeth Van Lew and Pauline Cushman.[20] Moreover, as Elizabeth Young has shown, just as many female as male writers took up the war as a subject in the late nineteenth century, whether their main characters were cross-dressing soldiers, spies, or "confidence women"—that is, "counterfeits" skilled in disguise.[21] These stories undoubtedly provide a source for many of Kalem's "school of action" war films. Aptly titled, *The Girl Spy* was the first in an irregular series starring (and written by) Gene Gauntier as a heroine named Nan who repeatedly baffles Union officers, after overhearing their plans, by hiding in a farmer's well, disguising herself as a boy among apple sacks on a cart, and leaping out of a tree onto an untethered horse, and galloping off to disclose Federal troop movements to the Confederates.[22] Another was *The Girl Spy before Vicksburg* (December 1910), which the *New York Dramatic Mirror* welcomed, partly because the "girl spy" was such "a fascinating, lively, resourceful and daring miss, equal to all possible and impossible emergencies."[23] Gauntier reprised this kind of role in *The Little Soldier of '64* (June 1911)—where, much as in the legend of "Molly Pitcher," she "dresses as a man and follows her husband into battle," and saves his life—as well as in *To the Aid of Stonewall Jackson* (July 1911), which was one of a half dozen story films shown by the Brooklyn Board of Education to thousands of people at various recreation centers in late 1911.[24] Even in a contrasting film such as *By a Woman's Wit* (April 1911), a Union spy who disguises himself as "a happy darkey" and then "a commissary agent" has to be rescued by a Southern woman whose sympathies lie with the North.[25]

One of the earliest surviving Kalem films about the Civil War, *The Railroad Raiders of '62* (June 1911), may lack either Gauntier or a girl spy, but it deserves mention as a remarkably sustained "school of action" war film.[26] In this story, six disguised Union soldiers sneak behind enemy lines to capture a Confederate locomotive but are pursued and shot before they can reach safety. Here, several "deep space" compositions establish a "realistic" distance between the opposing forces, especially when the Union men start to cross a plank bridge early on and have to hide among the pilings when Southern troops come into view in the far background. Much as does Biograph's *The Lonedale Operator* (March 1911), the film then uses crosscutting between Union and Confederate forces to deftly build suspense, accentuated with several dolly and tracking shots of the speeding locomotives. Perhaps most unusual are the low-angle full shot/long shots of the plank bridge under which the Union men first hide as the Confederate troops march across its span and on which, at the end, the last of them are felled.[27]

The *Mirror* was frankly amazed by the film, finding it "both exciting and thrilling and so well conceived that for the time it appears almost as an actuality."[28] Indeed, *The Railroad Raiders of '62* was so successful that it prompted the company to specialize in a series of "railroad thrillers" that could exploit the winter headquarters of one production unit in Jacksonville, Florida, and another in Alabama.[29] Most of these railroad thrillers, however, would have more contemporary subjects, as in *The Lost Freight Car* (October 1911), called simply "sensational" in Canton, or *The Grit of the Girl Telegrapher* (September 1912).[30]

Although they rarely eschewed action altogether, Biograph's Civil War films tended to focus on domestic or family-oriented stories. These "borrowed heavily from Civil War stage melodrama," as Mayer argues, for filmmaker D. W. Griffith was "*steeped* in . . . [such] theatrical tropes and structures" as paired households and families riven by conflict.[31] Moreover, they appropriated a key trope of gender blurring: the erosion, in Young's words, of "the boundary between male 'battlefront' and female 'homefront.' "[32] A fine early example occurs in *The Fugitive* (November 1910), which parallels two opposing soldiers departing from home, separates them from the overall battle for single combat in which the Northerner kills the Southerner, and then has the survivor flee for safety to the dead man's home.[33] The film's prior attention to the Southern mother now creates what the *World* called a dramatic, psychological struggle: once she discovers her dead son and learns who has killed him, she has to decide the fugitive's fate and finally allows him "to escape, for the sake of that other mother in the North."[34] The film's emphasis on "mother love" comes into sharp focus when compared with others that also tell stories of family loyalties divided by the war, such as Selig's *1864* (April 1911), where a dying Southerner blesses his own sister's love for a Northern opponent.[35] Biograph's *The House with Closed Shutters* (August 1910) was even more ambitious, "combining beautifully choreographed action in the battle scenes," which the *Mirror* found "remarkably realistic," with what Tom Gunning aptly calls "a claustrophobic Southern Gothic plot."[36] Here, in a characteristic bit of cross-dressing, the sister of a cowardly Confederate soldier takes his place in battle and dies in his uniform; in an unusual move, their mother then maintains the fiction of her son's honor while forcing him to live out his days unseen behind the closed shutters of the house. Given its critique of Southern manliness, not unexpectedly the film was a hit with audiences in the North: the *World,* for instance, reported that "no other picture" that week "so roused the enthusiasm of a large audience" at one of Keith's New York theaters.[37]

Biograph's *His Trust* and its sequel, *His Trust Fulfilled* (both January 1911), continue this theme of (more or less) honorable Southern sacrifice, but now the central figure is an "old Negro servant" (played in blackface).[38] Here, a Confederate officer is killed and leaves his family in the servant's care; the old black man saves the wife and daughter from a Union attack, supports them during the war, secretly finances the grown daughter's move into white society (after the mother dies), and, after the war, watches (from afar, not unlike the later Stella Dallas) her wedding to an English cousin. Although the "loyal underling" intensely devoted to the Lost Cause was a racist cliché of stage melodrama, the latter film is unusual (for the time), as Kristin Thompson argues, in having a white lawyer acknowledge the servant's trust with a handshake near the end; moreover, it keeps the daughter ignorant of the later sacrifices made by the black servant, a figure of displacement for both her father and mother.[39] A similar figure resolves the problems of a very different couple in *Swords and Hearts* (August 1911). This film may follow "the symmetries of stage melodrama," Mayer writes, but its opposing households and fathers are Southern, divided by class (plantation owner, "poor white" farmer), as are its young women, rivals for the love of the plantation owner's son, Hugh Frazier, also a Confederate officer.[40] Both fathers die when the "poor white" leads "bushwackers" to attack the plantation, but his daughter, Jennie Baker (Dorothy West, reprising her role from *The House with Closed Shutters*), saves Hugh from capture by Union soldiers shortly thereafter by donning his uniform, mounting his horse, and leading them astray. At the war's end, the aristocratic Irene Lambert abandons her claim on Hugh to become engaged to a victorious Union officer; his plantation in ruins, Hugh is reduced to subsistence farming until a faithful black servant restores the hidden Frazier family valuables and now reveals Jennie's earlier heroic action to him. After disparaging the conventional symbol of reunion (the gendered marriage of North and South), this film presents the emergence of a "New South" in which the "lost home" of white patriarchy is created anew with the aid of schematically aligned supporters, a "poor white" woman and a former slave working more or less in tandem.[41]

These two kinds of war stories work in near-perfect unison in Biograph's rightly famous *The Battle* (November 1911), which not only raised the Civil War film to a level that anticipated the Bison-101 two-reel Indian pictures but, for Vachel Lindsay, set the standard for a "one-reel work of art."[42] Here the story focuses on a young Union soldier who flees the scene of battle, shames his sweetheart (Blanche Sweet) by cowering in her nearby house, but then redeems himself by driving a last surviving wagon of ammunition (from General Grant's encampment) through enemy fire and back to the lines just in time to repel a final Confederate attack. The trade press unanimously admired the film's "spectacular" battle scenes, initially conveyed in "deep-space" compositions often taken from a high-angle camera position and then accentuated by crosscutting during the coward's perilous journey back to the front lines.[43] Advertised as a "masterpiece" that "ranks far above any other war picture ever made," *The Battle* was a smash hit with audiences, especially in the North: after weekend screenings, it had to be rebooked, in

FIG. 36. Theatre Voyons ad, *Lowell Courier Citizen* (8 November 1911), 9.

major downtown theaters in both Lowell and Lynn; more than a month after its release, the *Cleveland Leader* could still recommend it as "exceptional," "so much better than even the manufacturers claimed."[44] Uncharacteristically for Griffith, the story focused on Union characters, but several choices made the film more easily acceptable to different audiences. Reversing the usual pattern, Union rather than Confederate forces are put on the defensive, and the coward-turned-hero has to rescue them from a disastrous defeat. Moreover, the trade press reviews tended to eliminate most references to the Civil War or to the North and South. Instead, the film was described as an "elaborate and realistic war picture" that depicted a story of youthful "cowardice and subsequent redemption." In short, *The Battle* invited spectators not only to marvel at the unrivaled spectacle of the battle scenes but to identify with either the hero or the heroine (or both), suffering along with the hero as he finally proves his bravery—and masters a profound crisis of masculinity—or sharing the heroine's initial disgust and then her pleasure when her "faith in his manhood and courage is fully restored."

The Triumph of the Confederacy

Throughout most of 1912, Kalem (with few exceptions) became an exclusive source of Civil War films. Initially, these continued to be shot in Florida, to be directed by Kenean Buel, and to work variations on the "Molly Pitcher" or "girl spy" stories, but without Gauntier. In *The Battle of Pottsburg Bridge* (February 1912), for instance, the sister of a young Confederate officer wounded in battle completes his mission by setting fire to one end of a bridge; then the Confederates blow up the other, trapping the Union troops.[45] Similarly in *The Drummer Girl of Vicksburg* (June 1912), another sister takes the place of her dead brother and is wounded "disabling the enemy's gun," which exposes her identity.[46] *The Two Spies* (January 1912) enacted a "romance of reunion" by having a Confederate "girl spy" fall in love with "a spy from the Northern army," both disguised as farmers; they not only aid one another but also "part with an agreement that he shall come for her after the war."[47] Beginning with *A Spartan Mother* (March 1912), the Kalem films also came with a bonus, for twenty-five cents: piano scores specially arranged by Walter C. Simon.[48] The company promoted both film and music well in advance with a "special presentation" for "about 150 exhibitors" in the New York City area and followed that with "considerable special advertising matter."[49] The promotion seems to have worked, given the rare theater ads in cities from Lawrence to Des Moines, and its choice as one of four "photo-play stories of the week" in Cleveland.[50] Moreover, Rothapfel's "special music and effects" made it a "big feature" attraction for three days at the Lyric in Minneapolis.[51] Yet *A Spartan Mother* also gave an unusual twist to the story of a cowardly Confederate soldier by having his mother confront him with portraits of his heroic father and elder brother (killed in action), put a flag in his hands, and "drive him back to the ranks at the point of a revolver"—where he, too, could die honorably.[52] Despite the film's evident success in the North, a reviewer in the *World* admitted that he feared it would go over well only in the South.[53]

In the summer of 1912, probably inspired by the success of the Bison-101 westerns, Kalem began expanding its Civil War films into two-reel spectaculars.[54] The first of these was *The Siege of Petersburg* (July 1912), which has Lieutenant Van Dorn and Dan Frost (a "poor white" caring for his crippled sister) as rivals for the love of a plantation owner's daughter, Charlotte Pemberton (Anna Nilsson), all within the context of the Battle of Appomattox.[55] Although the *World* criticized this film for its lengthy scenes of exposition and relatively condensed battle spectacle, it seems to have had a successful run, and even was circulating three months later in cities from Lynn to Cleveland.[56] Indeed, the surviving first reel sustains interest by several means: framing the Pemberton porch and garden from inside the house (two vertical beams create a triptych "deep space" for the characters' movements), then sketching Van Dorn's sympathy for the crippled sister and Charlotte's hesitant attraction to Frost (she is engaged to Van Dorn).[57] In the end, once he realizes whom Charlotte really loves, Van Dorn sacrifices himself in the concluding siege battle. The film also uses unusual camera positioning around a bridge, first seen in *The Railroad Raiders of '62*, especially in reverse-angle, high-angle long shots, to depict the initial battle and Frost's rescue of a wounded Van Dorn as the bridge collapses from an exploding cannonball. In the much better reviewed *The Darling of the C.S.A.* (September 1912), Nilsson gets to play a "girl spy" who, in disguise, gains entrance to a Union fort and offers to betray the notorious spy figure they are seeking (herself), while securing information about an ammunition stockpile for the desperate Confederate army.[58] After the latter fails to capture the fort, the heroine returns and gives herself up to the Union forces, knowing that her threatened death will galvanize the Confederates who idolize her—and this time they mount a victorious attack. This film, too, was promoted as a special feature in cities from Lowell to Minneapolis, and it even shared top billing one Sunday at competing downtown theaters in Canton.[59]

That fall two different one-reelers brought these "Southern war pictures" to a kind of culmination. Kalem's *The Confederate Ironclad* (October 1912) combines the spectacle elements of previous films—mass attacks, locomotive chases, bridge burnings—with the novelty of a climactic river battle as Union gunboats attack the Confederate ship, a replica of the *Merrimack* probably constructed for an anniversary reenactment.[60] It also pits Elinor (Nilsson), a Northern spy, against a Southerner named Rose who, when Lieutenant Yancey (her "sweetheart") is wounded, single-handedly runs a powder train across a burning bridge to save the ironclad. Publicity for the film highlighted this "war on the river" reenactment, which Simon's music accentuated, Martin Marks notes, with a march based on "Auld Lang Syne."[61] But earlier scenes are even more impressive: Rose and Yancey's first meeting on a foreground platform overlooking the big rail yard, the high-angle long shots of a diagonal line of cannon confronting the distant Union attack, and the deft integration of long and close shots during the locomotive run.[62] In a rather awkward resolution, however, Rose and Yancey "generously" allow Elinor to escape with a fleeing Union officer. By contrast, Biograph's *The Informer* (November 1912) tells the grim story of a cowardly Southerner who does not exonerate himself.[63] Here, a soldier leaves his sweetheart (Mary Pickford) in the charge of his brother (who has a crippled hand), but the "faithless brother" (Henry Walthall) falsely reports him dead and slowly persuades her of his own love.[64] When the brother returns badly wounded, pursued by Union forces, she denounces the "informer" and seeks refuge for her lover in the "old negroes' quarters," while a black boy goes in search of Confederate troops. Holed up in a cabin, she bravely holds off the attackers until the Confederates arrive, and the "faithless brother" dies ignobly in the en-

suing battle.[65] The brother's villainy (stereotypically aligned with physical deformity) is so abhorrent that it makes the resolution of *His Trust Fulfilled* or *Swords and Hearts* impossible. Instead, the film ends with a defeated soldier (his uniform ragged, his sword gone), whom Pickford can barely comfort, and several women at a railing overlooking a river, awaiting soldiers who will never return.

In May 1912, an anonymous reviewer in the *Minneapolis Journal* broached a complaint quite opposite that of certain southern exhibitors two years earlier: "Granted that the civil war period is full of material for romantic picture-dramas, the question is, why do so many of these show the triumph of the confederates and the discomfiture of the northern troops?"[66] The complaint certainly had some basis, for the Civil War films released by Kalem and Biograph during those years, almost without exception, were "Southern war pictures."[67] That such a question rarely arose, and never in the trade press, however, reveals just how deeply embedded "Southern war pictures" were within reunion culture. The widespread acceptance in the North of the Lost Cause ideology and its nostalgia for a vanishing, allegedly honorable past, go a long way toward explaining their appeal across much of the United States. As stories of reconciliation, for the most part, these films presented a cultural "reconstruction" of the South and its subjected white "aliens" (not unlike many immigrants, or perhaps even an illegitimate child like my grandmother), making them acceptable once again for assimilation within a framework of "national harmony and patriotism." And the myth of the Lost Cause took on added resonance in film titles that evoked ancient tales of heroism, such as *A Spartan Mother,* and in the *World's* comparison of *The Dar-*

ling of the C.S.A. to the *Nibelunglied* and *Saga of the Volsungs.* Yet the unique focus on the heroic stories of girl spies and other "counterfeit" women, especially in Kalem's Civil War films, also must have worked to attract not just men but women, perhaps especially young working women in the North, as an audience. If, in one sense, the South undergoes a kind of "feminization" in these films that is perfectly consistent with what Silber calls the gender ideology of reunion culture, in another sense, it also serves as a fictional space within which "new kinds of public activity [become] possible for women" (as indeed they did during the Civil War), with variants of the New Woman springing into action, just as in the Wild West.[68]

The Resurgence of Male Heroism

In the summer of 1912, the Bison-101 company hinted that it was planning to produce a new series of spectacular "war pictures" that would exploit the Civil War "in the same careful manner" that had made the company's two-reel Indian pictures so popular.[69] The acrimonious struggle between the NYMP and Universal delayed those plans, however, and Kalem took advantage of the delay to release the first two-reel Civil War films. By the fall of 1912, both Universal's Bison production unit and Ince's new Broncho and Kay-Bee production teams finally were ready to make good on the earlier promise, and beginning in September, for nearly a year each of the three companies produced, on average, nearly one multiple-reel Civil War film per week. Beyond this steady rate of production, which reached a crescendo in the spring and summer of 1913, these films differed from the earlier Kalem and Biograph films on several counts. First, the stories often were constructed to stage more than one large-scale battle scene; the main characters now were just as likely to be Northern as Southern (at least in their wartime allegiance); disguise sometimes became more complicated, making characters' identities even more malleable; far more films than before worked toward an ending enactment of the gendered "romance of reunion"; and yet almost as many concluded, much like the earlier Indian pictures, in unmitigated suffering, sacrifice, or loss. Second, and perhaps most important, the lead characters were predominantly male: brothers, romantic rivals, fathers, and sons. The absence of principal female characters, let alone girl spies (with a few exceptions), is striking, especially given the continuing presence of crucial Indian women in Kay-Bee and Bison (Universal) westerns of the period. Third, a few films engaged more openly in reexamining, and even questioning (in at least one case), the past and present role of blacks in American society. Finally, certain films evidenced an increasing awareness of their storytelling as a public performance of memory work, forging links between one generation and another, shaping their representations of the war as a past calamitous event for *use* in the present.

Several of these points are exemplified in Broncho's very first release, *Sundered Ties* (September 1912). In the *World*, Harrison commented on this new interest in "dramas . . . of the Rebellion, . . . [a] historical epoch of a patriotism-inspiring nature" from a company (or its predecessor) that had done such admirable work earlier in the year with "the rough and tumble character of cowboy epics."[70] He also identified the "essence of the drama" in *Sundered Ties* as the conflict within John Stevens, a lieutenant in the Union army, over whether he would be "loyal to the flag" or stand with his family in the South—"a cruelly hard and difficult position," Harrison added, faced by many Southerners who had been educated at West Point or Annapolis. Despite a mother's pleas, a father's arguments, and a sweetheart's entreaties, Stevens chooses to fight for the North, and the battlefront eventually approaches his Southern home. Assuming the role of a volunteer sharpshooter for the Confederates, his younger brother is shot and his body carried to the Union lines, where Stevens, recognizing him, comes to know "the bitter price of patriotism." At war's end, Stevens' father and mother are invited to a birthday dinner for his sweetheart (although both families are destitute), for which an "old black butler and the inevitable 'mammy'" promise to find food, but the "fat coon" is caught stealing a chicken—in a racist cliché of "comic relief."[71] Stevens himself, in a timely return, not only "liberates" the man from jail but also secretly provides a feast for the families. When he finally arrives, "hesitating at the threshold" of the dining room, "his mother is first to give him a warm welcome, his sweetheart next, and the old Colonel [his father] yields in a tender final scene." Here, a semblance of the old South is restored, with its devoted black servants, and a new South is envisioned in the expected marriage, all produced by a prosperous Northerner who just happens to be a Southerner in disguise.

In later Broncho and Kay-Bee films, this deeply gendered romance of reunion often was worked out in exchanges of aid and protection, against a background of "very realistic and fiercely contested battles." In Kay-Bee's *When Lee Surrenders* (November 1912), for instance, the plot turns on how uniforms are read as signs of identity.[72] After a Southern woman reluctantly hides a wounded Union officer, Confederate troops find his coat, but he escapes when they fail to recognize him in the uniform of a sentry he has knocked out. The next day, Union troops find his coat and arrest the heroine's father for murder; after a victorious battle, however, the Union officer intercedes on behalf of the old man and then asks her to marry him—and her reply gives the film its title.[73] Kay-Bee's *The Dead Pays* (December 1912) involves another wounded Union officer taken in by the family of a more severely injured Confederate officer.[74] Trusting the Northerner who has fallen in love with her, the heroine keeps a Confederate spy (in disguise) from divulging Union battle plans but is herself compromised and faces arrest; protecting her, the Union officer gives himself up as a traitor. When the Con-

FIG. 38. Kay-Bee, *Sundered Ties*, 1912 (production still), *Photoplay* (October 1912), 30.

federate spy forces himself on the heroine, she extracts a written confession (promising to elope with him) and then shoots him in a struggle—and the document exonerates the man she loves. In Broncho's *The Sinews of War* (April 1913), the romance develops during the siege of Richmond, specifically in a warehouse turned into a prison for Union soldiers (whose burning was one of the film's spectacular scenes) and then in the bedroom of the warehouse owner's daughter.[75] The desire of a dying mother to see her son, an imprisoned Union officer, leads the heroine to organize his escape and later concealment in her bedroom, where her own brother (carrying dispatches) also is forced to hide. After exchanging clothes with the brother (at the heroine's insistence), the officer is captured, identified, and credited with intercepting the dispatches; to pay his debt, he keeps Union troops from arresting the brother, who has had to shoot a Confederate officer making unwanted advances to the heroine. In the end, the officer promises to return, after seeing his mother one last time.

As a crucial trope of these multiple-reel Civil War films, the transformation of identity through disguise also played a role in the few "girl spy" stories that circulated.[76] Selig contributed a pair of these, based on historical figures: *Pauline Cushman, Federal Spy* (March 1913) and *Belle Boyd, Confederate Spy* (May 1913).[77] The first film begins with the famous incident in which Cushman (already a committed spy), while performing in *Camille* at the Woods Theater in Louisville, dares to toast the Confederacy on stage.[78] Exposed, arrested, and confined at one point, she escapes with "valuable secrets" in the disguise of a Confederate drummer boy. Later, arrested and confined again, she picks up a secret transmission—"by means of a steel ramrod which she runs through a hole in the wall of her room and up against the telegraph instrument"—allowing Union troops to counter a Confederate ambush.[79] The second film exploits another unusual device: a ceiling hole through which Boyd can discover crucial Union plans, depicted in repeated overhead shots from the room above. The rest of the film is more conventional, however, relying on audience knowledge of Boyd's ride to the battlefront, saving Stonewall Jackson in his defense of the Shenandoah Valley.[80] In contrast to these "historical films," Gauntier resurrected her "girl spy" character in her first independent production, *A Daughter of the Confederacy* (March 1913), a three-reel film that the *World* claimed was "bigger [and better] in every way" and the *Morning Telegraph* wished had lasted even longer.[81] Here, the girl spy captures a Union captain who has tapped into a Confederate telegraph line, but he escapes up a chimney, passing the girl spy's room and then that of several Confederate officers discussing battle plans. After she herself is taken prisoner, the Union captain allows her to escape, and she joins the ensuing battle dressed in a friend's uniform. Both she and the Union captain are wounded, and their mutual love is revealed as they and other soldiers are carried off on railway flat cars to hospital. In short, when the Confederate girl spy of so many popular one-reelers finally drops her guise to adopt a stable identity, it turns out to serve the "romance of reunion."

Far more Civil War films, especially those of Kay-Bee and Broncho, taking their cue from revivals of Bronson Howard's popular play, *Shenandoah* (1889), sought to exonerate and honor an initially unmanly Southerner or Northerner, within a masculinist framework that denied women an active role.[82] In Kay-Bee's *For the Cause* (December 1912), a Confederate lieutenant falsely accuses his rival of cowardice in a duel, which estranges the latter from the woman they both love but fails to keep him from becoming a battlefield hero.[83] When the accused, captured as a spy and threatened with execution, "makes a sensational escape," the real coward puts on his hat and coat, leaves a note of confession, and dies in his place. In Kay-Bee's *The Great Sacrifice* (January 1913), two brothers in love with one woman take opposite paths: one joins the Confederates; the other (who has married her) is forced to enlist in the Union army, in place of a man whom he owes a gambling debt.[84] During a fierce bridge battle, the gambler is captured but escapes imprisonment (with the aid of his brother), only to be captured by Union forces that mistake him, in disguise, for a Southerner. After the war, he returns

FIG. 39. Empress Theater ad, *Toledo News-Bee* (24 May 1913), 4.

home to find his wife (convinced he is long dead) remarried to the brother who had helped him escape. Once more indebted, he sacrifices his own love and happiness for the greater good of this new union. Kay-Bee's *The Favorite Son* (February 1913), whose battle scenes impressed the *Mirror* with an "astonishing realism," worked a different variation on this story, bringing it in line with *The Informer*.[85] Here two brothers, again in love with one woman, enlist in the Union army, where one proves a coward and gets both of them captured and imprisoned. The "good" brother lets the other take his place in an escape, and the latter, without shame, reports his brother dead and convinces the woman to accept his hand. After a prisoner exchange, the "good" brother returns home, pursued by "guerrillas" who, after being repulsed in an attack, kill the fleeing coward, which sets up the "proper" union of lovers. In Universal-Bison's *A Coward's Atonement* (February 1913), by contrast, two brothers who have joined opposing armies get to die side by side on the battlefield, the one a former coward now wrapped in the Confederate flag.[86]

Despite this emphasis on manly heroism, a remarkable number of films during this period depicted the bleak devastation wrought by the war, in stories that broke up expectant romances or destroyed families, sometimes with a pathos that tipped over into bitter irony. In the "first release under [the Kay-Bee] trade-mark," *On Secret Service* (November 1912), for instance, a series of deceptions and ambush plots (one of which has a horse and rider "turn a complete somersault") ends with a Union spy executed by firing squad and a Southern heroine, who has fallen in love with him, weeping over his body.[87] In the same company's *Blood Will Tell* (November 1912), a father who has disowned his only son for desertion joins the Confederate army in his place. Once the Union troops seize the home, however, the son "undergoes a spiritual regeneration": overcoming a sentry, he dons his uniform, seizes the Union's battle plans, and rides through the fighting to the Confederate picket line. The father fires at what he believes to be a Union officer, and, in the *World*'s words, "the boy goes down to death at his father's hand while saving the day and the family honor at one time."[88] In Universal-Bison's *The Light in the Window* (March 1913), a young boy leaves his family to go north (unable to accept the whipping of slaves); later, during the war, he captures his own father as a spy and cannot prevent his being killed.[89] Grief-stricken, the boy steals away to console his mother, who each night has left a lighted lamp in the window, hoping for his return; mistaking him for a spy, she shoots and kills him, and an old black servant keeps her from discovering the truth— night after night, she goes on waiting by the window. In Bison's *The Northern Spy* (May 1913), rather shockingly, a Southern family, upon discovering that a wounded spy is their long-lost son, turn him over to Confederate troops to be shot.[90] In the same company's unusually "quiet picture," *The Picket Guard* (July 1913), by contrast, a young man leaves his wife and child to serve as a Union picket along the Potomac. His absence one day goes unrecorded, and "the dread of the young wife," in the *Mirror*'s words, "who waits [and waits] for the boy lying along the river bank strikes a deep chord of sympathy in the spectator."[91]

An increasing number of films carried the concerns about misfortune, blind loyalty, and misrecognition beyond the war and into the present. In Broncho's *The Pride of the South* (March 1913), for instance, battles scenes, "so swift, so tremendous in action," contrast with a touching story that, according to Harrison, was unusually "dependent on characterization."[92] This is especially true of the final scenes, in which a Confederate colonel finally reconciles with his daughter (who had married a Northerner, killed in the war), but only through the intervention of his feisty granddaughter and several black children with whom she has been raised.[93] "Deeply this touches the heart," wrote the *Morning Telegraph* of Kay-Bee's *The Lost Dispatch* (March 1913), in which a Confederate soldier is "dismissed from service on a false charge of cowardice and . . . later spurned by his sweetheart," whose own brother has been killed in the war.[94] Only in old age does she find, sewn into the lining of her dead brother's coat, a dispatch that clears his name—which allows her to reconcile with the old man just before he dies. In Universal-Bison's *The Last Roll Call* (April 1913), an officer deserts to attend his dying wife and has to flee as Confederates search for him. Twenty years later, he returns to find his grown daughter about to marry, yet "no one knows him but the old negro mammy, whom he swears to secrecy"—and he dies alone.[95] The same company's *Taps* (April 1913) makes explicit the appeal to a new generation assumed in this memory work. An old soldier, long ignored by townspeople, finally gets to tell the story of his youth to "two youngsters playing war." That story is far from the heroic tale they expect, for he "lost the girl he loved and honor because of the dishonesty and cowardice of his brother." In short, in the *Mirror's* words, "an undeserving man received all the honors and happiness while the deserving man gets nothing but obscurity and sorrow."[96] Broncho's *The Veteran* (November 1913) works out the ironic consequences of a simple misunderstanding. A technical error halts the pension of an old veteran, who cannot find work to support himself and his sick wife. At a veterans banquet, his former compatriots take up a collection for him, after he is discovered hiding food for his wife in his coat. They all follow him home, and the banquet band strikes up "Old Dutch" in front of the house; but inside his wife is "cold in death . . . her finger resting on an open Bible."[97]

From *Sundered Ties* to *The Last Roll Call*, most Civil War films continued to depict any black characters required for their plots as "dutiful darkies" of one kind or another. This was the case, for instance, in Kay-Bee's *A Black Conspiracy* (May 1913), whose provocative title proved a comic sleight of hand.[98] Not only does the film involve several former slaves in a "conspiracy" to join separated Southern sweethearts after the war, but, without a trace of irony, the opening slave market scenes get reworked in the end as a property auction that brings the lovers together. A very different conspiracy lay at the center of Rex's *In Slavery Days* (May 1913), distributed by Universal. Both the *World* and the *Mirror* found this melodrama of tainted blood (the old racist story of the octoroon who switched her baby for a white one) and its images of plantation life "remarkably and sympathetically appealing."[99] The "unconsciously usurping slave girl" grows up "headstrong, willful," and betrothed to the hero.[100] Overwhelmed by guilt, the octoroon finally reveals the deception; the rightful young woman is rescued from being sold as a slave; and, as the result of a quarrel, both mother and daughter die in a steamboat fire. Initially, Kay-Bee's *With Lee in Virginia* (April 1913) seems to unfold as a well-crafted story of Southern romance thwarted by the war and by a villainous Union rival.[101] It even reworks an attraction from "girl spy" film—the heroine overhears Union plans (officers have taken over her house) by listening through a vent—and a dramatic confrontation from *The Dead Pays* (she kills the villain in close quarters, with a bayonet, her anguished face accentuated by spot lighting).[102] Yet her savior is not the hero but an old black servant who hides her, allows himself to be arrested, and is soon executed. Rather than conclude with the battle, in which the Confederates are victorious (but destroy her home), the film ends with an unusual "epilogue": in midshot (following an ironic intertitle, "Peace"), the black man's wife sits in front of her cabin and, prompted by a dissolve in and out of a long shot of his grave site (where the lovers join her), she drops her head into her hands in mourning. In this film, a "new South" emerges not through reunion with the North but through the sacrifices of former black slaves.[103]

The culmination of multiple-reel Civil War films, at least prior to *The Birth of a Nation,* came fittingly in Ince's *The Battle of Gettysburg* (July 1913), one of the earliest American films of more than four reels. Its "special release" was timed to coincide with the "Peace Jubilee" held at the Gettysburg battle site and offered a level of spectacle that even reenactments could not approach.[104] A number of films based on actual battles had paved the way for this feature, but perhaps the most important was Universal-Bison's three-reel *Sheridan's Ride* (January 1913). The first two reels set up a double "romance of reunion," involving General Sheridan and a Southern woman, plus her close friend with rival lovers on opposing sides in the war. Writers at the time gave this section of the film mixed reviews, but all were swept away by the last reel's reenactment of the Battle of Cedar Creek, where Federal forces were routed, and Sheridan's famous twenty-mile ride to rally his troops. The *Mirror* pointed to "the strikingly graphic infantry and cavalry charge and retreat through the drifting smoke," during which one rival is wounded and his Confederate counterpart is killed by an explosion.[105] It also described the "novel effect" created by having the camera "kept just ahead of Sheridan and his galloping men" during several long takes that serve as an unusual dramatic climax.[106] Unfortunately, no print of *The Battle of Gettysburg* survives, making it difficult to confirm the trade press claims that this was Ince's "masterpiece" and "undoubtedly the greatest spectacular film yet produced."[107] Apparently, the first two reels focused on a conventional love story, but the last three, according to the *Morning Telegraph,* "most graphically portrayed. . . the horrors of war with all its Shermanesque qualities." Lubin's two-reel *Reunited at Gettysburg* (August 1913) is extant, but it focuses on the reunion of former combatants in the present, and a romance (reversing the usual roles) between a Southern son and a Northern daughter.[108] Particularly striking, however, is a flashback story in which the two fathers share a drink and a smoke during a momentary truce, but the Northerner shoots the other in the back just before he can return to his post. The degree to which this film favors the South is surprising, and even the *Mirror* admitted that it would "be hard for any audience to forgive the Northerner for his low-down trick."[109]

Yet perhaps this "Southern perspective" was less surprising than it might seem. For in representing a Southerner forgiving an instance of Northern aggression, Lubin's film suggests not only how acceptable the Lost Cause ideology had become but also how important Southern white masculinity was to a renewed sense of national patriotism. For, in Silber's words, the rampant "Anglo-Saxonism" of the period "seemed to confirm the natural unity of southern and northern white[s]."[110] That patriotism had emerged full-blown

FIG. 40. New York Motion Picture Corporation ad, *Moving Picture World* (7 June 1913), 1061.

during the Spanish-American War of 1898, in which Southern men won praise for their commitment to a new cause: an editorial in the formerly abolitionist *Independent,* for instance, celebrated that war as "a splendid outburst of Americanism in which the South equaled the North."[111] Not long after Miles, in January 1913, had described the Spanish-American War as "the final stage" in the process of unifying North and South, Universal announced a "change in policy" that explicitly linked the two wars: its "big Bison productions" no longer would have Civil War (or western) subjects; instead, they would "relate to the occupation of the Philippines and Cuba by the American Army."[112] Although this change of policy proved incomplete, a good number of these new war pictures were released that summer, the first of which, *The Stars and Stripes Forever* (May 1913), worked a variation on the "girl spy" stories of Civil War films.[113] However, according to the *World,* this girl spy was "a Cleopatra like creature" whose "failure to get information to the Filipinos at a crucial moment" (which involves a deft use of mirrors) allows the Americans to escape an ambush.[114] Others followed, such as *The Grand Old Flag* (June 1913)—which tells of "the adventures of two young Americans, picked up from floating wreckage" off Cuba, and concludes with a "good reproduction of the capture of San Juan Hill"[115]—and *The Battle of Manila* (July 1913), whose "fierce battles with the Stars and Stripes waving through the smoke in the midst of the fray," according to the *World,* were precisely the "stuff that excites" many audiences.[116] These films seized on and exploited the phenomenon of flag worship so prevalent at the time, a form of patriotism promoted perhaps most vehemently by Civil War veterans of the GAR.[117]

"Worthy of Exhibition in Every School in the Country"

In their commitment to multiple-reel Civil War films, Broncho and Kay-Bee in particular, according to the *Mirror,* achieved a high degree of "consistency in getting out good productions" that integrated love and romance, "homely touch[es] of naturalness," and scene after scene of thrilling action—"masterly, vividly, and artistically."[118] Harrison may have found many of these (along with Universal-Bison's) "marred by the inevitable trio of young people in whom it is difficult to rouse interest," and tried to suggest better stories "connected with those sad pages of our national history,"[119] but they clearly had a notable impact in exhibition from late 1912 through at least the summer of 1913. One only has to notice the report that, in October, "*Sundered Ties,* made good with New England managers, many of whom [among them, that of the Boston Star] grabbed the picture."[120] Or one can note Universal's special showing of *Sheridan's Ride* at the Ohio Motion Picture Exhibitors League convention in Columbus, in January 1913.[121] As a result, during several weeks of crowded screenings in Cleveland, one manager called it "the greatest spectacle ever put on film . . . a story to fascinate old and young [that] should be seen by all."[122] The *Leader* even quoted "a New York critic" describing *Sheridan's Ride* as a distinctive American film for its "acme of concentration of the three salient elements—intellectual production, veracity and modified sensationalism."[123] The film also was heavily promoted in cities from Toledo to Des Moines.[124] Or, the reception of *The Battle of Gettysburg* by 300 New England exhibitors at a special Mutual screening in Boston in late May. Reportedly, it "won the unstinted praise of the very critical and blasé audience," and several invited war veterans pronounced the battle scenes "the most realistic . . . ever produced."[125] Weeks later, the film "packed the National Theater" in the city, and the commandant of the Navy Yard called on "every student of history, as well as every person with a spark of patriotism in him," to see it.[126] In Washington, Chase's booked *The Battle of Gettysburg* for a special two-day engagement in early June; in Providence, the Opera House ran the film for more than a week in June and scheduled a "special performance" on Saturday morning for "school children"; in Canton, the new Alhambra featured it all week in early July and invited "old soldiers" to attend "free of charge" (from 9:00 A.M. to midnight) on Independence Day.[127]

The regular patterns that developed in their exhibition, however, provide even better evidence of the Civil War films' popularity, especially as American subjects, much like multiple-reel westerns, that could compete favorably with European feature imports. In Minneapolis, for instance, beginning in early November 1912, with *On Secret Service* and *When Lee Surrenders,* the Crystal became an exclusive venue for Broncho and Kay-Bee war pictures nearly every Sunday through Tuesday.[128] In Lynn, later that month, the Central Square made a similar commitment to the same companies' war pictures.[129] In those cities and others, from January through July or August 1913, Civil War films became so numerous that audiences for the best theaters often had several to choose from each week. Not only that, but they could count on seeing one title from either Broncho/ Kay-Bee or Universal-Bison, on a specific night of the week at a specific theater; moreover, they also could count on most titles showing up later at one or more theaters, again on a regular basis. In downtown Lynn, for instance, the Central Square competed with the Dreamland, the exclusive venue for "big Bison productions," with both often showing their first-run war pictures on the weekends.[130] In Baltimore, beginning in January 1913, one or two first-run war pictures were available weekly at downtown theaters, with the Dixie and the Little Pickwick (which shared owners) alternating a Broncho or Kay-Bee title on either Wednesdays and Thursdays or Fridays and Saturdays; another one or two films, usually on weekends, often were featured at a suburban theater in South Baltimore as well. In Toledo, beginning in February, Civil War films were prominent, along with westerns, in the weekend listings of up to a dozen residential theaters. In Des Moines, beginning in March, the downtown Unique was presenting a Broncho or Kay-Bee war picture every Thursday; by April, the Family was doing likewise with a Universal-Bison war feature every Tuesday.

Cleveland offers an interesting test case not only because the films were readily available through major rental exchanges (for northern Ohio)[131] but also because the *Leader* printed capsule reviews of many as they circulated through the city's best theaters. At one point in February, for instance, a half dozen war pictures were in first run, with *For the Cause* (at the Randall) and *The Favorite Son* (at the Doan) presented as Sunday specials, *The Sharpshooter* at the Marquis on Tuesday, and *Coward's Atonement* at the Corona on Wednesday.[132] Although most films ran for up to a month (through different theaters), several from Broncho and Kay-Bee—including *The Sinews of War* and *A Blue Grass Romance*—returned that summer; and Warner's *The Daughter of the Confederacy* ran consistently from March through May.[133] Initially, the capsule reviews tended to stress the sensational spectacle of the films' battles: in early February, for instance, in *Blood Will Tell* (shown at the Park National on Sunday), "wonderful battle scenes are shown, with riders shot from their horses and a close range conflict that is exciting"; in *When Lee Surrenders* (shown at the Madison on Wednesday and Thursday), "hundreds of men and horses are seen, and horses are killed by bursting shells making a wonderfully realistic subject."[134] By March 1913, however, in response to a minister who had complained that most of "the pictures he had witnessed in the local theatres were simply 'animated dime novels,' " the *Leader* specifically defended the Universal-Bison, Broncho, and Kay-Bee Civil War films, along with westerns, "as worthy of exhibition in every school in the country. As examples of real warfare with its attending patriotism and daring and bravery, they are lessons no youngster ever can forget. They teach love for the country's flag, respect and admiration for the living heroes and veterans. Each is a lesson in discipline."[135] That so many of these war pictures were shown on Sundays, when families seem to have attended in proportionally high numbers, attests not only to their popularity but also to their perceived value as uniquely "educational" features.

Determining more precisely what the audience was for these Civil War films and what about them may have appealed to specific moviegoers—be that "educational" or otherwise—is difficult to ascertain. Yet, as for westerns, the audience must have been relatively broad, given the number of titles available for viewing each week and at a variety of locations and times, especially on weekends. African Americans would have been an exception, of course, but Anna Everett's recent study does not mention any complaints or protests from the black press about Civil War films prior to *The Birth of a Nation*.[136] Moreover, segments of that audience differentiated by sex, age, class, and/or education could have been attracted to different features of these films, perhaps in combination: from thrilling sensation scenes or poignant stories of romance to "faithfully reproduced" historical events and "patriotic lessons" for the future—far from insignificant for the generation that soon would be engaged in fighting World War I. Accounts of specific audiences, other than those already cited, do prove difficult to come by. Still, the few surveys from the period on children's preferences are suggestive. In San Francisco, for instance, surveyed children in the third through eighth grades ranked war and historical films third, behind westerns and comedies, among the kinds of films they preferred.[137] In Portland, Oregon, those in the first through ninth grades ranked war pictures second, behind comedies, and just slightly above westerns.[138] Interestingly, nearly one-third of those in Portland who preferred war pictures were girls. Civil War films may have had a special appeal for immigrant youth, if those (Polish, Jewish, Italian, and others) that made up the core working-class audience for Kay-Bee and Broncho films at the Star Theatre in Pawtucket are any indication.[139] Tony Horwitz's meditation on his great-grandfather's interest in the war also is suggestive. For one of the first things this Jewish immigrant from Russia did upon arriving in New York in the 1880s was purchase a book on the war. Horwitz speculates that he may have been "drawn to the Civil War as a badge of citizenship," sensing perhaps that its history was like "an American Talmud that would unlock the secrets of his adopted land," and that, in "experiencing" the war, he was undergoing what Robert Penn Warren once called "the very ritual of being American."[140]

The prominence of disguise in so many Civil War films may have been especially salient for some audiences, no more so than for working-class and white-collar immigrant youth, and particularly young women. Civil War films shared this trope with other sensational melodramas—detective and crime thrillers but, notably, not westerns—yet disguise almost always served a worthy cause, whatever a character's alignment in the conflict. The frequency and ease with which characters in these films, whether male or female, Northern or Southern, could change their identity and "pass" as someone they were not were remarkable—so much so that it became the target of parody in Keystone's "masterly burlesque," *The Battle of Who Run* (February 1913), where "Mabel Normand appears in an officer's uniform, and has some trouble picking out the real hero."[141] Yet sometimes this "passing" through disguise also was sustained to the point of testing an audience's approval, perhaps no more so than in Broncho's *The Imposter* (November 1913).[142] Here, on the battlefield a Union officer finds a dead rebel who looks like his twin, and he takes some letters written by the man's half-blind mother. Commissioned to carry dispatches through the rebel lines, he is wounded and seized by Confederates but claims to be the dead man, whose resonant name was John Calhoun. Furloughed, he basks in the mother's love (he himself was raised an orphan) and, when her daughter returns from boarding school, falls in love with her. Later, when he is about to inherit the Calhoun estate, he confesses his duplicity to the young woman, but, convinced he is no scoundrel, she persuades him to continue to play his part, for the old woman's sake. After her death, as he prepares to leave, the young woman finally confesses her love and agrees to return North with him. What could easily have turned into a controversial "carpetbagger" plot instead becomes a psychologically poignant "romance of reunion."

For certain audiences, this practice of "passing" through disguise must have offered a model of transformation that, however fictional (and even sometimes overly complicated), was grounded in history and hence strongly suggested that anyone could refashion him- or herself as an American. In short, one of the chief tenets in these films' "romance of reunion," in which an "alien" white South could be "assimilated" into a new nation dominated by the industrial North, had its corollary in the experience of many immigrants who, in order to become American, had to become someone other than what they had been—and more "white" in the bargain. That characters, and not only those in the popular girl spy films, could "pass," and begin to transform themselves, simply through a change of clothing, by adopting a new costume, must have been especially resonant for young immigrant women. For historians from Kathy Peiss to Nan Enstad have shown how, during this period, to the chagrin of moral reformers, working women embraced consumer culture and especially a "taste for fashion" in ready-made clothing—from hats and "French heels" to the latest shirtwaists, skirts, and overcoats—as a means of escaping both the oppressive caste system of their "old country" origins and the often oppressive conditions of their current workplace factories or offices.[143] Moreover, by saving and investing what seemed a disproportionate part of their income in new clothes, Enstad argues, they actively declared themselves "American ladies."[144] For such women, trying on a new identity probably received as much encouragement from the "dressing up" inherent to so many Civil War films as it did from the more explicit desire expressed in such films as Biograph's *The New York Hat* (1912). And, as Clara Laughlin's *The Work-a-Day Girl* (1913) suggests, dressing up or passing could work to their advantage in attracting young men who might do more than take them out to dinner, a nickel show, or a dance; they might even play the hero of their own romance—and "union."[145]

By late 1913, multiple-reel Civil War films were decreasing in number; by the end of 1914, they had fallen to but one-quarter of those released the previous year.[146] Several reasons for this decline seem plausible. Civil War commemorations and reenactments seem to have peaked in 1913; by the summer of 1914, they must have paled in comparison to the real war that broke out in Europe. The films themselves also seem to have reached a point of exhausted repetition in their storytelling, saved largely by expensive and well-executed action scenes, still the "crucial attraction" of sensational melodrama. The *Mirror*, for instance, criticized the story of Lubin's four-reel *The Battle of Shiloh* (January 1914) as "hackneyed" and forgettable; but, it had to admit that, for "patrons [who] like thrills," the film was sure to succeed, so "brimming over with thrills" were its "dare-devil fighting, miraculous escapes, and stirring battle scenes."[147] In the two-reel *Fitzhugh's Ride* (February 1914), the same company even exploited the well-known name of a Union general to dress up its hero in a familiar story of two men in love with one woman, this time saved by the hero's spirited horseback ride up the aisle of a church to snatch the heroine away from the deceiving rival.[148] Although Civil War films had turned some actors into "movie personalities"—among them, Gene Gauntier and Anna Nilsson—none of these actors became solely identified with the "genre," as "Broncho Billy" Anderson had or Tom Mix and William Hart soon would for the western. Still, for a brief period, they must have played a significant role in joining together disparate peoples in that "imagined community" of reunion culture, in bringing a sense of "lived experience" (however fictional) to the "Civil War as a unifier," and in laying the groundwork for what would become a deliberately planned and highly controversial "national epic," *The Birth of a Nation*.

Document
Louis Reeves Harrison, "*Sundered Ties,*" *Moving Picture World* (14 September 1912), 1056–57

It is interesting to note the drift of moving pictures from Indian plays towards dramas of the Revolution and the Rebellion, especially in the case of a company that has shown the early struggles of settlers and redskins on a large and important scale, because this tendency closely coincides with that of American stage representations during the last hundred years. The rough and tumble character of cowboy epics, with their strong vitality and abundance of movement, corresponds to the earliest pictures of physical heroism in the history of the American drama to be succeeded in popularity by pictures of historical epochs of a patriotism-inspiring nature, and an ultimate study of social conditions during our struggle for existence as a nation, such as "Sundered Ties" just produced by the New York Motion Picture Company.

Sundered were ties of blood at the beginning of the Rebellion as well as those of individual interest, of social duty and of lofty patriotism. It was a time for men to reach decisions of vital importance in a few days and assume great risks in defense of hasty judgment. The young man of the south being educated at West Point or Annapolis occupied a cruelly hard and difficult position. As a good soldier he was bound to defend the flag irrespective of local prejudice or influence. As a man of character he must repay the government equipping him with an education by loyal service in the field. On the other hand, he must do battle against those he loved, who had brought him into the world, to whom he owed the very essence of what was manly and high-spirited in his nature.

The Southern cadet had to settle for himself whether he would stand by that part of the country that gave him birth or be loyal to the flag which he had sworn to protect under any and all emergencies. As to the relative nobility of his motives in either course, "Sundered Ties" does not deal, but it depicts the perplexity of a young officer's situation when invoked by his family to aid the Southern cause in opposition to his own perception of what was right and just under the circumstances.

In the self-conflict of John Stevens at the beginning of the Civil War lies the essence of the drama—a man's struggle between those sweet influences that appeal to his emotional nature and the sterner ones which regulate his sense of justice affords dramatic material in wellnigh exhaustless quantity. Too much cannot be made of it in the critical moments of a play. John Stevens, lieutenant in the regular army, U.S.A., arrives at his Southern home just before the war, when brave and intelligent men all over the land were at the parting of the ways.

. . .

Document
"Feature Films: *The Battle of Gettysburg*," *New York Dramatic Mirror* (11 June 1913), 27

The Battle of Gettysburg (New York Motion Picture Corporation)—The producers of this five-reel picture seem to be correct in their claim that it presents war scenes on a larger scale than even before attempted on the screen. In many respects it is a wonderful production, vivid in the extreme and, for the most part, extraordinarily exciting. Spectators will respond to the blood-stirring appeal of the troops engaged in a warfare that to all appearances is actual, and they will marvel at the enterprise and skill that have made possible the production of so lifelike a film. No amount of printed description could bring home, as does this picture, the magnitude of the Battle of Gettysburg and the terrifying slaughter it brought. Thomas H. Ince is the director, and he may properly regard it as his masterpiece. The country used as a setting is perfectly adapted to suggest a battlefield with the long stretches of fields broken by occasional hills and the general effect of distance. To all appearances thousands of soldiers have been used in depicting the three days' struggle of July 1, 2, and 3, 1863. We see the famous generals of the Civil War in consultation, and the maneuvering of the troops to gain advantageous positions; then charge after charge with maddened horses plunging through the pall of smoke that comes from booming cannon. Gunners, stripped to the waist, work like mad men until they are laid low by bullets, and others take their places; men fall by the hundred, and the attack is renewed by fresh troops sent to their support, and so it goes until the famous charge and repulse of Pickett's division. If a camera man had been on the side line during the actual battle his film could scarcely have given a more effective impression of the horrors of war. As to the story that occupies most of the first two reels of the picture and then is almost forgotten, not much need be said. It is the conventional situation for Civil War stories in which a girl has a lover in the Northern army and a brother with the Confederates. The story is well handled and sufficient to form a structure on which to hang incidents of a personal nature, but the worth of the film goes far deeper: it is found in a wonderful visualization of the greatest battle in American history.

He's Seen a Lot

I've seen the swirling ocean
    Come thundering up the beach
And rivers in commotion
    Go racing reach on reach;
I've seen the fair sun shining
    Above the storm and wreck;
I've watched where men were mining
    In caverns deep and black.

I've watched girls making toffee
    Old Santa's pack to fill;
I've watched men harvest coffee
    In Java and Brazil;
I've seen the Berbers selling
    Their coursers swift and sleek,
And little brown men felling
    Mahogany and teak.

Upon the Danube River
    I've looked with ravished eyes;
I've gazed with soul a-quiver
    On Italy's fair skies;
I've stared with awe and wonder
    On Fujiyama's height;
I've seen auroras sunder
    The north with blades of light.

Some folk decry my pleasure
    My want of thrift deplore;
Expenses I should measure
    And nurse my income more.
Though panics shake the nation,
    While I've a dime it goes
To round my education
    At the moving picture show!

THE KINETOGRAM,
New York Morning Telegraph
(8 September 1912), 4: 3

Entr'acte 4

Another "Forgotten" Part of the Program

Nonfiction

Everything a waste of time except *Pathé's Weekly*.
Portland, Oregon (1914)

In the recreation surveys across the country in the early 1910s, children usually ranked comedies, westerns, and war films as their preferences among moving pictures. Yet they also often gave surprisingly high marks to nonfiction films, whether described as educational, instructive, scenic, or travel.[1] In San Francisco and Portland, Oregon, for instance, such films ranked third and fourth, respectively; in Providence, children in grades five through eight (with whose urging, one wonders) put them first. In her 1911 observations of moviegoers on New York's Lower East Side, Mary Heaton Vorse even found an Italian youth in his early twenties, a "moving-picture show expert," who insisted that what he liked best, going to "a show every night," was "a good travel film or an a'rioplane race or a battle-ship review—dat's de real t'ing!"[2] Furthermore, nonfiction films could be profitable. From Long Beach, California, a neighborhood theater manager wrote to George Kleine, in May 1910, that Eclipse's *Trawler Fishing in a Hurricane* brought him more business in three days than the same company's immensely popular *The Fly Pest:* "You cannot give us too much of these kinds of pictures."[3] Until recently, cinema historians have tended to ignore or downplay nonfiction films during this period, assuming that they were declining in importance in the face of the increasing numbers of story films of all kinds and of longer lengths. During the past decade, however, a number of workshops and festivals have encouraged a closer look at this second "forgotten" component of the picture theater program.[4] Prompted by this renewed interest, my aim here is to draw once again on both trade press and newspaper discourse to sketch out what kinds of nonfiction films were shown as well as promoted to moviegoers—often

sharing advertising space with fiction films, and sometimes even monopo-
lizing that space—in a variety of exhibition venues in the early 1910s. With
this sketch come several suggestions as to these films' function and significance within a period of intense Americanization, especially in terms of what
was acceptable or valuable in representing the "foreign" to audiences.[5]

One sign of a sustained interest in nonfiction film was the publication of
George Kleine's 336-page *Catalogue of Educational Motion Pictures,* in April
1910.[6] This catalog included more than 3,000 films produced by MPPC manufacturers now made available for rental to "universities, colleges, scientific
and library institutions as well as to traveling lecturers."[7] Yet these targeted
customers hardly were seen as an exclusive market; rather, such films, Kleine
wrote, were "intended . . . for the education of the adult as well as the youth,
for exhibition before miscellaneous audiences."[8] The trade press generally
agreed with Kleine about the importance of "educational subjects" for a
wider audience, especially as a means of "uplift," or elevating "public taste."
Shortly after Kleine's catalog appeared, for instance, *Moving Picture World*
published the letter of a Washington moviegoer who recommended selecting a "good scenic . . . educational or industrial film" for a "family" theater's
program of two or three reels.[9] Nearly all his suggestions were French films,
and one year later the *World* itself complemented Pathé-Frères for offering
"more good educational and scenic subjects than any other film manufacturing firm in the business."[10] Perhaps most telling was *Motography*'s decision,
in October 1911, to introduce a new column called "Current Educational
Releases" that would review the previous month's educational film subjects:
that is, those "which tend to instruct the observer and convey to him a further knowledge of the commoner sciences—geography, history, natural history, scenery, foreign customs and sports, industrial activities."[11] Supplemented by related articles, this column continued for at least a year;
although French films received considerable attention initially, *Motography*
increasingly encouraged the production of "educational" films by American
manufacturers.[12]

Yet the interest in nonfiction evidenced by exhibitors and their audiences,
at least in terms of newspaper ads in New England, northern Ohio, and the
upper Midwest, seems to have been even greater than what the trade press
suggested. Certain news events films circulated widely, whereas others had a
more local appeal. In the early summer of 1910, for instance, the funeral of
Great Britain's Edward VII was promoted in picture theaters from Lowell to
Des Moines; two months later, the Kinemacolor coronation of George V
began a four-month-run on the Tremont Temple's vaudeville program in
Boston.[13] Several films of the Delhi Durbar ceremony in the British colony
of India received even more attention in Cleveland.[14] The "homecomings"

of other figures such as Cardinals Farley and O'Connell were celebrated especially in Boston and Lowell, where the Irish had gained some political control.[15] Disaster films of one kind or another also were sure to attract audiences: those of the Austin (Texas) flood of late September 1910 or the sinking of the *Titanic* in April 1912 could be found almost everywhere; those of the January 1912 Equitable Building fire in New York received special notices in Cleveland and Lowell; yet those of the Triangle shirtwaist factory fire in New York or the Scranton mine disaster (both in the spring of 1911) were advertised only in Youngstown.[16] Films of sports events such as baseball's World Series were so popular that both the Comique and the Olympia in Lynn one week booked the 1912 version (the Boston Red Sox played the New York Giants); Rothapfel even featured the 1912 Olympic Games at the Lyric in Minneapolis, probably because they were held in Stockholm.[17] Military preparedness films appealed to far more than an Italian youth on the Bowery: see, for instance, *Scenes from Our Navy* or *Launching a Battleship* at the Odeon in Canton and *Mobilization of the American Fleet* or *U.S. Artillery Maneuvers* at the Central Square in Lynn.[18] And the heightened war fever of this period was fueled by a number of films widely distributed in 1911–12: see *The Last Rites of the Maine* and the *Italian-Turkish War,* the latter of which was especially promoted, from late 1911 through late 1912, in cities with large Italian immigrant populations, from Boston and Lowell to Cleveland, Youngstown, and Canton.[19]

Other kinds of nonfiction were, if anything, even more appealing, and in some cities more than others. Industrial films, for instance, were unusually big in Cleveland. In late 1911, the *Leader* included several French films—among them, Pathé's *The Story of a Typewriter*—in its first reviews of "films worth seeing."[20] It was then, too, that the downtown Princess (which advertised in the city's labor weekly) promised "an industrial or educational film" every Thursday.[21] Most films celebrated American interests and, according to ads, seemed to target audiences in secondary commercial districts: *Logging and Milling* at the Park National, *Industries of the South and West* at the Enjoy-U, and *Building the Greatest Dam in the World* at the Tabor.[22] Industrials also were nearly as prominent in Lynn and Lowell: in October 1911, the Lynn YMCA even presented a special program of ten reels on automobile manufacturing.[23] Some films heralded scientific discoveries or exploited the new perceptual and representational capabilities of moving pictures: X-ray films were promoted several times at the Superior in Cleveland; a natural history series appeared at the Grand Opera House in Canton; Pathé's "famous" *Wild Birds in Their Haunts* (in color) was advertised at the Voyons in Lowell and shown on a Saturday at the Dome in Youngstown.[24] At the Lyric in Minneapolis, Rothapfel must have assumed that nature films appealed to his middle-class audiences, since he featured two versions of the Pathé film, as well as others such as *Birth of a Silk Worm.*[25] Yet travel films were by far the most popular of all.[26] In Lowell, the Voyons gave its audiences views of distant countries from Finland to Indochina, while the Scenic offered nostalgic "tours" of Ireland and Naples, Italy.[27] In Lynn, the Comique and Central Square took audiences on trips within the United States as well: from the Mohawk Valley and New York Barge Canal to Old Albuquerque and Yellowstone National Park.[28] Finally, for several months in the spring of 1912, the downtown Empress in Toledo even designated its Wednesday program as a "Travelogue Day."[29]

Given the continued attraction of nonfiction during this period, it is not surprising that Pathé-Frères seized the opportunity to compile a series of "foreign and domestic" short subjects into a weekly newsreel in early August 1911.[30] Initially promoted as an "illustrated magazine," *Pathé Weekly* was closely modeled on the format of the newspaper: "Read It in the Papers," a Des Moines exhibitor proclaimed, and "See It Here."[31] *Pathé Weekly* quickly won the support of the trade press: the *World* described it as a "novel innovation" demonstrating "the wonderful scope of the motion picture and its power as an educator," and *Billboard* called it a success within a few short weeks.[32] Yet signs of its impact were obvious in exhibition venues across the country. In Lowell, for instance, the Voyons added the newsreel to its weekly programs as early as late August.[33] Two weeks later, in Des Moines, it was being advertised as the last act on the Orpheum's vaudeville programs.[34] In Lynn, the Comique adopted the newsreel by late September; in Youngstown and Canton, it was introduced in early October, respectively, at the Dome and Orpheum.[35] *Pathé Weekly* may not have appeared in Toledo theater ads until January 1912, but the Royal and Empress then offered it on different days: the one on Mondays, the other on Fridays and Saturdays.[36] In Cleveland, beginning in late January 1912, Pathé took the unusual step (perhaps modeled on its monthlong but more general newspaper campaign two years earlier)[37] of using the *Sunday Leader*'s moving picture page to promote its newsreel as "one of the most important contributions to the entertainment and enlightenment of the world produced by any film maker."[38] For the next four weeks, the company then placed prominent ads in the *Leader*, describing the six to ten subjects that would be shown that week "at all well managed motion picture theaters."[39] A similar ad also made a rare appearance one week in February in the *Canton Repository*.[40] By then, observations like this were appearing in the trade press: because they so regularly watched *Pathé Weekly*, grammar school children sometimes "were better informed on current events than most adults."[41]

Pathé Weekly's overwhelming success led other companies to test their own newsreels. First to enter the field was another French company, Gaumont, which also advertised its *Weekly* in the *Cleveland Leader* for three weeks in February 1912.[42] Soon *Gaumont Weekly* began showing up in theaters such as the Mall in Cleveland, the Colonial and Crown in Toledo, the Park in

FIG. 41. *Pathé Weekly* ad, *Moving Picture World* (29 July 1911), 179.

Youngstown, and the Grand Opera House in Canton.[43] Between the spring and fall of 1912, the realignment of Independent distributors created some confusion as to exactly when a third newsreel first arrived. Just prior to its breakup, the Sales Company was offering Gaumont's newsreel as the *Animated Weekly*, but Universal seems to have taken control of that brand name during the summer and at some point started releasing its own newsreel.[44] By the end of the year, however, it is clear from ads in cities from Lynn to Canton to Des Moines that Gaumont, Universal, and Mutual all were offering their own newsreels to rival *Pathé Weekly*.[45] This was but one sign of what the *Mirror* described, in October 1912, as a veritable "public craving for illustrated news."[46] But there were certainly others. In Des Moines, that spring, the Colonial and Family competed for customers, using *Pathé Weekly* and *Animated Weekly*, respectively: the one featured Thursday through Saturday; the other, every Saturday.[47] Borrowing a suggestion from Pathé's own trade press ads, the Colonial singled out the "spring millinery shows" in Paris as a "special for the ladies" in its audience.[48] There also was evidence of local newsreels. During the spring of 1912, for instance, a *Cleveland Animated Weekly* was advertised for several months at the Mall and Crescent.[49] One year later, the Alamo Film Company of San Antonio announced it would be producing the *Texas Tattler*, a weekly newsreel for distribution throughout the state.[50] Yet still the "public craving" remained unsatisfied, and, in June 1913, Pathé decided to release its *Weekly* not once but twice a week. Interestingly, the announcement was "news" not only in the trade press but also in papers such as the *Cleveland Leader*.[51]

Nonfiction subjects of more than one reel also began to make an appearance by 1910. Boxing and wrestling films were among these, with the *Gotch-Zbyszko Fight* and *Kilbane-Attell Fight* perhaps the most widely circulated between 1910 and 1912.[52] The *Johnson-Jeffries Fight* (1910) also was shown in a large number of venues across the country, Dan Streible writes, even as it provoked increasing demands for censorship because of white fears that such matches upset basic assumptions of racial difference.[53] By the time of the *Johnson-Flynn Fight* (1912), these fears led Congress to quickly prohibit the further distribution of fight films—and theaters like the Orpheum in Toledo were forced to cancel their screenings.[54] Rodeo and Wild West show films presented no such controversy, even when the black cowboy Bill Pickett was featured. Selig's two-reel *Ranch Life in the Great Southwest* (with trick riding by cowboys Pat Long and Tom Mix) played at the Colonial in Des Moines for a full week in August 1910 and for several days at the Voyons in Lowell two months later.[55] In early 1911, in Des Moines, *Cowboy and Indian Celebrations in Cheyenne* was the feature attraction at the Grand Opera House, and *Buffalo Bill's Wild West and Pawnee Bill's Far East*, at Foster's (a legitimate theater).[56] In late 1911, 101 Ranch's three-reel *Fall Round-Up* played at the downtown Princess and Bijou Dream in Cleveland, as well as the Park in

FIG. 42. Colonial Theater ad, *Des Moines Register and Leader* (21 May 1912), 3.

Youngstown.[57] Selig's *The Diamond S Ranch* probably was the most popular of these multiple-reel films purporting to document cowboy life: in March 1912, in Lynn, it played one week simultaneously at both the Comique and the Olympia; in Cleveland, it opened at the downtown Cameraphone in late February and, within a month, had appeared at a number of second-run theaters across the city.[58] Even after Bison-101 had established the viability of multiple-reel fictional westerns, nonfiction films such as *The Life of Buffalo Bill* or *The California Rodeo* still could be advertised in late 1912 as feature attractions in Cleveland theaters.[59]

The most notable of the longer nonfiction films, however, clearly were the travel or expedition pictures.[60] Selig's two-reel *Roosevelt in Africa* (April 1910), which was promoted as an "authentic record" of the former president on a safari (although it was not), initiated an interest in pictures depicting dangerous journeys to that "dark" continent. *Buffalo Jones Lassoing Wild Animals in Africa* explicitly sought to exploit that: in February 1912, it was booked at the Colonial in Des Moines for an entire week.[61] Such films would serve as an impetus to fictional jungle or animal pictures (see chapter 5), but equally important, in providing a basis for the "special" multiple-reel travel film, was Lyman H. Howe's "Travel Festival," which after some fifteen years of developing a strong middle-class audience, according to Charles Musser and

Carol Nelson, reached its peak touring major cities in the early 1910s.[62] Boasting an organization that operated several teams simultaneously in different regions, Howe would rent a legitimate theater or vaudeville house in a city and "road show" his programs of "illustrated lectures" for at least several days and often for weeks or even longer.[63] In Cleveland, in May 1911, the "Travel Festival" played for a full month at the Colonial; in nearby Youngstown, it returned every six months for several days at the Grand Opera House.[64] Although his programs were composed of short subjects (primarily nonfiction), Howe organized them within a thematic trajectory that changed from year to year and could be varied from location to location or even from week to week. In June 1912, in Cleveland, for instance, one week's program focused on the burial of the *Maine* and a tour of Germany; another, on a review of the U.S. Navy; a third, on tours of the Alps, Tibet, and Singapore.[65] As Musser and Nelson argue, Howe's "most persistent rival," at least through the summer of 1912, was the Kinemacolor company, which "road showed" programs of short subjects, the most important of which was *The Durbar in Kinemacolor,* to the same middle-class audiences attracted to Howe's "Travel Festivals."[66]

Several long nonfiction travel films released that spring, however, began to win audiences away from Howe. One was the two-reel *Capt. Scott's South Pole Expedition* (March 1912), filmed by Herbert Ponting for Gaumont.[67] An early screening came in mid-June, in a four-day run at the Empress in Toledo.[68] Ten days later a print was showing at the Olympic vaudeville house in Cedar Rapids; a month later, it was rebooked at the Palace.[69] In September, it played one weekend at Cook's Opera House in Rochester.[70] By early 1913, Ponting himself was lecturing the film at the Dreamland in Lynn, and the film repeatedly was rebooked throughout 1913, often with other lecturers, from Toledo to Washington and San Francisco, where it ran for another month.[71] The six-reel *Carnegie Alaska-Siberia Expedition,* which documented animal life in the Arctic as filmed by Capt. F. E. Kleinschmidt, was featured all week at the Columbia in Toledo as early as February 1912.[72] Throughout the summer and fall, it played a variety of venues—including the Maxine Elliott Theatre in New York City, the Mall in Cleveland, and the Grand Opera in Youngstown—but was hampered, Musser and Nelson note, by technical problems.[73] The most popular of these films undoubtedly was the five-reel *Paul J. Rainey's African Hunt,* which the *World* described as "a truly wonderful set of perilous nature studies taken in darkest Africa."[74] This special feature opened in April 1912 at the Lyceum in New York City, lectured by its cameraman, J. C. Hemmett, and ran for an unprecedented sixteen weeks.[75] That fall, it played for a week at the Shubert in Rochester and the Metropolitan in Minneapolis and two weeks at the Opera House in Providence; by early 1913, the film was returning to legitimate theaters such as the Valentine in Toledo—and for even longer runs.[76] In February 1913, the *Lawrence Eagle*

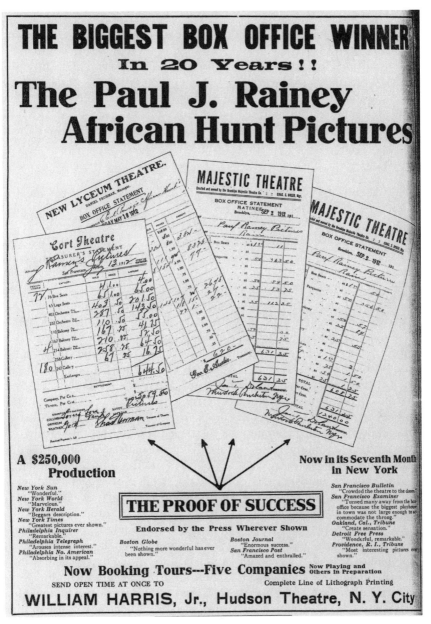

FIG. 43. *Paul Rainey African Hunt* ad, *New York Dramatic Mirror* (25 September 1912), back cover.

promoted the weeklong run of this "Darkest African Motion Picture" at the Colonial with a full page of pictures and text; a month later, in Sioux City, Iowa, the Grand Opera House ads cited the film's record runs elsewhere— ten months in New York and three months each in Boston and Chicago— while advertising its own weeklong run.[77] The extraordinary success of *Paul Rainey's African Hunt* even prompted Adolph Zukor to finance the distribution that summer, through a special company intriguingly called Arab Amusement, of British photographer Cherry Kearton's *Animal Pictures*, which "review[ed] animal life" from Africa to Borneo and India.[78]

If the variety program format characteristic of many moving picture theaters resembled that of monthly magazines or Sunday newspapers, moviegoers could "read" nonfiction subjects much like short articles, the difference being that visual illustration dominated the verbal text, rather than vice versa, and the time of "reading" was scheduled and condensed into a few minutes.[79] "To see is to know," G. Brown Goode (assistant secretary of the Smithsonian) had said of world's fairs' "object lesson" exhibits, and the travel films, industrials, scientific films, and others seemed to demonstrate that principle within the context of moviegoers' everyday life.[80] For both the industry and Progressive reformers, consequently, such films proved to be a critical means of defending moving pictures against those attacking their immorality or lack of worth. Much like "quality films," nonfiction films offered "elements of edification" that, in the language of the trade press, ensured that moviegoing would be "moral in its influence." Indeed, in cities from Des Moines to Lynn, picture theaters often used nonfiction rather than story films to promote moviegoing to the "better classes," at least through 1912.[81] Perhaps even more important, the weekly release pattern of *Pathé Weekly* and other newsreels—that is, their *seriality*—worked to further regularize moviegoing throughout 1911–13. This meant that moviegoers could count on seeing a new compilation of short nonfiction subjects at a certain time each week, much like they could count on reading one or more sections of a Sunday newspaper. Along with manufacturers' trademarks, popular genres such as the western and war film, and emerging personalities or stars, newsreels could serve as a "guarantee of satisfaction" at the movies, and so promote regular, repeated attendance.[82] Moreover, in tandem with multiple-reel imports, from *Dante's Inferno* to *Quo Vadis?*, the longer nonfiction films demonstrated the viability of the "road show" or "state rights" distribution system that prepared the way for the regular distribution of feature fiction films. Indeed, *Paul J. Rainey's African Hunt* proved almost as successful as the best of those European features.

Many of these nonfiction films, and especially newsreels, marked the "foreign" either as only minimally distinct from the "American" (for instance, news events, from public ceremonies to disasters) or as worthy of import and incorporation (for instance, Paris fashion). Travel films, however, often stressed the "otherness" of their subjects—in landscapes, "nonwhite" peoples, and animals—particularly in the context of weekly programs dominated by American story films. For most audiences—from middle-class whites to working-class patrons like that Italian youth on the Bowery—such moving pictures could simulate travel itself, turning spectators into tourists who could share the experience of "other" worlds as the "real t'ing" or a "moveable feast" for the eyes—and at minimal expense. In depicting expeditions and big-game hunts, special features from *Capt. Scott's South Pole Expedition* to *Paul J. Rainey's African Hunt* may have downplayed any sense of an explicit colonialist or imperialist mission but certainly assumed its ideological underpinnings—not only making the "unknown world" visible and readily available for consumption and appropriation but also ensuring that racial difference continued to determine the hierarchy of the world's peoples. These specials, consequently, served a specific function for middle-class white audiences. They reframed the sensational—so often associated with the "masses" and "bad taste," if not worse, as chapter 5 will show—and transformed its "foreign" excesses of violence and morbidity into an acceptably voyeuristic form of "exotic" spectacle.

Document
"Reviews of Special Feature Subjects," *New York Dramatic Mirror* (24 April 1912), 27

Paul J. Rainey's African Hunt (Jungle Film Company, Special; Lyceum Theatre, N.Y., commencing April 14)—

The dangers encountered, the obstacles combated, and the patience required to procure these marvelous motion photos of wild animal life can be appreciated by none save he who has, himself, tramped for days beneath a withering equatorial sun or has felt the tiny electric shudders chasing up and down his spine as he confronted an infuriated lion with no intervening barrier except a light camera. Ten thousand miles through the arid wastes and pampas of British East Africa were traversed to achieve the feat of photographing these tropical animals in their native haunts, and the views obtained easily transcend any series of wild animal pictures previously exhibited.

Astounding beyond credence are the pictures taken with a masked camera in and around the "water-hole" in the desert. Here in this depression animals of many species are seen to congregate for a common purpose. Elephants, giraffes, rhinos, zebras and monkeys mingle promiscuously with each other, contest for drinking room at the burrows, brawl, bask and saunter aimlessly around, utterly oblivious to the presence of a human being in the vicinity.

Intensely thrilling, also, are the pictures of the chase, the conquest of a lioness and the capture of the cheetah by Mr. Rainey's pack of blooded fighting dogs, unassisted by the men of the party. To see the dogs climb the matted tree in which the cheetah has sought refuge and boldly compel the cornered animal to leap into the foaming mouths of the waiting pack below is a spectacle long to remain engraved on one's mind—thrilling, but not gruesome.

The pictures, consisting of five reels, are accompanied by a lecture by Mr. Hemmett, the man who actually took the views for Mr. Rainey. His talk is a whimsical mixture of humor and exposition, delightful to listen to because the speaker is so intensely in earnest.

The Maid of the Movies

. . .

Oh! The Movie Maid is the girl for mine—
Not in the matrimonial line—
A husband would have to be divine
      To abide with such a wife;
But if I were a life insurance man,
I'd devise a perpetual payment plan
To insure the pictorial heroine—
      And retire rich for life.

WILLARD HOLCOMB,
New York Morning Telegraph
(14 December 1913), 5:6

Chapter 5

The "Usable Present" of Thrillers

From the Jungle to the City

The foreign manufacturers have been taught their lesson. More and more care is being shown in preparing films for the American market. . . . They are eliminating objectionable scenes, and through their American agents, who strive to give clear, decisive criticisms of the films sent here, the European producers get closer to the American ideal.[1]

The words are Herbert Blaché's, from a prominently displayed interview in the *New York Dramatic Mirror* (February 1913), and his positions—vice president of the Gaumont Company in the United States, president of Film Supply, and soon to be cofounder of Exclusive Supply—made it easy to assume that, in his words, he "should know something about the American market for foreign films." Nearly a century later, this kind of claim persists as a familiar trope in histories of early American cinema, even in Bowser's *The Transformation of Cinema, 1907–1915*, where one can find this sentence: "Pathé Frères and other foreign producers were quick to observe American tastes and morals, and as the American market was the biggest . . . , the films sent here would be those that they knew to be acceptable."[2] Strictly speaking, this was true of the early 1910s, if by "acceptable" one means acceptance by the National Board of Censorship. Yet if one follows the discursive traces of how European sensational melodramas, especially French ones, circulated and were received during this period, the claim becomes more difficult to substantiate. Indeed, Blaché himself might have found his words a bit embarrassing just six months later, when Gaumont released the first of its now famous *Fantômas* series on the US market—to a far from welcome response.

Within the context of "American tastes and morals," as the previous chapters have shown, sensational melodramas were a major object of concern during the early 1910s. What the trade press called *thriller melodramas* were particularly suspect because, unlike Civil War films and westerns (if to a lesser extent), they were so often of European manufacture. Yet thrillers were quite popular, particularly with what were described as the "ordinary moving picture audience," "average crowd," or "public"—all terms that served to mask the "masses" of working-class and white-collar youth who frequented the picture shows.[3] While generally "not elevating in taste and . . . worthless as examples of art," the *Mirror* argued in early 1912, thrillers still could be produced in such a way as to "appeal to all classes" as a "perfectly legitimate type of drama."[4] The class division not so artfully elided in this trade press discourse, however, also had a corollary, more fractious component: a perceived difference between American and "foreign" (specifically, French) values and tastes in the kinds of thrillers produced. Indeed, both the *Mirror* and *Moving Picture World* assumed a "European public . . . not yet educated up to the American standard," a public to which French manufacturers in particular catered with the worst thriller melodramas—full of criminal activity, excessive violence, and morbidity.[5] If thriller melodramas mapped out opposing "positions in the dialectical drama of modernity," as Tom Gunning puts it, the crime thriller that focused on "the criminal who preys on [modernity's] new systems of mobility and circulation" became closely associated with the French, whereas the detective film that focused on "the detective, whose intelligence, knowledge, and perspicacity allow him. . . to uncover crime and restore order," became the prerogative of the Americans.[6] A similarly schematic distinction in terms of exploiting or curbing violence, I would argue, also came to mark French and American animal or jungle pictures. All three kinds of thriller melodramas eventually would play crucial, if somewhat complicated, roles in the development of series films, multiple-reel films or features, and serials.

As exports on the US market, consequently, French crime thrillers, unlike Italian historical spectacles, seemed a serious moral and social threat to the work of uplifting and Americanizing the masses (many of them recent immigrants). Throughout this period, their *otherness*, particularly in contrast to the detective films and animal pictures produced by US manufacturers, provoked a kind of culture war waged in the trade press and local newspapers. On the one hand, that culture war served to codify what would be acceptable, even legitimate, and distinctly *American* about thriller melodramas in moving pictures—and what was not, and should be excluded. On the other hand, it generally allowed the circulation of "illegitimate" crime thrillers on the margins of exhibition, with some exceptions, as long as that circulation did not disturb the overall disciplining of any foreignness that might lurk in audiences.

"Elevating" Thriller Melodramas

If sensational melodrama already was a popular American cultural form, with a certain class affiliation, long before its prominence in moving pictures, the "problem" of foreign, particularly French sensationalism also was not without precedent. During the heyday of the dime novel, for instance, publishers reprinted European fiction as often as they printed "original" American work because costs were lower even if texts had to be translated. French *fait divers* fiction made up an unusually large portion of that translated material, according to ongoing research by Carol Armbruster at the Library of Congress, and its alleged immorality and morbidity often were cited in testimony by librarians at US congressional hearings in the late 1880s.[7] The result of those hearings was a copyright law that banned such piracy not only to support American writers but to protect American readers from "unhealthy" foreign influences. A similar "problem" arose twenty years later, as I myself have argued, when Pathé-Frères' French films became the predominant fare of the nickelodeons from 1905 to 1908 or so.[8] Here, the newly emergent trade press, along with certain national magazines, engaged in a loosely coordinated culture war to control what was again seen as undue French influence. An early *Variety* review, for instance, condemned Pathé's *Christmas Eve Tragedy*—which ended with a horse, cart, and driver thrown off a cliff into the sea—as no more fit for children than the "interior view of a slaughterhouse" and so reprehensible as to justify censorship.[9] The film was a prime example of French Grand Guignol melodrama that the trade press increasingly descried as "inappropriately sensational." American "ethical melodrama," it was argued, was very different because, even though filled with equally sensational attractions, it concluded with a "bright, happy denouement."[10] In that it drew on all that was considered risqué, deviant, and morally suspect in French culture, therefore, French sensational melodrama had to be curbed and for much the same reasons as before: to support American manufacturers as well as to protect American audiences.

Despite this history, the culture war that erupted in the early 1910s at first may seem surprising. After all, the Motion Picture Patents Company, founded in late 1908, had set weekly limits on the number of imported reels of French films; and the National Board of Censorship, instituted in early 1909, was forcing manufacturers, both French and American, to cut or make other changes in their films and even withdraw some from circulation.[11] Pathé had seemed to capitulate to the American market in 1910 not only by reducing its weekly releases from France—and including more stencil-color "classical" adaptations such as *Cleopatra* (1910)—but also by constructing an East Coast studio to produce its own American films, "with American actors and scenarios."[12] Later that same year, the company also won accolades for arranging a special score of Verdi's music to accompany its stencil-color adaptation of *Il Trovatore*.[13] Moreover, according to a *World* editorial, in June 1910, Gaumont films now rivaled those of Biograph in "pictorial quality"— the "chiaroscuro . . . always true to nature and well-balanced."[14] Yet a residual animosity toward the "otherness" of French culture persisted, always ready to be tapped. When, in early 1910, the National Board of Censorship passed Pathé's "ghastly" Russian tale, *Ouchard the Merchant,* for instance, *Variety* harshly criticized the board for having the gall to unleash such "bestialities" on the public.[15] That summer, more generally, the *World* warned the Independents about the danger of imported films: "foreign productions are more foreign in the young United States" than elsewhere because "the scheme of life in this country excludes all definite recognition of extraneous affairs."[16] In a crusade against moving pictures the following fall, the *New York World* repeatedly invoked the stereotypes of bad taste and immorality associated with the French, attacking a bullfight film erroneously attributed to Pathé and once again lambasting *Christmas Eve Tragedy,* which it failed to recognize as a two-year-old "junk film."[17] Still, these attacks amounted to little more than scattered potshots, especially in the context of the trade press's much more sustained criticism of westerns.

If westerns underwent a transformation into something more than the "ordinary," something capable of attracting a mass audience rather than just the masses, other forms of sensational melodramas experienced a similar kind of "elevation" into a "perfectly legitimate type of drama" during this period. One of these was the animal or jungle picture, in which Selig in particular specialized (exploiting its wild animal farm in Los Angeles), and whose subject of wild savagery also frequently appeared in Sunday newspaper stories: the prey in "Leaping Lioness Cheated of Prey by Bare 40 Inches," for instance, was none other than Paul J. Rainey.[18] In 1911, Selig began releasing an "African series" of such films, and the third title, *Captain Kate* (July 1911), received high praise in an unusual two-page write-up in *Moving Picture World.*[19] Framed by a story of circus people capturing wild animals, its main attraction was the "graceful and lithe" Kathlyn Williams: left alone at a remote trading post by her father's sudden death, this resilient yet vulnerable woman was defended from a lion attack by her own pet leopards. Much like the American cowboy girl, Williams was physically active, both a "child of nature" and a master of savagery (whether animal or human), and pointedly not a European colonizer. As evidence that this was no "cheap melodrama," *Captain Kate* was shown as part of the prestigious Lyric's opening night in Minneapolis.[20] The next film, *Lost in the Jungle* (October 1911), was heavily promoted and described by Selig himself as the "climax of the series."[21] Whereas the *World* reveled in its thrilling situations, in which Williams this time was threatened by wild leopards and rescued by an elephant, the *Mirror,* with its eye on potential middle-class audiences, stressed the undeniably powerful effect of the film's "jungle atmosphere and . . . dangers" that held "the spectator breathless at times."[22] As a testament to its popular appeal as a "great animal sensation," perhaps especially for working-class audiences, *Lost in the Jungle* was one of the very few films rebooked by special request or held over for extra screenings that fall in downtown picture theaters from Lowell and Lynn to Canton.[23]

Newspaper stories and pulp fiction constituted an even more obvious intertext for detective films. Particularly prominent were detective series such as the *Nick Carter Library* or *Tip Top Weekly* (with Yale-educated Frank Merriwell), serialized stories involving Raffles (a kind of American Sherlock Holmes) or others such as "Blindfolded" (in the *Toledo Blade,* beginning in March 1911), or short stories published in Sunday newspapers like the *New York Morning Telegraph.*[24] Yet other newspaper stories focused on successful investigations by famous detectives, extolled the latest "new method of scientific apprehension of criminals" (e.g., Bertillon's photographs), or raised the question of whether "science aids the criminal or the criminal detector."[25] Despite such comments as the *World's,* that "well produced detective stories always have a certain fascination,"[26] manufacturers initially were slow to exploit them in the early 1910s. Few detective films seem to have been released before the fall of 1911, except for Edison's *The Black Bordered Letter* (January 1911) or Reliance's *The Gloved Hand* (March 1911), in which a detective, at a public reception, collects a guilty woman's thumbprint by means of a waxed glove.[27] This reluctance remains unclear, but it may have been due to an avoidance of drawing too much attention to criminals or a perceived lack of sufficient "sensation" in the process of detection—"reestablishing the traces of individual identity beneath the obscurity of a new mobility," in Gunning's words,[28] tying identity securely to a particular body, and, as a consequence, determining criminal responsibility. Equally, it may have been due to the absence of a charismatic hero on the order of G. M. Anderson. The latter looked like it would be addressed when Imp's most popular male star, King Baggott, appeared in *King the Detective* (November 1911). This film also relied on the detection of a thumbprint, but this time to exonerate a young woman of killing her father (she had secretly married a man over his objection); yet its main attraction, according to the *Mirror,* was Baggott, "whose work is ever sincere and natural."[29] Although the film was successful enough—appearing in venues from the Hart in Toledo to the Majestic's opening program in St. Paul[30]—it would be another year before Baggott's detective would return, and longer before he would have his own series.

None of these thriller melodramas ran more than the standard length of one reel, but they shared the screen that fall and winter with multiple-reel films that began to establish the "special feature" as a regular format in exhibition. Several French films were among them and—much like *Temptations of a Great City*—sometimes elicited a conflicted critical response. Such was the case with Pathé's *In the Grip of Alcohol* (December 1911), a two-reel reworking of temperance stage melodramas in which an entire family is destroyed by a father's drunkenness. The *Mirror* found it "one of the most powerful picture sermons ever," and the *Cleveland Leader* echoed that praise at the beginning of the film's month-long run in that city.[31] Although admitting the force of its "terrible lesson," the *World* thought its story so "sordid [and] disagreeable" as to overwhelm audiences with a "feeling of disgust."[32] Surprisingly, there was no such concern over the effect of Éclair's three-reel *Zigomar,* which, in a series of sensation scenes, recounted the exploits of a master criminal (played by Arquillière) who, often in the disguise of a modern capitalist entrepreneur—"clever, reckless, and thoroughly immoral in his lust for lucre"—continually eluded capture.[33] Everyone hailed the film as "a masterpiece of sensationalism," a "notable film" that masterfully "[held] the mirror up to modern life."[34] Prominent ads for *Zigomar* ran for more than a month in the *Cleveland Leader,* and the film itself was said to "pack" no less than three downtown theaters on consecutive Sundays in December and January, before circulating through other theaters and then returning three months later for a three-day run at the suburban Knickerbocker.[35] In early January 1912, the *Morning Telegraph* reported that the film was "assured" of success.[36] Confirmation of that came that month in a three-day run at the Crown in Toledo and consecutive Sunday showings at different theaters in Youngstown,[37] and later in featured engagements at the Auditorium in Canton and at the Elite in Des Moines.[38]

How does one account for *Zigomar*'s critical and commercial success, for its acceptance as "appropriately" sensational? After all, Zigomar was not only the leader of a gang for whom murder simply could be the means to an elaborate robbery but a sexual predator as well, and he was responsible for a number of sensation scenes that masked his repeated escapes from the Paris police: a spectacular fire at the Moulin Rose music hall and an explosion that destroyed his subterranean headquarters in the deserted, ironically named Saint Magloire cathedral.[39] Moreover, the catalog of "inappropriate" French behavior or "bad taste" so often invoked by American writers certainly was in vogue at the time—as a weekly column in the *Chicago Daily News* attests, describing at length "an average French tragedy" in moving pictures.[40] In its ads, F & E downplayed *Zigomar*'s criminality, describing it as a "thrilling European detective story."[41] Moreover, Éclair may have deleted certain scenes or shots and reworded some intertitles for the US market, yet not all that much must have been cut or changed for it was released, as in France, in three reels. The sheer novelty of the "special feature," especially one whose subject probably was unfamiliar to American audiences—and to many reviewers, for the fictional series on which the film was based had not been translated—must have contributed to *Zigomar*'s success. An added attraction must have been the film's craft in using the new "feature" format, making it a model for how filmmakers could develop an intensely exciting narrative over several thousand feet of film. All this must have outweighed any hesitations or doubts felt by a critic such as Bush, who usually detested sensational melodramas, for he cited *Zigomar* as a prime example, along with *Dante's*

FIG. 44. Feature and Educational Film Co. ad, *Billboard* (6 December 1911), 81.

Inferno and others, of the "quality" that had to be maintained in the continued production of "long films."[42] That attitude toward French crime thrillers
would not endure, however, and the reemergence of a "French threat" can
be traced not only in the reception of later French films (and news events)
but also in that of "improved" American thriller melodramas.

American Masters and the French "Foreign" Threat

The extraordinary success of *Paul J. Rainey's African Hunt* during the spring
and summer of 1912 undoubtedly spurred Selig to continue exploiting the
"novelty and realism" of its sensational animal pictures. One of the most important was *Kings of the Forest* (November 1912), a two-reel "spell-binder" directed by Colin Campbell, starring Betty Harte as Sonia and "Baby" Lillian
Wade as her daughter.[43] Set among Boer farmers in the "wilderness" of South
Africa, its story turns on Sonia's husband's jealousy of a former friend, but its
chief "attractions" are threatened animal attacks—first by a leopard on the
child left alone at home, then by lions on mother and child as they attempt
to return to her parents' farm. *Kings of the Forest* circulated widely as a General
Film "special feature," highlighting programs at the Lyric in Minneapolis, the
Starland in St. Paul, and the Orpheum in Canton, and returning to the
Comique in Lynn the following April.[44] In Los Angeles, Lillian Wade made a
stage appearance after each screening at Clune's Main Street Theater, further
softening the film's sensationalism with a sentimental touch.[45] In 1913, Selig
upped its production of two-reel animal pictures, with *Wamba, a Child of the
Jungle* (May 1913), *Alone in the Jungle* (June 1913), and *The Terrors of the Jungle*
(November 1913), all starring Bessie Eyton.[46] In the "soft-toned" *Wamba, a
Child of the Jungle*, set in "British East Africa," Eyton plays a "halfbreed" who
leaves her drunken husband, Portuguese Pete, is taken in as the nurse for a
doctor's child (Lillian Wade again), and has to defend the child against her
husband as well as against marauding lions (who get to kill the latter in the
end).[47] This film also circulated widely as a General Film "special feature," and
ads often highlighted its half dozen sensation scenes.[48] *Alone in the Jungle*, in
the *World's* words, "surpasse[d] all its predecessors in thrilling encounters,"
among which was the "astounding sight" of a lion chasing Eyton through the
jungle, onto a cliff, and across a river, until it is shot just as she is caught.[49] This
film also made its villain a "halfbreed negro overseer," marking what was excluded—rather than included, as in *Wamba*—from the construction of a white
social order characteristic of such thrillers. The popularity of Selig's films led
competitors to produce their own animal pictures: Solax's *The Beasts of the
Jungle* (January 1913), "a thriller of the thirty-third degree"; World's Best
Film's *The Wizard of the Jungle* (April 1913), starring "Capt. Jack Bonavita, the
world's most famous lion tamer"; and Universal's *In the Coils of the Python* (August 1913), with "a nice, little 350-pound python."[50]

FIG. 45. Selig Polyscope ad, *Moving Picture World* (2 November 1912), 417.

Both Gaumont and Pathé also emulated and profited from the vogue for Selig's animal pictures, but they also sought to "modify" their own thrillers and minimize any "threat" they might pose on the US market. Throughout 1912, Gaumont released a series of "lion pictures" that, in the specific case of *The Lion's Revenge* (June 1912), won the *Mirror's* admiration: "Sensational as it may seem, the circumstance has been treated with much dignity, that both impresses and arouses one's credulance by its plausibility and truth."[51] As signs of the series' appeal, the *World* described the "widely-heralded, sensational, intensely exciting two-reel hand-colored feature entitled IN THE LAND OF THE LIONS" (September 1912) as a "spine tingler" that could not "be beaten," and the Columbia Theater in Cedar Rapids rebooked the film "by special request"—and even advised parents to "bring the children."[52] Pathé's *The Grotto of Torture* (November 1912)—in which a Hindoo priest punishes a "native" woman who has married an "English lover" by having her child seized by a "vicious leopard" and then luring her to a secret grotto from which both have to be rescued—also enjoyed some renown. In Cleveland, for instance, it first was screened as a "special feature" at the Knickerbocker in November, and then played at other major theaters throughout the following month.[53] Soon, however, the trade press began to complain that such "wild animal pictures [were] being overdone," something never ascribed to those of Selig or other US manufacturers. Gaumont's *In the Claws of the Leopard* (January 1913) the *Mirror* described as simply "a series of villainous machinations leading up to . . . the spectacle of a woman wrestling with a leopard and being mauled about the floor of several rooms by the beast to furnish excitement."[54] This kind of diatribe contrasted sharply with the acclaim usually accorded French historical films. As long as the sensational was integral to stories of a distant era (even if tragic)—as also was the case with Civil War films—French films were not just accepted but lauded. Gaumont's two-reel, stencil-color *The Margrave's Daughter* (March 1912) won exceptional praise: Bush, for one, declared it a "cinematographic masterpiece."[55] *The Prison on the Cliff* (July 1912) also gained this grudging respect from the *Mirror:* "The Gaumont Company has again taken a rather sensational situation and idea, and developed it into a most gripping and thoroughly convincing whole."[56]

During this vogue for animal pictures, detective stories also finally began to attract the interest of more US manufacturers—and as the basis for a series format. The French already were exploiting detective film series in Éclair's *Nick Carter* (1908–09), Eclipse's *Nat Pinkerton* (1911–13), and Pathé's comic variation in *Nick Winter* (1910–13), but few titles ever reached the United States.[57] Vitagraph seems to have led the way by having Maurice Costello, its principal male star, play Lambert Chase in the first of an announced series, *On the Pupil of His Eye* (July 1912).[58] Here, a murderer is tricked into returning to a dead man's body (Chase plants a story suggesting that the guilty man's image is fixed on the victim's pupil) and is caught and fixed on film by an unexpected flashlight camera. By April 1913, with the release of *The Mystery of the Stolen Jewels,* the series had accumulated a total of eight titles.[59] King the Detective returned in IMP's *The Opium Smugglers* (October 1912), a "melodrama of the old-fashioned sort," in the words of the *Morning Telegraph,* with Baggott bravely enduring "a series of adventures that Nick Carter would be jealous of."[60] Baggott worked variations on his detective figure in *Officer 174* (November 1912) and especially *The Rise of Officer 174* (May 1913), in which he captures some crafty art thieves by hanging on to the side of their speeding automobile, foils an attempt by an underworld boss to kill him at home, and finally exposes the boss's tricky plan to bribe him, through a stenographer's secret recording of the plotting by dictagraph.[61] In December 1913, Imp finally put Baggott in a more regular series, beginning with the two-reel *King the Detective in the Jarvis Case,* which received special promotion in the *Cleveland Leader* and "featured" just before New Year's at the Seville in Minneapolis.[62]

It was Edison, however, that invested more than other companies in the format.[63] This is hardly surprising, given the company's successful development of a monthly series, *What Happened to Mary?* (first released in July 1912), in which its top female star, Mary Fuller, plays a "modern girl," a stenographer in New York City, who voluntarily uses her skill and cunning to aid strangers in need. In an early "tie-in" that generated reciprocal publicity, each episode's story was published simultaneously in *Ladies' World,* a monthly magazine with a readership of nearly 1 million, largely working-class women.[64] Yet whereas the films stressed Mary's athleticism and agency, Shelley Stamp argues, the magazine stories showed her "preoccupied with romance and beauty."[65] As *What Happened to Mary?* drew to a close in the summer of 1913, Edison plotted a second monthly series, *Who Will Marry Mary?,* that aligned its heroine more closely with that of *Ladies' World,* but it also developed what was planned as a biweekly series of "Kate Kirby" detective stories, beginning with *The Diamond Crown* (July 1913), written and directed by J. Searle Dawley and starring Laura Sawyer.[66] The daughter of a retired police officer, with no discernible romantic interest, Kirby works as a "freelance" detective for his former department and sometimes calls on his assistance, as in *On the Broad Stairway* (July 1913), to solve the case of a bride stabbed to death on the eve of her wedding.[67] When Dawley and Sawyer joined Famous Players that summer,[68] Edison devised *The Chronicles of Cleek,* a "new series of detective mysteries," selected from the writings of Thomas W. Hanshew, published simultaneously in *Short Stories Magazine* and starring Ben Wilson.[69] In the first, *The Vanishing Cracksman* (November 1913), "the notorious criminal" falls in love, in the midst of a robbery, with the niece of a brain specialist (or phrenologist), who reads in "the shape of his head" the promise of "a great career as detective."[70] Others in the series, according to the *Mirror,* then avoided "the melodramatic" associated with Nick Carter—

and any further romantic interest—and instead "developed upon the lines of a Sherlock Holmes or a Raffles mystery."[71]

Most of these detective series were made up of one- or two-reel films, distributed as a more or less important component of General Film or Universal's weekly variety package. With *The Chronicles of Cleek,* however, audiences could count on a new film to be released on the last Thursday of each month. Detective films of three or more reels were also slow in developing. Atlas produced one of the first, a three-reel *Nick Carter* (March 1912), with "the great American detective solving the $100,000 jewel mystery"; but its state rights release was cut short by a threatened lawsuit from Street & Smith, publishers of the pulp fiction series.[72] More successful was another state rights release, Feature Photoplay's four-reel *Lieutenant Petrosino* (December 1912), which chronicled the exploits of an actual Italian-American detective who was assigned to rid the New York City docks of the Black Hand's criminal influence and eventually was killed in Palermo, Sicily.[73] This film also encountered difficulties, partly because of the downbeat ending: it was largely ignored in the trade press; it was never advertised in cities from Canton to Lowell; and the manager of the Mall in Cleveland was arrested for refusing to halt a three-day run of the film, when the mayor "deemed [it] objectionable."[74] Yet *Lieutenant Petrosino* did circulate widely for at least six months: it initiated a regular schedule of features in three-day runs at the Colonial in Toledo, played for two days (just prior to a return engagement of *Dante's Inferno*) at the Dreamland in Lynn, did very good business (coupled with *The Inauguration of President Wilson*) at the Star in Pawtucket, and served as a late-week special for such very different theaters as the Colonial in Des Moines and the Hart in Toledo.[75] Kalem's three-reel *Exposure of the Land Swindlers* (March 1913) had a living detective in a lead role—William J. Burns, "the twentieth century Sherlock Holmes"—supported by Alice Joyce, in a story that revealed "his course of procedure when confronted by a difficult crime."[76] After opening well at such theaters as the Lyric in Minneapolis and the Olympia in Lynn (lectured by Geoffrey Whalen), the film ran into distribution problems when General Film accused Kalem of circumventing its contract.[77] Interestingly, Dawley and Sawyer continued the "Kate Kirby" series with Famous Players, but for only two three-reel films, *An Hour Before Dawn* (October 1913) and *The Port of Doom* (November 1913).[78]

During the slow development of multiple-reel detective films by US producers, the French, by contrast, seemed eager to profit from *Zigomar's* success and what they may have construed as a growing American appetite for crime thrillers. Not long after Detroit's "official censor" declared "crime-impelling" movies were "obsolete,"[79] one particular news event seemed to encourage this assumption. In April and May 1912, the capture of the infamous Bonnot gang that had terrorized Paris and other nearby cities received unusual attention in US newspapers.[80] In fact, the *Cleveland Leader* filled the first

The Auto Cracksman Loots—Sometimes Slays—and Is Off Like a Flash

FIG. 46. "The Auto Cracksman Loots—Sometimes Slays—and Is Off Like a Flash," *New York Tribune* (3 November 1911), 2: 1.

two pages of its "Cosmopolitan Section" one Sunday with an extended account of the "Tiger Bandit" and his gang, written by Maurice Le Blanc, author of *Arsene Lupin*.[81] Previously, such criminals could be depicted as American—as in the "Auto Cracksman" story published in the *New York Tribune*, September 1911.[82] Now they became more and more fixed as "alien" or "foreign"—and typically French. United States manufacturers, of course, did not avoid crime films entirely: America's Feature Film, for instance, distributed nonfiction titles such as *Convict Life in the Ohio Penitentiary* (July 1912); and Biograph was not above producing one-reelers such as *The Musketeers of Pig Alley* (November 1912), which was advertised in Canton as "depicting the gangster evil that was the cause of Lieut. Becker going to prison."[83] Nor, of course, did other European manufacturers, but their multiple-reel films were consigned to marginal distributors. New York Film released German crime thrillers such as *Lights and Shadows of Chinatown* (July 1912), which did excellent business at the Pawtucket Star.[84] And Tournament Film, in Toledo, handled the German sensational melodramas of Asta Nielsen, which were successful enough that summer and fall and also turned up occasionally well into 1913. Multiple-reel French crime thrillers, however, proliferated on the US market: Éclair, for instance, imported a half dozen (most of them directed by Victorin Jasset) for release between May and July 1912, including *The Auto Bandits of Paris, Redemption, The Glass Coffin, Tom Butler, The Mystery of the Notre Dame Bridge,* and a second *Zigomar*.[85]

The trade press response to these new Éclair titles is difficult to assess. The

FIG. 47. "Bonnot, Tiger Bandit," *Cleveland Leader* (12 May 1912), C1.

breakup of the Sales Company disrupted the distribution of the company's French films, and eventually it set up a "Barnum of them all" affiliate, Universal Features, to handle them.[86] As a consequence, they generally fell outside the purview of trade press reviewers. The *Mirror*, however, did print a promotional piece on the "sensational auto bandits film" and a frame still "showing the capture of Bonnot, the bandit."[87] And the *World* contributed a positive review of *Redemption*, but that film differed from the others in that it exonerated a depraved woman who, in the end, dies nursing plague victims.[88] If neither a fascination with powerful criminal figures—which, in the case of *Zigomar* may have derived from its novelty as an early "feature," as well as from its "exoticism"—nor a condemnation of such figures can be found in the trade press, audiences certainly continued to be drawn to them.[89] In Toledo, the Colonial featured three of these Éclair crime thrillers, along with Pathé's *Charley Colms* (also based on the Bonnot gang), in June and rebooked *The Auto Bandits of Paris* in September.[90] In Cedar Rapids, the Palace promoted *Zigomar vs. Nick Carter* (*Zigomar II*) as "the greatest sensational European drama ever imported"; in Louisville, Kentucky, the Majestic called *Tom Butler* the "sensation" of the week.[91] In Lynn, for at least two months that summer and fall, the Central Square featured one Éclair crime thriller after another, supplemented by Asta Nielsen films.[92] In Cleveland, the downtown Princess specially advertised *The Phantom Bandit* (*Zigomar II*) and *The Mystery of the Notre Dame Bridge* in August, and the Norwood (a neighborhood theater on the northeast side) played the latter film together with *The Auto Bandits of Paris* one week in November. Not only did both of these Cleveland theaters cater to working-class audiences, but the Alpha, the only theater in the black ghetto to advertise, also showed nearly every Éclair crime thriller between July and November, rebooking *Redemption* (which "every woman should see") and *The Phantom Bandit* by "special request."[93] Increasingly, this suggests, French crime thrillers were being linked not to the mass audience promoted by the trade press but to the "less desirable masses."

Toward the end of 1912, the trade press may have taken note of this phenomenon, for certain writers now expressed a heightened anxiety over "the sensational situations," the "excessive violence" and "morbidity," so characteristic of French crime thrillers. In November, Bush voiced his growing unease at the "influx of foreign 'features'. . . dealing with crime"; two months later, that unease had turned to alarm.[94] Occasionally, the alarm sounded at the local level, as when the *Des Moines News,* in December, noted that a three-reel French film playing at the Golden ought to be banned.[95] Although specific films were mentioned only rarely, these attacks more than likely alluded to French films as the most visible in circulation. There was no such criticism, for instance, of Great Northern's *Gar-El-Hama* (November 1912), which not only enlisted sympathy for its daring criminal at the outset but also made sure to imprison him in the end.[96] Moreover, they appeared just as Gaumont imported a new group of sensational melodramas for release on the US market.[97] Trade press reviews of these Gaumont crime thrillers were decidedly mixed. Whereas the *News* praised the scenic effects and thrills of Léonce Perret's *In the Grip of the Vampire,* pointing out its uniqueness in experimenting with moving pictures (reenacting a crime) to restore the heroine (Suzanne Grandais) to sanity, the *Mirror* found its plot poorly constructed, and the *World* complained that never was a film "so burdened with inadequate and be-fogging sub-titles."[98] Perret's three-part *Main de fer* series—released as *The International Conspiracy, The White Glove Band,* and *When Thieves Fall Out*—was one of the earliest "continued story type of film" (certainly in multiple reels),[99] staging repeated, inconclusive showdowns between a police inspector nicknamed "The Iron Hand" and one nefarious villain after another (all played by Perret). Although the series earned a somewhat better response, the *World* confessed that the second film was "not substantial so much as absorbingly interesting."[100] No one took notice, for instance, of the third film's deft use of disguise or its unusual chase, in which three discrete masked images are orchestrated within the same frame. Instead, the *Mirror* used the film as an occasion to compare "the humanness and rugged virility of the American melodrama" to "the carefully dove-tailed plot of the Continental scenario writer"—and then damned it for not measuring up to the "Continental" standard.[101]

Despite this trade press anxiety, the Gaumont crime thrillers seem to have been popular that winter and spring, at the very moment when the far more numerous Kay-Bee, Broncho, and Universal-Bison westerns and Civil War films were making such an impact. Also popular were Éclair's *Balaoo* and *Zigomar III* (released slightly later in May 1913), along with others still in circulation. This was especially true for theaters catering to working-class audiences. In Lynn, the Dreamland featured several Gaumont titles, along with a repeat booking of *The Auto Bandits of Paris,* from January through February 1913. In Pawtucket, the Star did exceptionally good business with *Tom Butler* and *The International Conspiracy,* respectively, also in January and February. In Youngstown, the Princess played one Éclair or Gaumont crime thriller after another, including *In the Grip of the Vampire* and *The White Glove Band,* each Sunday, January through March.[102] In Toledo, the Hart ran several older Éclair thrillers in December 1912, with *The Auto Bandits of Paris* specially featured one Friday through Monday, while the Orpheum and Colonial showed several new Gaumont thrillers in February and March—and the Colonial featured *Zigomar III* in June. Yet not all these venues could be said to cater to the working class. In Des Moines, for instance, as the Colonial began to regularly schedule multiple-reel films for three day-showings, it booked *Zigomar III* shortly after *Satan's* successful run in May and added *Balaoo* in June. At the same time, in some cities, French crime thrillers either arrived after long delays or were shown in theaters that never advertised in local newspapers. In Cleveland, for instance, *The White Glove Band* and *When Thieves Fall Out* did not appear at the Mall, for Sunday shows, until late April and July, respectively. In Canton, *The Auto Bandits of Paris, The White Glove Band,* and others did not show up until July and August, and then only at the Airdome, a temporary open-air theater.[103] In Minneapolis and St. Paul, no trace of their presence survives at all, except for a Sunday-only showing of *Zigomar III* at the Mazada in late May. By the time of *Fantomas's* entrance that summer, French crime thrillers were in danger of fading into phantoms.

Who's There? And Who's Not

The trade press anxiety over the "sensational situations" that now seemed a constant in French crime thrillers coincided with an article, in April 1913, by Harrison, one of the *World's* more influential writers. Dubbed "The Fascinating Criminal," this article renewed the attack on all those who continued to indulge in what he called "rotten realism" and so make heroes of criminals, which the Éclair and Gaumont films certainly came close to doing. The "fascinating criminal," he claimed (inadvertently repeating the Detroit censor of a year before), was "a thing of the past," which intelligent producers should be eliminating from the screen.[104] This attitude seems to have been widespread and may have been a factor in how the trade press— and Gaumont itself, as that interview with Blaché suggests—framed the discussion of the company's sensational melodramas throughout 1913. In opening his review of Louis Feuillade's three-reel *The Rajah's Casket* (May 1913), for instance, Hugh Hoffman in the *World* claimed that the French company had taken "a liking to detective plays," based on the recent offerings by US manufacturers—in effect, rewriting what recently had been said about Gaumont's crime thrillers. The film was praised because its hero was a detective rather than a powerful criminal and his gang, and because there was "not an illogical or jarring anachronism in the entire piece."[105] Even stronger praise was accorded Itala's four-reel *Tigris* (March 1913)—"continually engrossing, frequently enlivened by unexpected thrills"—partly because its infamous criminal (another "terror of Paris") commits suicide at the end, and the detective hero begins a romance with Tigris's innocent sister.[106] All this could be read as an incentive to the French to shift the subject of their sensational melodramas from one side of the law to the other, something that actually occurred in the films that Éclair began to offer on the US market. After the third film in the *Zigomar* series, Éclair turned away from its seemingly omnipotent or mysterious criminals to feature government spies challenged by an international conspiracy in *Protea* (November 1913). Unfortunately, at least in the context of the US market, what Gaumont put on offer was *Fantomas*.

Indeed, the nadir in the reception of French crime thrillers probably came with the release of the (later famous) *Fantomas* series.[107] Its lukewarm (at best) reception contrasts sharply with the excitement that greeted several rival American sensational melodramas. To downplay the criminal and sensational in advertising the first *Fantomas* film, *Under the Shadow of the Guillotine* (July 1913), Gaumont described it as part of a "Cracksman vs. Detective Series," which not only toned down the violence of Fantomas's crimes (and played on the "Master Cracksman" subtitle of *Tigris*) but also depicted him as an elegant, black-masked gentleman.[108] Moreover, an advertisement in the *Mirror* listed the cast, perhaps to draw on audience familiarity with René Navarre, the "Phantom Crook" (who had played the detective in *The Rajah's Casket*).[109] Still, the responses to this "crook play" were anything but enthusiastic.[110] The *Mirror*'s reviewer found it merely of "medium interest." Although he could not refrain from praising the photography, stage settings, and acting, he faulted the film's story construction (once again), while ignoring the fact that it was intended as part of a series: "Much of the important action takes place 'off stage,' and is explained in subcaptions. The entire first part is occupied with a depiction of how Fantomas robs a countess of her jewels, an incident having no bearing upon the main thread or theme . . . . The ending is weak for the melodrama arrives at nothing."[111] The *Mirror* then actually refused to review the second and third films in the series. The *World* printed brief, mildly positive reviews of the first two films,[112] and then Hanford C. Judson described the third, *The Mysterious Fingerprint*, as having little appeal except for what Frank Woods called "the least cultivated persons" of the outmoded nickelodeons:[113] "where pictures with a decided punch are wanted, where startling and terrible sensations presented with logic enough to make them connect up. . . in a seemingly organized whole are desired, this third installment of 'Fantomas' will be welcome, will even stir enthusiasm."[114]

The series' circulation seems to have mirrored this trajectory of condescension and more or less confirmed its limited appeal. In Cleveland, only *Fantomas I* registered (in very fine print) for two nights in late August at the downtown Mall; after that, hardly any French crime thrillers ever were mentioned in the *Leader*.[115] Although the first two films in the series played at the Orpheum in Canton, in October and December, respectively, each was featured just one night in the middle of the week.[116] In Youngstown, *Fantomas II* similarly appeared at the Orpheum for just one Sunday in December.[117] In Toledo, *Fantomas III* followed *Protea* at the Hart in late January 1914, but the promised fourth film in the series failed to appear there and never showed up elsewhere, unless it was unadvertised.[118] In Lowell, *Fantomas III* may have been a hit at the new 1,500-seat Owl in March 1914, but ads for the film promoted its "ballroom scene in which graceful couples do the latest steps. . . the hesitation waltz, the tango and others."[119] In cities from Lynn to Des Moines and Minneapolis, furthermore, the *Fantomas* series left no trace at all in the newspapers. By the time that the *Mirror* seems to have reevaluated its position, reviewing *Fantomas V* (March 1914), what it now saw as the "distinctiveness" of the series, "whereby the director, by deft touches here and there, seems to establish a close relation between the spectator and the mystery,"[120] rapidly was dissolving away. By July 1914, Gaumont's ad for the fifth (and last) film was pathetically tiny and placed in the back pages of *Motion Picture News*,[121] eerily marking both the devalued status of *Fantomas* on the US market and the vanishing point of French crime thrillers as a whole. The fascination with the sensational criminal—especially one who eluded capture and retribution—had turned, less than two years after *Zigomar's* triumph, into the repudiation of a "foreign" *other* that definitely could not be assimilated as *American*.

Gaumont also had the bad luck to release *Fantomas II* and *Fantomas III* just as a (sometimes hysterical) debate erupted over the alleged threat to moral decency and the bases of social order from a number of popular "white slave" films.[122] Consequently, it is instructive to compare the phantom-like presence of *Fantomas* with one of the more controversial American features, Universal's *Traffic in Souls* (December 1913). The *News* declared that "a few years ago such a picture as this would have been impossible," and the *World* admitted that its subject, the "white slave" trade, even now would "arouse bitter antagonism" from those committed to "battling with the evil . . . in the old-time secret way."[123] Yet the latter's reviewer argued that the film showed "practically

GAUMONT'S GREATEST DETECTIVE DRAMAS

OF ALL CRACKSMAN vs. DETECTIVE SERIES, THE GREATEST

FANTOMAS

No. 1
"FANTOMAS
UNDER
THE
SHADOW
OF THE
GUILLOTINE"

ORDER NOW

No. 1
"FANTOMAS
UNDER
THE
SHADOW
OF THE
GUILLOTINE"

ORDER NOW

THE PHANTOM CROOK

FIG. 48. Gaumont ad, *Moving Picture World* (31 July 1913), 119.

nothing of the lure of underworld life," upheld "the forces of law and order" throughout its six reels, and sustained the suspense of its dramatic story with "unusual power." The *Mirror* concurred: the film "succeeded admirably in handling a subject of morbid interest and difficult situations with nothing that would pander to the evil senses and everything that tends to bring out the finer feeling of the spectator."[124] Similarly, *Motography* declared that there was "a lesson to young and old in every foot of its length."[125] As Shelley Stamp has shown, *Traffic in Souls* was unusually popular in New York.[126] But the film also scored a hit in many other cities, usually booked in legitimate theaters, just as were *Quo Vadis?, Les Misérables,* and other big features. In Cleveland, the Colonial had it for the last two weeks of December, and the *Leader,* well aware of its New York success, printed a story about how "Cleveland Loves 'Traffic in Souls.' "[127] Similarly, in Toledo, the Auditorium ran the film for a week and a half in late December and then rebooked it for another week in early January; in Rochester, the Shubert had it for a full week in December.[128] In Boston, the film held the screen at the Globe for no less than nine weeks (from December through February), with five shows a day, and reportedly was seen by nearly 140,000 people.[129] In nearby Lowell, it played at regular picture theaters: one week at the New Jewel in mid-March, and then another week at the Merrimack Square in early April.[130] In St. Paul, the Metropolitan ran *Traffic in Souls* for a week in early February and then moved the film across the Mississippi River to its sister theater in Minneapolis for another four days in early March.[131] In late May, it finally showed up in Des Moines at the Berchel for a week at the end of the legitimate theater season.[132]

Traffic in Souls has received a good deal of attention recently from American film historians, and their analyses have focused rightly on the context of "white slavery" hysteria surrounding the film, its relation to other white slave productions (on stage and screen), its narrative construction and ideological contradictions, and its representation of the pleasurable as well as dangerous effects of modern technologies of transportation and communication on the mobility of (specifically, female) bodies.[133] Yet another context is equally valuable, especially for highlighting its difference from French crime thrillers: the development of the "scientific" American detective film as an "appropriate" variant of sensational melodrama. The *World* seemed implicitly aware of that in noting that the story of *Traffic in Souls* centered on an ordinary woman's brave attempt, aided by her "policeman-sweetheart," not only to rescue her younger sister but also to gather evidence, using her father's dictograph invention (already anticipated in King Baggot's *The Rise of Officer 174*),[134] against the criminal ring of traffickers in women. If, in French films, policemen and detectives seemed powerless to control master criminals like Fantomas, in American films like *Traffic in Souls,* criminals eventually were rendered powerless as the police, in concert with ordinary citizens, and assisted by new recording devices, restored the orderly, legiti-

FIG. 49. Globe Theatre
ad, *Boston Journal*
(17 January 1914), 4.

mate flow of peoples (even immigrants from abroad) into and within the
modern city. However morbid or excessively violent the trade press considered French crime thrillers, as long as their circulation was held in check,
certainly relative to films like *Traffic in Souls,* and their criminals remained
free to exploit the mobility and anonymity of modern life only within the
confines of "old Europe," their deleterious effect on the "less desirable
masses" might be kept to a minimum.

It is no less instructive to compare *Fantomas* with Selig's *The Adventures of
Kathlyn,* which not only starred Kathlyn Williams (still remembered for her
heroism in *Lost in the Jungle*) but also just happened to set its first episodes in
the "land of lions" that Gaumont may once have hoped to "own."[135] Unlike
the *Fantomas* series, whose titles were released at irregular intervals over the
course of nearly a year, the thirteen two-reel episodes of *Kathlyn* appeared at
regular biweekly intervals in General Film's variety programs, beginning in
late December 1913.[136] In an innovative "campaign of motion picture advertising, moreover," a full-page "installment of [the] serial story" was
printed in perhaps as many as fifty newspapers—among them the *Chicago Tribune, Boston Globe, Minneapolis Journal,* and *Youngstown Vindicator*—each Sunday prior to the showing of a new episode.[137] The detective film offered one
precedent for such serials, as Bowser suggests,[138] but another particularly per-
tinent to *Kathlyn* was the animal picture in which Selig specialized and in
which Williams once again was starring—*In the Midst of the Jungle* (October
1913) and *Thor, Lord of the Jungle* (December 1913).[139] For here again, in what
Selig itself described as a "costly series of sensational wild animal features"
(as early as August 1913),[140] Williams was "continuously beset by dangers and
seemingly insurmountable odds," at the hands of "the savage denizens [both
animal and human] of Jungle Land."[141] This time, however, "the domain of
perilous adventure and thrilling photodramatic narrative" was India,
stripped of colonial traces and suffused with an "atmosphere of Orientalism"
that reminded the *World* of the "mysticism" of the "Arabian Nights."[142] Although less taken with these films than the *World,* the *Mirror* agreed that

FIG. 50. *Adventures of Kathlyn* ad, *Chicago Tribune* (7 January 1914).

Williams's screen "personality" was "the true attraction," "the mainspring of the action and of interest," whether threatened with death or engineering her own escapes from danger.[143]

Within weeks, exhibitors were sometimes surprised to find that *The Adventures of Kathlyn* was well on its way to being "the hit of the year" or season—"the best innovation of its kind . . . to increase the interest, enlarge the sales and stimulate universal curiosity and cash reciprocation of anything ever advanced in the moving picture business."[144] In Chicago alone, four times more prints of each episode were released than of any other film; upon returning from a trip to Europe, George Kleine was astonished at how the serial was increasing the city's theater attendance and changing the attitude of newspapers toward moving pictures.[145] In Minneapolis, each episode circulated according to a set schedule over a two-week period—beginning at the Lyric (Monday to Wednesday); moving on to the New Lake (Friday and Saturday), the Palace (Sunday), and the Vista (the next Monday and Tuesday); then jumping the river to the Saint Paul Majestic (Thursday and Friday).[146] In the region of Detroit, ads listed its daily appearance in one theater after another for the entire month of January.[147] In Boston, "a number of theaters" reportedly were "using it as [their] only feature"; in Cincinnati, the serial drew "crowded houses. . . in spite of alternately rainy and hot weather."[148] That *Kathlyn*, again unlike *Fantomas*, successfully appealed to the new mass audience and not merely the masses Barbara Wilinsky has demonstrated in her fine analysis of the coproduction strategies innovated by Selig and the *Chicago Tribune*.[149] Whereas Selig had a core audience assumed to be working-class and white-collar, the *Tribune* had a "largely white, native-born, middle-class readership."[150] Placing "teaser advertisements for *Kathlyn*" on the newspaper's "women's" page, making the story installments part of its Sunday "Special Features" section (in color), and jointly planting stories on the film's success—with headlines such as "Crowds Besiege Kathlyn Shows"—allowed both the *Tribune* and Selig to "blend their class-based audiences to attract men and women from all classes."[151] Indeed, as the "Kathlyn Vogue" turned into a "craze" or "rage," *Kathlyn* quickly became the source for one popular fad after another—including the "Kathlyn waltz," the "Kathlyn cocktail," and the "Kathlyn post card" (with advance orders of "one million")—and advertisers promoted all kinds of fashion tie-ins, "such as 'The Kathlyn bolero,' 'The Kathlyn tango pumps,' and various articles of feminine finery."[152]

Kathlyn's stunning success quickly provoked a craze for similar "serial queen" variants of the sensational melodrama.[153] Perhaps having gotten wind of Selig's plans, Mutual announced a "fifty-two reel serial" to be released weekly, beginning in early January 1914, and to star Norma Phillips (of Reliance) as *Our Mutual Girl*.[154] This serial eschewed sensation scenes, however, and served as a kind of showcase for modern urban life, drawing on elements of the newsreel and travel film to tell the story of a fictional character who moves from a simple life in the country to fashionable New York in the company of a wealthy aunt.[155] The serial that soon topped even *Kathlyn* in popularity, of course, was *The Perils of Pauline*, which Pathé American developed in conjunction with William Randolph Hearst for release through Eclectic, beginning in late March.[156] Much as with *Kathlyn*, full-page installments of *Pauline* were published in "seven of the largest Sunday papers" (all owned by Hearst), along with others such as the *Detroit News,* just prior to each episode's Monday release.[157] Similarly, as the "wonderfully natural," active, ingenious heroine, Pearl White was *Pauline*'s chief attraction, as she single-handedly fought off villains out to steal the fortune of her dead foster father and repeatedly had to rescue her would-be fiancé.[158] Besides, there was an added gimmick to attract audiences: spectators clever enough to solve certain mysteries that cropped up in each episode's story could win big prizes of $1,000.[159] Within weeks, fifteen prints of the initial episode were reported circulating in San Francisco, and another ten were running in St. Louis; and audiences could see *Pauline* in up to sixty theaters in the Detroit area.[160] By July, Eclectic could boast that *Pauline* had "broken all records for bookings and patron pulling power."[161] Not to be left behind, Universal developed its own serial, *Lucille Love, The Girl of Mystery,* starring the team of Grace Cunard and Francis Ford, and contracted with the A. P. Robyn Newspaper Syndicate to publish installments of each of its fifteen episodes in nearly forty papers, from the *Boston Post* and *Cleveland Leader* to the *Toledo News-Bee* and *St. Louis Times.*[162] In the *Cleveland Leader,* full-page ads not only promoted this "marvelous, blood-tingling 'Movie' " (while displaying a fashionably gowned Cunard) but also listed each episode's circulation through nine theaters on Sunday (including the Mall, Bijou Dream, and Alhambra) and two each on the other six days of the week (including several in nearby Youngstown and Akron).[163]

The Mantra of American Sensational Melodrama

"Melodrama of the best sort is always uplifting; right triumphs and evil is either frustrated or gains its just reward."[164] During the culture war of the early 1910s, this deceptively simple definition served as a mantra with which to separate—and thus marginalize—French crime thrillers from American sensational melodramas. Exceptions to the rules were rare, and historically situated, as in the case of *Zigomar* or Éclair's *Protea* in late 1913: as if responding to implicit directives from the trade press, the latter film featured a government spy, not a criminal—and a woman no less who, much like her American counterparts, was more than proficient at disguises and daring escapes in enemy territory. The *Mirror*'s respectful praise gave substance to *Protea*'s popularity: "it teems with action, yet the excitement is of a healthy sort that does not repel."[165] As did the film's three-day run at the Knickerbocker in Cleveland, its repeated bookings at the Hart in Toledo, a report in the *World* that *Protea* did "the biggest business of the year" for the Bijou Dream in Philadelphia and had to "booked. . . for a three-day repeat," and a testimonial from Mrs. E. L. Taylor, manager of the Jewel Theatre, that it was "the best show that ever played in Flint [Michigan]."[166] *Fantomas* by contrast, proved to be a kind of limit case for what American reviewers—and audiences, to a lesser extent—found unacceptable, morally threatening, and even repellent in French crime thrillers, yet its reception was hardly unusual. Indeed, the polarities of "appropriateness" in this culture war over sensational melodrama were symptomatic of what was fast becoming an inflated sense of American moral and social superiority in relation to the rest of the world, including the "old world" of Europe. That superiority not only served to justify certain kinds of moving pictures as a "social force" for both the masses and the new mass audience but also proved a usefully deceptive mask for the imperialistic ventures in which the United States was then currently engaged. And that would support the US film industry's "invasion" of Europe and other countries, just then getting under way, and ultimately sell US cultural imperialism as a "global good." For, as the export manager for the Nicolas Power Company bragged, in early 1914: "There [was] an enormous demand for films of sensational subjects such as war dramas, wild West, jungle stories, good detective and other stories with strong emotional interest."[167]

Appropriately "modified," the action and behavior in American sensational melodramas, it would seem, made action on a broader front just as appropriate.

Document

W. Stephen Bush, "Advertising and Criticising,"

Moving Picture World (23 November 1912), 750

For the benefit of numerous readers and advertisers The Moving Picture World desires to make it as plain as English words can wield the matter that the buying of advertising space in small or large quantities confers no right to praise and commendation, or indeed to any notice at all in the editorial or critical columns of the paper. While this is true of all and any products offered in the advertising section of The Moving Picture World, it is especially true in regard to films. The judgment of The Moving Picture World is not for sale. Films will be reviewed purely on their merits. If producers of films are under the impression that liberal use of the advertising columns will in any way influence the criticisms of this paper, they are harboring a misconception, which we have always done our best to discourage. The Moving Picture World owes whatever usefulness and prestige it may possess to the confidence of the exhibitor in the integrity of its motives and the soundness of its judgments. Following the policy of its late founder, we will always want to build up rather than tear down, but as we strive to lift the picture up we cannot sit by idly and see it dragged down.

We refer in particular to a large and recent influx of foreign "features" and to some domestic film abortions dealing with crime and gunplays, with prison horrors and life in the underworld. The makers of these films call them "features." If there is any thing to distinguish these productions from others it only is their bad preeminence. They are lurid and sensational in the worst sense of the word and, as a rule, they are plainly and frankly immoral. They appeal directly to the ignorant, the morbid and the depraved. They are a stench in the nostrils of the audiences in the ordinary American motion picture theater. Multiple reel features are now on the flood tide of popularity. Hoping to be carried along by the current, the makers of these offensive features imagine they can create a fictitious value for their product by heavy advertising. On the strength of such advertising they expect and almost demand extended and complimentary reviews of their productions. We wish to serve notice on this type of producers that their expectations and demands will be ignored. Nor will they be able through liberal advertising to secure immunity from hostile criticism, whenever their releases demand hostile criticism for the good of the industry at large. A producer of films who must make his money at the expense of the good name and fame of the motion picture is the most dangerous enemy. Against him and all his works we will not hesitate to turn the destructive edge of the critical pen.

Too much filming of the underworld and the portrayal of crime just for the sake of a thrill or a sensation have been two great reproaches on the industry in the past. The Moving Picture World has done its share toward the wiping out of these reproaches, and it proposes to keep a ceaseless vigil at its post of duty.

We wish to make it clear that we are not prejudiced against foreign features as such. On the contrary, this paper has been the first to recognize and proclaim the superior merits of such features as "Dante's Inferno," "Homer's Odyssey," "The Crusaders, or Jerusalem Delivered," "The Miracle" and other great classic, historic, allegorical and spectacular productions. One cannot, however, look through the columns of the moving picture journals of Europe without a fear lest many of the "sensational features," now exploited there to the disgust of the friends of the motion picture, will find their way here. The advance guard seems to have reached here. It will be our unpleasant duty to refuse them the hospitality of these shores. In England, where the public are not used to pictorial presentations of crime and cinematographical delineation of sex problems, a note of alarm has been sounded by our esteemed contemporary, The Bioscope. In England these objectionable features are called "exclusives," and speaking of their bad influence the British paper says:

> We think that some of the widely advertised "exclusives" hide under their claim of sensationalism something infinitely more degrading. . . . In what lies their attraction? Is it in the stirring story, the sensational deeds, the strong plot or the wonderful photography? All these are quite legitimate attractions, and have no lowering influence; with them we have no quarrel. But it is the blatant innuendoes, and often the nauseous episodes, which are crowded into a few exclusives that create evil. . . . Let us make an end of these films, which are degrading to both exhibitor and audience.

We recognize in a few of these objectionable features much technical skill, good acting, splendid photography and the brains of able directors. We regret sincerely that so much cleverness and industry are wasted. Open and flagrant indecency, however, vitiates even the most artistic pictures. The methods of European censorship, however rigorous they may be in shutting out films which seem to belittle "duly constituted authority," are notoriously lax in matters of morality. Almost anything will pass muster. The resulting licentiousness in film productions has raised storms of protest even in Continental Europe, and the public, whose morality is underestimated by the police, will have no more of these offensive "features." It is a great mistake to try and market them here. What is too raw for Continental Europe will not get past an American board of Censorship.

The Photoplayers

The Answer

"The Play's the thing,"
    Said Bill, the Bard,
"The play's the money getter,
    But for bringing in
    Good coin and hard,
The photoplay is better."

    Why is this so?
    Well, this is why
The film plays are good payers—
    Their directors
    Take more pains to
Choose with care their players.

Now where is there
    A better bunch
Of actors and actresses?
    Don't try to guess—
    For guessing but
Your ignorance confesses.

    There can't be found
    A better lot
Than for the screens are playing;
    And that is why
    Both you and I
Our nickels keep on paying.

Photoplay Magazine
(July 1913)

Entr'acte 5

Trash Twins

Newspapers and Moving Pictures

The fictional young woman who introduced chapter 1 could have been imagined reading a newspaper and deciding where to go to the movies in any number of cities other than Des Moines in the spring of 1913. In Lynn, she could have been a shoe factory worker perusing the frequent ads in the *Daily Item* for four major downtown moving picture theaters or arguing with friends over the advice about current pictures in "The Critic's Comment" column published every Saturday. In Toledo, she could have been a salesgirl reading either the special Saturday page published by the *Blade* for "Practical Picture Pointers" about the "Principal Picture Plays" at downtown theaters or the daily block ads in the *News* for what was playing at her neighborhood picture theater. In Minneapolis, she could have been a stenographer or "typewriter" turning to the "Motion Pictures" page in the *Sunday Tribune* for information on the programs at a dozen downtown and suburban picture theaters. The trade press generally was slow to pick up on this. In May 1911, *Moving Picture World* moaned that the daily press was "woefully ignorant of the doings in the moving picture world" (and not just in its own pages).[1] As late as October 1912, the *New York Dramatic Mirror* claimed that the " 'movies' continue to flourish" without "the benignant approval" of the daily newspapers, that the "pictures are left very much to speak for themselves."[2] Yet, by the spring of 1913, trade journals as different as the *World* and *Motography* acknowledged that local newspapers were now promoting *photoplays* or *movies* (the distinction could be significant) by running special pages and/or columns on a regular basis.[3] Yet, if a mutually profitable relationship was well established between moving pictures and newspapers by 1913–14,[4] signs of its emergence—however tentative, irregular, and uneven, like those for feature films—are quite visible as early as 1911, despite the *World's* complaint, and even before.

Whereas previous chapters and entr'actes have drawn on newspapers as a heavily mediated source of information, this final entr'acte focuses on the weekly or even daily stream of discursive material itself. If one assumes that the daily newspaper was "so arranged that it appeal[ed] to every member of the family—father, mother, sister, and brother"—and that its crucial function was to mediate the complexity of urban life, offering a kind of map or menu by which people of all kinds could make sense of a city and their position within it, then ascertaining how moving pictures are discursively described and promoted on a daily or weekly basis becomes a way of "knowing" more about the place of moviegoing within everyday life.[5] Consequently, my aim in this entr'acte is to sketch the more prominent patterns in the cinema's developing institutional relationship with newspapers (again, principally in selected cities from the Northeast to the upper Midwest), during the transition from what Jan Olsson aptly has called a discourse dominated by *flânerie* and then reform to one that was more or less professionalized.[6] This entr'acte thus covers a range of practices and formats, from the innovative or experimental to the regularized. It takes note of what seem to be general or national patterns and those, by contrast, that seem more local, involving variations from one region or city to another—and the latter include intriguing anomalies. Expanding on the ideas and insights already set forth in entr'acte 2, this more focused study of newspaper discourse also reveals as much about the assumed audiences for moving pictures, their moviegoing habits and "tastes," as it does about the films themselves or the industry that produced and circulated them.

During the heady years of the nickelodeon boom, exhibitors sometimes had used local newspapers as an initial means to promote their business, but, except in scattered cities and towns, few carried on the practice for long. Indeed, what strikes one today is the relative lack of even minimal ads for moving picture theaters in most city newspapers from 1908–9 through 1910–11. To be sure, individual exhibitors here and there paid for small ads to appear on a regular basis: in the fall of 1910, for instance, these included the managers of the Voyons (Lowell), the Comique and Olympia (Lynn), the Odeon (Canton), and the Colonial (Des Moines).[7] The "Moving Pictures and Vaudeville" column of block ads that began to appear daily in the *St. Louis Times* in August 1909, however, definitely was unusual. At first, only a half dozen theaters briefly listed their programs of either licensed or Independent films; within a month, however, that number had increased to more than two dozen, including some of the best downtown theaters, many suburban and neighborhood theaters, and even several airdomes—with some like the downtown Grand Central or Casino detailing each film, illustrated song or vaudeville act, and musical number on that day's program. By the following spring, there were nearly fifty theaters of various kinds and sizes in a column that took up more than a half page of the newspaper. Yet, oddly, these block ads rapidly shrank in number during the early summer months of 1910 and disappeared altogether within a year of their initial appearance. One explanation may be that, as a new Independent paper (first issued in 1907), the *Times* welcomed such a means of advertising revenue, but its relatively low circulation eventually proved insufficient for exhibitors.[8]

With slight variations, however, this strategy saw limited use elsewhere in St. Louis and other cities. In February 1910, fifteen of the same picture theaters filled the first page of the *St. Louis Republic*'s want ad section one Sunday with block ads for their "High-Class Moving-Picture Theatres"; a year and a half later, even more theaters paid for another special page of ads for what now were called the city's "Leading Moving Picture and Vaudeville Houses."[9] From the fall of 1911 through the spring of 1912, four picture theaters (the Isis, Scenic, Wonderland, and Novelty) in downtown Minneapolis paid for a single block ad (listing one or two film titles for each theater) on "The Stage" page of the *Sunday Journal*.[10] In the fall of 1912, three theaters in downtown Baltimore and another in South Baltimore began sponsoring a "Moving Pictures" column of block ads in the Sunday *Sun;* within six months, the column had added six more downtown theaters.[11] About the same time, ten theaters in downtown Rochester introduced a similar "Moving Picture Theatres" column of block ads in the Sunday *Herald*.[12] A unique version of this strategy appeared in Toledo in late January 1913 (as if for the benefit of my imagined salesgirl and her friends), when a dozen "picture theaters in the residence districts" sponsored a "Moving Pictures and Where to See Them" column in the daily *News-Bee*'s want ads.[13] At its peak, the column listed sixteen theaters divided into the city's "west side," "north side," "south side," and "east side" neighborhoods. For several weeks in September, a similar column of block ads also could be found in the Saturday edition of the *Boston Journal,* for up to twenty "motion picture houses in the residential districts" of the city.[14]

According to *Moving Picture World,* by early 1911 film manufacturers were shipping "vast quantities of literature . . . free to every exhibitor" (that from Selig is among the little that survives).[15] Although exhibitors generally tended to use this "free literature" for promotional purposes on site, some also tapped into it as a source for a variety of strategies and formats that they developed in conjunction with newspapers that year. If sometimes these read as the explicit product of manufacturers' interests, at other times they clearly reflected the interests of exhibitors and a particular newspaper—and the latter's sense of its readership and advertisers—or sought to balance the interests of all three parties. One such strategy or format can be seen in the Sunday column of gossip and information, "In the Moving Picture World," that the *Chicago Tribune* introduced in November 1911.[16] First signed by Gene Morgan and thereafter attributed to the "Reel Observer," this column ranged far and wide: noting the popularity of "wild West" pictures one week and supporting trade press "protests against the volume" of such films a month later; announcing industrial developments such as Edison's home projecting kinetoscope and the American Film Company's newly opened printing plant in Evanston; interviewing celebrities like Mabel Taliaferro, who visited the city for the premiere of Selig's *Cinderella* (in which she starred); and summarizing the annual police report on moving picture censorship in Chicago. What is particularly striking in this long-lasting column—and what probably restricted its publication to the *Tribune*—is the consistent attempt to offer a local angle on moving pictures: for instance, the only manufacturers ever mentioned—Selig, Essanay, American, Pathé-Frères—all had production facilities or distribution offices in or near the city.[17]

"In certain quarters," again according to the *World*, exhibitors also were urging newspapers to "take up the work of criticizing the films" just as they did "regular drama."[18] Although the ephemeral character of so many short films released each week during this period made that urging inherently problematic, several papers actually did take up the challenge. In June 1911, the *St. Louis Republic* began running a column called "Film Reviews and Latest Motion Picture Attractions" in the "Special Feature" section of its Sunday edition.[19] Unfortunately, the short reviews largely constituting this column were reprinted verbatim from the *New York Morning Telegraph*, but without crediting the source; when, several months later, the *Morning Telegraph* questioned the propriety of this practice in a prominent article, the *Republic* reduced its column substantially.[20] What it now did was something that other newspapers were trying out: probably using the publicity sent to exhibitors, they began to print regular columns on current films that ranged from outright ads to capsule reviews. One of the first of these appeared in September 1911 in the Sunday *Youngstown Vindicator*, as the "Week in Moving Picture Theaters," which essentially reprinted or summarized descriptions that the manufacturers circulated or that could be found in the trade press.[21] By late September, a biweekly theater column (Tuesdays and Sundays) in the *Minneapolis Journal* began to include brief local reviews of featured films at the Lyric, most likely prompted by Rothapfel's own promotional tactics, and then of programs at other picture theaters that advertised regularly in its pages.[22] A similar Tuesday column in the *Lynn Daily Item*, called "The Critic's Comment," also began to cover the "striking features" in several downtown picture theaters, beginning in late January 1912.[23]

One of the more interesting of such columns was "At the Photo Plays," published weekly (and often more frequently) in the *Toledo News-Bee*. From the first column, in November 1911, the texts read as little more than ad copy for one or more downtown theaters, but soon they were including bits of local commentary, and, by January 1912, nearly every column was headed by at least one small graphic image illustrating a film currently featured in exhibition.[24] Although a few, like that for Gaumont's *Christian Martyrs,* were based on production stills, most, like that for Pathé's *Passion Play,* were quite simple in design; yet over the course of the year, exemplified by Éclair's *The Auto Bandits of Paris* or Gaumont's *Their Lives for Gold,* they also could be appropriately, if roughly, dynamic.[25] None of the previous columns considered films other than those shown at theaters providing ad revenues, so one of the first with local reviews ranging beyond such theaters appeared under the banner of "The Movies" in the *Des Moines News,* beginning in late November 1912. Still anonymous, as were most of the others, this reviewer covered neighborhood theaters such as University Place, as in this brief note on Pathé's *Wild Birds at Home:* "an instructive motion picture [that] can not be commented on too highly. The picture shows numerous kinds of wild fowl in the native haunts—how they live, eat, swim, feed their young, etc. The picture is so arranged and well shown that not a second's time while it is being shown, does it become dry."[26] Moreover, he (most likely) invoked moral judgment with ease in criticizing one program presented by the Golden, a small downtown theater:

> Unfortunately, for the attendants of the movies, especially children, Des Moines does not have a censor that can pass on every film.
> The three reels of the French film at the Golden depicting such things as all the agonies of a suicide, in fact, two suicides, unfaithful women, etc., would certainly come under the ban of a censor.[27]

Arguably the most important innovative format, well beyond that initiated by the *Chicago Tribune,* came from the *Cleveland Leader,* which combined columns of block ads, capsule reviews, industry information, local stories, and much more into the first Sunday newspaper page to treat moving pictures as its exclusive subject. In September 1911, the *Leader* began printing a Sunday page of special admission coupons for a "selected circuit of [dozens of] moving picture theaters . . . in Ohio and Pennsylvania," a promotional page that gradually included short pieces of "news" about "the moving picture world" (sometimes culled from the trade press), as well as synoptic reviews reprinted (with credit) from the *New York Morning Telegraph.* In early December, the paper dropped these coupons to institute a full page headlined "Photo-Plays and Players" devoted to "news of Cleveland's leading picture theaters," as well as its own "reviews of the feature films of the week."[28] The editor was Ralph Stoddard, a former theater manager in Sandusky, Ohio, now a *Leader* reporter, who also would edit one of the first weekly newspaper columns devoted to real estate and building construction. This "Photo-Plays and Players" page was supported by ads for twenty-five to thirty picture theaters (a quarter of the city's total number), several film rental exchanges and slide manufacturers or renters, and the manufacturers willing to provide production photos of their new films. In return for this support,

FIG. 51. "Photo-Plays and Players" logo, *Cleveland Leader* (10 December 1911), S5.

and as "a guide to fans," Stoddard printed a column listing, and often commenting on, the Sunday or even weekly programs shown in these theaters—in effect, encouraging readers to anticipate or plan their moviegoing in advance, at least for selected theaters located downtown or in one of a half dozen secondary commercial and entertainment districts.

Although Stoddard's Sunday page flourished for nearly six months, the *Leader* severely reduced the space devoted to moving pictures between May and October 1912, perhaps out of some uncertainty about whether moving pictures could sustain this kind of interest. Then, in November, the *Leader* resumed its full-page format and, during the holiday season, even experimented briefly with a separate "Theatergoers Section" that gave two pages to moving pictures and made them the equal of vaudeville and stage plays. Soon Stoddard also introduced several new columns. One singled out major figures in the city involved in film distribution and exhibition—men such as E. Mandelbaum, who had founded Lake Shore Film & Supply as well as Feature & Educational Films, became a stockholder in the Mutual Corporation, and eventually set up World Special Films; Sam Bullock, who had managed one of the first nickelodeons in the city and now owned a chain of picture theaters; or Samuel Morris, owner of the Home and president of the Cleveland League of Motion Picture Exhibitors. Another that ran for seven weeks, and was written by Stoddard himself, offered a short history of moving pictures entitled "Aladdin's Wonderful Lamp Eclipsed." For two years, the "Photo-Plays and Players" page shifted, arbitrarily it seemed, between one section of the Sunday edition and another: news, sports, metropolitan, women's, and even the want ads. In late November 1913, however, it finally found a secure position in the society section, either before or after the page devoted to drama. This probably was the clearest sign (other than its choice of "photoplay") that, at least for the *Leader,* audiences for moving pictures were indistinguishable from those for the legitimate theater, that moving pictures had become a reputable form of entertainment for even the upper levels of a newly emergent middle class: the educated, the professional, the social elite.

For some time, the *Cleveland Leader* may have been the only newspaper with such a special weekly page.[29] In March 1912, the *Boston American* began running a page in the "Editorial and Drama Section" of its Sunday edition, with short texts and graphic illustrations linked to specific films, but it lasted no more than three weeks.[30] Soon after the *Leader* reinstated its Sunday page in late 1912, several New York papers, according to the *Dramatic Mirror,* began accepting "illustrated articles on different phases" of moving pictures,[31] but it was in the upper Midwest, as W. Stephen Bush acknowledged, that other papers finally followed the *Leader*'s model. In February 1913, the *Des Moines Register and Leader* began offering a half page each Sunday to a column of "newsy" items, probably selected from the trade press.[32] Its initial banner, "At the Moving Picture Playhouses," soon was replaced by "News of the Photoplays and Players," whose terms were more in line with those of the *Leader.* A month later, the *Minneapolis Sunday Tribune* introduced a full page in its weekly "Society Section," headlined simply "Motion Pictures," which, much like the *Leader,* included short articles, production stills and other graphic illustrations, synoptic reviews, and columns of ads from the picture theaters and rental exchanges.[33] In May, the *Toledo Blade* began running a similar page of short articles, star photos, short reviews, and local ads, whose headline banner changed slightly from week to week.[34] For the first two months, it appeared in the Saturday edition, but in June it was shifted to Wednesday, perhaps so that some picture theaters could advertise their weekend programs in advance.[35] Not until early September 1913, apparently, did a major newspaper in the Northeast, the *Boston Journal,* institute a special page devoted to moving pictures, usually following its "Dramatic Page" in the Saturday edition.[36] Topped by a scrolling banner (with cowboys prominent among other figures), "News and Doings in the Motion Picture World" included long and short articles, production photos, star shots, and ads from rental exchanges and local theaters. Although advertising support initially may have been largely local, it soon devolved on the companies distributing feature-length films, such as Famous Players, Warner's Features, and World Special Films.

Another format that emerged in late 1911 probably came directly from the manufacturers, spurred by the sudden success of *Motion Picture Story Magazine,* whose monthly editions initially were full of fictional versions of MPPC films.[37] At the same time that it introduced its weekly moving picture column, in November 1911, the *Chicago Tribune* also began publishing "a Photo-Play in Story Form" each Sunday in its "Features" section.[38] This was an early version of the fictional tie-in—in this case, a one-page text based on a film about to be released by Essanay or Selig[39]—each one designed to instill in readers the desire to experience the same story at the movies. Shortly thereafter, American Film tried a similar strategy, on a less regular basis, but in more than sixty newspapers across the country.[40] For a brief period in early 1912, each Saturday the *Boston Evening Traveler* also printed a fictional tie-in from one of the MPPC companies as "The Traveler's Moving Picture Story."[41] None of these fictional tie-ins took hold until the *Chicago Tribune* and Selig teamed up, in late 1913, to publish each "chapter" of *The Adventures of Kath-*

FIG. 52. "News and Doings in the Motion Picture World" logo, *Boston Journal* (15 November 1913), 5.

lyn just as that week's serial episode was being distributed to picture theaters. The astounding popularity of that film—together with the "chapters" that circulated in dozens of other newspapers[42]—quickly led to similar fictional tie-ins for Pathé's *The Perils of Pauline* and Universal's *Lucille Love*. What is less well known is that it also prompted the *Cleveland Leader*, in early February 1914, to adopt a related strategy to directly reach the "60,000 to 80,000 [people who] attend a moving picture show each day" in the city—and thereby possibly raise its own circulation—by printing each morning "a complete new story of the best motion picture film" that would be "shown at the theaters the same afternoon and evening."[43] Within weeks, "Today's Best Moving Picture Stories" could offer readers as many as three or four stories per day, ranging from one-reel comedies to features, and from nearly every US manufacturer.[44] The format interested Famous Players and Pathé enough to briefly negotiate similar deals, respectively, with the *Boston Journal* and a half dozen Hearst newspapers.[45]

One final innovation also first appeared in late 1911, although it would not become regularized until a year later. This was the syndicated column that, much like the fictional tie-in, could be distributed to a large number of newspapers. Perhaps the first of these came from the Frederic J. Haskin newspaper syndicate of Washington, D.C., one of whose staff writers, Louis Brownlow, compiled a twelve-part series on various phases of the moving picture industry that, the *World* alleged, "was printed in forty newspapers of the first class" throughout the country.[46] In the *St. Paul Pioneer Press,* this series was signed by Haskin and ran on the editorial page for twelve straight days in the middle of October 1911.[47] The first two stories offered a historical sketch of the moving picture's development; the next three focused on how films are made and what kinds; another dealt with censorship; two more covered film distribution and exhibition; the tenth took up educational uses; the eleventh sketched moving pictures' "universal" reach (from Africa to China and Japan); and the last looked to the "future." This series was important not just for offering an early, relatively lengthy, United States–centered account of moving pictures as a new mass entertainment (with all the conventional ideological assumptions of the period firmly embraced) but primarily for being circulated to such a broad, general readership. Stoddard undoubtedly was influenced by the Haskin series in writing his own seven-part "history" several

"Oh, There's That Smiley, Golden-Haired Girl Again!"

Right here in the pages of The Daily News the editor is going to introduce YOU to that Golden-Haired Girl, and that Beautiful Child and that Athletic Young Hero, and that Gun-Toting Cowboy and scores more—all OLD FRIENDS OF YOURS!

Why, OF COURSE, we mean the MOVING PICTURE FOLKS you see each week in your favorite theater, the people you recognize again and again as the picture machine makes them act nightly before your eyes.

We're going to tell you all about them—what they are like personally, how they live, what they do between times. With us you will visit them in their native haunts, interview them, sketch them.

Some bright youngsters gave moving pictures an apt, vivid name, and is has spread all over the United States. He called them—

"THE MOVIES"

So The Daily News, recognizing "the movies" as the biggest, most popular amusement in the world, will tell you all about it from every angle. A member of our staff has been at work on the subject for weeks, traveling, investigating, interviewing—getting facts and pictures about this rival (in size) of the automobile industry, which nightly entertain 5,000,000 American people, gathered in 20,000 theaters. This writer, Miss Gertrude M. Price, has worked on the subject till she has become an expert—YOUR "MOVIE" EXPERT. She will keep at it, entertaining and posting you on this theater we all enjoy.

Read the first "movie" story in today's paper—and keep your eyes open right along for the appearance of YOUR FAVORITES.

FIG. 53. "The Movies," *Des Moines News* (11 November 1912), 2.

months later in the *Cleveland Leader.* Yet no other syndicated series or column appeared until November 1912, when the Scripps-McRae newspaper chain proclaimed that its "moving picture expert," Gertrude M. Price, would be entertaining readers with stories about the "MOVING PICTURE FOLKS" because "'the movies' [were] the biggest, most popular amusement in the world."[48]

The format and focus of the Scripps-McRae column arguably would have an impact greater than any developed previously. For one thing, by February 1913, Price was working in Los Angeles, writing from the "great California studios."[49] For another, she wrote almost exclusively about American actors in moving pictures, the personalities or "stars" that were attracting so much audience interest (the subject of chapter 6). Her brief texts also were marked by the colloquial language of everyday speech, as was her consistent use of the slang term "movies" rather than "photoplays," and they were illustrated with one or more halftone images (probably drawn from publicity photos) that usually emphasized actors' faces. Her stories or "personality sketches," along with others that were unsigned but followed the same format, appeared frequently, sometimes daily, and could be slipped into almost any page of a newspaper—occasionally, even on the front page. Moreover, they not only were distributed among the Scripps-McRae chain of newspapers in the Midwest but also were available to perhaps hundreds of others that subscribed to the United Press Association, which six years earlier had gathered the Scripps telegraphic services into a single nationwide entity.[50] Indeed, much like the movies themselves, Price's stories circulated as mass-culture commodities throughout the country, almost simultaneously, yet at the same time could be framed or tweaked for local consumption: an added line in the *Des Moines News,* for instance, read: "You have seen this actress at: The Colo-

Movies! the New Crop They Are Growing in the Land of Oranges
By Gertrude M. Price.

Los Angeles, Dec. 13.—I am out here in the West to "size up" the Western moving picture studios. But I don't know where to begin and I know I shall never finish! A conservative man tells me there are 73 companies between San Francisco and San Diego!

Be that as it may, Southern California is alive with picture players!

Directors who have been in the business a long time say this part of the country is the natural place in which to take pictures, because they can work about 360 days out of the year, and the sunlight is nearly always "on tap." In addition to that there is the sea, and there are the mountains within easy access.

"How do people like having a moving picture concern in their midst?" I asked the manager of a big concern down on the coast.

"How do they like it?" he answered: "Why they like it fine, and when they know anything is wanted for the movies, they just fall over themselves to be nice."

There are moving picture plants and ranches and studios dotted around all the way down the coast, I find.

Some of them have as many as 12 or 13 companies working on them.

GERTRUDE M. PRICE.

Others only have one or two. There are independents and so-called trust concerns working side by side, all taking advantage of the sunshine and the scenery.

The people in the towns in which moving pictures are made have all sorts of odd experiences.

For instance, while I was walking down the street in Santa Monica a day or two ago, a gypsy rushed out of a store with something concealed under his arm.

Two policemen jumped from behind a building nearby and gave chase. Somebody called "Thief!" And everyone in the block stopped to see what was the matter.

"Huh!" said a grizzled man to a young boy standing near. "Hope them police gets that feller."

"They sure will, mister," replied the boy. "'Cause you see them's 'movie' police."

Later in the day as I walked on the beach, I saw a great crowd out at the end of the pier. And upon looking closer, I could see a woman in the water, battling, as if life depended upon it, with the waves.

I started down the pier to find out all about it when I overheard a girl say, "There are those 'movie' actors drowning themselves again for a picture."

On the crowded streets of Los Angeles, in the exclusive residence sections of Pasadena, up in San Francisco, and down at San Diego, it is all the same. You never can tell when you are going to overtake, or be overtaken, by an auto load of made-up picture players going to the scene of action.

And if you are out in the country, as likely as not, you'll fall in with a regiment of bluecoats making a forced march, or run into the thick of a big battle scene.

The "movie" folks are privileged people in California and they seem to have given an added picturesqueness to the country.

FIG. 54. "Movies! The New Crop They Are Growing in the Land of Oranges," *St. Paul News* (14 December 1913), 3.

nial, The Lyric, The Family." Furthermore, with variations from newspaper to newspaper, they ran quite regularly throughout 1913 and well into 1914. For more than a year, then, Price probably was far more widely read, especially by moviegoers, than anyone in the trade press. The probable effects on moviegoing readers I will explore in the next chapter.

According to the trade press, in 1913 other syndicated services, perhaps emboldened by Scripps-McRae's "movie expert," may have begun supplying newspapers with material on moving pictures for special columns and/or pages. That spring, Arthur Leslie's syndicated service (in New York), for instance, boasted of plans to furnish "60 newspapers, weekly, with 'roasts' on films" that already had appeared in the trade press.[51] Although Leslie later claimed that he had "induced over a hundred of the more enterprising newspaper editors to allow him to inaugurate . . . the first motion picture page,"[52] his claim has yet to be verified and certainly ignores the Scripps-McRae precedent. Late that same year, the Syndicated Publishing Company also placed an ad in *Motion Picture News* depicting its service funneling information to scores of papers, but that too remains to be documented.[53] What is certain is that, although Price herself stopped writing stories in March 1914, the Scripps-McRae newspapers reintroduced what had been her column that summer, now signed by a "picture play reporter" named Esther Hoffmann.[54] Moreover, other women soon followed her pioneering lead as newspaper columnists and reviewers: from Mae Tinee (the pseudonym of Frances Peck) and Kitty Kelly at the *Chicago Tribune,* in March and July 1914, respectively, or Louella Parsons (a scenario editor in Essanay's Chicago office) at the *Chicago Herald,* in December 1914,[55] to cub reporter Dorothy Day, whose "News of the Movies" column first appeared in the *Des Moines Tribune* in the summer of 1915.[56] By then, of course, most companies had publicity departments that aimed to ease the work of all these columnists and reviewers: in the summer of 1914, for instance, Mutual claimed to be shipping "a weekly news sheet for 6,000 editors of daily and weekly newspapers to clip from, and a cut and matrix service to go with it."[57] And reports were beginning to appear that the principal readers of all this "moving picture news" (again, see chapter 6) were "women and girls."[58]

Not all press discourse contributed to standardizing the relationship between moving pictures and newspapers, of course, so it is worth glancing at certain bits and pieces of anomalous material that fall outside the patterns sketched up to this point—for that material can be revealing in its own right. Some of these bits and pieces demonstrate the unusual popularity that the movies had achieved by the early 1910s. There was the front-page contest sponsored by the *Toledo Blade,* in early 1911, with cash prizes for the best "dramatic reviews of moving picture shows."[59] There were countless comic strips, editorial cartoons, and stories that relied on readers' familiarity with a specific film or the general sense of film exhibition. In the Scripps-McRae papers, for instance, "Osgar and Adolf" parodied the conventions of historical films and westerns, as well as the dying scene in *Queen Elizabeth.*[60] In the *Cleveland Leader,* an uncredited writer contributed a scenario story, "The Triumph of the Movieman," divided into twelve short scenes and illustrated with cartoon figures of exhibitor Sam Morris at the projector and five current stars as main characters.[61] Others seem unexpectedly informative or oddly insistent on educating their readers. There was the lengthy story in the *Lynn Daily Item,* for instance, that not only named and reprinted photos of the projector operators at the five downtown picture theaters but also described in detail their equipment and the phases of their work.[62] And there was the unique series of full- and half-page stories in the *Canton News*'s Sunday magazine—with titles such as "How Moving Pictures Are Teaching the Bible" or "How Moving Pictures Teach Kindness, Sympathy, and Generosity"—which seemed to assume an uneasy middle-class readership that, even in early 1914, still needed to be persuaded that moving pictures not only were reputable but also could be useful.[63]

By 1914, moving picture news may have been "eagerly gobbled up by the [newspaper] reader who [was] interested in the movies," as the *World* claimed,[64] but the "trash twins" were still working at working in sync, cooking up ever more delectable (and mutually profitable) menus for continual consumption.

Document
"Moving Picture Sections," *Motography*
(5 April 1913), 219–20

Not long since we were accustomed to open our local newspapers with a sense of hostility and suspicion, scanning the editorial columns for innuendo or open attack against the industry. Today we see not merely favorable comment, not merely occasional short stories of the films, but whole Sunday pages, and even "Moving Picture Sections," installed as regular features of metropolitan dailies.

Casually viewed, this change of heart, or development of interest, seems but a national tribute to a constantly growing business and a recognition of the people's choice in entertainment. An investigation of the newspaper motive shows in many cases, however, an ulterior purpose. That purpose, naturally, is to secure advertising.

With the encouragement of example, several of the many bright minds engaged in trade publicity work have conceived the plan of establishing motion picture departments or press syndicates in connection with the big newspapers of the country. But to overtures in this direction the newspaper publishers have made as a rule, but one reply. "Show us the business," they say, "and we will give space to your department. But first we must be assured of so many dollars of advertising."

So some of the newspapers are running motion picture departments and getting a little advertising. A few bold spirits are even running their "sections" without any advertising. But, with a few exceptions, the newspaper's tendency is to demand payment in full, in advance, for its film exploiting.

Of course the newspaper publisher feels sure that the motion picture business is overflowing with easy money, that it appeals directly to his readers and that those readers ought to be worth something to the rich and open-handed film man. In this attitude he is just naturally and humanly selfish. He does not take into account the fact that all the films shown in the country are made by the same few manufacturers, while every other newspaper in the country has as much right to film advertising as his particular paper. The result, should *every* newspaper succeed in establishing a motion picture section with advertising accompaniment, is beyond imagination—and certainly beyond any possible commercial merit.

Let us take another view of the situation. Our national entertainment is motion pictures. Our national pastime is baseball. All the newspapers give unlimited space to baseball news and stories, and they do it without any advertising, because their readers demand it by buying the papers that print most about it.

The only reason people buy newspapers anyway is because the newspapers print what the people want to read. They want to read about local and national happenings, about their favorite sports, about entertainments. The newspapers already print the news and the sports; but they want pay for printing the entertainments. Is this attitude logical?

Exploitation in the newspapers is good for the motion picture trade in many ways. It helps it to permanent establishment, converts its enemies, reassures its doubters, confuses its reformers, spreads its popularity and helps to standardize its operations. But even that is no reason for demanding paid advertising from the manufacturer. The function of the newspaper is not to serve any particular coterie of business men, but to serve the public at large.

The newspaper publisher today demands tribute from the motion picture trade because he can do so without protest; in serving moving picture news to the public he has little or no direct competition.

But presently, in each community large enough to support two or more newspapers, one of them will see a way to gain friends and increase circulation by printing that same motion picture news on its merits, as baseball news is printed. When that happens, the competing papers must fall into line. And happen it will, before very long, from the very nature of the popular interest in the subject.

The legitimate advertising prospect for the local newspaper is the picture theater itself. We believe the exhibitor should advertise to his own local public—and he can do that only by patronizing the newspapers. Even in the big cities, where suburban theaters would be paying for much waste circulation if they advertised in the larger papers, small "neighborhood" weeklies are frequently found that afford splendid mediums. So much of a field has the newspaper in film advertising. But the national manufacturer the local paper cannot reasonably expect to get.

The M. P. Girl

I saw her first on Broadway,
    And then in Chinatown;
I've met her in the Bowery,
    Joking with a clown.
She has wintered in Alaska,
    And summered in Ceylon,
And one spring in Madagascar
    She played a game of "con."
I've seen her beating up a cop,
    I've seen her drive a car.
And when the engine did a flop
    She got an awful jar.
She once fell down a mountain side
    And landed on her head.
But when they picked her up and cried
    She was not even dead.
She'll run a boat or dance a jig.
    She'll sit and spoon all night.
She doesn't seem to care a fig
    About what's wrong or right.
She's married nearly fifty men,
    She's children by the score,
And yet she's only ten plus ten,
    And modest to the core.
    Ah, yes, I worship her shadow,
    And I spend all my money, although
    It's only in pictures I see her,
    On a film in the M. P. show.

HILSON MUNSEY,
New York Dramatic Mirror
(12 June 1912), 33

Chapter 6

"The Power of Personality in Pictures"

Movie Stars and "Matinee Girls"

In early 1913, moviegoers from Des Moines or St. Paul to Toledo, Cleveland, or Pittsburgh could have paused, reading their local Scripps-McRae newspaper, and looked more closely at a story signed by Gertrude Price and headlined "Stunning Mary Pickford." The story would have heartened those who agreed that Pickford had "probably the largest following among feminine moving picture players," would have amazed even those who did not know that the former "Biograph girl" was taking in a salary of $10,000 a year, and would have disheartened nearly all with the news that she was quitting the movies—yet not for good—to become a New York stage star in David Belasco's production of *The Good Little Devil*.[1] Had any of those moviegoers—especially my imagined young working women—had the opportunity, in January, to catch *The New York Hat,* the last film Pickford made with D. W. Griffith at Biograph before signing with David Belasco, they also might have collected a free postcard of the star at one of their local picture theaters showing licensed films.[2] Pickford, of course, was just one of many picture players whose frequent appearances on screen had become so appealing to movie fans. Indeed, the stars and the star system that was being put in place to support them arguably offered an alternative to the strategies guaranteeing audience satisfaction mapped in previous chapters—that is, manufacturers' or distributors' brand names, variations on recurring stories and situations (especially those of sensational melodramas), and, eventually, regularized special features. And this strategy arguably may have been the most significant of all for a rapidly expanding fan culture in creating and sustaining the ever-renewed desire to "go to the movies."

The general outlines of the star system's emergence in the early 1910s are familiar enough through the historical research and theoretical work of such scholars as Richard deCordova, Janet Staiger, Eileen Bowser, and Kathryn

Fuller Seeley.[3] Their studies have shown that, although the legitimate theater and vaudeville provided precedents for such a system, "picture personalities" were somewhat different from stage performers: as commodities, they served as a "viable means of product differentiation" across a series of films, certainly, but their singular bodies and faces also served as hermeneutic lures for fans to find out more and more about their favorites, as deCordova has written, continually accruing knowledge as well as renewing their pleasure from one film to another, from one week to the next.[4] As informative and insightful as their work has been, however, it has relied almost exclusively on a selective reading of the trade press as well as early fan magazines. What I propose here is to offer a more finely nuanced analysis of the nature and function of the star system, and those who were its fans, by extending the discourse on stars to include largely unexamined material in selected daily newspapers and by rereading some that may seem familiar in the trade press as well as the first fan magazine. Moreover, I want to reconsider that system in conjunction with the concept of *personality*, "both the unique qualities of an individual and the performing self that attracts others," a concept that circulated widely at the time and that, Warren Susman long ago suggested, "found brilliant expression" in the development of moving pictures after 1910.[5] Finally, my analysis also unfolds (as have previous chapters), at least in part, within the context of the Americanization process so characteristic of the period, for much of this discourse on movie stars introduces an intriguing spin on the contentious process of imagining a national identity.

Shaping the Star System:
The Fan Magazine and the Newspaper

Both deCordova and Bowser have sketched the initial phases of the industry's response to what *Moving Picture World* perceived, by 1909–10, as a growing demand by moviegoers for more information about their "favorite actors and actresses."[6] In late 1909, for instance, Kalem printed a group photo of its principal actors for exhibitors to display in their theater lobbies.[7] In March 1910, Laemmle launched an infamous publicity campaign to promote Florence Lawrence (formerly of Biograph) as the major star of IMP, his new production company.[8] This campaign included several "events"—from a faked news story of Lawrence's death in a traffic accident to her surprise visit to St. Louis—all reported in the *World* and the *St. Louis Post-Dispatch*. The latter event was particularly significant in that Lawrence was explicitly labeled a "film star" in an extensive series of articles in the *St. Louis Times*.[9] Advance stories prepared the paper's readers for the special two-day appearance of "the girl of a thousand faces"; thousands of fans greeted her with an ovation when she arrived by train on March 25 (the reception allegedly rivaled that for either Commander Peary or President Taft); and hundreds heard her speak at the Gem Theater, where she signed photographs for up to "500 women."[10] Over the next three-plus weeks, the *Times* printed a series of thirteen photographs of Lawrence in different film roles, as if to compensate admirers who failed to get one with her autograph.[11] Within weeks, Vitagraph mounted a similar promotion of its "Vitagraph Girl," Florence Turner, including the added attraction of a specially commissioned "waltz song" that Turner herself performed to "wild applause" at personal appearances in the New York City area.[12] Other companies soon followed suit—Kalem, with Gene Gauntier, its longtime "Kalem Girl" (and chief scenario writer); Reliance, with Marion Leonard (also a former Biograph player)[13]—and, in November 1910, Vitagraph modified this promotional scheme by sponsoring "Vitagraph Nights" (also in the New York City area), with another of its stars, Maurice Costello, making special personal appearances.[14]

Forced by moviegoers to circulate the names, still images, and even physical bodies of their most popular actors, manufacturers thus accepted, in Bowser's words, the "shift from brands to stars in the public mind" and gradually began to revamp their nascent publicity systems to better support and enhance the distribution and consumption of their product.[15] Vitagraph stars made more personal appearances. Seeing Turner at the small Park Row Theater in Manhattan, in October 1910, prompted Thomas Bedding, for instance, to congratulate himself on foreseeing the public curiosity about "the personalities—the corporeal personalities—of the good people who make those 'silver shadows' for our entertainment."[16] Five months later, "1,700 people turned out to meet Mr. Costello" at the Academy in Jersey City.[17] The company also now sold individual photographs of its stars to exhibitors for lobby displays.[18] If certain practices continued, others were introduced through the trade press or exhibition venues. On its Sunday page, beginning in late February 1911, the *New York Morning Telegraph* reproduced publicity photos of a half dozen stars each week, alternating between those supplied by MPPC and Independent companies.[19] The *World* briefly joined the trend, from December 1910 to February 1911, by publishing several columns of "Picture Personalities" that singled out Pickford, Costello, Pearl White, and Arthur Johnson.[20] As early as April 1911, *Film Index* reported, lantern slides (made by Scott & Van Altena and DeWitt C. Wheeler) of the licensed manufacturers' leading "photoplayers" allowed exhibitors to promote their "coming attractions" on screen.[21] By the end of the year, "beautiful lantern slides" as well as photographs of licensed "photo players" were widely available to exhibitors.[22] Moreover, even the *New York Dramatic Mirror* recognized the impact of such picture personalities by allowing a publicity photo of Pickford to grace one of its December front covers.[23]

It was also in early 1911 that *Motion Picture Story Magazine*, as several historians have noted, gave a big boost to the emergence of the star system.[24] Editor Eugene Brewster devoted most of the monthly's pages to prose ver-

FIG. 55. Mary Pickford, *New York Dramatic Mirror* front cover (6 December 1911).

sions of current licensed films, but he did offer readers full-page photographs of individual stars. Initially called "Personalities of the Picture Players," this front section quickly became the "Gallery of Picture Players" and expanded from a half dozen to a dozen pages.[25] That "personality" was the word chosen here and by the *World* ("star" was suggested by *Nickelodeon*)[26] to designate moving picture actors was telling. The term, Susman found in his research, was widely used in self-improvement manuals between 1900 and 1920 as a means of resolving the problem of how the individual could be distinguished from the *crowd* in modern society.[27] This new interest in *personality,* replacing the formerly dominant concept of *character,* stressed self-fulfillment and self-expression, especially through the notion of the performing self that also had developed in psychology.[28] In her textbook, *An Introduction to Psychology* (1902), according to Susan Glenn, Mary Whiton Calkins had asserted that "imitation of other selves [is] a richly personal experience . . . a conscious attempt to make oneself into this fascinating personality."[29] Whereas Calkins drew on theatrical metaphors, the self-improvement manuals often seemed to be alluding to the movies, Susman suggests, by associating a string of adjectives besides "fascinating" with personality: "*stunning, attractive, magnetic, glowing, masterful.*"[30] Yet, if movie stars embodied this modern performative model of personality in exemplary ways, they also, paradoxically, became larger-than-life figures of *authenticity* through what the *Dramatic Mirror* described as "the secret of intimate personal expression [conveyed] through the medium of the camera and the screen" (most specifically in close shots of the face),[31] as well as through the collectible images (also emphasizing the face) and texts circulated in such new monthlies as *Motion Picture Story Magazine.*[32]

Perhaps provoked by this mass magazine's success, more and more discursive material on picture personalities became accessible to moviegoers by late 1911 and early 1912. In August, *Motion Picture Story Magazine* itself initiated a new column, "Answers to Inquiries," from readers interested primarily in learning more about the stars.[33] In September 1911, *Photoplay Magazine,* a new monthly published in Chicago, began printing its own "Gallery of Picture Stars," drawn exclusively from the Independents.[34] That fall, Essanay sent exhibitors a "cut" of its leading actor-writer-director, G. M. Anderson, "together with a very interesting feature news story," and versions of that "novel advertising" ploy could be read in newspapers such as the *Youngstown Vindicator* and *Canton News-Democrat.*[35] When the *Cleveland Leader* launched its groundbreaking Sunday page devoted to moving pictures, Stoddard took care to placate fans with at least one photo story of a picture player each week: over the first six months, his choices ranged from those already mentioned (Pickford, Anderson, Costello, Gauntier, and Leonard) to Kathlyn Williams, Lillian Walker, and Alice Joyce. Just before Christmas, the *Leader* even played Santa Claus to its readers, filling one page of its Copperplate Pictorial Section with ten "Stationary Portraits of Moving Picture Stars" (all but one women).[36] Yet the most striking sign of this increase came in newspaper ads that exhibitors in certain cities designed to promote their programs. In September 1911, for instance, in Lynn the Comique one Sunday identified Joyce as appearing in one of its films, Kalem's *Branded Shoulder;* in

Youngstown, that same day, the Orpheum headlined Lawrence and Johnson in Lubin's *Divided Interests*. In December, in Toledo the Hart called attention to Pickford (and Owen Moore) in showing the first film she had made for Majestic, with the blatant title, *The Courting of Mary;* while in Cleveland, the Ezella highlighted its pair of Vitagraph stars, Turner and Costello, in *Auld Lang Syne*, and both the Cameraphone and the Cozy boasted of having John Bunny in a Vitagraph comedy. Several months later the Lowell Voyons advertised Pickford's appearance in *Iola's Promise* (her first film after returning to Biograph); the Youngstown Dome, Mary Fuller in a new Edison film; the Toledo Empress, Pickford in Biograph's *Mender of Nets;* and the Minneapolis Lyric, Bunny in yet another Vitagraph comedy.

In a growing number of cities, then, exhibitors were beginning to do more than simply circulate the names of their picture theaters or the brands of films they regularly offered each week in their variety programs. Instead, they were finding it more and more advantageous to use newspaper ads to exploit their audience's desires to see their favorite actors, as often as possible. These ads provide one means of gauging the popularity of various movie stars during this period, and two names appear more frequently than any other: John Bunny and G. M. Anderson. Bunny seems to have been a favorite among a broad range of people, from the steelworkers and their families at the Youngstown Dome to the "high-class" audiences at the Minneapolis Lyric. Anderson, by contrast, was especially popular in northern Ohio, where he was nicknamed "Bullets" rather than Broncho Billy, whether at the Orpheum or Dreamland in Cleveland, the Princess or Park in Youngstown, or the Orpheum in Canton.[37] Yet neither, intriguingly, placed in the first popular picture player contest, which the *Morning Telegraph* opened to its readers in September 1911.[38] A grand prize of a $200 diamond would go to the picture player who collected the most votes from moviegoers, apparently gathered by exhibitors and mailed to the newspaper. Moviegoers did more than simply vote, however, for over the course of several months, the *Morning Telegraph* received "many hundreds of letters . . . relative to the personality of motion picture artists in the contest."[39] The winner, announced in December 1911, was Florence Turner, "the charming leading lady of the Vitagraph Company," whose 233,509 votes far surpassed those cast for Thanhouser's Marguerite Snow (97,950), Majestic's Mary Pickford (64,007), Pathé's Octavia Handworth (44,853), Mabel Normand (34,049), and Selig's Kathlyn Williams (28,224).[40] By comparison, the most popular male actor, Maurice Costello, garnered only 12,065 votes.

A second popularity contest organized in January 1912 by *Motion Picture Story Magazine*, however, produced very different results.[41] Again, prizes were awarded to the most popular picture players, but they were more "honorific"; moreover, moviegoers could mail their votes directly, but subscribers could fill out a special coupon that counted as ten votes—although report-

edly few did.[42] Fans also were encouraged to write comments about their favorite stars, and each month the magazine printed several pages of examples, much of it in doggerel verse. The winner this time was "Dimples"
Costello, with 430,816 votes, followed by Essanay's Dolores Cassinelli
(333,898), Lubin's Mae Hotely (204,955), Essanay's Francis X. Bushman
(130,361), and G. M. Anderson (98,989).[43] Pickford and Handworth may
have been among the top dozen vote-getters, but Normand and Williams—
along with Bunny—barely reached the top fifty. *Motion Picture Story Magazine's* alignment with licensed manufacturers partly accounts for this dis-
crepancy between contests, but probably more important factors are
differences—in region, and especially in gender—in the population of read-
ers/spectators that cast votes. For, along with others of her sex, the "Photoplay Matinee Girl" that *Film Index* one year earlier had described as both "the
product [and] the producer of the present exploitation of the personality of
the picture player" may already have become a keen devotee of the monthly
magazine.[44] Although these two contests intensified fans' desire to learn
more about their favorite actors and possess their own images, it was *Motion
Picture Story Magazine* that made the most of the opportunity. In early 1912,
it introduced a "Chats with the Picture Players" section, with three or four
"personalities" the subject of casual interviews.[45] "Postcards of stars' photos"
may have been purchased as early as April 1911, according to Bowser,[46] but
manufacturers certainly were feeding fans' fascination by early 1912. Vitagraph offered "souvenir postal cards" (a dozen for only twenty-five cents) and
featured Costello in its ads after he won the *Motion Picture Story Magazine* contest.[47] Even the magazine itself exploited its readers' desires by selling a booklet collecting its "Gallery of Picture Players" (146 portraits in all) and then
offering its subscribers one color photo each month, beginning, of course,
with Costello.[48]

Strikingly absent from either of these contests, with one exception, were
any European movie stars. As demonstrated in *The Red Rooster Scare*, audience
preferences shifted, or were encouraged to shift, around 1909–10 from films
made in Europe (and especially France) to those made in the United States.
Few European moving picture actors had a following by the end of the nickelodeon period—the exception, Max Linder, was most known[49]—and after
1910 it was unusual for their names to appear in newspaper ads. In October
1910, for instance, in Lowell the Voyons was one of the last to advertise Linder in a Pathé comedy; in January 1912, in Cleveland the Fulton listed a Gaumont film, *Jimmie on Guard,* "introducing the famous boy actor" who earlier
had received rare photo promotions in *Motion Picture Story Magazine* and *Billboard,* but he remained unnamed.[50] Although her long career was coming to
a close, Sarah Bernhardt was still famous enough in the United States,
largely through her frequent tours as a stage performer, that exhibitors
everywhere could bank on her name to promote the few multiple-reel films

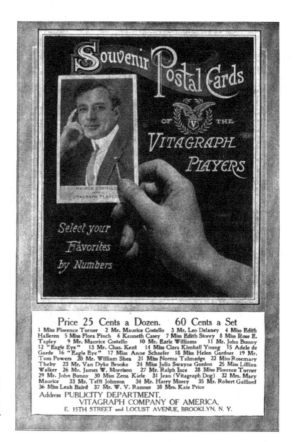

FIG. 56. Souvenir Postal Cards of Vitagraph Players, *Motion Picture Story Magazine* (June 1912), 159.

in which she agreed to perform in the early 1910s—notably *Camille* and *Queen Elizabeth* (see chapter 1). Yet, along with Réjane (*Mme Sans-Gêne* often came paired with *Camille*), she was the only French star to appear in moving picture ads in cities such as Lawrence and Lynn, which had significant French-Canadian immigrant populations.[51] One new European star momentarily did seem primed to break into the American market in 1912: Asta Nielsen.[52] In Toledo, in April, the Hart called her the "German Bernhardt" in one of her first imported "features," *Women Who Pay;* two months later the Empress called her the "Swedish Bernhardt" in another import, *Gypsy Blood.*[53] By the time, in late August, the Central Square in Lynn described the same film as "America's Film Sensation," Nielsen no longer needed such comparisons.[54] Yet she faded from public discourse by the end of the year, perhaps because only one small firm in Toledo seems to have distributed her films and even though, as late as October, the Toledo Empress boasted that it would be showing "all of the great Asta Nielsen features."[55]

By late 1912, then, the picture players to be admired and possibly emulated, even by "the foreigner" seeking insight into "the customs and habits of the country of his adoption,"[56] had to be no less American than anything else on the screen.

The "Moving Picture Expert,"
"Moving Picture Folk," and Their Audience

From late 1912 to early 1913 there occurred another surge in signs of the stars' significance to the industry and in the discursive material circulated directly or indirectly to moviegoers. While this surge paralleled and indeed helped to create conditions for the regular production and distribution of multiple-reel and feature-length films,[57] it served even more to shore up the variety program of single-reel films. One sign came in Cleveland, in a Victor Film Service ad that simply listed the "stars" featured in Universal programs.[58] Another appeared in the prestigious *New York Dramatic Mirror*. Readers found several of its covers, formerly reserved for stage actors and managers (with the exception of Pickford in late 1911), now graced by picture players. The first, "Helen Gardner as Cleopatra," came in late July, shortly after an ad for her forthcoming feature-length film ran on the magazine's back cover.[59] Others followed that fall after the *Mirror* acknowledged that the "motion picture star" was "attaining great popular distinction" and published lengthy interviews with Florence Lawrence, John Bunny, and Florence Turner.[60] Interestingly, the first stars may not have been familiar to most *Mirror* readers: Pauline Bush, best known as a western heroine for American Film, and Mary Fuller, who, though dressed in a leopard-skin coat and posed by a new sports car, was then starring in Edison's monthly series, *What Happened to Mary?*, serialized in *Ladies World*, the mail-order monthly most read by rural, small-town, and working-class women.[61]

Contests based on "picture personalities" continued to thrive. In August, the *New York Morning Telegraph* announced a contest to choose the most popular moving picture player of 1912.[62] Again, the prize, a $1,000 Christman & Sone grand studio piano, would go to the actor accruing the most votes from fans. The winner this time, however, was a surprise: Essanay's Martha Russell (208,748 votes), followed by Vitagraph's Lillian Walker (141,724), Thanhouser's Florence La Badie (114,882), Edison's Mary Fuller (60,858), Reliance's Gertrude Robinson (35,422), and Selig's Kathlyn Williams (31,538).[63] Regional differences played a role in the voting, the newspaper claimed, with the majority of votes for Russell coming from "the South, Southwest, and West," whereas those for Walker and La Badie came primarily from "the Eastern and Midwestern states." Yet, as before, most voters probably were men: the top male actor, Lubin's Edwin August, placed eleventh; Costello was nineteenth; and Anderson, twenty-second.[64] In September, *Mo-*

tion Picture Story Magazine created a "Prize Puzzle Contest" that required contestants to be unusually familiar with movie actors' names.[65] Their task was to fill fifty-seven spaces left blank in a brief history story, somewhat ironically titled "A Tale of the First French Settlers," each one with the different "name of a Photoplayer." As an added incentive, the prizes would be awarded to the fans who chose "the largest number of names correctly": five dollars in gold, a leather-bound volume of the magazine's *Popular Player Portraits,* subscriptions to *Motion Picture Story Magazine.* From the list of winning contestants, one can deduce something about the magazine's readership and perhaps about movie fans in general. Most lived in the Northeast, the mid-Atlantic states, and the upper Midwest, but a few came from elsewhere—Florida, Tennessee, Mississippi, Washington, California. Moreover, just as in the *Toledo Blade*'s earlier criticism contest, the majority were young, unmarried women.[66] Prompted by these contests, more local ones also began to appear. In February 1913, for instance, five theaters in Des Moines banded together, asking contestants to identify the images of five stars seen regularly on their screens—here, too, the winners were dispersed across the city, and the majority were women.[67]

Although the *Dramatic Mirror* and *Motion Picture Story Magazine* continued to interview actors (the former restricted itself to the bigger stars), and the latter answered more and more queries about them and kept printing fans' adulatory doggerel, signs of the public fascination with "picture personalities" cropped up in other venues as well.[68] In October 1912, *Motography*'s associate editor, Mabel Condon, rather belatedly launched an interview column entitled "Sans Grease Paint and Wig" that first featured American's Warren J. Kerrigan and then went on to include Essanay's Beverly Bayne, Selig's Adrienne Kroell, Broncho Billy "in Real Life," and American's Louise Lester.[69] In April 1913, the column turned into a one-page "gallery of [four] picture players," with short takes on the likes of Bunny, Normand, Mack Sennett, Ford Sterling, and Anna Little.[70] In August, *Photoplay Magazine* finally began to interview actors, beginning with Pickford, just as she was returning to the movies as a "famous player."[71] More directly targeting audiences, some exhibitors expanded their local ads to include the cast lists for selected films on their programs. As early as 1911, manufacturers such as Edison had begun providing "full cast lists in the advertisements for every film" and even attaching credit titles to certain films; by August 1912, *Motion Picture Story Magazine* also was listing the characters' and actors' names at the beginning of certain "Photoplay Stories."[72] In April and May 1912, two theaters in Canton, the Orpheum and the Odeon, experimented with this practice on a limited basis, printing the actors' names for a few Edison, Selig, and Vitagraph films in their regular ads.[73] By October, Odeon ads frequently were giving the cast lists for at least one or two MPPC films.[74] In late December, the Odeon's manager, A. H. Abrams, even advertised the cast lists for all six films on his

FIG. 57. "Name the Star" contest, *Des Moines News* (10 February 1913), 3.

Christmas holiday program.[75] Finally, at least according to one firm closely linked with licensed and Independent companies, exhibitors could purchase "postcards of popular photoplayers" so cheaply that they now could be "given away free" to patrons.[76]

Arguably, the most important star discourse introduced in late 1912, however, came in the syndicated stories or "personality sketches" written by Gertrude Price, the "moving picture expert" for Scripps-McRae newspapers. Although these stories can be found in dozens of papers, those circulated in the *Des Moines News* were especially numerous—accordingly, they will be a prime source for the analysis that follows. As pointed out in entr'acte 5, Price wrote exclusively about American picture personalities or stars (illustrated by halftone sketches), and her stories were far more available to moviegoers than anything that exhibitors passed on from the manufacturers or trade press and probably even more than what *Motion Picture Story Magazine* was circulating.[77] The personalities that Price wrote about, beginning in November 1912, first were associated with the licensed manufacturers—early examples ranged from Costello and Bunny to Fuller and Cassinelli—but gradually she added those working for the Independent companies—from IMP's King Baggot to Keystone's comedienne Mabel Normand.[78] There are several striking patterns in her choice of stars. One is the frequency of child actors, from Helen Armstrong, the tiny "starlet of the 'Flying A,'" or Baby Lillian Wade of Selig's "wild animal pictures" to Judson Melford, a "natural . . . clever picture-player" who just happened to be the son of one of Kalem's chief filmmakers.[79] In fact, not only did Price write more than a dozen stories on child actors in the movies, but she also seems to have signed several pieces as "Aunt Gertie," most notably a story about Thomas A. Edison, "who invented the phonograph, and the electric light, and the moving picture, too."[80] Using the pseudonym of Aunt Gertie, from May through July 1913, she composed a series of condensed fairy tales for children, from "Snow White" to "The Little Mermaid."[81] And she even contributed a story on five-year-old Princess Ileana of Romania, in which children were asked to imagine a real princess sitting right beside them in a movie theater.[82]

Another pattern, however, is much more prominent. At least one out of four or five actors or stars is described as acting in westerns, and the illustrations support this by having men and women like Edwin August (now Powers), Warren J. Kerrigan (American), or Jack Richardson and Pauline Garfield Bush (also American) decked out in cowboy hats and others like Red Wing (Pathé American) or Mona Darkfeather (Universal) in full Indian costume.[83] Price's texts also underscore that emphasis, as in her description of Kalem's Ruth Roland as "an athletic girl" who "runs, rides, and rows with all the freedom and agility of a boy"—for instance, in one of her "riding pictures," *The Girl Deputy*.[84] Now Des Moines picture theaters, unlike those in other cities (including those with Scripps-McRae papers), did not heavily promote westerns. Essanay's Anderson, for instance, whether called "Bullets" or Broncho Billy, was rarely advertised as a headliner in the city. The multiple-reel westerns of Kay-Bee, Broncho, and Universal-Bison occasionally were celebrated, but not as frequently or intensely as they were in cities such as Toledo, Cleveland, or elsewhere. Price's many stories suggest, then, especially coming after several "Flying A" stories were published in the *News* in early 1912,[85] that she was not alone in her fascination with cowboy, cowboy girl, and Indian figures and that indeed there was a substantial audience for westerns in the city—or an audience that her stories at least fostered. In

FIG. 58. Pauline Bush, *Motion Picture Story Magazine* (March 1913), 5.

late 1913, she even wrote an exclusive series of nine stories on location about Buffalo Bill Cody's epic reenactment of several battles in the Indian wars of 1876 to 1891, produced by Essanay with US government support.[86] This series is a rare record of what then became *Indian Wars Pictures,* which was shown privately to government officials and clubs, beginning in January 1914, but whose several versions never were widely distributed or exhibited.[87]

Most striking, however, are the number of stories, at least two-thirds of the total by my count, devoted to women. As might be expected, still familiar stars turn up—from Pickford and Williams to Joyce and White—but most now are forgotten, and several, such as Pauline Bush, appear more than once.[88] Among them one can count the "regal-looking Miriam Nesbitt," who, supposedly "bored by the world," turned to the movies and "likes rough and ready parts."[89] Or Jesslyn Von Trump, "a capital rider" at American, who "likes herself in a cowgirl costume very much, indeed."[90] Or that "tall woman of the picture players," Anne Schaefer, who is said to enjoy playing lead roles and character parts for Vitagraph's western unit.[91] Or "dainty, daring" Clara Williams, Lubin's "leading lady," "who can beat the boys at anything on a horse."[92] Or Leona Hutton, who finds that "being 'almost killed' 365 days in the year is only a hum drum regularity" in her busy life at Kay-Bee.[93] For the most part, the women Price writes about are young, active, and independent—celebrated as skilled horsewomen and fearless "daredevils," often seen in westerns and adventure films. In fact, some are not unlike the champion cowgirl riders and sharpshooters, such as Bessie Herberg and Lucille Parr, prominently promoted in performances of the 101 Ranch Wild West that toured the country to great acclaim at the time.[94] Moreover, complementing these women are others who had become successful filmmakers and/or scenario writers in the industry: Nell Shipman; Lois Weber, who recently had joined Universal after several years at Rex and Reliance; and the earliest female filmmaker Alice Guy Blaché, who had made all of Gaumont's films in Paris between 1896 and 1906 and now was head of Solax, her own production company in New Jersey.[95]

The general readership of Scripps-McRae newspapers, according to Gerald Baldasty's research, suggests that Price's extensive "gallery of picture players" may well have assumed a particular targeted audience.[96] In a 1906 letter to Robert Paine, the nationwide editor of his chains, E. W. Scripps himself (sounding a bit like Charles Foster Kane) described his "string of small, cheap, working-class newspapers" as "friends, advisors, and even special pleaders of the ninety-five percent of the population that were not rich or powerful."[97] Indeed, most of the papers that Scripps bought or started up after 1900 pledged allegiance to the "common people," promising to act as the "organ, the mouthpiece, the apologist, the defender and the advocate of the wage earning class."[98] This pledge extended to giving substantial coverage to labor issues and strongly supporting organized labor.[99] Like many others, the Scripps papers also paid special attention to women readers: as Paine once wrote, "The woman in a house who swears by a paper is worth five men who buy it on the street."[100] But the Scripps-McRae papers were different, Baldasty argues, in "making a particular effort at providing content of interest to working-class women."[101] That content ranged from weekly short stories and editorial cartoons to articles on how to run a household on a limited income or on how many women now worked outside the home.

In the specific case of Des Moines, the News had a "large clientele among . . . workingmen," at least according to a 1911 history of the city, and was "a vigorous supporter of labor interests."[102] In articles published as early as 1907, the News also gave unusual attention to women (presumably also their readers) with blue-collar, white-collar, and even professional jobs in the city.[103] It was this clientele of working men and women that most likely was the principal audience for moving pictures in Des Moines in the early 1910s. From the fall of 1911 on, for instance, moving picture theaters such as the Colonial, Family, and Elite began to place ads on a regular basis in the evening News rather than in its rivals, the jointly owned, more business-

oriented morning *Register and Leader* and evening *Tribune*. Only in February
1913 did the *Register* establish its own Sunday column devoted to moving pictures, and the nomenclature it used assumed an audience of moviegoers
quite different from that in the *News*. Initially called "At the Moving Picture
Playhouses," the column soon became "News of Photoplays and Photoplayers"—yet it, too, could not ignore its readers' desire for publicity photos of
the stars.[104] In its choice of words, the *Register* was following the trade press,
writing manuals, and other papers like the *Cleveland Leader,* in using the
newly coined "photoplays," that cast moving pictures as a legitimate form of
art, with educational effects, in order to build a middle-class audience.[105] The
News—and Price herself—opted instead for "movies," a term often linked al-
literatively with "menace" by others,[106] but which was familiar to them as the
popular slang spoken by most moviegoers.

So what can be said further about the movie fans who may have doted on
Price's syndicated stories about American movie stars? Certainly the texts
(and their elaborated, punchy titles) and the images of all these female stars,
in or out of westerns, could have appealed to men reading the *News*. One
cannot ignore that. And those devoted to child stars could have targeted
"*Daily News* youngsters," encouraging them to go see the latest movie starring, for instance, "The Thanhouser Kid."[107] Yet they also invited the consent
of mothers, in that they describe moviemaking as a kind of "family affair" and
promote moviegoing as a safe, acceptable, as well as enjoyable experience.
Recall the late 1913 Mutual ad, in St. Paul, that explicitly elicits such mater-
nal consent. Moreover, at least one story about Adrienne Kroell toyed with
the conventions of romance, addressing "girls, girls, Des Moines girls—
how'd you like to have the reputation of being the 'most engaged girl' living?"[108] But, overall, the stories seem to target other kinds of women. After
all, most of the movie stars Price promotes are described as athletic young
women, carefree but committed to their work, frank and fearless in the face
of physical risk. Strikingly, nearly all are unattached, and without children.
In short, they seem to have the "freedom" assumed as "natural" for young
men. How desirable all this must have been for the young unmarried working women who formed a significant part of the core readership of Scripps-
McRae newspapers as well as an emerging fan culture, perhaps especially
those in white-collar or even professional jobs in the growing service industries of Des Moines and other cities. For them, the desire to "go to the movies"
would have been double: not only did the film roles that women played function as projective sites of fantasy adventure for spectators (that lashed read-
ing/viewing/consuming into a pleasurable activity) but, as a new kind of active, attractive worker or even professional, the stars—and even Price herself,
whose newspaper work had an uncanny parallel to that of Mary Fuller in yet
another Edison series, *Dollie of the Dailies*[109]—served as successful role models to emulate. Indeed, although never named as such, most arguably could

FIG. 59. Mary Pickford, *Motion Picture Story Magazine* (April 1913), 9.

be read as popular, influential figures of a specifically American New Woman.[110]

The political stance of the *News* as well as that of Price herself provide a further perspective on the continual parade of all these "picture personalities." As a strong advocate of women's suffrage, another characteristic of Scripps-McRae papers, the *News* had printed stories about special screenings of suffragette films such as *Votes for Women* at the Unique Theater in June 1912.[111] Furthermore, not only did it give front-page coverage to the famous suffragette march on Washington in early 1913; Price also apparently joined the march to interview one of its leaders.[112] In writing about actors such as Pauline Bush, then, the following admiring remark was hardly surprising: that, much like herself, she was "an ardent suffraget."[113] Indeed, Price acknowledged women in the industry as political figures, promoting the early 1914 election of several to public office in the newly incorporated Universal

City near Los Angeles.[114] Moreover, in one of her last signed stories, on 30 March 1914, she explicitly described the "wonderful field which the moving picture has opened" as a "great new field for women folk"[115]—from stars and lesser actors to writers and filmmakers—where a woman's "originality . . . her perseverance and her brains are coming to be recognized on the same plane as [a] man's." Here, they might explore what "the *new woman* means," as feminist anthropologist Elsie Clews Parsons put it in 1916: that is, "the woman not yet classified, perhaps not classifiable, the woman *new* not only to men, but to herself."[116] Consequently, in circulating, weekly and sometimes even daily for more than a year, a series of influential "new women" for female fans of the movies—perhaps especially those "photoplay matinee girls"—Price's syndicated stories take on special significance for the ways they interconnect movies, working women of different classes, and the suffragette movement.

Parallel, yet Diverging Legacies

The extensive circulation of star discourse in *Motion Picture Story Magazine* and Scripps-McRae newspapers together worked to strengthen a number of national, regional, and local practices promoting moving pictures: personal appearances at theaters, rather anxious discussions in the trade press, and more and more popularity contests. Francis X. Bushman, for instance, made a much-publicized tour in early 1913, "packing them in at the Victoria" in Rochester, delighting crowds during "a sensational run in Pittsburgh theaters," and giving "an entertaining lecture . . . on the manufacture of motion pictures," as well as speaking his lines on stage while several of his films were shown during three evenings at the Cameraphone in Cleveland.[117] An especially telling instance of "star power" during this period can be found in the accounts book of the Pawtucket Star. In late May, when the Thanhouser Kid appeared one Friday, the theater's receipts suddenly jumped to more than triple the usual amount for that day—and the highest of the week.[118] Reporting on "the power of personality in pictures" and the public's "natural desire . . . to see the object in the flesh," the *Dramatic Mirror* initially warned that the "illusion [so] valuable [for telling a story] on the screen" could be undermined by "too great a familiarity" with the players; yet by early 1914 it seemed willing to accept the fact that "the player's personality" had become "one of the manufacturer's strongest advertising points and even more directly—the exhibitor's."[119]

Contests demanding knowledge of the picture players proliferated. In December 1912, even the *Cleveland Leader* began running a weekly contest asking moviegoers to identify the photos of a half dozen or more actors and the theater where each one's current film was appearing; for prizes, there were "200 books containing six admission tickets good for any league theater in the city."[120] By January, the *Leader* reported receiving 3,000 entries, and for the next month the contest also asked participants to name the film titles and their manufacturers of four reproduced scenes.[121] In the first half of 1913, *Photoplay Magazine* sponsored its own "popularity contest," won by Kerrigan (195,550 votes), followed by Thanhouser's Marguerite Snow (189,391) and James Cruze (165,291), Baggot (158,475), and Lawrence (136,645).[122] At the same time, *Motion Picture Story Magazine* held yet another "Popular Player Contest" for an alleged half-million subscribers and "at least a million" readers.[123] Although the magazine admitted that a majority of those voting were women, the declared winner still was something of a surprise: Romaine Fielding (with 1,311,018 votes), who often starred as a psychologically scarred character and/or a Mexican American hero in Lubin westerns, followed by Vitagraph's Earle Williams (739,895), Kerrigan (531,966), and Joyce (462,380).[124] *Ladies World* soon came up with an intriguing variation on this phenomenon, a "Hero Contest," by publishing a Louis Tracy story in serial form, from January through May 1914, and inviting readers to vote on which of seven actors would be best suited to play the lead character.[125] After an extensive promotion—lantern slides were distributed to thousands of exhibitors, and "three-colored cards telling the story" and containing all seven actors' photos were circulated on New York subway cars—Bushman won the role with 1,806,630 votes, followed by Kerrigan (1,262,740), Costello (1,088,400), and Pathé's Crane Wilbur (575,650).[126] Finally, in April 1914, the *St. Louis Times* began conducting a "Favorite Player" contest, in which each week's winner had his or her photo printed in the Tuesday issue.[127] After ten weeks of balloting, readers then got to decide which of the ten winners—several of whom had once lived in the city (Baggot, Anne Schaefer, Lubin's Rosemary Theby, and Vitagraph's Naomi Childers)—would be voted the area's "most popular moving picture player."[128]

One particular legacy of Price's syndicated stories, however, is the trajectory that can be traced between so many of her subjects, the women who were such active heroines in a variety of sensational melodramas, and the slightly later "serial queens." With a good deal of insight, Jennifer Bean has argued that one of the industry's more successful ploys during this period was "to shift [public] attention along the axis of production from the mechanical base and financial backers of film to the people who enacted real-life situations," giving "a name and a face to spectacle."[129] And the players' bodies' so often put at risk in "real-life" physical "stunts" were as likely to be female as male. The trade press certainly exploited this risk, and sometimes exaggerated it, in order to satisfy as well as fuel fans' curiosity. In June 1911, *Film Index* recounted the bloody injuries that Kathlyn Williams suffered—as well as "the nerve and grit" she displayed—in making Selig's *Lost in the Jungle,* when a leopard pounced "on her head and shoulders full weight."[130] Six months later, both the *World* and the *Mirror* reported that, despite breaking an ankle during the filming of a runaway stagecoach in Essanay's *Broncho Billy's Christmas Dinner,* Edna Fisher "continued acting during three subse-

FIG. 60. "Miss Billie Unafraid," *Des Moines News* (17 November 1912), 7.

quent scenes without revealing the extent of her injuries."[131] In April 1912, Louis Reeves Harrison had to praise Anna Little in Bison-101's *The Crisis:* "a corking rider, full of vim in action," who "sweeps on the screen like a whirlwind."[132] Price's countless stories of athletic young female "daredevils" simply extended and even celebrated the spectacle of thrilling risks and dangers to women's bodies that occurred in filmmaking, and several of the "personalities" she singled out—Kathlyn Williams, Ruth Roland, Alice Joyce—would become even more renowned as serial queens or, in the case of Joyce, as a "series queen."[133] Although her analysis focuses on such later figures, Bean's conclusion neatly fits Price's subjects: they repeatedly experience the threat of accident and disaster, "but, more importantly, [they] survive and, better yet, thrive on it."[134] Constantly coping with catastrophe and performing spectacular feats, most of Price's movie stars make over the American New Woman as "an exceptional subject of modernity."[135]

A second, rather different legacy stems much more from *Motion Picture Story Magazine* and a shift in the Scripps-McRae syndicated column that occurred in 1914. Just as she suddenly appeared as a "Moving Picture Expert" in late 1912, so too did Price suddenly disappear in the spring of 1914. Unsigned stories about the movies continued to circulate in Scripps-McRae newspapers for several months, and in late July the syndicated column returned, now signed by "picture play reporter," Esther Hoffmann.[136] So little is known about Price, or Hoffmann, that it is difficult to explain this shift in personnel. Price may well have used her "movie reporting" as a means to make her way as a professional newspaperwoman,[137] but she also may have lost interest in the new amusement industry. Whatever the case, her writings and those of her successor point to significant changes that may have determined her options. For one thing, Price displayed a noticeable lack of attention to feature films; by contrast, her persistent fascination with westerns, especially one- and two-reelers, or with relatively minor stars, also in one- and two-reelers, may have seemed passé by 1914.[138] For another, Scripps-McRae papers seemed to undergo a general shift in coverage, as if targeting a different readership—perhaps as women, even working women, increasingly were delinked from suffrage (after the failed 1913 campaign) and aligned ever more firmly with consumption and domestication (hence, kept "in place")—and Price's interests may have become less and less in sync with those of her employers. Moreover, although Hoffmann continued her predecessor's practice of writing stories about movie stars, she wrote less frequently and focused on far less active female figures, such as "little Marguerite Courtot" and Lillian Gish, the "most beautiful blonde in the world."[139] Perhaps most tellingly, her stories, unlike Price's and more like those in the *Cleveland Leader*, now consistently appeared on a relatively new "Society" page "For Women."

Perhaps most revealing, in terms of this second legacy, were the myriad ways in which female picture personalities in particular were becoming more and more associated with fashion, proper behavior, and all "the good things in life." An explicit instance of this appeared, in December 1913, when Mutual announced its *Our Mutual Girl* series not only in the trade press but also in the New York dailies and the *Saturday Evening Post*.[140] Initially starring Norma Phillips (Reliance), and later Carolyn Wells, the series whisked a simple young country girl into the New York City home of a wealthy aunt, who showed her "the most prominent people," "the greatest showplaces," and "the smartest shops," in order to turn her into "a society belle." In short, *Our Mutual Girl* was "a fashion subject" that allowed moviegoers, most likely young women (among them, imagination conjures the figure of my grandmother), to share the actor's good fortune in touring the metropolis.[141] The industry would later use this "fashion interest" to target the largely female audience for serials and series, as Ben Singer has shown,[142] but an even earlier syndicated column in Scripps-McRae papers would tightly knot the growing relationship between movie stars and moviegoers around the subject of beauty, "pantomime and personality." In April 1913, Price had described Essanay's multitalented Beverly Bayne as a "clever horsewoman";[143] by July 1914, however, the "Beautiful, Graceful Beverly Bayne, Society Actress of the

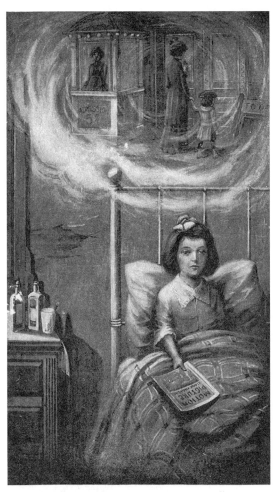

"ABSENCE MAKETH THE HEART GROW FONDER"

FIG. 61. "Absence Maketh
the Heart Grow Fonder,"
Motion Picture Story Maga-
zine (February 1914), 112.

Movies," was contributing a series of articles, cowritten with Idah M'Glone
Gibson, on feminine appearance and behavior.[144] Previously, this kind of column had been owned exclusively by stage performers, from Lillian Russell
to Billie Burke or (briefly) even Sarah Bernhardt.[145] Now, signaling a significant cultural shift, even "the most popular movie heroine," in the words of
Francis X. Bushman, could speak as the authority on such matters.[146] And
what should Bayne's initial pieces focus on but how young women could develop "a pleasing personality" through the "practice [of] pantomime," because "personality beats lotions"?[147] And how would they do that? "Watch the

girls on the 'movie' screen."[148] All too soon *Motion Picture Story Magazine* would confirm this shift by posing former "daredevils" like Joyce and Normand as prime illustrations of "Dame Fashion and the Movies."[149]

In June 1914, a *Moving Picture World* correspondent in Washington described "the moving picture news" now appearing so frequently in the city's daily newspapers as confined within the realm of the "feminine," whose most avid readers were "mother and the girls."[150] If one can accept the "evidence" of *Motion Picture Story Magazine*'s contests and inquiries, the syndicated stories in Scripps-McRae newspapers, as well as the "great mass [of letters] from children and women" then being written to Mary Pickford—now "America's Sweetheart"[151]—the consistent object of their gaze and spectacle of their fascination was the "picture personality."

Document
"Personality a Force in Pictures," *New York Dramatic Mirror* (15 January 1913), 44

Names appear under the pictures on these pages, but if the names were missing, if the faces were left to identify themselves, how many *Mirror* readers would be able to point to each one of the pictures and say, "that is So-and-So"? For most of those who read this it would be a simple matter. The faces are as familiar as those of old friends and as welcome. The players shown here prove the power of personality in pictures: their appearances are awaited by thousands of people, and the companies to which they belong have few stronger assets than their services.

The secret of intimate personal expression through the medium of the camera and the screen is elusive. A pleasing face is not in itself sufficient, nor can an individuality be made distinct by means of conventional gestures and facial expressions. The players selected to appear on this page have distinctive personalities that they have learned to express in distinctive ways.*

When Florence Turner plays a part she makes it sympathetic because everything she does is in harmony with the figure on the screen. She behaves as she would if actually experiencing the emotions of the character interpreted. Her facial expressions and her movements combine to create a human being with whom one may sympathize, and the audience does not stop to separate the actress from the part she is playing. It is Florence Turner under a different name, perhaps, and in new surroundings, but always the

---

* The players selected to accompany this article were Gene Gauntier (Feature Players), August Carney (Essanay), John Bunny (Vitagraph), Kathlyn Williams (Selig), Jane Fearnley (IMP), Edwin August (Powers), Lottie Briscoe (Lubin), Ormi Hawley (Lubin), G. M. Anderson (Essanay), and Alice Joyce (Kalem).

emotions are expressed in terms natural to the medium of their expression. Gradually the spectator comes to know such a player as he knows a friend and the more complete the acquaintance, the more thorough the enjoyment to be gained from a film performance. Fleeting facial expressions that might indicate little at first, gain in meaning as features become familiar, until we can guess at thoughts without the need of words to express them.

In a way it is like a sign language in which the more obvious meanings are common property. Any actor can indicate mirth, or anger, or fear, or despondency, but to suggest the finer shades of such emotions requires an ability to feel what is to be expressed, a power of expression on the part of the player and then the comprehension of the spectator, born of familiarity with the actor.

The players we have chosen as striking examples of effective personality in pictures are not imitative and generally their success has been due to an unusual personality expressed by strikingly individual methods. A substitute may work along the same lines and do it cleverly, but the result will not be the same because the method is acquired, rather than natural, and that indefinable harmony of personality and action is lacking.

Consider John Bunny, for instance. A scenario writer would have a difficult time in devising a scenario out of which he could not get a laugh. Mr. Bunny is a comedian through and through. He has a keen sense of humor and a genial way of expressing it that makes a Bunny picture a certain treat, even if there is nothing exceptional about the story. He has become such a familiar figure on the screen that he cannot enter a popular restaurant in any of the larger cities of the United States without hearing whispered comments, "There goes Bunny." But it is a mistaken notion to believe, as many people appear to, that his effects are gained solely by reason of an oddly humorous face, and without the display of an art that makes the most of his natural gifts. Mr. Bunny certainly has an exceptional personality, but equally he is an artist who takes his work seriously, and so do all the others whose names are of as much value as the trade mark of the company for which they work.

Augustus Carney, or Alkali Ike, as he is called, has created a cowboy type that has inspired imitators, but the character remains firmly identified with its originator. Like John Bunny, Alkali Ike is recognized wherever he goes and his appearance in pictures is awaited with eagerness by admirers of Western comedy films at their best.

The list of those whose personalities have become an important feature of current pictures might be continued at length, but we are going to let readers supply the names of their missing favorites. The star system may be abused and overworked in pictures, just as it sometimes is abused and overworked on the stage, but thus far its influence has been beneficial rather than harmful. The players whose pictures appear on these pages have honestly won the popularity that is theirs, and there are others whose likenesses would be included if space permitted.

And along this line it would be interesting to know to what extent an interest in individual players is responsible for the frequent attendance of patrons at motion picture houses. Judging from the number of letters of a personal nature received by the Mirror, it must be great. It seems that many people are more concerned about the figures they see on the screen than the connected series of incidents they are engaged in relating. If some of these enthusiasts stopped to ask themselves whether they were more entertained by a good photoplay acted by strangers or a mediocre one in which some favorite appeared, there is a good chance that the verdict would be in favor of the popular player. That may not be an altogether healthy condition, but it is one that exists and must be recognized by the men who produce pictures.

Document
Gertrude Price, "'Miss Billie Unafraid'—Torn by a Tiger
but Nervy as Ever to Act the Most Daring Things Ever
Seen on the Stage!—Heroine of Movies," *Des Moines
News* (17 November 1912), 7

Earth, sea or sky have no terrors for Kathlyn Williams, the beautiful star of the Selig photo players, whose pet ambition is to be the first successful woman hydroaeroplane operator in the world.

One look at her fearless face is a good omen of the fulfillment of her plan. "Billie" or "Unafraid," as her friends call her, has run the gamut of moving picture sensations all the way from flying machines to acting in a cage where there were untamed lions.

She has never refused to risk her own safety for the sake of a good picture.

In the old animal film, "Lost in the Jungle," she was compelled to crouch down within a few feet of a tiger, and drop behind a protecting rock when it turned. There was some misunderstanding, on one of the signals, and before she could save herself the animal leaped upon her and tore a gash in her scalp which required six stitches of the surgeon's skilful needle.

Another time in "The Girl with the Lantern," she was obliged to lie across a railroad track, until a train traveling at great speed, was within 50 feet of her. The only assurance she had of safety was the promise and quick action of the other actors who were to rescue her at that moment.

If there had been a single misstep or the slightest delay, Kathlyn Williams would have been crushed to death.

"But what is this daring actress like, out of the pictures?" you ask. A perfectly unspoiled girl as natural and genuine as a child; a remarkable horsewoman and a good conversationalist.

Her hair is the real kind of golden. She laughs as if life were a great, big song. And she talks as if the living of it were the best thing on earth.

At home the moving picture star, who will dare anything to make her last picture the greatest, reads and plays and cooks and eats and primps like any other girl. This winter while she creates new roles at the Edendale studio near Los Angeles, and plays the leading part in some big new animal pictures, she promises to learn to operate the hydroaeroplane. She has already made the preliminary plans.

Chatting about the pictures to me she said:

"Seeing himself in the moving pictures is the most helpful and the most discouraging criticism an actor can have. It's the severe test of looking at yourself from the outside and at a distance.

"Mannerisms positively stare at you from a picture when they would pass unnoticed on the stage. The searching light of the picture camera seems to have reveled in your faults.

"Daylight hours, the opportunity to live at home, the wonderful variety of characters and the chance for study are the chief inducements the pictures offer to the player.

"I like being a photo player because I like doing things difficult, unexpected things. Maybe that's the reason I am going to be the first woman hydroaeroplanist. The strange sensation of flying through space fascinates me.

"I am not afraid.

"Look," she whispered as I started toward the door, "hardly anyone knows—my life is charmed!

"See my talisman?"

She lifted into the light a tiny bit of ivory wonderfully carved in the shape of a fish. It is the gift of a woman who saw Kathlyn Williams in a moving picture adventure on a screen in a remote little hamlet in England.

Document
Gertrude Price, "Sees the Movies as Great, New Field for Women Folk," *Toledo News-Bee* (30 March 1914), 14

There never was a day when all the feminine folks of "worldom" could turn time and thought into money as they can now!

The mental market place of the nation has been thrown open to woman with wares to sell. Her originality and her perseverance and her brains are coming to be recognized on the same plane as man's.

And there's nowhere that you can find this happy new equality of originality and ability as in the wonderful field which the moving picture has opened.

New Woman's Field

The "movie" world is the great new woman's field!

It is bubbling over with novel opportunities for pretty girls, active girls, persevering girls, blonde girls, brunette girls, short girls and tall girls, athletic girls and studious girls.

There are a hundred and one things a girl can do in the "movies."

She may be one of scores of the sad or merry maids whose bright faces are mirrored on the screen.

She may be one of the competent girls in the big factory of the large moving picture plant, busily matching and tinting the thousands of yards of film.

She may be an adept in the art of costume, and find a place in the busy wardrobe room which must be ready to supply any style of dress of any period at notice.

No End to the Needs

Or she may be the clever "brains" of the story of the film itself! And in this department there seems to be no end of the needs. This is the place where originality, spelled with a big "O" and underlined, wins big favors and a ready pay check.

"Something new, something new," is the constant cry of the moving picture producers, some of whom are expected to finish three pictures a week.

There is no limit to the number of scenarios needed, it seems. Therefore, there is no limit to the number of girls who may try their hand at this new avocation.

NOTES

Abbreviations

For the purposes of space, the following acronyms are used for frequently referenced magazine and newspaper sources from the period as well as film archives.

Trade Press

B	Billboard	MPW	Moving Picture World
Bio	Bioscope	N	Nickelodeon
CJ	Ciné-Journal	NYDM	New York Dramatic Mirror
FI	Film Index	NYMT	New York Morning Telegraph
M	Motography	PM	Photoplay Magazine
MPN	Motion Picture News	V	Variety
MPSN	Motion Picture Story Magazine		

Newspapers

BA	Boston American	DMT	Des Moines Tribune
BJ	Boston Journal	E	L'Etoile (Lowell)
BP	Boston Post	LAT	Los Angeles Times
BS	Baltimore Sun	LCC	Lowell Courier-Citizen
CC	Cleveland Citizen	LDI	Lynn Daily Item
CG	Cleveland Gazette	LE	Lawrence Eagle
CL	Cleveland Leader	LoST	Lowell Sunday Telegram
CN	Canton News-Democrat	LS	Lawrence Sun
CR	Canton Repository	LT	Lawrence Tribune
CRR	Cedar Rapids Republican	LyST	Lynn Sunday Telegram
CT	Chicago Tribune	MJ	Minneapolis Journal
DFP	Detroit Free Press	MT	Minneapolis Tribune
DMN	Des Moines News	NCH	New Castle Herald
DMRL	Des Moines Register and Leader	NYT	New York Times

PP	Pittsburgh Press	SPN	St. Paul News
PT	Pawtucket Times	SPPP	St. Paul Pioneer Press
RDC	Rochester Democrat and Chron-	TB	Toledo Blade
	icle	TNB	Toledo News-Bee
RH	Rochester Herald	TUL	Toledo Union Leader
SFC	San Francisco Chronicle	WS	Washington Star
SLR	St. Louis Republic	YV	Youngstown Vindicator
SLT	St. Louis Times		

Archives

AMPAS	Academy of Motion Picture	MoMA	Museum of Modern Art
	Arts and Sciences	NFM	Nederlands Film Museum
GEH	George Eastman House	NFTVA	National Film/Television
LoC	Library of Congress		Archive

Introduction

1. Benedict Anderson, *Imagined Communities: Reflections on the Origin and Spread of Nationalism,* rev. ed. (London: Verso, 1991), 1–7, 42–43.

2. Ibid., 25, 44–45.

3. Ibid., 202–3. Awareness of the challenge offered by the United States' unusually diverse population sometimes cropped up in the US trade press, as in this quote: "No other country on the globe has as great a number of varied nationalities, creeds, and sects in touch with each other, and purveyors of amusements cater to all of them"—"Observations by Our Man About Town," *MPW* (15 August 1914), 949. In the late twentieth and early twenty-first centuries, the concept of an "imagined community of nationality" has reemerged to become unusually conflicted, exacerbated by the current US government's promotion of an internal "culture of fear" in the "war on terrorism" (specifically, in the 2004 presidential election) and its divisive, arrogantly misguided, deceptive war on/in Iraq.

4. Eric Hobsbawm, "Mass-Producing Traditions: Europe, 1879–1914," in Eric Hobsbawm and Terence Ranger, eds., *The Invention of Tradition* (Cambridge: Cambridge University Press, 1983), 279.

5. See especially Philip Gleason, "American Identity and Americanization," in Stephen Thernstrom, ed., *Harvard Encyclopedia of American Ethnic Groups* (Cambridge, Mass.: Harvard University Press, 1980), 38–47.

6. Matthew Frye Jacobson, *Whiteness of a Different Color: European Immigrants and the Alchemy of Race* (Cambridge, Mass.: Harvard University Press, 1998), 68.

7. Alexander Saxton, *The Rise and Fall of the White Republic: Class, Politics, and Mass Culture in Nineteenth-Century America* (London: Verso, 1990), 10.

8. Jacobson, *Whiteness of a Different Color,* 41, 68.

9. Ibid., 75.

10. See also Noel Ignatiev, *How the Irish Became White* (New York: Routledge, 1995); and Matthew Frye Jacobson, *Special Sorrows: The Diasporic Imagination of Irish, Polish, and Jewish Immigrants in the United States* (Cambridge, Mass.: Harvard University Press, 1995).

11. Gleason, "American Identity and Americanization," 39.

12. Miriam Bratu Hansen, "The Mass Production of the Senses: Classical Cinema as Vernacular Modernism," in Christine Gledhill and Linda Williams, eds., *Re-inventing Film Studies* (London: Arnold, 2000), 339–44. In 1929, Will Hays gave a concise, early summary of Hansen's point: "America is in a very literal sense the world-state. All races, all creeds, all the manners of men that exist on the globe, are to be found here—working, sharing and developing side by side in a reasonable degree of understanding and friendship"—see Hays, *Moving Pictures: An Outline of the History and Achievement of the Screen from Its Earliest Beginnings to the Present Day* (New York: Doubleday, Doran, 1929), 506.

13. See, for instance, Judith Mayne, *The Woman at the Keyhole: Feminism and Women's Cinema* (Bloomington: Indiana University Press, 1990); Miriam Hansen, *Babel and Babylon* (Cambridge, Mass.: Harvard University Press, 1991); Janet Staiger, *Bad Women: Regulating Sexuality in Early American Cinema* (Minneapolis: University of Minnesota Press, 1995); Kathryn Fuller, *At the Picture Show: Small-Town Audiences and the Creation of Movie Fan Culture* (Washington, D.C.: Smithsonian Institution, 1996); Lauren Rabinovitz, *For the Love of Pleasure* (New Brunswick, N.J.: Rutgers University Press, 1998); Shelley Stamp, *Movie-Struck Girls: Women and Motion Picture Culture after the Nickelodeon* (Princeton, N.J.: Princeton University Press, 2000); and Jennifer Bean, "Technologies of Early Stardom and the Extraordinary Body," in Jennifer Bean and Diane Negra, eds., *A Feminist Reader in Early Cinema* (Durham, N.C.: Duke University Press, 2002), 404–43.

14. Shelley Streeby, *American Sensations: Class, Empire, and the Production of Popular Culture* (Berkeley and Los Angeles: University of California Press, 2002), 7, 27, 32.

15. Ben Singer, *Melodrama and Modernity: Early Sensational Cinema and Its Contexts* (New York: Columbia University Press, 2000). I have had to exclude at least two other kinds of films quite popular during the early 1910s, but they certainly deserve further attention. One is the romance, or "visual love story," which Mark Garrett Cooper has begun to analyze in *Love Rules* (Minneapolis: University of Minnesota Press, 2003). The other is the short comedy or comic series, which Rob King, for instance, has studied in a recent UCLA dissertation on Keystone.

16. Astute studies of the dime novel can be found in Michael Denning, *Mechanic Accents: Dime Novels and Working-Class Culture in America*, 2nd ed. (London: Verso, 1998); and Bill Brown, "Reading the West: Cultural and Historical Background," in Bill Brown, ed., *Reading the West: An Anthology of Dime Westerns* (Boston: Bedford Books, 1997), 1–40.

17. The term "10–20–30 melodrama" came from the price of seating in the theaters that catered to this kind of popular drama, which prospered on a national scale by the late 1890s, as theater circuits and syndicates combined to finance, book, and promote "the mass production of touring companies"—Singer, "Ten-Twenty-Thirty Melodrama," in *Melodrama and Modernity*, 149–88.

18. The research on New York is extensive; that on Chicago less so, especially in the early 1910s—see, for instance, J. A. Lindstrom, "Where Development Has Just Begun: Nickelodeon Location, Moving Picture Audiences, and Neighborhood Development in Chicago," in Charlie Keil and Shelley Stamp, *American Cinema's Transitional Era: Audiences, Institutions, Practices* (Berkeley and Los Angeles: University of California Press, 2004), 217–38; and Moya Luckett, "Cinema and Community: Progressivism, Spectatorship and Identity in Chicago, 1907–1917" (unpublished

manuscript). Robert C. Allen has been especially insistent on studying diverse rural communities in the South, most recently in his opening address at the Commonwealth Conference on American Cinema and Everyday Life, University College London, 25 June 2003.

19. W. Stephen Bush, "The Moving Picture and the Press," *MPW* (8 March 1913), 975.

20. Glenmore Norton, "The Moving Picture Revolution," *N* (1 May 1910), 225. This text was reprinted from *Success* magazine.

21. See, for instance, "Opening of the Strand," *MPW* (18 April 1914), 371.

22. See, for instance, "The New Year," *M* (10 January 1914), 17.

23. See, for instance, "Personality—Box-Office Magnet," *NYDM* (10 January 1914), 52.

24. Julian T. Baber, "Efficient Publicity Work," *MPW* (30 May 1914), 1270.

25. The "title" was given to my grandfather in a newspaper article, "Window Experts Build Ever Changing Show," *CR* (22 October 1941), n.p.

Chapter 1: American Variety and/or Foreign Features

1. "The Movies," *DMN* (4 May 1913), 6.

2. Colonial ad, *DMRL* (2 May 1913), 12.

3. Berchel ad, *DMRL* (15 September 1912), n.p.

4. "The Movies," *DMN* (4 February 1913), 5; Namur's University Place Theatre ad, *DMN* (4 February 1913), 6.

5. Ivo Blom, *Jean Desmet and the Early Dutch Film Trade* (Amsterdam: Amsterdam University Press, 2003), 25.

6. Janet Staiger, "Combination and Litigation: Structures of US Film Distribution, 1891–1917," *Cinema Journal* 23.2 (Winter 1984), 41–72; Robert Anderson, "The Motion Picture Patents Company: A Re-evaluation," in Tino Balio, ed., *The American Film Industry*, 2nd ed. (Madison: University of Wisconsin Press, 1985), 133–52; Eileen Bowser, *The Transformation of Cinema, 1907–1915* (New York: Scribner's, 1991), 80–84, 191–233; and Michael Quinn, "Distribution, the Transient Audience, and the Transition to the Feature Film," *Cinema Journal* 40.2 (Winter 2001), 35–56. For a more recent study, see Scott Curtis, "A House Divided: The MPPC in Transition," in Keil and Stamp, *American Cinema's Transitional Era*, 239–64.

7. Although not my initial intention, this chapter offers a different model from that put forth by Ben Singer, whose exclusive reliance on production data skews his analysis of "the relationship between shorts and features" in exhibition during the 1910s—see Singer, "Feature Films, Variety Programs, and the Crisis of the Small Exhibitor," in Keil and Stamp, *American Cinema's Transitional Era*, 76–100.

8. According to William Fox, the weekly "license tax of $2" was levied "on every moving picture machine sold" to exhibitors, "some of which [were using] two machines" by 1909—see "Federal Suit to Dissolve the Picture 'Trust,' " *NYMT* (18 August 1912), 4.2: 2.

9. This column first appeared as "Review of the Bills at Moving Picture Shows," *SLT* (6 November 1909), 3.

10. "News of the Moving Picture Theatres," *SLT* (8 January 1910), 4, (5 March 1910), 4, and (12 March 1910), 3.

11. Ellis Cohen, "The Moving Picture Field," *NYMT* (2 January 1910), 4.1: 4. See the Jewel ad, *LoST* (27 March 1910), 4; and "The Jewel," *LoST* (10 April 1910), 7.

12. For information on the Sales Company, conceived as early as December 1909, see "The Motion Picture Distributing and Sales Company," *MPW* (7 May 1910), 724; "The Sales Company," *MPW* (21 May 1910), 822–23; "The Sales Company To-Day," *MPW* (4 June 1910), 929; and "Motion Picture Distributing and Sales Company," *MPN* (15 April 1911), 23–24. The Sales Company apparently did not recall and retire the film prints it leased—"The Goat Man, On the Outside Looking In," *M* (November 1911), 237.

13. The first column of "Moving Picture and Vaudeville" ads appeared in the *SLT* (1 August 1909), 9.

14. "Moving Pictures and Vaudeville," *SLT* (26 April 1910), 13, (30 April 1910), 21, and (10 May 1910), 13.

15. "Moving Pictures and Vaudeville," *SLT* (14 May 1910), 13.

16. "Status of the Motion Picture," *B* (3 December 1910), n.p.

17. Sales ad, *MPW* (2 July 1910), 3.

18. Sales ad, *MPW* (9 July 1910), 91; Associated Independent Film Manufacturers ad, *MPW* (9 July 1910), 90.

19. Sales ad, *MPW* (17 September 1910), 611.

20. "New 'Broadway Theater' an Elaborate Structure," *LT* (22 July 1910), n.p.; "The Central Square Theatre, Lynn's Newest Playhouse," *LDI* (17 December 1910), 9.

21. See the Scenic ad, *LoST* (14 August 1910), 2; and the Star Theatre ad, *LoST* (11 September 1910), 2.

22. Jack Tierney, "The Moving Picture Situation in Toledo, O.," *B* (28 January 1911), 6. That the Isis, Crown, and Hart were Independent theaters can be gathered from slightly later ads in the *Toledo Blade* and *Toledo News-Bee*.

23. Elite Theatre ads, *DMN* (6 August 1911), 6, and (3 September 1911), 6.

24. Sales ad, *MPN* (6 May 1911), 27. Another factor in Sales's success was Eastman Kodak's amended agreement with the MPPC, in February 1911, which allowed the company to sell film stock to independent manufacturers—see Bowser, *The Transformation of Cinema*, 83.

25. See, for instance, "List of Films and Their Release Dates," *B* (18 March 1911), 67–68; "Data from Manufacturers' List of Releases," *MPN* (6 May 1911), 24–25; and "Federal Suit to Dissolve the Picture 'Trust,' " 4.2: 2. *Billboard* also was one of the first to argue that the MPPC had "made an irreparable mistake in their formation of the subsidiary corporation termed 'General Film Co.,' " largely because it failed to consider exhibitor resistance to its weekly fees—see "Motion Pictures in 1910," *B* (1 April 1911), 10.

26. "Washington and Philadelphia," *FI* (27 August 1910), 6; Moore's Film Exchange ad, *FI* (1 October 1910), 12; Tierney, "The Moving Picture Situation in Toledo, O.," 6; and "Cleveland," *MPW* (20 May 1911), 1126.

27. "Pathé American Studio Announced by Mr. Berst," *FI* (9 April 1910), 1, 3; "New Pathé Studio," *NYDM* (9 April 1910), 21; and "New Pathé Studio," *FI* (6 August 1910), 3.

28. According to Frederic J. Haskins, licensed films were leased to exhibitors on a scale of highest to lowest prices: a "first-run" film had never been exhibited before;

a "second-run" film was supplied from two to seven days after its original release; a "third-run" film was from one week to four weeks old; a "thirty-day" film was a month old; and a "commercial" film was more than a month old. Exhibitors, he claimed, tended to arrange their weekly schedule so as to lease "one first run, one second run, and two commercials" for each daily change of program. See Haskins, "Film Makers Divided into Two Hostile Camps," *SPPP* (17 October 1911), 6.

29. See the General Film, Lake Shore, and Victor ads, *CL* (10 December 1911), S5.

30. National Film Distributing ad, *NYMT* (3 September 1911), 4: 3.

31. See the Sales ad, *NYMT* (17 December 1911), 3; and the National Film Distributing ad, *NYMT* (17 December 1911), 12. See also E. V. Morrison, "The Motion Picture Situation," *B* (9 December 1911), 28. National Film Distributing may have lost momentum when B. E. Clements left the company in late November—see "Clements Withdraws," *B* (2 December 1911), 14.

32. "Herbert Miles Resigns," *B* (7 October 1911), 14.

33. "Gaumont American!" *B* (6 January 1912), 14. One reason Gaumont gave for leaving Kleine was that the company wanted to sell more than the current average of forty copies worldwide of each film it produced.

34. "Proposed Combination," *B* (20 January 1912), 14.

35. "Gem Refused Admission," *B* (20 January 1912), 14; "Sales Company Denies," *B* (27 January 1912), 14. Gem was forced to release its films through an agreement with Rex, which was allowed three releases per week by Sales but had been making only one.

36. A. K. Greenland, "Is the Open Market Inevitable?" *B* (3 February 1912), 6; and the Sales ad, *NYMT* (3 March 1912), 4.2: 2.

37. Staiger, "Combination and Litigation," 53–54; Bowser, *The Transformation of Cinema*, 221. For information from the period, see "A Successful Organizer," *MPW* (26 April 1912), 357. One of the first ads for Western Film Exchange appeared in the *NYMT* (30 April 1911), 4: 7.

38. "Third Moving Picture Faction Formed," *B* (23 March 1912), 48; "Majestic Withdraws from Sales Company," *NYMT* (24 March 1912), 4.2: 2; and "New Corporation Enters Field of Film Exchanges," *NYMT* (24 March 1912), 4.2: 4.

39. "Big Independent Announcement," *NYDM* (3 April 1912), 27.

40. "Fourth Film Faction Formed," *B* (18 May 1912), 22; "Film Field Now Entered by Two New Rival Forces," *NYMT* (19 May 1912), 4.2: 1; "Independent Division?" *NYDM* (22 May 1912), 27; "Manufacturers and Exchangemen Meet," *B* (25 May 1912), 10; "War in Film Circles," *B* (25 May 1912), 11; and "Independent Factions Organize," *MPW* (1 June 1912), 807.

41. See, for instance, "Universal Issues Strong Program," *MPW* (15 June 1912), 1036–37; the Universal Film ad, *MPN* (15 June 1912), 43; and the Universal Film ad, *M* (17 August 1912), 6–7.

42. See, for instance, the Film Supply ads, *MPN* (18 May 1912), 48; *NYMT* (19 May 1912), 4.2, 2; *M* (June 1912), 7; and *MPN* (15 June 1912), 5

43. See, for instance, the Film Supply ad, *MPW* (3 August 1912), 404.

44. "Lake Shore Film Merges with Mutual Company," *CL* (19 May 1912), S5; and the Lake Shore Film ad, *CL* (23 June 1912), S6.

45. Blaché served as president; Ingvald C. Oes (Great Northern), as vice president; C. J. Hite (Thanhouser), as treasurer; and the board of directors included S. S.

Hutchinson (American) and Harry Aitken (Majestic)—see "Independent Factions Organize," 807.

46. See, for instance, "Withdrawal from the Universal Film Company Precipitates Row of Size," *NYMT* (30 June 1912), 4.2: 1. See also Bowser, *The Transformation of Cinema,* 223–24.

47. "Mutual Closes Deal," *B* (10 August 1912), 11.

48. See, for instance, the Mutual Film ad, *MPW* (17 August 1912), 611.

49. "Correspondence: New England," *MPW* (3 August 1912), 459.

50. "Correspondence: New England," *MPW* (23 November 1912), 785; Central Square ad, *LDI* (23 November 1912), 2; and "Correspondence: New England," *MPW* (4 January 1913), 68.

51. "Five Companies Go from Film Supply to Mutual," *NYMT* (22 December 1912), 4.2: 1. Film Supply was a much less aggressive, relatively open firm, which ultimately did not work to its benefit—see E. V. Morrison, "The Film Business in the Future," *B* (14 September 1912), 20.

52. Powers began to lose his battle with Laemmle for control of Universal perhaps as early as February 1913, but he, Swanson, and Horsley certainly were gone from the company by June. For a while, Powers retained financial interests in the Powers and Victor film manufacturers, as well as the Victor Film Service (Cleveland and Buffalo) and Rex Film Service (Albany), all still contracted with Universal. See "Powers Out; Universal Suit Dropped," *NYMT* (16 February 1913), 4.2: 1; "Independent Exchange Pool," *MPW* (29 March 1913), 1315; "First Complete Story of the Laemmle-Powers Fight," *NYMT* (15 June 1913), 4.2: 1; and "Fight over Universal Halts, but Not for Long," *NYMT* (22 June 1913), 4.2: 1. For an early profile of Powers, see "Who's Who in the Film Game," *M* (June 1912), 261–62. For a capsule account of Universal's internecine struggles, see Bowser, *The Transformation of Cinema,* 223–24.

53. See "Lack of Harmony Reported in Film Supply—Blache, Oes, and Raver Form New Firm," *NYMT* (30 March 1913), 4.2: 1; and the Exclusive Supply ad, *NYMT* (30 March 1913), 4.2: 3. Another sign of weakness was the announcement that Mutual had acquired Gaumont's exchanges in Canada—"Mutual Gets Seven Exchanges in Canada Owned by Gaumont," *NYMT* (11 May 1913), 4.2: 1.

54. See the General Film and Victor ads, *CL* (8 December 1912), S7; and the Lake Shore ad, *CL* (15 December 1912), S5.

55. "Some Good Things Coming; Week's Gossip in Filmland," *CL* (2 February 1913), B4. Another sign of stability was the extensive listing of licensed and independent film exchanges (in which Mutual and Film Supply overlapped significantly) in the "Classified Trade Directory," *Moving Picture Annual and Yearbook for 1912* (New York: Moving Picture World, 1912), 124–26.

56. See the Music Hall, Star, and Pastime ads, *PT* (14 December 1912), 5; and the Globe ad, *PT* (4 January 1913), 5.

57. See the Mutual/Unique ad, *DMN* (26 January 1913). 6.

58. See the Mutual and Laemmle Film Service ads, *MJ* (4 May 1913), 8: 10.

59. See, for instance, the Universal ad, *DMRL* (20 April 1913), 8; and the Mutual ad, *DMRL* (4 May 1913), 7. This also was the moment when NYMP signed a two-year distribution contract with Mutual and agreed to increase its production from six to twelve reels per week—see "N.Y. Motion Picture Co. Signs with the Mutual," *NYMT* (13 April 1913), 4.2: 1.

60. See the Essanay ad, *DMRL* (20 April 1913), 8.

61. See the Reliance ad, *DMRL* (20 April 1913), 8. Universal, Mutual, Essanay, and Reliance all ran their final ads in the *DMRL* (20 July 1913), 12.

62. "The Backbone of the Business," *M* (20 September 1913), 191.

63. See the Mutual ads, *MJ* (15 November 1913), 12, and (29 November 1913), 8; and the ad for Mutual comedies, with a drawing of Ford Sterling's face, in the *CT* (4 January 1914), 1: 8.

64. The analogy actually had been made as early as "Periodical Topicals," *M* (August 1911), 56.

65. See, for instance, John M. Bradlet, "The Open Market," *MPW* (18 February 1911), 349–51. For a concise discussion of the "closed" and "open" market systems in Europe, see Blom, *Jean Desmet and the Early Dutch Film Trade*, 27–33.

66. See Bradlet, "The Open Market," 349–52; and "The Feature Film—Its Possibilities," *B* (22 April 1911), 14, 51.

67. Here my analysis parallels that of Corrina Müller, who argues that the development of long features, especially because of their "socio-cultural implications," was "the principal agent of transformation" in early German cinema—summarized in Blom, *Jean Desmet and the Early Dutch Film Trade*, 31–32. See also Corrina Müller, *Frühe deutsche Kinematographie. Formale, wirtschaftliche und kulturelle Entwicklungen 1907–1912*, Stuttgart/Weimar: J. B. Metzler, 1994. See also Ben Brewster, "Periodization of Early Cinema," in Keil and Stamp, *American Cinema's Transitional Era*, 66–75.

68. "Notes," *NYMT* (12 March 1911), 4.1: 4; and "An Important Italian Subject," *NYDM* (15 March 1911), 34. See also "Motion Picture Reviews," *B* (22 April 1911), 14. The recently restored, tinted 35mm print of *The Fall of Troy* shown at the 2005 Le Giornate del cinema muto clearly suggests why this film made such a stunning impact at the time: a massive army assaulting the high walls and gates of Troy, consistent deep-space compositions, and the spectacle of Paris and Helen embedded within a giant half shell floating through the ether attended by dancing putti.

69. "Scenes from the World's Greatest Motion Picture," *YV* (16 April 1911), 12; and Park Theater ad, *YV* (16 April 1911), 13.

70. See the Jewel ad, *E* (15 April 1911), 4; and Scenic Theatre ad, *LoST* (30 April 1911), 7.

71. "The Film of the Week," *MPW* (29 April 1911), 935. At the Ideal Theater (also in Chicago), the film "broke all house records as people came back two and three times to see it again"—Bowser, *The Transformation of Cinema*, 201. *The Fall of Troy* was still playing that summer, for instance, at the Isis Egyptian Theatre in Toledo—see the Isis ad, *TB* (17 June 1911), 12.

72. Dorothy Donnell, "The School of Moving Pictures," *MPSN* (July 1911), 95.

73. "Critical Reviews of Independent Films," *NYMT* (23 April 1911), 4: 7.

74. See the P. P. Craft ads, *MPW* (17 June 1911), 1377, 1380; and the Sales ad, *B* (8 July 1911), 32–33.

75. See the Monopol Film ads, *NYDM* (12 July 1911), 25; *B* (15 July 1911), 3; and *MPW* (15 July 1911), 47.

76. See the Monopol Film ads, *NYDM* (19 July 1911), 24, and (23 August 1911), 22; and *B* (26 August 1911), 51.

77. See "The Theater," *Washington Star* (3 September 1911), 2: 2; the Belasco ad,

Washington Star (3 September 1911), 2:2; and "Washington," *NYDM* (6 September 1911), 24.

78. The film also was favored with excellent reviews and articles—e.g., W. Stephen Bush, "Dante's Inferno," *MPW* (29 July 1911), 188–89; Rev. Elias Boudinet Stockton, "Impressions of 'Dante's Inferno,' " *MPW* (16 September 1911), 780; and W. Stephen Bush, "Music and Sound Effects for Dante's Inferno," *MPW* (27 January 1912), 283–84. Pliny P. Craft later was heralded as the originator of the state rights idea in "The Father of the Feature," *MPW* (11 July 1914), 272–73.

79. See "Dante's Inferno," *LT* (9 September 1911), 4; and the Mall ad, *CL* (17 September 1911), N4. The Jake Wells Amusement Company, headquartered in Norfolk (Virginia), also seems to have distributed the film throughout the South—see the Monopol Film ad, *NYDM* (23 August 1911), 22; and "Dante's Inferno Dates," *CL* (1 October 1911), B6. For further information on Jake and Otto Wells, see Terry Lindvall, "Cinema Virtue, Cinema Vice: Race, Religion, and Film Exhibition in Norfolk, Virginia, 1908–1922" (paper presented at the Commonwealth Conference on American Cinema and Everyday Life, University College London, London, 27 June 2003).

80. " 'Dante's Inferno' in Boston," *MPW* (2 December 1911), 714.

81. William Gane seems to have been licensed to rent the film in Greater New York—see the William J. Gane ad, *NYMT* (7 January 1912), 4.2: 4.

82. "Correspondence: Toledo," *MPW* (13 July 1912), 164. An extensive listing of the "State Right Owners" for *Dante's Inferno* can be found in *Moving Picture Annual and Yearbook for 1912*, 137.

83. *The Crusaders* enjoyed several lengthy glowing reviews: "The Crusaders," *B* (8 July 1911), 48; "A Great Epic in Moving Pictures," *MPW* (15 July 1911), 14–16; and "The Film of the Hour," *B* (29 July 1911), 11.

84. See the World's Best Films ad, *NYMT* (3 September 1911), 4: 2. According to F. C. McCarrahan, manager of Kleine Optical in Chicago, much of the popularity of *The Crusaders* was due to the company's manager, Tom Quill—see C. J. Ver Halen, "The Movie Situation in Chicago," *B* (23 March 1912), 29, 90.

85. See the Feature & Educational Film ad, *B* (16 September 1911), 54; the Auditorium ad, *CN* (17 September 1911), 24; and "Great Interest Being Shown in The Crusaders," *CN* (24 September 1911), 24. Feature & Educational Film was founded in Cleveland late that summer by "Manny" Mandelbaum, who also owned Lake Shore and several major picture theaters in the city.

86. "Turkish Crusaders Shown on a Film," *BA* (10 December 1911), E6; "Turkish War Now Seen in Films," *BA* (17 December 1911), E6; "At the Jewel," *LST* (24 December 1911), 6; and "Amusements," *LS* (1 January 1912); 4.

87. "Here's a Handy Guide for the Theatregoers" and "Turkish Crusaders Shown on a Film," *BA* (10 December 1911), E6; and "Turkish War Now Seen in the Films," *BA* (17 December 1911), E6.

88. Star ad, *PT* (5 March 1912), 5; Isis ad, *MJ* (31 March 1912), 8:11; Family ad, *DMN* (26 May 1912), 12; "At the Orpheum," *TNB* (8 June 1912), 7; and Central Square Theater ad, *LDI* (10 August 1912), 2.

89. See "Odyssey in Pictures," *B* (7 October 1911), 15; the Monopol ads, *B* (3 February 1912), 40–41, (10 February 1912), 55, and (24 February 1912), 43; and the Monopol ads, *NYDM* (14 February 1912), 31, (21 February 1912), 29, and (28 Feb-

ruary 1912), 33. A "striking Odyssey poster" also was reproduced in *NYDM* (28 February 1912), 30. *Homer's Odyssey* had the lengthiest list of "state right owners," according to "Classified Trade Directory," *Moving Picture Annual and Yearbook for 1912*, 139. Monopol was said to have "made a great deal of money," but it foundered sometime in 1912 or early 1913, apparently because of a rift between Craft and the "man of many interests," Pat Powers, the company's primary investor—see "Monopol Film Co. Split among Its Promoters," *V* (15 August 1913), 14.

90. See the Auditorium ad, *MJ* (21 April 1912), 4; and the Metropolitan ad, *MJ* (2 June 1912), 8: 8.

91. See the Columbia ad, *CRR* (17 September 1912), 3; the Jewel ad, *E* (15 October 1912), 2; and the Colonial ad, *DMN* (2 November 1912), 2.

92. W. Stephen Bush, "Gauging the Public Taste," *MPW* (11 May 1912), 505. Two years later, Frank E. Woods also acknowledged the impact of such "pretentious three and four reel subjects . . . from Europe," distributed according to a "state rights plan," in "What Are We Coming Up To?" *MPW* (18 July 1914), 442.

93. See the French-American Film ads, *B* (3 February 1912), 10; and *NYDM* (14 February 1912), 30.

94. See the French-American Film ads, *NYMT* (25 February 1912), 4.2: 2 and 3, (3 March 1912), 4.2: 5, and (17 March 1912), 4.2: 3; W. Stephen Bush, "Bernhardt and Rejane in Pictures," *MPW* (2 March 1912), 760; and "Reviews of Feature Subjects," *NYDM* (10 April 1912), 26.

95. See the Valentine ad, *TNB* (16 March 1912), 6; "Bernhardt and Rejane Films Admired by Big Audiences," *NYMT* (12 May 1912), 4.2: 4; and "Bernhardt-Rejane Pictures Popular," *B* (29 June 1912), 22.

96. See the Alhambra ad, *CL* (7 April 1912), S8; the Princess ad and "Bernhardt Film a Hit," *CL* (14 April 1912), S6; and the Mall ad, *CL* (19 May 1912), S5.

97. See the Auditorium ad, *CN* (19 April 1912), 16; and the Orpheum ad, *YV* (12 May 1912), 18.

98. Dreamland ad, *LDI* (2 November 1912), 2.

99. See, for instance, W. Stephen Bush, "Do Longer Films Make Better Show?" *MPW* (28 October 1911), 275; and "The Year 1912," in *Moving Picture Annual and Yearbook for 1912*, 15.

100. " 'Spectator's' Comments," *NYDM* (9 August 1911), 20; and Epes Winthrop Sargent, "Will Specials Lead to Runs," *MPW* (2 September 1911), 606–7. Sargent also argued that special releases would not harm cheaper theaters—see Sargent, "The Special Release and the Small Exhibitor," *MPW* (30 September 1911), 965.

101. Epes Winthrop Sargent, "Advertising for Exhibitors," *MPW* (24 February 1912), 666, and (2 March 1912), 763.

102. See the Orpheum ad, *CN* (1 October 1911), 24; and the Lyric ad, *YV* (3 December 1911), 19.

103. See the Star ad, *PT* (17 February 1912), 5; the Orpheum ad, *TNB* (8 June 1912), 7; and the Alpha Theater ad, *CG* (31 August 1912), 3.

104. The demeaning phrase comes from " 'Spectator's' Comments," *NYDM* (9 August 1911), 20. The only review of the film appeared in *B* (24 June 1911), 22. There were few "State Right Owners" for *Temptations of a Great City,* and they were concentrated in the upper Midwest (Standard Film Exchange of Chicago was most prominent), according to *Moving Picture Annual and Yearbook for 1912*, 137. As an example

of a state rights booker who may never have distributed the film in and around Kansas City or Des Moines (the areas of his offices), see the Chas. L. Marshall ad, *MPW* (7 October 1911), 59.

105. *Temptation of a Great City* drew better than average receipts at the Star that winter, bested only by those for *Dante's Inferno* and Kalem's *Arrah-Na-Pogue* (which played only one Saturday)—Star Theatre Treasurer's Statement Ending 24 February 1912, Box 10, Keith-Albee Collection, Special Collection, University of Iowa Library.

106. See "Will Present Big Productions," *MPW* (13 January 1912), 109; and the Great Northern Special Feature ad, *B* (10 February 1912), 43.

107. The initial F & E ads for *Zigomar* appeared in *NYMT* (25 November 1911), 4.2: 3; *MPN* (25 November 1911), 25; and *B* (9 December 1911), 81. F & E ads promoted *Zigomar* in the *Cleveland Leader* from late December through early February, and the company probably paid for a photo-story on the "great detective film" in *CL* (4 February 1912), S6. Small F & E ads for *Zigomar* continued in the *New York Morning Telegraph* well into July 1912.

108. "F & E Open Branch Office," *B* (13 January 1912), 15; and "F & E Film Co. Growing," *CL* (17 March 1912), S6.

109. J. Parker Read Jr., "The Feature Film," *B* (24 February 1912), 11, 54. See also "Achievements of 'Nineteen-Eleven'," *MPW* (13 January 1912), 106; and " 'Spectator's' Comments," *NYDM* (12 June 1912), 24.

110. Several of these state rights firms had offices in the same building (145 West Forty-fifth Street) where Monopol was headquartered, near Times Square in New York City.

111. Feature Film ads, *B* (16 March 1912), 30, and (27 April 1912), 62.

112. "Classified Trade Directory," *Moving Picture Annual and Yearbook for 1912*, 127–28.

113. See the New York Film ads, *B* (3 February 1912), 58, (27 April 1912), 62, and (6 July 1912), 52.

114. "Another Feature Company," *MPW* (6 April 1912), 26–27; and the Century ad, *MPW* (6 April 1912), 63. Feature Photoplay did likewise, beginning with *Zigomar*, for the area around New York City—see the Feature Photoplay ad, *MPW* (16 March 1912), 1001.

115. Warner's Features ad, *MPW* (20 April 1912), 242.

116. World's Best Film ad, *B* (20 April 1912), 58.

117. H. F. H., "The Asta Nielsen Pictures," *MPW* (23 March 1912), 1054; and the Tournament film ad, *MPW* (20 April 1912), 197.

118. See the Park ads, *YV* (28 February 1912), 14, (3 March 1912), 19, (31 March 1912), 20, (7 April 1912), 21, and (14 April 1912), 23; and the Orpheum ad, *YV* (12 May 1912), 18.

119. See the Family ad, *DMN* (28 April 1912), 6; and "At the Photo Plays," *TNB* (1 June 1912), 2.

120. See "At the Photo Plays," *TNB* (20 April 1912), 2, and (18 June 1912), 7; the Park ad, *YV* (7 April 1912), 21; the Orpheum ad, *YV* (30 June 1912), 16; and the Central Square ad, *LDI* (27 April 1912), 2.

121. In Chicago, exhibitors had the option of running the three reels of *Two Orphans* on the same program or "separately in conjunction with a mixed program"— see Jas. S. McQuade, "Chicago Letter," *MPW* (21 October 1911), 196. Selig's two-reel

The Danites was still being released on consecutive days in late February 1912—see Jas. S. McQuade, "The Danites—A Revival," *MPW* (24 February 1912), 660.

122. The manager of the Lyric, S. L. Rothapfel, reported directly to William Selig that he increased his orchestra to "twenty pieces" in order to present *Cinderella* properly—see the 9 December 1911 letter from Rothapfel to Selig, in the Clarke Collection, file 47, scrapbook 2, Margaret Herrick Library, Academy of Motion Picture Arts and Sciences (AMPAS).

123. Earlier in December, *Cinderella* had played to "record breaking houses" at the Mission Theatre in Salt Lake City—see the 8 December 1911 letter from Dean R. Daymer to Selig Polyscope, Selig Collection, folder 39, Margaret Herrick Library, AMPAS.

124. "At Leading Theaters," *CL* (31 December 1911), B7; the Mall ad, *CL* (7 January 1912), B7; the Cameraphone ad, *CL* (14 January 1912), S5; the Home ad, *CL* (21 January 1912), S6; the Cozy ad, *CL* (4 February 1912), S6; and the Superior ad, *CL* (25 February 1912), S6.

125. Charles Young, "Among the Chicago Houses," *MPW* (30 December 1911), 1065.

126. "When C. Columbus Came Over Here," *NYMT* (1 October 1911), 4.2: 2; Jas. S. McQuade, "Chicago Letter," *MPW* (21 October 1911), 196; James S. McQuade, "The Coming of Columbus," *MPW* (4 May 1912), 407–10; and "Reviews of Special Feature Subjects," *NYDM* (15 May 1912), 27. The Knights of Columbus financed the film and arranged for the replicas of the original caravels, constructed for the 1893 Columbian Exposition, to highlight the pageant.

127. "Big Licensed Features," *NYDM* (22 May 1912), 25; and "More Special Features," *NYDM* (29 May 1912), 25.

128. See, for instance, "The Coming of Columbus," *M* (May 1912), 199–205, and the front cover. Selig already had published a booklet recommending how to exhibit *Cinderella*: Cecil Metcalf, *Complete Lecture and Manual of Instruction on How to Exhibit Selig's Cinderella* (Chicago: Selig Polyscope, 1911)—Selig Collection, folder 39, Margaret Herrick Library, AMPAS.

129. See the Lyric ad, *MJ* (5 May 1912), 8; and "Columbus at the Movies," *MJ* (7 May 1912), 4.

130. "Doings at Los Angeles," *MPW* (8 June 1912), 914. In New York, Gane's Manhattan also held the film "for an entire week"—see "Critical Reviews," *NYMT* (19 May 1912), 4.2: 4;

131. Colonial ad, *DMRL* (19 May 1912), 5.

132. See the Orpheum ads, *CN* (26 May 1912), 14, (2 June 1912), 16, (9 June 1912), 12, and (16 June 1912), 12; and "Orpheum Theater," *CN* (16 June 1912), 12. The Odeon also showed the film two weeks prior to its run at the Orpheum—see the Odeon ad, *CN* (2 June 1912), 16.

133. "Wonderful Moving Pictures," *CN* (16 June 1912), n.p.

134. The exhibitor's decision was based on the $1,000 profit he had made earlier by showing *Dante's Inferno* at his own theater and the erroneous assumption that he would make even more with a similar film at a larger theater and with even more advertising—see Epes Winthrop Sargent, "Advertising for Exhibitors," *MPW* (24 August 1912), 762.

135. Evidence of such concern, specifically about Italians, can be found, respec-

tively, in Chicago and New York—"Americanize Aliens by Moving Pictures," *NYMT* (17 December 1911), 4.2: 1; and Stephen Allen Reynolds, "The Undesirable Emigrant," *NYMT* (14 April 1912), 2: 8. For a superb analysis of how Italian films constructed Italian immigrant audiences in New York, see Giorgio Bertellini, "Italian Imageries, Historical Feature Films, and the Fabrication of Italy's Spectators in Early 1900s New York," in Melvyn Stokes and Richard Maltby, eds., *American Movie Audiences: From the Turn of the Century to the Early Sound Era* (London: British Film Institute, 1999), 29–45. See also the last four chapters of Bertellini's dissertation, "Southern Crossings: Italians, Cinema, and Modernity (Italy, 1861–New York, 1920)" (New York University, 2001).

136. However, none of these east side picture theaters—Columbus, Luna, Luxor, Napoli, and Roma—advertised in the city's main newspaper, the *Youngstown Vindicator*.

137. See the General Film ads, *NYDM* (14 August 1912), 34, and (16 October 1912), 30.

138. General Film ads, *NYDM* (6 November 1912), 30, and (13 November 1912), back cover.

139. Quinn, "Distribution, the Transient Audience, and the Transition to the Feature Film," 45. See also Bowser, *The Transformation of Cinema*, 203–4.

140. Quinn, "Distribution, the Transient Audience, and the Transition to the Feature Filme," 46. See, for instance, the General Film ad promoting Kalem's three-reel *The Land Swindlers*, as an "extra," in the *CL* (15 March 1913), M10. If, in June, company ads stressed quality, reasonable prices, and efficiency, in October 1913 they claimed, "It's the Average That Counts!"—see the General Film ads, *M* (14 June 1913), 9, and *NYMT* (12 October 1913), 5: 5.

141. C. J. Ver Halen, "The Film Situation in Chicago," *B* (14 September 1912), 93. Shortly thereafter, a *Morning Telegraph* writer praised the "wonderful advances" made by multiple-reel films—"Plural Reel Subjects Are Solution of Film Question," *NYMT* (13 October 1912), 4.2: 2.

142. "Famous Players to Be Shown in Film Pictures," *NYMT* (7 July 1912), 4.2: 1; Famous Players Film ads, *NYMT* (7 July 1912), 4.2: 3, and (21 July 1912), 4.2, 3; "Theatrical Stars in Pictures," *NYDM* (10 July 1912), 26; "Prominent Theatrical Stars in Films," *B* (20 July 1912), 10; and Famous Players ad, *MPW* (27 July 1912), 311. See also "The Woman of 10,000 Deaths," *NYMT* (27 October 1912), 2: 7.

143. "Prominent Theatrical Stars in Films," 10; Famous Players ad, *B* (20 July 1912), 19; "Music for 'Queen Elizabeth,' " *NYDM* (7 August 1912), 26. The significance of Frohman's entry into the moving picture business was quickly noted by the trade press—see, for instance, " 'Spectator's' Comments," *NYDM* (17 July 1912), 24; Robert Grau, "Theatre Men in Pictures," *MPW* (28 September 1912), 1205; and Hugh Hoffman, "Daniel Frohman and the Photoplay," *MPW* (26 October 1912), 335. But see also "Adolph Zukor, the Benefactor of Posterity!" *MPN* (25 January 1913), 14–15.

144. "Bernhardt Film Licensed," *NYDM* (7 August 1912), 27; and Bowser, *The Transformation of Cinema*, 225–26.

145. "Bernhardt Film in Chicago," *B* (10 August 1912), 11; Famous Players ad, *MPW* (17 August 1912), 679; "Bernhardt Film in Loew Houses," *NYDM* (28 August 1912), 27; and "Queen Elizabeth Film in New York," *B* (31 August 1912), 10. See also

the 28 September 1912 letter from Zukor to N. N. Brooks (of Boston)—Zukor Collection, folder 1, Margaret Herrick Library, AMPAS.

146. "Bernhardt as Queen Elizabeth," *NYDM* (17 July 1912), 31; W. Stephen Bush, "Queen Elizabeth," *MPW* (3 August 1912), 428–29; and the Famous Players Film ad, *MPW* (3 August 1912), 411. The film also was fictionalized in *Photoplay Magazine* (August 1912), 37–43. See also the Berchel ad, *DMN* (14 September 1912), 5; the Colonial ad, *CL* (27 October 1912), M4; and the Valentine ad, *TNB* (14 December 1912), 4.

147. See "Correspondence: New England," *MPW* (9 November 1912), 565, and (30 November 1912), 888; the Rex ad, *YV* (24 November 1912), 26; the Hippodrome ad, *RH* (8 December 1912), 22; the Casino ad, *WS* (12 January 1913), 2:3; and the Grand ad, *CN* (16 February 1913), 13.

148. "World's Greatest Actress at Dreamland This Week," *CL* (10 November 1912), B5; Dreamland ad, *CL* (10 November 1912), M5; Quincy ad, *CL* (15 December 1912), S5.

149. Quinn, "Distribution, the Transient Audience, and the Transition to the Feature Film," 49–50.

150. See "Miss Blanche Walsh," *B* (29 June 1912), 22; the Masko Film ads, *NYMT* (7 July 1912), 4.2: 4, and (22 September 1912), 4: 5; "Blanche Walsh, Another Pioneer in a New Field," *NYDM* (7 August 1912), 5; and the Masko Film ad, *MPW* (19 October 1912), 212.

151. See "Resurrection Exhibited," *B* (27 July 1912), 11; the Garden ad, *WS* (29 September 1912), 2:7; "Chronique Théâtrale," *E* (22 October 1912), 4; the Colonial ad, *RDC* (8 December 1912), 22; and "The Movies," *DMN* (29 June 1913), 6. Reviews of the film were mixed: "Blanche Walsh a Success," *NYDM* (24 July 1912), 27; and W. Stephen Bush, "Resurrection," *MPW* (10 August 1912), 522–25.

152. " 'Cleopatra' Is Given a Try-Out," *NYDM* (20 November 1912), 31. See the United States Film ads, *NYMT* (15 December 1912), 4: 2; and *NYDM* (4 December 1912) back cover, and (26 February 1913), back cover. Reviews ranged from the lackluster to the exceptional—see, for instance, Louis Reeves Harrison, "Helen Gardner's Idealization of Cleopatra," *MPW* (30 November 1912), 859–60; and " 'Cleopatra' Is Exceptional Five-Part Feature Release," *NYMT* (15 December 1912), 7: 4. Previously, Gardner had received excellent notices for the lead role in Vitagraph's *Vanity Fair.*

153. See the Duchess ad, *CL* (22 December 1912), M5; the Garden ad, *WS* (23 March 1913), 2: 3; the Gordon ad, *RH* (30 March 1912), 22; and "Correspondence: New England," *MPW* (10 May 1913), 607. The film did return for three days to Washington—see the Garden ad, *WS* (13 April 1913), 2: 3. By late February, the film had been sold in the South and West, but not in the Northeast and upper Midwest—see the United States Film ad, *NYDM* (26 February 1913), back cover.

154. "Cleopatra's Story on the Screen," *MJ* (18 May 1913), 8: 10; the Alhambra ad, *TNB* (23 August 1913), 4; the Palace ad, *CRR* (14 September 1913), 7; and the Star ad, *DMRL* (24 May 1914), 7.

155. " 'Cleopatra' Film Banned in Canada," *NYMT* (15 June 1913), 4.2: 3.

156. See, for instance, "Big Shakespearean Film," *B* (31 August 1912), 11; and "Richard III. in Pictures," *B* (7 September 1912), 10. See also Hanford C. Judson, "A Princess of Bagdad," *MPW* (29 November 1913), 991.

157. See, for instance, the Crown Feature Film ads, *NYMT* (2 June 1912), 4.2: 4, *B*

(6 July 1912), 51, and *MPW* (13 July 1912), 181; and the World's Best Films ad, *NYMT* (6 October 1912), 4: 3. Crown Feature, however, did claim "exceptional success" in marketing its film—see "Film Is a Success," *NYMT* (11 August 1912), 4.2: 3.

158. See, for instance, the New York Film ads, *NYMT* (2 June 1912), 4.2: 4, and (13 October 1912), 4: 3. Continental Kunstfilm produced this German adaptation of Reinhardt's production.

159. M. H. Woods was the theatrical producer involved in this suit—see "First Blood in Fight over 'The Miracle' Film," *NYMT* (13 October 1912), 4: 1; " 'The Miracle' Film Is Shown for First time," *NYMT* (20 October 1912), 4: 1; the Harry G. Schultz ad, *NYMT* (12 January 1913), 4.2: 5; and "Suit over 'The Miracle,' " *NYDM* (26 February 1913), 27.

160. See the General Film ad, *NYDM* (5 February 1913), 30.

161. Bowser, *The Transformation of Cinema*, 133.

162. See the Coliseum ad, *DMN* (12 March 1913), 6; "Correspondence: New England," *MPW* (19 April 1913), 292; and the Crystal ad, *CRR* (7 May 1913), 3.

163. Saxe's Lyric ads, *MJ* (27 April 1913), 10, and (11 May 1913), 10.

164. See the Ambrosio American ad, *NYMT* (5 January 1913), 4.2: 3.

165. See "Important Films of the Week," *NYMT* (5 January 1913), 4.2: 5; "Ambrosio Picture Is Impressive," *NYDM* (8 January 1913), 31; W. Stephen Bush, "Satan," *MPW* (18 January 1913), 243–44; and " 'Satan' Brings Change of Heart to Former 'Knocker,' " *NYMT* (2 February 1913), 4.2: 2.

166. See the Colonial ads, *DMRL* (2 May 1913), 12, and (7 June 1913), 5.

167. " 'Satan' a Winner," *CL* (25 May 1913), C4.

168. See "Scenes from Kleine's 'Quo Vadis?' at the Astor Theatre, Starting April 21," *NYMT* (20 April 1913), 4.2: 4; " 'Quo Vadis?' Proves to Be Striking Picture," *NYMT* (27 April 1913), 4.2: 1; and " 'Quo Vadis' at the Astor," *MPW* (3 May 1913), 467.

169. See the George Kleine ads, *NYMT* (27 April 1913), 4.2: 7; *NYDM* (30 April 1913), 24; *MPW* (3 May 1913), 496–97; and *NYMT* (11 May 1913), 4.2: 7. See also James S. McQuade, "Quo Vadis?" *MPW* (17 May 1913), 681–82; and "113,000 See 'Quo Vadis?' in Baltimore," *NYMT* (29 June 1913), 4.2: 5.

170. See the George Kleine ad, *MPN* (7 June 1913), 4; "George Kleine's Production 'Quo Vadis,' " *MPN* (7 June 1913), 13; and "No State Rights for Kleine 'Quo Vadis?' " *NYMT* (8 June 1913), 4.2: 2.

171. See "Quo Vadis a Big Hit at the Tremont," *BJ* (15 July 1913), 7; and the Tremont ad, *BJ* (6 September 1913), 4. See also the Hippodrome ad, *CL* (20 July 1913), W4; "*Quo Vadis?* Now Enacted in the Movies," *CL* (20 July 1913), Copperplate Pictorial Section: 2; the Hippodrome ad, *CL* (10 August 1913), W5; and the Alhambra ad, *CL* (24 August 1913), M3.

172. See the Berchel ad, *DMRL* (27 July 1913), 6; the Auditorium ad, *LAT* (3 August 1913), 3: 1; the Columbia ad, *SFC* (3 August 1913), 19; the Alhambra ad, *TB* (9 August 1913), 22; the Providence Opera House ad, *PT* (23 August 1913), 7; and the Mason Opera House ad, *LAT* (31 August 1913), 3: 1.

173. See the Star ad, *PT* (11 September 1913), 3; the Metropolitan ad, *MJ* (26 September 1913), 8: 9; the Lyceum ad, *RH* (28 September 1913), 23; the Opera House ad, *LE* (10 October 1913), 10; and the Metropolitan ad, *SPN* (19 October 1913), 7.

174. See the Tivoli ad, *SFC* (7 December 1913), 18; the Lyceum ad, *TB* (8 De-

cember 1913), 6; the Metropolitan ad, *SPN* (14 December 1913), 5; the Fitzbaugh ad, *RH* (11 January 1914), 21; " 'Quo Vadis' at the Regent," *MPW* (7 February 1914), 680; and "Rothapfel Rehearsing," *MPW* (14 February 1914), 787.

175. Epes Winthrop Sargent, "Advertising for the Exhibitors," *MPW* (10 January 1914), 162.

176. Bowser, *The Transformation of Cinema*, 211–12.

177. World Special Films premiered Pasquali's version at Wallach's Theatre in New York and then booked it on Klaw and Erlanger's theater circuit—see the World Special Films ad, *MPW* (11 October 1913), 183. Reviews generally were more favorable to Ambrosio's production than to Pasquali's—see, for instance, Louis Reeves Harrison, "Last Days of Pompeii," *MPW* (11 October 1913), 135; "The Last Days of Pompeii," *MPW* (25 October 1913), 363; "Feature Films on the Market," *NYDM* (8 October 1913), 33, and (22 October 1913), 32. World Special Films was owned and managed by Phil Gleichman of Detroit and "Manny" Mandelbaum of Cleveland—see "World Special Films Corporation Opens; To Supply Features," *NYMT* (28 September 1913), 5: 1.

178. See, for instance, "First Eclectic Film," *NYDM* (15 January 1913), 60. Initially, the firm may have been called Cosmopolitan Film, set up by K. W. Linn to distribute the films of Max Linder—see the Cosmopolitan Films ad, *NYMT* (15 December 1912), 4: 2.

179. Eclectic became embroiled in a lawsuit when illegal copies of *The Mysteries of Paris* appeared in Cleveland and New York—see "Eclectic Protects Rights," *NYDM* (9 July 1913), 27; and "Feature Film Notes," *MPN* (30 August 1913), 15.

180. "Feature Film Reviews," *NYMT* (13 April 1913), 4.2: 2; Louis Reeves Harrison, "Les Miserables," *MPW* (26 April 1913), 362–63; and "A Lesson from 'Les Miserables,' " *MPW* (5 July 1913), 50.

181. Jas. S. McQuade, "Chicago Letter," *MPW* (2 August 1913), 520; and Grauman's Imperial ad, *SFC* (14 December 1913), 18.

182. "The Eclectic Film Co. and 'Les Miserables,' " *MPN* (25 October 1913), 38; the Grand Circus Theater ad, *DFP* (9 November 1913), 5: 11; and "Correspondence: Louisville," *MPW* (29 November 1913), 1030. In Detroit, the film also returned to a second theater several weeks later—see the New Forest ad, *DFP* (28 December 1913), 5: 7.

183. See the Tremont Temple ads, *BJ* (30 August 1913), 5, and (22 November 1913), 4; and "Les Miserables," *BJ* (13 September 1913), 5. Gordon's Olympic circuit held rights to the territories of New England and New York—" 'Les Miserables' at Last to Be Shown in New York," *MPW* (1 November 1913), 503. See also "Show 'Les Miserables,' " *NYDM* (28 January 1914), 31.

184. Eclectic kept distribution rights to the Southern states to itself—see "Eclectic Opens Offices in the South," *MPN* (13 December 1913), 37.

185. Ignoring the distribution practices of Warner's Features and Famous Players leads Singer to claim that "features had not made much of an incursion into mainstream movie-theater exhibition" until "around 1915"—Singer, "Feature Films, Variety Programs," 84.

186. See, for instance, the Warner's Features ads, *MPW* (27 July 1912), 364–65, and (19 October 1912), 212. Warner's Features also were included in the column "Feature Film Company Release Dates," *MPN* (16 November 1912), 31.

187. See, for instance, the Warner's Features ads in *NYMT* (15 December 1912), 4: 10; and *NYDM* (18 December 1912), back cover; and "Gauntier Feature Players," *MPW* (21 December 1912), 1169.

188. See Warner's Features ad and "Gauntier Film Here," *CL* (2 March 1913), M11; Warner's Features ad and "Gene Gauntier as Girl Spy in New Warner Feature Film," *CL* (9 March 1913), M5; "Demand for Features," *NYDM* (23 April 1913), 29; "Warner Back from Long Trip," *MPW* (26 April 1913), 359; and the Warner's Features ad, *NYDM* (1 October 1913), 31.

189. " P. A. Powers to Head New Warner's Features, Inc.," *NYMT* (3 August 1913), 4.2: 1; "P. A. Powers to Provide Exclusive Films," *MPN* (9 August 1913), 15; "Pat Powers New Head Warner's Feature Co.," *CL* (10 August 1913), C4. See also "Helen Gardner Goes on Warner's Programme," *NYMT* (2 November 1913), 5: 2; and the Warner's Features ads, *NYMT* (9 November 1913), 5: 3; and *BJ* (15 November 1913), 5. For a summary of the company's history, see "Warner's Features, Inc.," *MPW* (11 July 1914), 262.

190. See "Warner Service Soon," *CL* (21 September 1913), N6; and the Warner's Features ad that begin in the *CL* (28 September 1913), N6. Abe Warner's article on features was reprinted in a condensed form as "Increasing Demand for Good Features," *CL* (3 August 1913), C4. A report also claimed that a new 2,100-seat theater in Cleveland, the Miles, would be contracting with Warner's Features, but this apparently did not materialize—see "$500,000 Theatre for Cleveland," *MPN* (8 November 1913), 42. See also the Miles ad, *CL* (21 December 1913), S10.

191. See the Bijou ad, *PT* (20 September 1913), 3; the Opera House ad, *LoST* (2 November 1913), 5; "Correspondence: New England and Canada," *MPW* (4 October 1913), 54; and the Colonial ad, *DMN* (25 October 1913), 2. See also the Warner's Features ads that begin in the *NYMT* (21 September 1913), 5: 3; and the *BJ* (18 October 1913), 5.

192. See the Fitzbaugh Hall ad, *RH* (30 November 1913), 19. The term "progressive exhibitor" comes from a Warner's Feature ad, *Motion Picture News* (25 October 1913), 10.

193. See, for instance, the Warner's Features bulletins in *MPW* (28 February 1914), 1161, and (14 March 1914), 1423; the Alhambra ad, *TNB* (7 June 1914), 5; and the Warner's Features ad, *CL* (28 June 1914), S8.

194. See "Davis Will Manage the Bijou Theatre," *PT* (27 December 1913), 3; and the Opera House ad, *LoST* (22 February 1914), 5.

195. Quinn, "Distribution, the Transient Audience, and the Transition to the Feature Film," 50. See also "Famous Players' Regular Releases," *MPN* (2 August 1913), 31; "Famous Players to Put Out Regular Releases," *NYMT* (3 August 1913), 4.2: 1; and the Famous Players ad, *MPW* (26 August 1913), 854–55. Much like Universal and Mutual, Famous Players ran strip ads in Sunday newspapers such as the *Des Moines Register and Leader*, from late April through late July 1913.

196. See the Famous Players ad, *MPW* (6 September 1913), 1030–31.

197. See, for instance, "Feature Films on the Market," *NYDM* (10 September 1913), 28, and (17 September 1913), 28; George Blaisdell, "Mrs. Fiske Triumphs as 'Tess,' " *MPW* (13 September 1913), 1155; and George Blaisdell, "In the Bishop's Carriage," *MPW* (20 September 1913), 1266.

198. See the Knickerbocker ads in the *CL* (31 August 1913), C5, and (14 September 1913), M2; and "Mary Pickford in Town," *CL* (14 September 1913), C4.

199. See the Saxe's Lyric ad, *MT* (7 September 1913), S9; the Famous Players ad, *BJ* (13 September 1913), 5; the Gordon ad, *RH* (21 September 1913), 22; Talley's Broadway ad, *LAT* (21 September 1913), 3: 3; and Grauman's Imperial ad, *SFC* (21 September 1913), 18.

200. See, for instance, the Star ad, *PT* (4 October 1913), 3; "New Majestic Plans," *SPN* (19 October 1913), 3; the Olympia ad, *LyST* (9 November 1913), 2; and the Orpheum ad, *CN* (5 December 1913), 19. Even more theaters in New England are listed in the Famous Players ad, *MPW* (4 October 1913), 97.

201. See, for instance, the Famous Players ads in the *BJ* (1 November 1913), 5, (8 November 1913), 5, (15 November 1913), 5, and (22 November 1913), 5.

202. Such Famous Players titles, and their claims of "elevating the picture art," apparently were what Frank Woods was ridiculing in "What Are We Coming To?" *MPW* (18 July 1914), 442–43.

203. See the four-page supplement in the *DMRL* (2 May 1914).

204. George D. Proctor, "What the Coming Season Means to Motion Pictures," *NYMT* (7 September 1913), 5: 1.

205. "The New Year," *M* (10 January 1914), 17. See also Robert Grau, "New Era for Motion Pictures," *NYDM* (4 March 1914), 4.

206. See Adolph Zukor's own assessment in "Famous Players in Famous Plays," *MPW* (11 July 1914), 186. It is worth noting that Marcus Loew initiated a rather different system by booking features, from a variety of sources, for regularized distribution through his extensive circuit of theaters—"How Loew Booms Feature Films," *NYMT* (21 December 1913), 5: 2.

207. See, for instance, the Paramount ads in *MPW* (25 July 1914), 528–29, in *CT* (5 September 1914), 5, and *DMRL* (6 September 1914), 7.

208. Ben Singer also makes this point, using statistical data, in "Feature Films, Variety Programs," 78–84. The conclusions one can draw from these data, however, are limited because Singer restricts his study to the production of American films, in terms of titles and reels (excluding European films on the US market), and to the problem of exhibiting "feature" films in relatively small theaters, dubiously assuming that the latter attracted the majority of moving picture audiences.

209. *Variety* was particularly insistent on reporting General Film's change in policy: "Service Exercises Picture Exhibitors in New York," *V* (9 May 1913), 14; "Unlicensed Feature Films in Ass'n Licensed Houses," *V* (11 July 1913), 1; " 'Service De Luxe' Planned as Feature by Gen. Film Co.," *V* (29 August 1913), 14; "Feature Pictures Now May Be Seen in All Theaters," *CL* (31 August 1913), C4; and Proctor, "What the Coming Season Means to Motion Pictures," 5: 1.

210. See, for instance, "General Film Starts Exclusive Service for Exhibitors October 13," *NYMT* (5 October 1913), 5: 1; "General Film Exclusive Service," *MPW* (11 October 1913), 139; and "Report on General Film Exclusive Service," *MPW* (25 October 1913), 385.

211. The Film Man, "Comment and Suggestion," *NYDM* (31 December 1913), 24. See also Louis Reeves Harrison, "Your Program," *MPW* (14 February 1914), 785; William N. Selig, "Present Day Trend in Film Lengths," *MPW* (11 July 1914), 181–82; and Carl Laemmle, "Doom of Long Features Predicted," *MPW* (11 July 1914), 185.

Entr'acte 1: Mapping the Local Terrain of Exhibition

1. William E. Sage, "The Triumphal Processioning of the Silent Players," *CL* (21 May 1911), M8. In conjunction with this article, Sage gathered together photographs of a dozen movie stars (all women) and reprinted them as "Film Fairies: Stars of the Stilly Screen," in the Copperplate Pictorial Section of that same Sunday edition of the *Leader*.

2. William E. Sage, "What Moving Pictures Mean to Regular Playhouses," *CL* (8 August 1911), M8.

3. For an excellent study of this region, including Cleveland and other cities in Ohio, see J. C. Teaford, *Cities of the Heartland: The Rise and Fall of the Industrial Midwest* (Bloomington: Indiana University Press, 1993).

4. Roy Stafford, "At the Moving Picture Show," *YV* (30 October 1910), 25.

5. Maggie Valentine, *The Show Starts on the Sidewalk: An Architectural History of the Movie Theatre* (New Haven, Conn.: Yale University Press, 1994), 31. The best one-volume history of exhibition more or less skips this period between the nickelodeon and the palace or "national theater chains"—see Douglas Gomery, *Shared Pleasures: A History of Movie Presentation in the United States* (Madison: University of Wisconsin Press, 1992). Even though her chapter on exhibition supposedly focuses on "the newer 'palatial' theaters," Eileen Bowser does devote several informative pages to both nickelodeons and moving picture theaters after 1910—see Bowser, *The Transformation of Cinema*, 121–36.

6. Ellis Cohen, "In the Moving Picture Field," *NYMT* (23 January 1910), 4.1, 4.

7. See, for instance, Joseph Medill Patterson, "The Nickelodeons, the Poor Man's Elementary Course in the Drama," *Saturday Evening Post* (23 November 1907), 10–11; Walter Prichard Eaton, "The Canned Drama," *American Magazine* (1909), 493–500; William Allen Johnson, "The Moving Picture Show, the New Form of Drama for the Million," *Munsey's* (August 1909), 633–40; Asa Steele, "The Moving-Picture Show," *World's Work* (February 1911), 14218–32; and Mary Heaton Vorse, "Some Picture Show Audiences," *Outlook* (24 June 1911), 441–47. The Vorse essay is collected in Gregory Waller, ed., *Moviegoing in America: A Sourcebook in the History of Film Exhibition* (London: Blackwell, 2002), 50–53.

8. See Michael M. Davis, *The Exploitation of Pleasure; A Study of Commercial Recreations in New York City* (New York: Russell Sage Foundation, 1911); Louise de Koven Bowen, *Five and Ten Cent Theaters: Two Investigations* (Chicago: Juvenile Protective Association, 1911); Rowland Haynes, "Recreation Survey of Kansas City, Mo.," in *Second Annual Report of the Recreation Department Board of Public Welfare* (Kansas City, 1912), 3–68; Francis R. North, *A Recreation Survey of the City of Waltham, Massachusetts* (Waltham: E. L. Berry, 1913); and William Trufant Foster, *Vaudeville and Motion Picture Shows: A Study of Theaters in Portland, Oregon*, Portland: Reed College Social Services Series 2, 1914. For an overview of these surveys, see Alan Havig, "The Commercial Amusement Audience in Early 20th-Century American Cities," *Journal of American Culture* 5.1 (1982), 1–19.

9. In 1910, Essanay held a contest to coin the best word to describe this new form of entertainment, and "photoplay" was selected for its alignment with cultural "uplift"; the judges hoped that one day "going to the photoplay" would be like "going to the opera"— *N* (15 October 1910), 226. See also " 'Photoplay' Wins in Essanay Con-

test," *Film Index* (15 October 1911o), 3. For an instructive analysis of the issues involved in early attempts to describe and define moving pictures, see Gregory Waller, "Photodramas and Photoplays, Stage and Screen, 1909–1915," in Leonardo Quaresima and Laura Vicki, eds., *The Tenth Muse: Cinema and the Other Arts* (Udine: Forum, 2001), 575–85.

10. My focus generally excludes, however, several excellent recent case studies such as Waller, *Main Street Amusements: Movies and Commercial Entertainment in a Southern City, 1896–1930* (Washington, D.C.: Smithsonian Institute, 1995); and Fuller, *At the Picture Show.* It also has to exclude most of the research on early cinema—for instance, that of Robert C. Allen and his students on North Carolina—presented at the Commonwealth Conference on American Cinema and Everyday Life, University College London, 25–28 June 2003.

11. "Picture Show Poor Man's Vacation Trip and Sure Cure for 'Blues' for All," *CN* (23 April 1911), 14. One of the theater owners interviewed in this story was A. H. Abrams of the Odeon, where my grandfather would soon work as a musician.

12. H. I. Dillenback, "Looking into the Future," *N* (15 March 1910), 143–44.

13. David S. Hulfish, "Motion-Picture Theater," *Cyclopedia of Motion-Picture Work*, vol. 1 (Chicago: American Technical Society, 1914 [1911]), 165–210. Hulfish was the "technical editor" of the trade journal *Nickelodeon* (1909–11), which then became *Motography; Motion-Picture Work* went through at least three editions by 1915. A major section of Hulfish's *Motion-Picture Work* is excerpted in Waller, *Moviegoing in America*, 54–62.

14. Frank E. Woods, "Pictures Divided into Three Grades," *NYDM* (9 July 1913), 25.

15. Epes Winthrop Sargent, "Advertising for Exhibitors," *MPW* (6 December 1913), 1141–42.

16. W. Stephen Bush," Gradations in Service," *MPW* (2 May 1914), 645.

17. Frederic J. Haskins, "Film Makers Are Divided into Two Hostile Camps," *SPPP* (17 October 1911), 6.

18. William T. Braun, "Building Codes and Picture Theaters," *N* (25 February 1911), 211. In Boston, theaters seating more than 800 paid higher licensing fees; in Peoria, Illinois, those seating more than 400 paid only slightly higher licensing fees— "Correspondence: In the Mississippi Valley," *MPW* (16 December 1911), 914; and "Correspondence: New England," *MPW* (20 January 1912), 215.

19. "Motion Picture Theaters in Greater New York," *MPW* (1 April 1911), 8. Philadelphia had a slightly different arrangement: the city charged a licensing fee of $100 for all theaters, whereas the state charged $500 for those seating more than 400 and only $35 for those seating fewer—W. H. Prescott, "Little Items Gathered in the East," *N* (15 February 1910), 105.

20. "Correspondence: Youngstown, O," *MPW* (25 November 1911), 650.

21. Braun, "Building Codes and Picture Theaters," 212. Sometime in 1911 this apparently changed so that both downtown and residential theaters could present vaudeville and moving pictures— James S. McQuade, "Motion Picture Affairs in St. Louis," *MPW* (4 November 1911), 362.

22. "New York Exhibitors Now Favor 450 Seats," *MPW* (12 April 1913), 148; and C. H. Blackwall, "New York Moving Picture Theatre Law," *The Bricklayer* 23 (1914), 47.

23. "The Moving Picture Theatre," *Architecture and Building* 43.8 (May 1911), 320; and Blackwall, "New York Moving Picture Theatre Law," 46–57.

24. "Population—Ohio," *Thirteenth Census of the United States, III: Population Reports by States* (Washington, D.C.: Government Printing Office, 1913), 363, 398, 427–28. The census may not have been interested in distinguishing people according to class or income, but it did differentiate "native whites" and "foreign-born whites." Of Cleveland's 560,000 people, nearly 200,000 were listed in the latter category, with more than half coming from Austria (many of them Czechs), Germany, Hungary (many of them Slovaks), Ireland, and Russia (which nearly always meant Russian Jews). These immigrant groups still had their own newspapers at the time—see "American Spirit Predominates the Foreign Language Papers in Cleveland," *CL* (21 December 1912), M2. Jewish immigrants, whether arriving earlier from Germany or later from Russia, were estimated to number 100,000 by 1912, a 40 percent increase from ten years earlier—see "Estimates 100,000 Jews in Cleveland," *CL* (28 October 1912), 2.

25. On the Dreamland and Duchess, respectively, see Charles F. Morris, "A Picture Theater in the Mission Style," *N* (November 1909), 137–38; and Jas. S. McQuade, "Chicago Letter," *MPW* (22 February 1913), 764. Although unspecified, the Orpheum was touted as having "the largest seating capacity of any downtown theater show in Cleveland"—see "Some Big 'Flickers' in Picture Business," *CL* (9 February 1913), W4.

26. On the Home and Superior, respectively, see "Some 'Flickers' in Picture Business," *CL* (17 November 1912), B5; and "Superior Rises from Small Start," *CL* (8 December 1912), B7.

27. On the National, Penn Square, Alhambra, Knickerbocker, U.S. Theater, and Monarch, respectively, see Charles Morris, "The National Theater in Cleveland," *N* (December 1909), 169–70; "Woodland to Have Fine New Theater," *CL* (3 September 1911), B4; "The Next Step," *M* (September 1911), 107; "Among the Picture Theaters," *M* (March 1912), 140, and (April 1912), 189; and the Monarch ad, *CL* (23 February 1913), M11. According to a later article, the Penn Square was owned by Emil Myer (who had first run a theater on Halstead Street in Chicago), had 624 seats, and was located on a high-traffic "business corner" near a "high-class residential section"—"Among the Picture Theaters," *MPW* (18 July 1914), 445. The reference to a "second downtown," originally called Doan's Corners, comes from David D. Van Tassel, ed., *The Encyclopedia of Cleveland History* (Bloomington: Indiana University Press, 1996), 359.

28. Just slightly more than 100 moving picture theaters were listed in the 1911–12 *Cleveland Official City Directory,* 2036–37. See also the reference to "120 moving picture theaters" whose "average seating capacity is estimated at 425," in "Figure It Yourself," *CL* (21 January 1912), S6.

29. See, for instance, the Orpheum ad, *CC* (28 December 1912), 2; and the Princess ad, *CC* (18 January 1913), 2. A block ad for a special Labor Day issue, in 1912, suggests that theaters in the northeast (Doan), east (Dixie, Glenside), and southeast (Market Square) commercial districts, and another on the city's far west edge (Lakewood, Madison), attracted working-class customers—see the *CC* (31 August 1912), 12. The downtown Bronx also was included in this ad.

30. Owned by C. Clayton Green, a well-known black businessman (with interests in a sofa bed company, laundry company, and restaurant), the Alpha Theater, 3206 Central Avenue, advertised almost weekly in the *Cleveland Gazette,* from July through December 1912. After Green suffered a stroke, the theater became the Ogden (man-

aged by Helen Ogden) in May 1913. According to the 1913–14 city directory, another theater one block away and across the street took the Alpha name shortly thereafter. See Kenneth Kusmer, *A Ghetto Takes Shape: Black Cleveland, 1870–1930* (Urbana: University of Illinois Press, 1976), 82–83, 142; and the Odgen Theater ad, *CG* (3 May 1913), 3.

31. Of the 300,000 people in Minneapolis, almost a 50 percent increase from ten years earlier, the 1910 census listed more than 115,000 as "foreign-born white," with the majority coming undoubtedly from Scandinavia—see "Population of Individual Cities" and "Color or Race, Nativity, and Parentage," *Thirteenth Census of the United States*, 64, 95. For the number of picture theaters in Minneapolis, see "Thorough Inspection of Motion Picture Theaters Reveals Some Minor Faults, But Not One 'Fire Trap,' " *MJ* (22 October 1911), 5.11. In the adjacent city of St. Paul (200,000 population), by late 1911, moving picture theaters had become a "routine part of neighborhood life"—see "Lure of Film Shows," *SPPP* (1 October 1911), 3.8.

32. Of the 170,000 people in Toledo, the 1910 census listed more than 30,000 as "foreign-born white," with nearly half coming from Germany and the next largest numbers, from Russia, Poland, Hungary, Canada, and Italy—see "Population—Ohio," *Thirteenth Census of the United States*, 363, 398. For the number of picture theaters in Toledo, see "The Moving Picture Situation in Toledo, O.," *B* (28 January 1911), 6.

33. For other similar cities such as Rochester, Washington, D.C. (eighty-seven theaters), and Boston (forty-seven theaters), see "Bilakem Loose Again," *FI* (23 July 1910), 6; "Motion Picture Conditions in Many Towns and Cities of All-America," *B* (28 January 1911), 8; "Rochester Dotes on Motion Pictures," *NYMT* (21 May 1911), 4: 6; and "The 'Movie' House; Its Development," *BJ* (6 September 1913), 4. Tom Moore, "the 'Original' moving picture man" in Washington, controlled four major downtown picture theaters, as well as five more in other parts of the city—see W. H., "Washington, D. C.," *MPW* (20 April 1912), 250.

34. The seating capacity of the Crystal and Lyric, respectively, come from "New Picture Theater Nearly Ready," *MJ* (16 August 1909), 12; and James S. McQuade, "The Belasco of Motion Picture Presentations," *MPW* (9 December 1911), 796.

35. McQuade, "The Belasco of Motion Picture Presentations," 796–98.

36. This survey of Minneapolis picture theaters beyond the downtown area derives from a comparative analysis of the theater listings in the 1909–14 city directories, a 1902 map of the city, and maps illustrating early ethnic neighborhoods in June Drenning Holmquist, *They Chose Minnesota: A Survey of the State's Ethnic Groups* (St. Paul: Minnesota Historical Society, 1981).

37. Another theater on the "east side," the Milo, was said to cater to recent Jewish immigrants—see "A Theater Showing Only Biblical Films," *M* (December 1911), 258.

38. "Lure of the Film Shows," 3: 8.

39. On the Royal, Colonial, Empress, and Princess, respectively, see "Little Journeys in Pictureland," *FI* (2 July 1910), 12; "At the Photo Plays," *TNB* (3 February 1912), 14; "Empress Theater Unfair," *TUL* (17 May 1912), 2; and the Princess ad, *TUL* (29 August 1913), supplement. A Toledo reporter who, in the 1950s, wrote a series of stories on early moving picture theaters put the capacity of the Crown at 200 seats—Mitch Woodbury, " 'Movietime, U.S.A.' Evokes Plenty of Memories," *TB* (14 October 1951), from the Mitch Woodbury Scrapbooks, Local History Department, Toledo

Public Library. Although not impossible, this seems doubtful, since the Crown was one of the first theaters to handle multiple-reel films and advertised regularly at least into the summer of 1912.

40. For a summary history of Toledo's commercial districts and ethnic communities, see Charles N. Glaab and Morgan J. Barclay, *Toledo: Gateway to the Great Lakes* (Tulsa, Okla.: Continental Heritage Press, 1982), 66, 68, 71, 95, 99.

41. The seating capacity of the Yale comes from Mitch Woodbury, "Put a Nickel in Nickelodeon," *Toledo Sunday Times* (8 April 1956), from the Mitch Woodbury Scrapbook, Local History Department, Toledo Public Library. The seating capacity for the Laurel comes from the "grand opening" ad, *TNB* (2 August 1913), 2. For a complete listing of moving picture theaters, see the *Toledo City Directory* from 1906 to 1914. The seating capacities of the better residential picture theaters in Boston also were around 600 to 700—see "How Movie Houses Build Up the Suburbs," *BJ* (20 December 1913), 5.

42. See the Hart ads, *TUL* (10 December 1912), 6, and (23 May 1913), 2. Toledo had "relatively strong unions" during this period—see Glaab and Barclay, *Toledo*, 62.

43. Of the 85,000 people in Des Moines, the 1910 census listed slightly more than 10,000 as "foreign-born white," with the greatest number coming from Scandinavia, Germany, and Russia—see "Supplement for Iowa," *Thirteenth Census of the United States*, 624. Like many Iowa cities, Des Moines was dominated by German-born immigrants, many of them with second- or third-generation families by 1910. For a more thorough analysis of motion picture exhibition in this city, see Abel, "The Movies in a 'Not So Visible Place': Des Moines, Iowa, 1911–1914," in Kathryn Fuller Seeley and George Potamianos, eds., *Beyond the Bowery*, forthcoming from University of California Press.

44. The Family was owned and managed by Jacob Milowslowsky, who, unlike A. H. Blank, Isaac Ruben, or Julius Singer (who first ran the Laemmle Film Service branch office), remained in the city rather than move to higher positions in the cinema industry.

45. Namur's downtown drugstore supposedly had the "largest soda fountain in the world" and was still "the most popular" in the city in 1914—see the Namur ads, *DMN* (30 June 1907), 11, and (30 June 1914), 3.

46. See, for instance, the Idle Hour University Place Theatre ad, *DMN* (12 September 1911), 8; Namur's (Highland Park) Theatre ad, *DMN* (15 November 1911), 6; "Photo Plays," *DMN* (18 February 1912), 6; and Namur's block ad, *DMN* (18 November 1912), 6.

47. According to the city directories, the theaters near University Place had names such as Rex, Crystal, and Cupid; those surrounding the state capitol, Mystic, Iris, Ideal, and Amuz-U. The Cupid was owned and managed by two women, Mrs. Dodson and Mrs. Baker—see "Charter Car to See Movies," *DMN* (2 April 1913), 5. The immigrant backgrounds of Des Moines neighborhoods can be gathered from the churches listed in the city directories: churches that still held services in Swedish or Norwegian as well as English, for instance, were located on the east side.

48. See "Elbert & Getchel to Make Changes at Unique-Majestic," *DMN* (30 April 1911), 6; "Photo Plays," *DMN* (27 January 1912), 3; the Casino ad, *DMRL* (4 December 1912), 4; the Theatre Royal ad, *DMN* (2 February 1913), 6; the large Casino ad,

DMN (16 March 1913), 6; "Star Theatre Sold," *DMN* (9 May 1913), 4; "New Movie House," *DMN* (15 June 1913), 13; "Majestic Will Be Turned into Movie Theater," *DMN* (3 September 1913), 5; "New Palace Is Beautiful Theater," *DMN* (26 October 1913), 6; and "Black Cat Movie House," *DMN* (2 November 1913), 2. The seating capacities for the Majestic, Unique, Casino, Family, and Palace come, respectively, from "New Vaudeville Theater to Open," *DMN* (20 August 1910), 6; the Unique ad, *DMN* (26 January 1913), 6; the Casino ad, *DMN* (16 March 1913), 6; "New Movie House," *DMN* (15 June 1913), 13; and the Palace ad, *DMN* (24 October 1913), 10.

49. In December 1913, *Moving Picture World* reported that there were "twenty-seven moving picture houses" in Des Moines, which is more than are listed in either the *Des Moines City Directory* for either 1913 or 1914—"Correspondence: Iowa," *MPW* (13 December 1913), 1293.

50. "New Garden Theatre Will Open This Afternoon," "Builders and Furnishers of New Garden Theater and Odd Fellows Building. The Finest in Iowa," and the Garden Theater ad, *DMRL* (2 May 1914), supplement.

51. This was not the case in the larger northern Massachusetts city of Worcester (145,000 population in 1910), where Roy Rosenzweig found not only large downtown picture theaters quite early but also both large and small neighborhood theaters, especially in "the multiethnic, working-class East Side"—Roy Rosenzweig, *Eight Hours for What We Will: Workers and Leisure in an Industrial City, 1870–1920* (Cambridge: Cambridge University Press, 1983), 192–93.

52. "Color or Race, Nativity, and Parentage," in *Thirteenth Census of the United States*, 95. See also Arthur L. Enro Jr., ed., *Cotton Was King: A History of Lowell, Massachusetts* (Lowell: New Hampshire Publishing, 1976).

53. On the Colonial, Merrimack Square, New Jewel, and Premier, respectively, see "A New Moving Picture House," *LCC* (8 October 1910), 6; Merrimack Square Theater ad, *LCC* (24 November 1911), 13; "New Theatre Will Be Built," *LCC* (23 May 1912), 6; and Henry, "New England and Canada," *MPW* (17 January 1914), 303.

54. "Color or Race, Nativity, and Parentage," 96. On the Broadway, New Nickel, and Victoria, respectively, see "New 'Broadway Theatre' an Elaborate Structure," *LE* (22 July 1910), n.p.; "The Nickel—The House Beautiful," *FI* (17 September 1910), 7; and "Victoria Theater, Lawrence, Mass.," *MPW* (22 April 1911), 886. See also Donald B. Cole, *Immigrant City: Lawrence, Massachusetts, 1845–1921* (Chapel Hill: University of North Carolina Press, 1963).

55. Lynn's population increased 30 percent from 1900—see "Population of Individual Cities," *Thirteenth Census of the United States*, 64. Of those 90,000, the 1910 census listed slightly more than 30 percent as "foreign-born white," somewhat lower than the 35 percent in Boston and substantially lower than the 40 percent in Lowell and nearly 50 percent in Lawrence—see "Color or Race, Nativity, and Parentage," 96. See also Keith Melder, *Life and Times in Shoe City: The Shoe Workers of Lynn* (Salem, Mass.: Essex Institute, 1979).

56. On the Central Square and Olympia, respectively, see "The Central Square Theatre, Lynn's Newest Playhouse," *LDI* (21 December 1910), 14; "Mammoth House for Lynn, Mass.," *FI* (22 April 1911), 13; and the Olympia ad, *LDI* (7 October 1911), 2. Until the Gaumont-Palace opened in Paris in November, the Olympia may have been the largest picture theater in the world. One other theater, the Pastime, opened in West Lynn, in either 1909 or 1910.

57. *Thirteenth Census of the United States,* 96. For the seating of the Star and Pastime, see "New Star Theatre," *PT* (23 November 1907), 5; and the Pastime ad, *PT* (16 September 1912), 5. For information on the immigrant populations of Pawtucket and Central Falls, see *Pawtucket, Rhode Island: Statewide Historical Preservation Report P-PA-1* (Providence: Rhode Island Historical Preservation Commission, October 1978), 26; and Louise Lamphere, *From Working Daughters to Working Mothers: Immigrant Women in a New England Industrial Community* (Ithaca, N.Y.: Cornell University Press, 1987). The two new theaters in Central Falls were the New Casino, near the Polish-Jewish immigrant neighborhood, and the Dexter, near Irish and French-Canadian working-class neighborhoods—see the *Pawtucket and Central Falls RI Directory* (Providence, R.I.: Sampson and Murdock, 1913), 731; and *Pawtucket and Central Falls RI Directory* (Providence, R.I.: Sampson and Murdock, 1914), 717.

58. "Population, Ohio," 418. Of the 80,000 people in Youngstown, the 1910 census listed 25,000 as "foreign-born white," with the greatest number coming from Hungary (many of these Slovak), Austria (many of these Czech), and Italy. The epithet for the city comes from a story in the *Youngstown Vindicator* (14 April 1907)—Clipping Files, Youngstown Public Library.

59. For an extensive summary of the Youngstown vaudeville houses and moving picture theaters, see "Correspondence: Youngstown, O.," *MPW* (25 November 1911), 650–51. For the Rex, see "Among the Picture Theaters," *M* (January 1912), 44. In 1911–12, the picture theaters catering to Italians had names such as the Columbus, Luna, Luxor, Napoli, and Roma—see the *Youngstown Directory* (1912), 1217–18. According to city directories, several of Youngstown's initial moving picture men were in the liquor business: C. W. Deibel had been vice president of the Gallagher Company, a wholesaler in liquor and drugs; Dan Robbins had run a saloon on East Federal. It was Dan Robbins who, with the Warner brothers, opened a small vaudeville house and several nickelodeons under the name of Cascade Amusements in nearby New Castle, Pennsylvania, in 1907—see "South Mill Street Theater Will Soon Open the Season," *NCH* (8 November 1907), n.p.; "Cascade Theater to Be Formally Opened to Public Tonight," *NCH* (19 November 1907), 1; and the Cascade ads, *NCH* (16 September 1908), 4. When the Warners returned to Youngstown, after developing a profitable rental exchange, Duquesne Amusement & Supply, in Pittsburgh, Harry Warner built the downtown Rex Theater with David Robbins, who had run the Robbins family grocery business on the city's far west side.

60. "Youngstown Ministers Report," *M* (April 1911), 16.

61. According to the Youngstown city directories, only one of these residential theaters had a name, the Hazelton Dome, which opened in 1912; the few others listed only their owner's name.

62. See "Correspondence: Youngstown, O.," 650; the photo-story on the reconstruction of the Dome in the *YV* (7 July 1912), 7; and the full-page ad for the opening of the New Dome Theatre, *YV* (22 December 1912), 24.

63. "Population—Ohio," *Thirteenth Census of the United States,* 363, 418–19. As in Youngstown, "Blue laws" forced the Grand Opera, Orpheum, and Auditorium to present special Sunday programs of moving pictures. See also "New Movie House for Crystal Park," *CN* (31 August 1913), 16. The Happy Hour, a former skating rink, was open weekday evenings and weekend afternoons and evenings—see the Happy Hour ad, *CN* (29 October 1911), 18.

64. Gomery, *Shared Pleasures*, 34–40. See also James S. McQuade, "Saxe Motion Picture Enterprises," *FI* (1 April 1911), 10–11; and Jas. S. McQuade, "Chicago Letter," *MPW* (9 December 1911), 808, and (15 March 1912), 1088. By early 1910, *Nickelodeon* already was noticing this trend to "the so-called syndicate plan" whereby a "string" of theaters was "operated by one company," a prime example being Automatic Vaudeville which controlled twenty-seven theaters, including the Unique in New York City—see Charles F. Morris, "A Pair of New York's Picture Theaters," *N* (15 March 1910), 141; and "Little Items Gathered in the East," *N* (1 April 1910), 172. See also "Marcus Loew, Coming King of Vaudeville," *NYMT* (8 May 1910), 4.1: 7.

65. "Some Big 'Flickers' in Picture Business," *CL* (24 November 1912), W6, and (22 December 1912), S6.

66. "Mandelbaum Sells Theaters," *CL* (2 November 1912), W7. Located in the suburban shopping district that would become the city's "second downtown," the Knickerbocker may have been a prototype of the theaters that would later anchor the Balaban & Katz chain—see Gomery, *Shared Pleasures*, 44.

67. A. H. Blank eventually would become a regional executive for the Publix Theaters controlled by Paramount—see *Who's Who in Des Moines* (Des Moines, Iowa: Robert Baldwin, 1929), 31; and "August 18, 1971," *Variety Obituaries, VII, 1969–1974* (New York: Garland, 1988). The Star's initial owner, Isaac Ruben, meanwhile, moved to Minneapolis to develop, with M. L. Finkelstein, a major chain of picture theaters there—see Montague Norton, "Picture Theaters of the Better Class," *N* (15 May 1910), 256; "New House for Minneapolis," *FI* (1 April 1911), 13; and "June 2, 1931," *Variety Obituaries II, 1929–1938* (New York: Garland, 1988).

68. "Toledo to Have $90,000 House," *M* (4 January 1913), 2; the Empress/Laurel ad, *TB* (20 August 1913), 7; and the Empress Amusement Co. ad, *TB* (10 September 1913), 7.

69. See, for instance, "Correspondence: New England," *MPW* (12 October 1912), 156. Nathaniel Gordon would return to his hometown of Rochester to build the Gordon Photoplay House (1,800 seats) in early 1913—see "Made 'Pile' in Picture Houses," *RH* (2 February 1913), 19; and the Gordon ad, *RH* (16 February 1913), 23.

70. The flagship Scenic Temple in Boston (1,444 seats) was one of two "luxury movie theaters" by 1910, and presented only three shows daily—see Richard Butsch, *The Making of American Audiences: From Stage to Television, 1850–1990* (Cambridge: Cambridge University Press, 2000), 160.

71. See, for instance, "Correspondence: New England," *MPW* (20 January 1912), 215, (21 December 1912), 1204, and (8 November 1913), 626; "Motion Picture Houses," *BJ* (13 September 1913), 4; and "Davis Will Manage the Bijou Theatre," *PT* (27 December 1913)—Clippings Book, Keith-Albee Collection, Special Collections, University of Iowa Library. A. A. Kellerman owned the Victoria (as well as the Pastime) until Hiram Abrams, who had interests in some twenty-one picture theaters around Boston and became associated with the Boston office for Famous Players, made it part of his Victoria Theater Company in late 1913—see "Prominent Personalities," *M* (12 July 1913), 12.

72. W. Stephen Bush, "Is the 'Nickel Show' on the Wane?" *MPW* (28 February 1914), 1065.

73. The Film Man, "Comments and Suggestions," *NYDM* (16 October 1912), 25.

74. One of the first trade press writers to argue for the value of such neighborhood

theaters was Margaret I. MacDonald, in "Objectionable Theaters," *MPN* (16 December 1911), 7. That moving picture theaters, along with urban transportation systems, contributed to the growth of secondary commercial districts in many cities is acknowledged in Thomas E. Dockwell, "Common Sense in Newspaper Solicitation," *Editor and Publisher* (18 January 1913), 19. A productive analysis of this phenomenon in one city can be found in J. A. Lindstrom, "Where Development Has Just Begun: Nickelodeon Location, Moving Picture Audiences, and Neighborhood Development in Chicago," in Keil and Stamp, *American Cinema's Transitional Era*, 217–38.

Chapter 2: The "Usable Past" of Westerns, Part 1

1. See, for instance, "Film Charts," *MPN* (29 April 1911), 21, and (20 May 1911), 20. Nine months earlier, the *New York Dramatic Mirror* had done a survey of all the films released on the market in July and had come up with a similar set of categories, except for westerns, which it subsumed under the more general term "melodrama"— see "Pictures Need No Censoring," *NYDM* (14 August 1910), 25. Six months earlier, in categorizing musical accompaniment for moving pictures, Clarence Sinn also subsumed "cowboy pictures" within melodrama, "more or less of a sensational order"— see "Music for the Picture," *MPW* (3 December 1910), 1285.

2. "Letters to the Editor," *MPW* (11 February 1911), 314.

3. "In the Far West," *Bio* (9 February 1911), 11–12.

4. "Motion Picture Reviews," *B* (11 March 1911), 15.

5. This chapter and the next extend the argument developed in the last chapter of Richard Abel, *The Red Rooster Scare: Making Cinema American, 1900–1910* (Berkeley and Los Angeles: University of California Press, 1999), 151–74.

6. Although primarily interested in proposing a theoretical model of genre useful for cinema studies, Rick Altman offers a relevant sketch of the western as a genre-in-the-state-of-becoming, in *Film/Genre* (London: British Film Institute, 1999), 36–38. See also Nanna Verhoeff's imaginative, insightful perspective on the western as a "genre-in-the-making," in *After the Beginning: Westerns before 1915* (Utrecht University, 2002). As Verhoeff's dissertation suggests, recently there has been growing interest in early westerns, notably in two books that appeared after these two chapters were written: Andre Brodie Smith, *Shooting Cowboys and Indians: Silent Western Films, American Culture, and the Birth of Hollywood* (Boulder: University of Colorado Press, 2003); and Scott Simmon, *The Invention of the Western Film: A Cultural History of the Genre's First Half-Century* (Cambridge: Cambridge University Press, 2003).

7. Herbert Blau, *The Audience* (Baltimore: Johns Hopkins University Press, 1990), 21. For a definition of "constellated communities," particularly as distinct from Anderson's "imagined community," see Altman, *Film/Genre*, 161–62, 198, 199. Ultimately, my analysis takes up the issue of how the western may have served (or not) as a "regulatory schema facilitating the integration of diverse factions into a single social fabric"—see Altman, *Film/Genre*, 208. The phrase "usable past" comes from Van Wyck Brooks's influential essay, "Creating a Usable Past," *Dial* 64 (11 April 1918), 337–41.

8. Hansen, "The Mass Production of the Senses," 340–44. Curiously, Hansen offers "slapstick comedy, adventure serials, and detective films," but not westerns, as examples of that "new sensibility" of "Americanism" or American modernity during the 1910s.

9. See, for instance, Hans Leigh, "Acting and Action," *MPW* (2 October 1909), 443; "Essanay Will Release Two Reels," *MPW* (6 November 1909), 638; and "Comments on the Films," *MPW* (8 January 1910), 17.

10. "Comments on the Films," *MPW* (13 August 1910), 350, and (24 September 1910), 688; and "Reviews of Licensed Films," *NYDM* (14 September 1910), 32.

11. Anderson wrote, directed, and starred in most of these early Essanay westerns, which, given his commitment to nomadic location shooting, were filmed near Denver, El Paso, Santa Monica, Santa Barbara, Redlands, and San Rafael, until he finally established a studio in Niles Canyon, thirty miles from Oakland, California, in the early summer of 1912. The best studies of Anderson are David Kiehn, *Broncho Billy and the Essanay Company* (Berkeley, Calif.: Farwell Books, 2003); and Smith, *Shooting Cowboys and Indians*, 37–69, 133–56. See also "The Essanay Story," probably written by Stuart Nixon, editor of the *Niles Township Register*, in March 1953, in the Hollywood Museum Collection, Margaret Herrick Library, AMPAS. Perhaps the earliest reappraisal of Anderson came in William K. Everson, *A Pictorial History of the Western Film* (New York: Citadel, 1969), 18, 20–21; that reappraisal was revised and amplified in Everson, *American Silent Film* (New York: Oxford University Press, 1979), 241–43, as well as in Kevin Brownlow, *The War, the West, and the Wilderness* (New York: Knopf, 1978), 249–53. A 35mm viewing print of *Under Western Skies* (920 feet) is available at the LoC.

12. "Comments on the Films," *MPW* (20 August 1910), 406.

13. Alan Trachtenberg, *The Incorporation of America: Culture and Society in the Gilded Age* (New York: Hill and Wang, 1982), 17–18. The catalog edited by William Truettner, *The West as America* (Washington, D.C.: Smithsonian Institution, 1991), is an extraordinary source of images from that iconographic tradition. For an analysis of earlier western films in the context of this tradition, see Abel, *The Red Rooster Scare*, 152–53.

14. Verhoeff, *After the Beginning*, 26.

15. See, for instance, the reviews of Bison's *The Flight of Redwing*, Nestor's *The Ranchman's Bride*, and Champion's *The Way of the West* in "Reviews of Independent Films," *NYDM* (23 November 1910), 31.

16. "Comments on the Films," *MPW* (26 November 1910), 1238.

17. "Variety's Own Picture Reviews," *V* (25 February 1910), 15.

18. "The Indian and the Cowboy," *MPW* (17 December 1910), 1399. See also the article reprinted from the *Los Angeles Times* as "The Press and the Picture," *MPW* (3 December 1910), 1290.

19. "Pictures That Children Like," *FI* (21 January 1911), 3.

20. "The Passing of the Western Subject," *N* (18 February 1911), 181–82.

21. "What Would the Film Producer Do without These?" *N* (11 March 1911), 278.

22. Exceptions would include the letters to "The Spectator" complaining, for instance, about "the awful flood of cowboy and Indian subjects that the film-makers still persist in turning out," in *NYDM* (12 April 1911), 30, and (19 April 1911), 30.

23. Representatives of several tribes appeared in Washington, D.C., protesting the depiction of Indians in westerns—see "Those Indignant Indians [reprinted from the *New York World*]," *N* (4 March 1911), 246; "The Indian and the Film," *B* (11 March 1911), 14; and "Indian War on Films," *MPW* (18 March 1911), 581. The immediate cause of this uproar probably was Selig's *Curse of the Redman* (February 1911), written and directed by Hobart Bosworth—Smith, *Shooting Cowboys and Indians*, 85.

24. In Canton, the managers of the Majestic and Dreamland were interviewed in "Picture Show Poor Man's Vacation Trip and Sure Cure for 'Blues' for All," *CN* (23 April 1911), 14. In Lynn, the Theatre Comique and Central Square Theatre called particular attention to westerns as well as Biograph films in their ads in the *Lynn Daily Item* between December 1911 and February 1912.

25. See, respectively, "Reviews of Licensed Films," *NYDM* (4 January 1911), 29; and "Critical Reviews of Licensed Films," *NYMT* (5 March 1911), 4.1: 4.

26. See the Selig ad on the inside front cover of *Nickelodeon* (June 1911). Other highly regarded examples of this new batch of westerns were *One of Nature's Noblemen* and *Range Pals,* both starring Hobart Bosworth—see "Critical Reviews of Licensed Films," *NYMT* (4 June 1911), 4: 7; and "Reviews of Licensed Films," *NYDM* (28 June 1911), 30.

27. "What an Audience Likes," *MPN* (3 June 1911), 13. Essanay's comic western series featuring Alkali Ike also came in for praise—see, for instance, "Critical Reviews of Licensed Films," *NYMT* (28 May 1911), 4: 7. Even reputable critics such as W. Stephen Bush, who usually preferred "art" films, occasionally recognized the "tragic power" of a western such as Kalem's *The Mexican Joan of Arc* (July 1911)—see W. Stephen Bush, "*The Mexican Joan of Arc,*" *MPW* (15 July 1911), 19.

28. See the Selig ad in *MPW* (29 July 1911), 227. Mix worked and trained at the Miller Brothers' 101 Ranch in Oklahoma before teaming up with Selig in 1910—see Paul Reddin, *Wild West Shows* (Urbana: University of Illinois Press, 1999), 190–91. See also Bowser, *The Transformation of Cinema,* 172.

29. A 35mm viewing print of *Saved by the Pony Express* (920 feet) is available at the LoC.

30. "Selecting the Programme," *MPN* (9 September 1911), 14. See also "Comments on the Films," *MPW* (12 August 1911), 377.

31. "Letters to the Editor: Cowboys Always Popular," *MPW* (12 August 1911), 383. The only evidence of criticism in the *World* that summer came in a letter from Cleveland, asking, "Why in the name of common sense are so many film producers Western mad?" and in Bush's diatribe against Indian stereotypes—see "Letters to the Editor," *MPW* (22 July 1911), 132; and Bush, "Moving Picture Absurdities," *MPW* (16 September 1911), 773.

32. See the Vitagraph ad in *NYDM* (15 March 1911), 31. Although companies such as Edison, Biograph, and Vitagraph (all located initially in the East and well known in film histories) did make westerns, Smith rightly singles out Selig and Essanay (headquartered in Chicago), along with Bison, as the most important early producers in the "genre"—Smith, *Shooting Cowboys and Indians,* 3–4, 58.

33. Simmon calls many of these films "Eastern Westerns," partly because their stories often followed the tradition of James Fenimore Cooper's novels and partly, I would add, because they tended to be shot on location in the eastern United States—see Simmon, *The Invention of the Western Film,* 12–31.

34. "Critical Reviews of Independent Films," *NYMT* (3 September 1911), 4.2: 4. In the summer and fall of 1911, according to its ads in *Billboard,* the Powers company manufactured at least one Indian picture per week.

35. "Critical Reviews of Independent Films," *NYMT* (4 June 1911), 4: 6, and (8 October 1911), 4: 6. A 35mm viewing print of *A Redskin's Bravery* (645 feet) is available at the LoC.

36. "Critical Reviews of Independent Films," *NYMT* (19 February 1911), 4: 4, and (19 March 1911), 4.1: 5. James Young Deer and his wife, Red Wing, both of whom had performed with the 101 Ranch Wild West and then worked on western films for Kalem, Lubin, Biograph, and Vitagraph before joining Bison, arguably were crucial to the popularity of the company's early westerns and helped establish the New York Motion Picture Company as one of the most successful of the Independents—Smith, *Shooting Cowboys and Indians,* 75–82.

37. "Motion Picture Reviews," *B* (17 June 1911), 50; and "Reviews of Independent Films," *NYDM* (21 June 1911), 32. Darkfeather was from "an old aristocratic Spanish family" in Los Angeles, but her study of Indian customs endeared her to many tribes and led to her being described as "the greatest exponent of Indian women in the motion picture business"—"Best 'Indian' in Films Is Not Real Redskin," *CL* (22 December 1912), S5.

38. "Little Dove's Romance," *MPW* (2 September 1911), 602; and "Reviews of Independent Films," *NYDM* (13 September 1911), 26. A 16mm viewing print of *Little Dove's Romance* (388 feet), from the Paul Killiam Collection, is available at the LoC.

39. "Reviews of Licensed Films," *NYDM* (29 November 1911), 26, 28.

40. "The Vogue of Western and Military Drama," *MPW* (5 August 1911), 271; Edward S. Curtis, *The North American Indian: Being a Series of Volumes Picturing and Describing the Indians of the United States and Alaska* (Cambridge, Mass.: Harvard University Press, 1907–30). See also Edward Buscombe, "Photographing the Indian," in Edward Buscombe and Roberta Pearson, eds., *Back in the Saddle Again: New Essays on the Western* (London: British Film Institute, 1998), 29–45. This preservationist impulse also was evident in several music collections published at the time: Alice C. Fletcher, *Indian Story and Song from the North America* (Boston: Small, Maynard, and Company, 1900); Frederick R. Burton, *American Primitive Music* (New York: Moffat, Yard, and Company, 1909); and John A. Lomax, *Cowboy Songs and Other Frontier Ballads* (New York: Sturgis and Walton, 1910)—see Alexander, *Here Lies the Country,* 58. See also George Lewis, "Music of the Red Man," *B* (1 October 1910), 9; and "Songs of the American Cowboy," *NYMT,* Sunday Magazine (14 April 1912), 5.

41. "Comments on the Films," *MPW* (2 July 1910), 24; and " 'Spectator's' Comments," *NYDM* (14 December 1910), 28. See also David Mayer, "The Broken Doll," and Sumiko Higashi, "The Song of the Wildwood Flute," in Paolo Cherchi Usai, ed., *The Griffith Project* (London: British Film Institute, 2000–2003), 4: 191–94, 218–19. Sixteen-millimeter viewing prints of *The Broken Doll* and *The Song of the Wildwood Flute* are available at the LoC. Scholars still have a tendency to focus on Griffith's Biograph westerns to the exclusion of others more popular and/or influential at the time, especially when they write about Indian pictures in the early 1910s: see, for instance, the otherwise excellent recent study by Alison Griffiths, "Playing at Being an Indian: Spectatorship and the Early Western," *Journal of Popular Film and Television* 29.3 (Fall 2001), 100–111.

42. A 35mm viewing print of Kalem's *Her Indian Mother* is available at the LoC.

43. Hired away from Bison by Pathé, Young Bear and Red Wing initially worked out of the company's New Jersey studio; in late 1910, they were sent to Los Angeles, where he established Pathé's western production unit near Selig's Edendale studio. Other than Bison and Bison-101, Pathé was the only company that consistently had Indians play Indian roles. See, for instance, "James Young Deer," *MPW* (6 May 1911),

999; the full-page Pathé ad for "Princess Red Wing," *NYDM* (1 May 1912), 33; Smith, *Shooting Cowboys and Indians*, 82–83, 89–99; and Simmon, *The Invention of the Western Film*, 30–31. The earliest surviving film probably directed by Young Deer, but shot in New Jersey, is *White Fawn's Devotion* (June 1910), available on program 3 of the *Treasures from American Film Archives* DVD (2000).

44. "Reviews of Licensed Films," *NYDM* (28 June 1911), 32; and "Comments on the Films," *MPW* (9 September 1911), 716. Another Pathé Indian picture worth noting is *The Chief's Talisman* (April 1911), which apparently told of a past story impinging on the present with such clarity that it had no need of intertitles—see "Reviews of Licensed Films," *NYDM* (26 April 1911), 31; and "Critical Reviews of Licensed Films," *NYMT* (30 April 1911), 4: 7. It also is worth noting that some of Young Deer's Indian pictures for Pathé, such as *Red Deer's Devotion* (1911), went so far as to promote interracial marriage, which most critics could not accept, and others proposed "that whites and Indians could best integrate on tribal rather than Anglo-American terms"—see Simmon, *The Invention of the Western*, 30; and Smith, *Shooting Cowboys and Indians*, 95.

45. "*The Legend of Lake Desolation*," *MPW* (29 July 1911), 191. See also "Motion Picture Reviews," *B* (19 August 1911), 15. Not long before, Mary Austin had promoted the "poetic drama . . . as the best mode of expression for Indian life—see Austin, "The Dramatic Values of Indian Life," *NYDM* (29 March 1911), 5. Under Young Deer's direction, Pathé continued to release such Indian films well into 1912, as exemplified in *The Red Man's Honor* and *A Redskin's Appeal*—see "Comments on the Films," *MPW* (18 May 1912), 628, and (29 June 1912), 1226–27.

46. See the American ad in *MPN* (8 April 1911), 23. See also "Data from Manufacturers' List of Releases," *MPN* (6 May 1911), 24.

47. See, for instance, "Motion Picture Reviews," *B* (20 May 1911), 50–51, and (27 May 1911), 51.

48. "Cowboy Pictures," *MPW* (10 June 1911), 1304; "Progress of the Independent Product," *MPW* (15 July 1911), 29.

49. "Reviews of Notable Films," *MPW* (29 July 1911), 190–91. Bowser analyzes *The Ranchman's Nerve* in *The Transformation of Cinema*, 172.

50. See, for instance, the American ads in *MPN* (26 August 1911), 17; *NYDM* (6 September 1911), 24; and *MPW* (16 September 1911), 770.

51. "Newsy Items from El Cajon Valley," *MPN* (30 September 1911), 28.

52. See, for instance, "First of Nestor Western Pictures with Genuine Western Atmosphere," *MPN* (9 December 1911), 34; "California Pictures," *B* (6 January 1912), 15; the American ad in *MPW* (20 January 1912), 229; and the Nestor ad in *MPW* (10 February 1912), 449.

53. See, for instance, the American ads in *MPN* (9 March 1912), 51; and *MPW* (16 March 1912), 980–81. At least three of these stories were published in the *Des Moines News:* "The Grub Stake Mortgage—A Moving Picture Short Story of Western Life" (17 January 1912), 10; "Where Broadway Meets the Mountains—A Moving Picture Story of the West" (27 January 1912), 3; and "How Lonesome Was Chased Off the Ranch" (9 April 1912), 4.

54. "Wild West Pictures," *MPN* (18 November 1911), 6. Even more letters agreeing with that article were cited in "Wild West Pictures," *MPN* (25 November 1911), 7. A reference to these "protests against the volume of 'wild west' films" can be found in "In the Moving Picture World," *CT* (24 December 1911), 2.2: 3.

55. "Facts and Comments," *MPW* (2 December 1911), 700. The diatribes lasted into February 1912, not only in the *News* but also in the *New York Dramatic Mirror*, where "The Spectator" wrote that, even if they were "better done" than before, there still were "too many melodramas and Wild West subjects" on the market—see " 'Spectator's' Comments," *NYDM* (7 February 1912), 28; and "The Wild West," *MPN* (24 February 1912), 21. See also the remark that cowboy films, although "distinctly not criminal," were hardly "elevating in taste and generally worthless as examples of art," in " 'Spectator's' Comments," *NYDM* (6 December 1911), 28.

56. "Reviews of Current Films," *M* (July 1911), 42; "At the Theatres," *LST* (2 July 1911), 6; "Vaudeville and Pictures," *MJ* (15 October 1911), 8; and "Tag Day at the Lyric," *MJ* (31 October 1911), 16. See also "Fighting Blood, a Novel Film," *NYDM* (14 June 1911), 29; and J. B. Kaufman, "Fighting Blood" and "The Last Drop of Water," in Cherchi Usai, *The Griffith Project*, 5: 79–84.

57. "Bison Company Gets 101 Ranch Wild West," *MPN* (2 December 1911), 24; "Bison Gets 101 Ranch," *NYDM* (6 December 1911), 29; "Bison Company Gets 101 Ranch," *MPW* (9 December 1911), 810; "Western Spectacles," *B* (9 December 1911), 46; "What Bison Wants," *MPW* (13 January 1912), 119; and "Bison-101 Feature Pictures," *MPW* (27 January 1912), 298. Reappraisals of Bison-101 and Thomas Ince can be found in Brownlow, *The War, the West, and the Wilderness*, 253–62; and especially in Smith, *Shooting Cowboys and Indians*, 105–32. For a thorough, well-told story of the Miller Brothers' 101 Ranch, see Michael Wallis, *The Real Wild West: The 101 Ranch and the Creation of the American West* (New York: St. Martin's Press, 1999).

58. "With the Western Producers," *MPN* (18 November 1911), 41. See also "Mr. Thomas H. Ince," *MPN* (26 October 1912), 21; and "Spectacular Pictures His Long Suit," *MPN* (8 November 1913), 18. Later Ince would promote himself as a founder of the western genre in an article in *MPW* (5 July 1915), 225—quoted in Brownlow, *The War, the West, and the Wilderness*, 256. See also the column of articles written by Ince, entitled "In the 'Movies'—Yesterday and Today," especially numbers 4 and 5— in the Hollywood Museum Collection, AMPAS.

59. "Reviews of Notable Films," *MPW* (29 July 1911), 193.

60. See, for instance, the Essanay ad in *MPW* (21 October 1911), 226.

61. See the Dome Theater ad, *YV* (9 April 1911), 14. A 35mm viewing print of *The Sheriff's Chum* (750 feet) is available at the LoC.

62. "Critical Reviews of Licensed Films," *NTMT* (16 April 1911), 4.1, 7. While praising the climactic fight, *Billboard* also found the film "entirely lacking in plot," with poorly connected events—"Motion Picture Reviews," *B* (15 April 1911), 17. By contrast, *Motography* praised the film for its construction as well as its "expressive" acting— see "Reviews of Current Films," *M* (May 1911), 96. For the *Mirror*, too, the film was "acted with intelligent restraint"—see "Reviews of Licensed Films," *NYDM* (12 April 1911), 32. Another Essanay western released about the same time, *Across the Plains*, "scored a big hit"—"Critical Reviews of Licensed Films," *NYMT* (9 April 1911), 4.1: 9.

63. "Letters to 'The Spectator,' " *NYDM* (24 May 1911), 33.

64. "The 'Most Photographed Man,' " *M* (November 1911), 245; "The Most Photographed Man," *NYDM* (22 November 1911), 26; and " 'Live' Advertising for Exhibitors," *MPW* (2 December 1911), 714.

65. See, for instance, the Majestic ads for "Little Mary" in *NYDM* (18 October 1911), 30, (25 October 1911), 30, and (15 November 1911), 29.

66. "J. Max Anderson," *YV* (15 October 1911), 14; and "This Man's Photo Seen Every Day for 300,000," *CN* (5 November 1911), 15. See also "Is Boys' Favorite," *CL* (24 December 1911), B7.

67. See, for instance, the Princess ads in *Youngstown Vindicator* from (15 October 1911), 15 to (7 January 1912), 17; and the Orpheum ads in *Canton News-Democrat* from (21 April 1912), 15 to (9 June 1912), 12. Several of these ads include a photo of "Bullets" Anderson.

68. See the Essanay ads in *MPW* (23 December 1911), 951, and (2 March 1912), 739. Smith attributes this strategy to Anderson himself and traces the name to a story written for middle-class readers by Peter B. Kyne and supposedly published in *Saturday Evening Post*—see Smith, *Shooting Cowboys and Indians*, 135, 144.

69. "Another good Western drama . . . with everybody's favorite, Mr. G. M. Anderson, in the leading role"—see the Odeon Theater ad, *CN* (29 October 1911), 10. A 35mm viewing print of *A Pal's Oath* (895 feet) is available at the LoC. An ironic variation on this story, rather unusual in Anderson's westerns, occurs in *A Wife of the Hills* (July 1912), in which Anderson escapes jail to take revenge on a friend and his unfaithful wife, only to give himself up after a gunfight outside their cabin when he discovers, in gratification, that a stray shot from the sheriff or his posse has struck the friend, who dies in the wife's arms. A 35mm viewing print of *A Wife of the Hills* is available at the Nederlands Film Museum (NFM). Another variation occurs in *Broncho Billy's Oath* (October 1913), in which Anderson does shoot his treacherous friend through a cabin window—see "Licensed Films," *NYDM* (29 October 1913), 38.

70. See, for instance, "Critical Reviews of Licensed Films," *NYMT* (22 October 1911), 4.2: 5.

71. "Critical Reviews of Licensed Films," *NYMT* (31 December 1911), 4.2: 5; and "Reviews of Licensed Films," *NYDM* (3 January 1912), 30.

72. A 35mm viewing print of *Broncho Billy's Christmas Dinner* is available at the NFM.

73. See, for instance, James McQuade, "Famous Cowboys in Motion Pictures," *FI* (25 June 1910), 9–10; the special poster for *Ranch Life in the Great Southwest* reproduced in *FI* (2 July 1910), 23; "Buffalo Bill Films," *B* (17 September 1910), 24; the J. Frank Hatch ad in *B* (17 September 1910), 45; "Buffalo Bill Pictures Draw," *MPW* (26 November 1910), 1242; and the Atlas ad, *MPN* (30 September 1911), 18. *Ranch Life in the Great Southwest*, for instance, played for an entire week, in August 1910, at the Colonial Theatre in Des Moines—see the Colonial ads in the *DMN* (10 August 1910), 8, and (15 August 1910), 5. *Buffalo Bill's Wild West and Pawnee Bill's Far East* then played for four nights, in March 1911, at two different legitimate theaters in Des Moines— see the Grand ad, *DMN* (15 January 1911), 4; and the Foster's ad, *DMN* (26 February 1911), 6. For *The James Boys in Missouri*, see "The James Boys in Missouri," *MPN* (2 September 1911), 8–9; and the week of 9 March 1912 in the 1911–1913 Treasurer's Accounts Book for the Star, box 10, Keith-Albee Collection, Special Collections, University of Iowa Library. An incomplete 35mm viewing print of *Ranch Life in the Great Southwest* (622 feet) is available at the National Film/Television Archive (NFTVA); a 16mm viewing print of the first reel of *Buffalo Bill's Wild West and Pawnee Bill's Far East*, at the LoC.

74. "Weekly Feature Films," *B* (20 April 1912), 14. See also the report on the one-

year contract between Bison and the 101 Ranch, in "Bison Co. Contracts with Miller," *B* (3 February 1912), 10.

75. "Bison-101 Feature Pictures," *MPW* (27 January 1912), 298. See also the Bison-101 ads in *MPN* (3 February 1912), 28; *MPW* (10 February 1912), 449; *NYMT* (17 March 1912), 4.2, 4; and *Film Fancies* (24 February 1912)—cited in Brownlow, *The War, the West, and the Wilderness,* 256. The *Sunday Telegraph* described *War on the Plains* as "a masterly production more than up to all expectations"—see "Critical Reviews," *NYMT* (25 February 1912), 4.2, 3. *The Golden Wedding* received the gold medal at the 1911 Cinematograph Exposition in Turin, Italy, which a Cleveland theater, the Tabor, publicized when the film played there in late 1911—"Reviews of Notable Films," *MPW* (9 December 1911), 799; and "At Leading Theaters," *CL* (31 December 1911), B7.

76. "Comments on the Films," *MPW* (23 March 1912), 1063.

77. See, for instance, the Bison-101 ads in *MPN* (23 March 1912), 40; and *MPW* (30 March 1912), 1131; and *"Blazing the Trail,"* *MPN* (13 April 1912), 7. The Bison-101 westerns quickly surpassed the "dramatic power and startling effects" of Griffith's "remarkable and absorbing" one-reel *Billy's Stratagem* (February 1912), as well as *Iola's Promise* (March 1912)—see "Reviews of Licensed Films," *NYDM* (21 February 1912), 29; and "Comments on the Films," *MPW* (28 February 1912), 690, and (6 April 1912), 40. See also Russell Merritt, "Billy's Stratagem," in Cherchi Usai, *The Griffith Project,* 5: 181–85.

78. Louis Reeves Harrison, *"The Indian Massacre,"* *MPW* (9 March 1912), 854–56. A 35mm viewing print of *The Indian Massacre* (1,716 feet) is available at the LoC.

79. Biograph's better-known, much praised *Iola's Promise* (March 1912) makes an interesting comparison here, for its "dull and timid Indian girl," played by a quite recognizable Mary Pickford, is indebted to a white miner for rescuing her from a band of cutthroats and, in return, later rescues him and his wife from her own tribe (spurred by the latter's gesture making the sign of the cross) and then dies, but not before revealing the source of the gold the miner is seeking in Indian territory. See, for instance, "Critical Reviews," *NYMT* (17 March 1912), 4.2, 5; and "Reviews of Licensed Films," *NYDM* (20 March 1912), 30. A 16mm viewing print of *Iola's Promise* is available at the LoC.

80. "Reviews of Special Feature Subjects," *NYDM* (24 April 1912), 27.

81. A 16mm viewing print of *Blazing the Trail* is available at the MoMA.

82. "Reviews of Sales Company Films," *NYDM* (20 March 1912), 33. See also "Comments on the Films," *MPW* (30 March 1912), 1166. A 35mm viewing print of the second reel of *The Deserter* (879 feet) is available at the LoC. For an interesting column describing the choices of musical accompaniment for Bison-101 westerns, especially "the climax of these beautiful plays," see Clarence E. Sinn, "Music for the Picture," *MPW* (25 May 1912), 717.

83. "Critical Reviews," *NYMT* (17 March 1912), 4.2, 2

84. This photo is printed in *MPN* (16 March 1912), 22.

85. See the Mall ad, *CL* (10 March 1912), S6; Reo Stadt, "Review of Films," *CL* (31 March 1912), S8; and "From Religious to Wild West, Range of Week's Films," *CL* (7 April 1912), S8.

86. "Programs of Leading Theaters," *CL* (17 March 1912), S6, (24 March 1912), S6, and (2 April 1912), W8.

87. "Correspondence," *MPW* (23 March 1912), 1085. See the Central Square Theatre ads in the *LDI*, 23 March to 8 June 1912.

88. "The Critic's Comment," *LDI* (4 June 1912), 5.

89. Colonial Theater ad, *TNB* (27 March 1912), 7. The Colonial was the biggest Toledo theater, seating 1,000.

90. "At the Photo Plays," *TNB* (20 April 1912), 2. See the ads for the Crown Theater from early March to early June 1912. See also "Correspondence," *MPW* (13 July 1912), 164.

91. "What's Offered This Week in the Local Show Shops," *MJ* (2 June 1912), 8.8. See the ads for the Crystal and the Isis in the Sunday edition of the *Minneapolis Journal*, from 25 February through 16 June 1912. The Unique, which rarely advertised, even featured three Bison-101 westerns, one after the other, one week in June—see " 'Movies' on a Ranch," *MJ* (13 June 1912), 12.

92. See the Family Theatre ads, *DMRL* (21 April 1912), 5; and *DMN* (21 April 1912), 6. *Blazing the Trail* also played at the east side Elite Theater two months later— see the Elite Theater ad, *DMN* (30 June 1912), 6.

93. See Abel, *The Red Rooster Scare*, 171–72.

94. See the Vitagraph ad in *MPW* (20 January 1912), 181; and "Reviews of Licensed Films," *NYDM* (24 January 1912), 39.

95. See the Solax ad in *MPW* (3 August 1912), 405; and "Licensed Film Stories," *MPW* (3 August 1912), 482. A 35mm viewing print of *Two Little Rangers* is available at the NFM.

96. "Critical Reviews," *NYMT* (14 July 1912), 4.2: 4. A 35mm viewing print of *Broncho Billy's Narrow Escape* is available at the NFM.

97. See "Ten Famous Kalem Beauties," *NYDM* (31 January 1912), 53; "Comments on the Films," *MPW* (9 March 1912), 866; and "Reviews of Independent Films," *NYDM* (22 May 1912), 29.

98. See the filmography compiled by David Turconi and Paolo Cherchi Usai for *Vitagraph Co. of America: Il cinema prima di Hollywood* (Pordenone: Edizioni Studio Tesi, 1987). Sturgeon was one of the first filmmakers to gain some kind of notoriety outside the industry—see, for instance, "The Real Man behind the Gun Is Director," *DMN* (23 May 1913), 4.

99. "How States Are Made," *MPW* (17 February 1912), 565. See also "Critical Reviews," *NYMT* (10 March 1912), 4.2, 4; and "Comments on the Films," *MPW* (23 March 1912), 1062, 1064. The importance of this film is signaled by newspaper stories about it—see, for instance, "How States Are Made," *CL* (18 February 1912), B6. A 35mm viewing print of *How States Are Made* is available at the NFM.

100. "Reviews of Licensed Films," *NYDM* (13 March 1912), 29. *How States Are Made* also was featured at the downtown Empress in Toledo one weekend—see "At the Photo Plays," *TNB* (13 April 1912), 5.

101. "From Harvard to Director's Place: Rollin S. Sturgeon Upsets Rules of the Game and Wins Out," *NYDM* (15 January 1913), 42.

102. "Reviews of Licensed Films," *NYDM* (22 May 1912), 20. See also "Comments on the Films," *MPW* (1 June 1912), 829. This film is notable for its use of eye-line matches and shot/reverse shots—see the perceptive review of its use of close shots and, by implication, eye-line matches, in "The Pick of the Programmes," *Bio* (4 July 1912), 63, 65. A 35mm viewing print of *The Greater Love* is available at the NFM.

103. The characters' names are given in "Licensed Film Stories," *MPW* (11 May 1912), 560.

104. "Reviews of Licensed Films," *NYDM* (24 April 1912), 29. A 35mm viewing print of *The Craven* is available at the NFM.

105. See the Vitagraph ad in *MPW* (20 April 1912), 199.

106. "Big Independent Developments," *NYDM* (3 April 1912), 27.

107. "'101' Bison Problem Solved," *NYDM* (10 April 1912), 25.

108. See, for instance, "New Corporation Enters Field of Film Exchange," *NYMT* (24 March 1912), 4.2, 4; "Film Field Now Entered by Two New Rival Forces," *NYMT* (19 May 1912), 4.2, 1; "Independent Division?" *NYDM* (22 May 1912), 27; "Break in Ranks of Sales Company," *MPW* (25 May 1912), 707; and "Independent Split Complete," *NYDM* (29 May 1912), 27.

109. See, for instance, the Universal ad, *NYDM* (12 June 1912), 31; and "Laemmle Controls Universal," *MPW* (21 June 1913), 1237.

110. See, for instance, the New York Motion Picture ad, *MPW* (6 July 1912), 59; "Doings in Los Angeles," *MPW* (20 July 1912), 235; "Universal Bison Litigation," *NYDM* (7 August 1912), 27; and "Fashions in Moving Pictures Change Quickly," *NYMT* (25 August 1912), 4.2: 3.

111. See, for instance, "Bison Pictures to Be Real Features," *NYMT* (11 August 1912), 4.2: 4; the Mutual ad, *MPN* (10 August 1912), 38; the Broncho ad, *MPN* (17 August 1912), 3; and the New York Motion Picture ad, *MPN* (19 October 1912), 4–5. For news of Francis Ford's shift from acting to directing, see "Doings in Los Angeles," *MPW* (8 June 1912), 913, and (5 October 1912), 32.

112. On the recommendation of Bob Birchard, I use Bison-101 to designate the westerns produced by Ince during the first half of 1912 and Universal-Bison to designate those produced and released by Universal in 1912–13, although Universal did use Bison-101 for a short time until the 101-Ranch threatened a lawsuit. The best filmography of Thomas Ince is Steven Higgins's "I film di Thomas H. Ince," *Griffithiana* 18–21 (October 1984), 155–94.

113. Louis Reeves Harrison, "Custer's Last Fight," *MPW* (22 June 1912), 1116–18; the New York Motion Picture ad, *MPN* (21 September 1912), back cover; and "Custer Film at Oxford," *CL* (13 October 1912), W8.

114. The last two-reel Bison-101 Indian picture, apparently, was *On the War Path* (June 1912)—see "Comments on the Films," *MPW* (6 July 1912), 43. After the one-reel *The Colonel's Peril* (June 1912), there was nothing from Bison-101 for two months—see "Comments on the Films," *MPW* (13 July 1912), 149.

115. See, for instance, the Orpheum ad and "Anderson at Orpheum," *CL* (10 November 1912), B5; and the Orpheum ad in the labor weekly *CC* (28 December 1912), 2. At least one film was promoted as a "special attraction," Griffith's *A Pueblo Legend* (August 1912), which followed the pattern of previous Biograph "poetic" pictures in seeking to depict Indian civilization before Columbus—see, for instance, "Another Biograph Masterpiece," *NYDM* (14 August 1912), 23; "Critical Reviews," *NYMT* (1 September 1912), 4.2: 4; and Tom Gunning, *D. W. Griffith and the Origins of American Narrative Film: The Early Years at Biograph* (Urbana: University of Illinois Press, 1991), 271.

116. Jas. S. McQuade, "The Fall of Black Hawk," *MPW* (6 July 1912), 31–33; J. S. McQuade, "Geronimo's Raid," *MPW* (14 September 1912), 1054–55; and G. F. Blaisdell, "Peril of the Plains," *MPW* (21 September 1912), 1167–68. Another multiple-reel western, *The Last Stand of the Dalton Boys,* was released by Atlas in June 1912.

117. See, for instance, the favorable review by James S. McQuade, "The Red Man's Honor," *MPW* (14 December 1912), 1064. *Their Lives for Gold* also was fictionalized in *PM* (August 1912), 23–29. Gaumont first had tried to break into this market for westerns with *Driven from the Ranch* (April 1912)—see "Comments on the Films," *MPW* (27 April 1912), 330.

118. "Reviews of Special Features," *NYDM* (31 July 1912), 31; and "At the Photo Plays," *TNB* (14 August 1912), 8, and (21 August 1912), 3. See also the more favorable review by G. F. Blaisdell, "Their Lives for Gold," *MPW* (10 August 1912), 515. *Their Lives for Gold* was among the half dozen films seized in Cleveland when the authorities arrested several prominent theater managers for showing crime pictures on Sunday—"Police Raids at Cleveland," *MPW* (21 December 1912), 1192.

119. The first inkling of this decision came in "Doings in Los Angeles," *MPW* (6 July 1912), 35.

120. "Reviews of Universal Films," *NYDM* (11 September 1912), 33; and "Comments on the Films," *MPW* (21 September 1912), 1176.

121. "Comments on the Films," *MPW* (21 September 1912), 1177.

122. "Comments on the Films," *MPW* (26 October 1912), 343, and (2 November 1912), 451; "Reviews of Universal Films," *NYDM* (5 February 1913), 32; and "Feature News and Reviews," *NYDM* (12 February 1913), 31.

123. "Mona Darkfeather Films," *NYDM* (14 May 1913), 26; and "Reviews of Universal Films," *NYDM* (20 August 1913), 36.

124. "Comments on the Films," *MPW* (26 October 1912), 343; and "Reviews of Universal Films," *NYDM* (27 November 1912), 33. An incomplete viewing print of *Early Days in the West* (1,248 feet) is available at the NFTVA.

125. "News and Reviews of Feature Films," *NYDM* (12 March 1913), 29; and "Comments on the Films," *MPW* (22 March 1913), 1221. For an opposing view, see "Feature Film Reviews," *NYMT* (16 March 1913), 4.2: 2.

126. A 35mm viewing print of *The Flaming Arrow* (1,800 feet) is available at the NFTVA. Although the *Mirror* complained about light-skinned Indians in this film, the trade press did praise Universal when it had real Indians play Indian characters, as in *A Redman's Love* (October 1912); showed empathy for the "rights of the original American," as in *The Rights of a Savage* (December 1912); or represented the "ceremonial dances of Pueblo Indians," as in *Indian Dances and Pastimes* (December 1912)—see "Reviews of Universal Films," *NYDM* (30 October 1912), 34, and (4 December 1912), 35; and "Comments on the Films," *MPW* (28 December 1912), 1294.

127. "Comments on the Films," *MPW* (21 September 1912), 1177–78, and (12 October 1912), 144. Throughout September and October, both Universal and NYMP released two-reel westerns under the Bison label, which created some confusion in the trade press.

128. "Important Films of the Week," *NYMT* (29 September 1912), 4.2: 10; and "Reviews of Supply Co. Films," *NYDM* (2 October 1912), 32. *Custer's Last Fight* also was fictionalized in *PM* (September 1912), 25–32.

129. "Supply Co. Films," *NYDM* (16 October 1912), 33. See also "Important Films of the Week," *NYMT* (13 October 1912), 4.2: 4.

130. "Supply Co. Films," *NYDM* (23 October 1912), 32.

131. Louis Reeves Harrison, "The Invaders," *MPW* (9 November 1912), 542. *The Invaders* also was among the half dozen films seized in Cleveland in December.

132. This film, much like *The Invaders,* has an Indian heroine, Bright Star, who is abandoned by an army lieutenant but then later tries to lead him to safety during an Indian ambush; a powder wagon explodes prematurely, however, and "she drags herself to the body of the dead Lieutenant and dies with her arms around him"—"Independent Film Stories," *MPW* (16 November 1912), 706; and "Reviews of Supply Co. Films," *NYDM* (20 November 1912), 36.

133. "Important Films of the Week," *NYMT* (17 November 1912), 4.2: 4.

134. Louis Reeves Harrison, "A Shadow of the Past," *MPW* (28 December 1912), 1277; and "Reviews of Mutual Films," *NYDM* (8 January 1913), 33. At least one other Indian picture should be mentioned in passing, the independently produced *Hiawatha,* an adaptation of the 1906 pageant play based on Henry Wadsworth Longfellow's famous poem—see " 'Hiawatha,' The Indian Passion Play in Pictures," *MPN* (1 March 1913), 15; "Hiawatha," *MPW* (29 March 1913), 338; and Harvey Harris Gates, "Unspoiled Indians in True Portrayals," *NYDM* (9 April 1913), 31.

135. "Reviews of Mutual Films," *NYDM* (22 January 1913), 33; and "Comments on the Films," *MPW* (1 February 1913), 465. This probably was not Mae Marsh, who allegedly was recognized in Broncho's *The Civilian* (November 1912), but perhaps the actress Winnie Baldwin, first praised in Kay-Bee's *In the Ranks* (January 8)—see "Comments on the Films," *MPW* (7 December 1912), 978, and (11 January 1913), 159. A very incomplete viewing print of *The Wheels of Destiny* (approximately 500 feet) is available at the NFTVA.

136. "Views of the Reviewer," *NYDM* (2 October 1912), 24; and "Important Films of the Week," *NYMT* (24 November 1912), 4.2: 5.

137. "The Critic's Comment," *LDI* (10 December 1912), 13.

138. See, for instance, the large Central Square ad, *LDI* (23 November 1912), 2; the Central Square ads thereafter through the end of March; and the Dreamland ads in the same newspaper, from late December 1912 through April 1913.

139. These observations are based on the "Moving Pictures" block ads published on the theater pages of the *Baltimore Sun*'s Sunday edition, from 5 January to 13 April 1913.

140. See, for instance, "Custer Fight Film Is an Educator," *CL* (6 October 1912), W7; "Custer Film at Oxford," *CL* (13 October 1912), W8; "Where Best Shows Are Found Today," *CL* (12 January 1913), M5; and the Lake Shore Film ad, *CL* (2 February 1913), B4.

141. Unique Theatre/Mutual Films ad, *DMN* (26 January 1913), 6.

142. See, for instance, "Saturday's and Sunday's Moving Pictures and Where to See Them," *TNB* (1 February 1913), 9.

143. "Saturday's and Sunday's Moving Pictures and Where to See Them," *TNB* (12 April 1913), 8.

144. See "The Movies," *DMN* (29 June 1913), 6; and the Comique ad, *LDI* (5 July 1913), 2. The MPPC manufacturers chose not to release multiple-reel westerns in competition with those of Universal-Bison, Broncho, and Kay-Bee, with the exception of Selig's two-reel remake of *The Cowboy Millionaire* (February 1913) and Kalem's three-reel *The Cheyenne Massacre* (April 1913)—see, for instance, Jas. S. McQuade, "The Millionaire Cowboy," *MPW* (25 January 1913), 344–45; "Feature News and Reviews," *NYDM* (12 February 1913), 31; and "Feature Films on the Market," *NYDM* (21 May 1913), 27.

145. For a more extensive analysis of the box office receipts contained in the Trea-surer's Accounts Book of the Star Theatre, from December 1911 to October 1913, see Richard Abel, "Patchwork Maps of Movie-Going, 1911–1913," in Robert Allen, Richard Maltby, and Melvin Stokes, eds., *American Cinema and Everyday Life*, forthcoming from University of Essex Press.

Entr'acte 2: Moviegoing Habits and Everyday Life

1. Waller, "Introduction: A Century at the Movies," in *Moviegoing in America*, 5.

2. The Bijou, for instance, definitely was open from 10:00 A.M. to 10:00 P.M., show-ing two reels of Independent films—see "Correspondence: Youngstown, O.," *MPW* (25 November 1911), 650. The Rex (five cents) shared those hours and at one point advertised special music each evening and Sunday afternoon.

3. "Nickels for Theatres vs. Nickels for Bread," *NYMT* (12 May 1912), 4.2: 2. In late 1909, David Hulfish offered far more conservative hours, "11:00 a.m. until 9:00 p.m." for a typical moving picture theater in a downtown shopping district; by 1913, he changed that to "9 A.M. until 11 P.M." for the "large exclusive picture house"—see Hul-fish, "Economy in Picture Theater Operation," *N* (1 January 1910), 15, and *Cyclopedia of Motion-Picture Work* (Chicago: American Technical Society, 1914 [1911]), 25.

4. See the Ezella ad, *CC* (23 November 1912), 2.

5. For this information on the Diamond, Orpheum, Crescent, and Laurel, see "Sat-urday's and Sunday's Moving Pictures and Where to See Them," *TNB* (12 April 1913), 8; and the Laurel ad, *TNB* (2 August 1913), 2.

6. See the Namur's Highland Park ad, *DMN* (15 November 1911), 6; and the Namur's block ad, *DMN* (18 November 1912), 6.

7. "Motion Picture Houses, in the Residential Districts of Metropolitan Boston," *BJ* (6 September 1913), 4.

8. "Licensed Film Releases," *NYMT* (19 February 1911), 4: 4.

9. The first of the Comedy Theatre's weekly ads appeared in the *NYMT* (12 March 1911), 4.1, 4. See also "First Runs at Gane's," *NYDM* (24 January 1912), 33.

10. For some in Massachusetts, this may have been a consequence of General Film's attempt, in late 1910, as Bowser writes, to "rationalize" distribution "by ruling that exhibitors could have only biweekly changes" of either first-run or second-run films—see Bowser, *The Transformation of Cinema*, 84.

11. See the twenty-page brochure on the Bijou Theatre published in early 1911; and "Ten-Cent Theatre Popular Institution," *NYMT* (1 September 1912), 4.2: 3. Many of the one-act plays reportedly were written by Harvard and Radcliffe students.

12. See the Lyric ad, *MJ* (17 September 1911), 5: 9; and "In Vaudeville Houses," *MJ* (26 September 1911), 12.

13. Such "special program nights" in theaters offering a variety program of daily-changed films were common at least through the summer of 1913—see John B. Rath-burn, "Motion Picture Making and Exhibiting," *M* (26 July 1913), 72.

14. W. W. Winters, "With the Picture Fans," *N* (1 September 1910), 123–24. See also " 'Spectator's' Comments," *NYDM* (7 August 1912), 24.

15. See also Bowser, *The Transformation of Cinema*, 126–28.

16. Quoted from the Bijou Theatre booklet and "Ten-Cent Theatre Popular Insti-tution," 4.2: 3.

17. F. H. Madison, "In the Northwest," *MPW* (7 September 1912), 994. The Lyric also boasted of its "footman at the door, pages, lady matrons, and colored girl ushers"—"The Lyric's Reopening," *MJ* (10 September 1911), 5: 8.

18. "Effect on Audiences of Moving Pictures," *NYMT* (24 December 1911), 4: 6.

19. Havig, "The Commercial Amusement Audience in Early 20th-Century American Cities," 8; and F. H. Richardson, "Women and Children," *MPW* (21 February 1914), 962. Richard Butsch repeats this claim but also notes other supporting surveys in Cincinnati and Madison—Butsch, *The Making of American Audiences,* 146. A 1914 Columbia University study of how often a selected group of working men in New York attended moving picture shows also lends some support to Richardson's cliché—see Charles Stelzle, "How One Thousand Workingmen Spend Their Spare Time," *Outlook* 106 (4 April 1914), 762–66. One report even claimed that "nine out of every ten persons that enter the moving picture shows . . . are women," but this must have been exaggerated, coming from the Minneapolis Board of Home Missions and Church Extension—"Blames the Women," *NYMT* (2 June 1912), 4.2: 3.

20. Jos. F. Hennegan, "Music and the Picture Show," *B* (3 February 1912), 13. Hennegan was arguing that this regular patronage demanded a new illustrated song at least every other day.

21. "Women and Children Get Picture Habit," *NYMT* (14 January 1912), 4.2: 1.

22. "Are Detroiters 'Movie Mad'?" *DFP* (5 October 1913), Features: 3.

23. Roy Stafford, "At the Moving Picture Show," *YV* (30 October 1910), 25; Frank H. Madison, "In the Mississippi Valley," *MPW* (24 August 1912), 783.

24. Havig, "The Commercial Amusement Audience in Early 20th-Century American Cities," 7–8. This seems remarkable, given the Massachusetts statistics revealing that many young working women (not living at home) were paid less than $6.00 a week, far less than the estimated required budget of $10.60—see Clara E. Laughlin, *The Work-a-Day Girl: A Study of Some Present-Day Conditions* (New York: Fleming H. Revell, 1913), 160–63.

25. Cited in Rosenzweig, *Eight Hours for What We Will,* 201.

26. Robert Wood and Albert J. Kennedy, eds., *Young Working Girls* (Boston: Houghton Mifflin, 1913), 106–7, 112–13; Ruth S. True, *The Neglected Girl* (New York: Survey, 1914), 66–67; and Harriet McDoual Daniels, *The Girl and Her Chance* (New York: Fleming H. Revell, 1914), 71. *Young Working Girls* was compiled from information gathered by 2,000 settlement social workers in New York City: one interesting conclusion was that working girls aged fourteen through sixteen were much less dependent than those aged sixteen through eighteen on young men for the expense of attending a moving picture show.

27. Viola Paradise, "The Jewish Immigrant Girl in Chicago," *Survey* 30 (6 September 1913), 701. Many historians, as well as writers at the time, have noted the unusual number of young women, many unmarried, among Jewish immigrants and also their exceptional desire to become "Americanized"—see, for instance, Rose Cohen, *Out of the Shadow* (New York: George H. Doran, 1918), 150–51; Andrew R. Heinze, *Adapting to Abundance: Jewish Immigrants, Mass Consumption, and the Search for American Identity,* (New York: Columbia University Press, 1990); Susan Glenn, *Daughters of the Shtetl: Life and Labor in the Immigrant Population* (Ithaca, N.Y.: Cornell University Press, 1990), 2, 159–66; and Barbara Schreier, *Becoming American Women: Clothing and the Jewish Immigrant Experience, 1880–1920* (Chicago: Chicago Historical Society, 1994), 6, 52.

28. Eustace Hale Ball, *The Art of the Photoplay,* 2nd ed. (New York: G. W. Dillingham, 1913), 116.

29. Frederic C. Howe, "Leisure," *Survey* 31 (3 January 1914), 415. It should not be forgotten that the downside of this increase in leisure time, especially for young working women, was "a state of affairs wherein the world's labour market [had] actually come to depend on the work of women outside the home"—see Laughlin, *The Work-a-Day Girl,* 53.

30. A summary of moving pictures' influence on children came in the November 1912 issue of *Mother's Magazine,* quoted in "Mothers, Children and Pictures," *M* (7 December 1912), 419. This potential source, as far as I know, remains unexamined.

31. Daniel J. Czitrom, *Media and the American Mind: From Morse to McLuan* (Chapel Hill: University of North Carolina Press, 1982), 42. Ipswich had a population of 6,000 in 1914.

32. Czitrom, *Media and the American Mind,* 42. Springfield had a population of just over 50,000 in 1910—*Thirteenth Census of the United States,* 63. "A similar survey of four Iowa cities (Iowa City, Dubuque, Burlington, Ottumwa) . . . showed that 30 percent of the boys and 21 percent of the girls in these communities went to the movies at least seven times a month, with 60 percent of the boys and 45 percent of the girls going at least four times a month"—Czitrom, *Media and the American Mind,* 42–43.

33. Foster, *Vaudeville and Motion Picture Shows,* 17, 27, 28. Portland had a population of slightly more than 200,000 in 1910—*Thirteenth Census of the United States,* 64. In the slightly larger city of Indianapolis, a Children's Aid Society investigation of the city's picture theaters one evening found approximately 8,500 children in attendance—"Gossip of Moving Picture Makers," *NYMT* (25 September 1910), 4.1: 4.

34. Robert O. Bartholomew, "Report of Censorship of Motion Pictures and of Investigation of Motion Picture Theatres of Cleveland, 1913"—cited in David Nasaw, "Children and Commercial Culture: Moving Pictures in the Early Twentieth Century," in Elliott West and Paula Petrik, eds., *Small Worlds: Children and Adolescents in America, 1850–1950* (Lawrence: University Press of Kansas, 1992), 18.

35. Foster, *Vaudeville and Motion Picture Shows,* 17, 22. Summarizing other surveys of large cities from this period, Havig concludes that "youth and young adults ranging in age from 15 to 25 years constituted the bulk of the movie audience in the years before World War I": in Milwaukee, Kansas City, and Detroit, for instance, they made up 50 percent of the audience—Havig, "The Commercial Amusement Audience in Early 20th-Century American Cities," 9.

36. Dorothy Donnell, "The School of the Moving Pictures," *MPSM* (July 1911), 96. Two years later, the president of the Kansas Welfare League audaciously claimed that "the motion picture shows have more to do with the teaching of the children of Kansas than their parents do"—"Children Taught More by Motion Pictures Than by Their Parents," *NYMT* (9 November 1913), 5: 1.

37. See "Fine Pictures," *LST* (23 July 1911), 7; and "Correspondence: New England," *MPW* (7 September 1912), 992. The Merrimack Square also took the trouble to say that "in securing [pictures] the management always keeps in mind the desires of the women and young folk patrons of the theatre"—"At the Theatres," *LST* (9 July 1911), 6.

38. "Correspondence: In the Mississippi Valley," *MPW* (15 June 1912), 1051.

39. See the Princess ad, *TNB* (10 May 1913), 4.

40. For a concise summary of such service, see Bowser, *The Transformation of Cinema*, 126–28.

41. This and two other cartoons appear in *MPSM* (September 1912), 147, 149, 151. One other cartoon shows a large group of people entering a moving picture theater, while an adjacent saloon has cobwebs on its doors; the second shows the John Smith family (with two children) entering a moving picture show, while the contrasting graphic shows John Smith alone going to a legitimate theater.

42. See the General Film ads, *NYMT* (20 July 1913), 4.2: 3, (27 July 1913), 4.2: 3, (3 August 1913), 4.2: 4, and (5 October 1913), 4.2: 3. One of the first General Film ads to use this graphic style appeared in *MPN* (26 April 1913), 5.

43. See the Mutual ads, *SPN* (15 November 1913), 12, and (29 November 1913), 8. Mutual also began to run a series of ads with its new logo, "the sign of the winged-clock," in *NYMT* (23 November 1913), 5: 3, and *MPN* (29 November 1913), 10. Mutual's publicity campaign apparently caught both General Film and Universal by surprise—"Mutual Publicity Campaign Jolts Competitors to Life," *V* (12 December 1913), 13.

44. On the matter of children, see the Minneapolis survey, in which children of school age were said to make up 40 percent of the overall audience for moving pictures—"Facts and Comments," *MPW* (8 February 1913), 548. This survey may have been prompted by a grade school teachers association questionnaire advocating censorship—see "Plan Inquiry into Picture Theaters," *MJ* (27 October 1912), 1: 10. The latter also probably led to articles promoting motion pictures as "an aid to the education of the growing generation"—see "Moving Picture Field Has Unlimited Scope Is the Theory of Minneapolis Theatrical Men," *MT* (2 March 1913), S7.

45. "Picture Show Poor Man's Vacation Trip and Sure Cure for 'Blues' for All," *CN* (23 April 1911), 14. This article was reprinted eight months later as "Views of Four Ohio Exhibitors," *M* (December 1911), 258.

46. "The Movies," *DMN* (11 November 1912), 2.

47. "Movie Man Freed in Color Case," *DMN* (27 June 1913), 4.

48. The first of these contest announcements appeared in the *TB* (18 February 1911), 1. They continued daily for the following week and then once or twice a week thereafter, through March 10.

49. This is implied, in the *Toledo Blade* announcements, by descriptions of "the fellow sitting next to you" and "one of those fellows who relax when they get into the barber chair," as well as the epithets for moving pictures as "either 'bully' or a 'bum show.'"

50. See "First Offering of Blade Picture Show Critics," *TB* (25 February 1911), 15; and "Will You Win?" *TB* (27 February 1911), 1. Another sign of the newspaper's surprise was its publication of the girls' photos, along with brief interviews, in "Moving Picture Criticism Winners," *TB* (27 February 1911), 7.

51. "Here Are Prize Winning Moving Picture Criticisms," *TB* (4 March 1911), 24; "Picture Show Critics Do Better This Week," *TB* (11 March 1911), 12; and "Last Moving Picture Prizes Won by Girls," *TB* (18 March 1911), 13.

52. See, for instance, the study of San Francisco cited in Foster, *Vaudeville and Motion Picture Shows*, 27. The Portland survey itself is difficult to interpret because it includes eighty kinds of films, many of them overlapping—see Foster, *Vaudeville and Motion Picture Shows*, 24–25.

53. I thank Rick Altman for drawing my attention to this rare accounts book, along with several clippings books for the Star Theatre, in the Keith-Albee Collection, Special Collections, University of Iowa Library, Iowa City, Iowa.

54. The Pawtucket Civic Theatre committee showed moving picture programs on Sunday evenings, beginning in the fall of 1913, in order "to make more intelligent 'citizens' of those who [were] not yet naturalized," with specific reference to Polish, Italian, Jewish, Syrian, Greek, and Armenian immigrants—see "Resolution Passed by the Civic Theatre Committee of Pawtucket and Central Falls, R.I., June 2, 1913," *MPN* (2 August 1913), 8; and "Pawtucket Has Civic Theater," *MPW* (20 March 1915), 172. Many of these immigrants were employed by the city's textile companies handling cotton and silk, with women as numerous as men overall in various occupations. Although most working women were unmarried, only Polish women tended not to drop out of the labor force after marriage. See Lamphere, *From Working Daughters to Working Mothers*, 87–90, 159–61.

55. Unfortunately, the Star's accounts book ends on the week of 13–18 October 1913.

56. The Star Theatre was owned and managed by Walter S. Davis and his recently widowed mother-in-law, Julia Reid, described as "one of the most successful lady financiers throughout . . . New England," who also served as treasurer—in other words the accounts book was hers.

57. The Pawtucket Civic Theater reported that its audiences preferred "war pictures" and "wild west scenes"—see "Pawtucket Has Civic Theater," *MPW* (20 March 1915), 1752.

58. Star ad, *PT* (19 March 1914)—Clippings Books, Series IV, Keith-Albee Collection, Special Collections, University of Iowa Library.

59. Hansen, "The Mass Production of the Senses," 341.

60. This quote comes from "Mrs. W. H. Bryant, head worker of the Neighborhood House, 906 Galapago Street," Denver, in "Nickels for Theatres vs. Nickels for Bread," 4.2: 2.

Chapter 3: The "Usable Past" of Westerns, Part 2

1. See, for instance, Reddin, *Wild West Shows*, 27–49, 86–117. French attitudes toward the American West and especially Indians also had been popularized in the novels of Gustave Aimard—see Ray Allen Billington, *Land of Savagery, Land of Promise: The European Imagery of the American Frontier in the Nineteenth Century* (New York: Norton, 1981), 219–40.

2. Jacques Portes, *Fascination and Misgivings: The United States in French Opinion, 1870–1914*, trans. Elborg Forster (Cambridge: Cambridge University Press, 2000), 87–103.

3. Francis Lacassin, "The Éclair Company and European Popular Literature from 1907 to 1919," *Griffithiana* 47 (May 1993), 61–87.

4. Ibid., 65.

5. For analyses of these films, see Richard Abel, *The Ciné Goes to Town: French Cinema, 1896–1914* (Berkeley and Los Angeles: University of California Press, 1994), 107–8, 123–24.

6. Deniz Göktürk, "Moving Images of America in Early German Cinema," in

Thomas Elsaesser, ed., *A Second Life: German Cinema's First Decades* (Amsterdam: Amsterdam University Press, 1996), 93–100.

7. "Topics of the Week: The Popularity of Western Films," *Bio* (18 August 1910), 4–5. This editorial was reprinted as "Popularity of Western Films," *NYMT* (28 August 1910), 4.1: 4. See also "What the People Want," *Bio* (27 October 1910), 73.

8. "A Notable Production," *Bio* (28 July 1910), 54–55; "Ranch Life in the Great Southwest," *Bio* (1 December 1910), 17; and "A Notable Essanay Photoplay," *Bio* (5 January 1911), 59, 61.

9. See, for instance, the Essanay ad, *Bio* (16 February 1911), 37.

10. See the American ads, *Bio* (12 January 1911), 6, and (4 May 1911), 186; and "The 'Flying A' Film," *Bio* (26 January 1911), 53. For Bison, see "Red Wing and the White Girl," *Bio* (27 April 1911), 163.

11. "London Likes Essanay Western Photoplays," *N* (18 March 1911), 311.

12. "London Ramblings," *MPN* (6 May 1911), 7.

13. "Moving-Picture Business Abroad," *M* (June 1911), 142. Nearly identical language appeared in J. D. Whelpley, "Moving Picture Business Abroad," *MPN* (16 September 1911), 24. See also "Moving Pictures across the Sea," *NYMT* (4 June 1911), 4: 5.

14. "Two Great 'Flying A' Releases," *Bio* (1 June 1911), 395; "Range Pals," *Bio* (13 July 1911), 93; "The Poisoned Flume," *Bio* (24 August 1911), 401; and the Essanay ad in *Bio* (14 September 1911), xxviii.

15. "Exporting an Imaginary America to Make Money," *NYT* (30 July 1911), 5: 4.

16. Kristin Thompson, *Exporting Entertainment: America in the World Film Market, 1907–1934* (London: British Film Institute, 1985), 29–34.

17. See the "Nouveautés cinématographiques" listings in *Ciné-Journal* from July 1911 through August 1912. Although Biograph also produced westerns during this period, they were not prominent initially among the company's releases in France.

18. The Swedish censorship records, written on large filing cards, began in early September 1911. During the early months, according to Jan Olsson, the censors viewed not only new releases but also older films that companies considered potentially profitable in rerelease. With the help of John Fullerton, in early June 2000, I examined several months of these records in the Department of Cinema Studies, Stockholm University. In December 2000, Marina Dahlquist assisted me in examining the Pathé archives at the Swedish Film Institute, specifically the *Pathé Lager Bok* (1910–11).

19. Zettlund & Thelanders Boktr ads, *Nordisk Filmtidning* 19 (January 1910), 16; 20 (February 1910), 14; and 21 (March 1910), 14.

20. In early June 2000, Mats Björkin assisted me in examining a selection of these cinema programs (uncataloged) in the Department of Cinema Studies, Stockholm University.

21. Göktürk, "Moving Images of America in Early German Cinema," 96.

22. "Exporting the American Film," *M* (August 1911), 90–92.

23. "American Films Popular Abroad," *CL* (11 February 1912), S6. See also "An American School of Moving Picture Drama," *MPW* (20 November 1909), 712.

24. "Moving Picture Preferences Abroad," *M* (November 1911), 214; and "South Africa's Picture Shows," *M* (February 1912), 78. For specific references to these Consulate Reports, especially for what they reveal about westerns, see "Moving Picture

Business Abroad," *MPN* (16 September 1911), 24; "The Motion Picture in European Countries," *MPW* (10 February 1912), 494; and " 'Spectator's' Comments," *NYDM* (26 June 1912), 20.

25. American Film Company ad, *Bio* (18 January 1912), 162.

26. Joyce Appleby, Lynn Hunt, and Margaret Jacob, *Telling the Truth about History* (New York: Norton, 1994), 108, 111; and Frederick Jackson Turner, "The Significance of the Frontier in American History [1893]," in *The Frontier in American History* (New York: Henry Holt, 1920), 1–38.

27. For an excellent discussion of the "frontier" as an "inherently mobile" term in any analysis of westerns, see Verhoeff, "Easterns," *After the Beginning*, 55–69. Although the West, and even westerns, generally may be seen as "a product of the modern city," as Verhoeff and others argue, the term "modern city" is far from stable or monolithic, as my descriptions and analyses of exhibition venues and audiences attest.

28. The American West, much like most of Africa, tended to be depicted as "empty" or blank in many mid-nineteenth-century maps. Whereas Catlin and Buffalo Bill's images of the West maintained this protean inexactitude, the Miller Brothers initially, and unsuccessfully, sought to restrict their image of the West to the southern Great Plains, the location of their immense family ranch in Oklahoma—see Reddin, *Wild West Shows*, 8, 164.

29. See, for instance, the Essanay ads in *Bio* (25 January 1912), xxii, (2 May 1912), vi, (2 June 1912), 734, and (18 July 1912), 1705. To be sure, Essanay sought to promote Anderson as "popularly known as Broncho Billy" as early as October 1911, just as he was being nicknamed "Bullets" in northeastern Ohio—see the Essanay ad, *MPW* (7 October 1911), 60.

30. See, for instance, the Essanay ads in *CJ* (3 February 1912), 2, and (6 July 1912), 42.

31. See, for instance, " In the Moving Picture Field," *CT* (14 April 1912), 10: 3; and "Comments on the Films," *MPW* (18 May 1912), 629. In July 1912, however, some of the *World*'s reviews were still referring to "those typical Western dramas in which G. M. Anderson has won popular favor in the Old and the New World"—see Jas. S. Mc-Quade, "The Smuggler's Daughter," *MPW* (20 July 1912), 233. For explicit references to the "Broncho Billy Photoplays" and to Anderson himself as the "American Cow Puncher," see the Essanay ad, *NYMT* (15 December 1912), 4: 3. For detailed information on Anderson's initial "studio" in Niles, see Kiehn, *Broncho Billy and the Essanay Film Company*, 77–104; and Smith, *Shooting Cowboys and Indians*, 135–36.

32. See, for instance, "Dramatizes Dime Novels," *CL* (23 June 1912), S6; "Of Interest to the Trade," *M* (4 January 1913), 25; and Mabel Condon, "Sans Grease Paint and Wig," *M* (15 February 1913), 111. David Horsley's brief attempt to forge a deal with Frank Tousey drawing on the *Wild West Weekly* series is described in Smith, *Shooting Cowboys and Indians*, 108–9. The first of the Nestor series, *Young Wild West Leading a Raid* (June 1912), survives in a 35mm viewing print (770 feet) at the NFTVA.

33. See, for instance, "Edison-McClure," *MPW* (29 June 1912), 1212.

34. *Broncho Billy* films were released almost weekly from late November 1912 through March 1913, then settled into a biweekly release schedule for the rest of the year.

35. See the review of *Broncho Billy's Narrow Escape* in "The Pick of the Programmes,"

Bio (1 August 1912), 367; and Essanay ads in *MPW* (29 June 1912), 1187; and in *NYDM* (4 September 1912), 31. For remarks on Anderson as an appealing "personality," see "Reviews of Licensed Films," *NYDM* (12 March 1913), 36. Although rarely as active as the cowboys in Buffalo Bill's Wild West, Anderson may have seemed to share with them, at least in the eyes of the English, a sense of hardened physicality and "natural" gentlemanliness—see Reddin, *Wild West Shows*, 93–94.

36. See the reviews of *Broncho Billy and the Bandits* and *Broncho Billy's Last Hold Up* in "Comments on the Films," *MPW* (18 May 1912), 629, and (24 August 1912), 770. As an explicit sign of his popularity with boys, see Clyde Martin's doggerel, "I'm the Guy," *M* (12 October 1912), 304.

37. Smith, "The Making of Broncho Billy," in *Shooting Cowboys and Indians*, 133–56.

38. The reference is to Eric J. Hobsbawm, *Social Bandits and Primitive Rebels: Studies in Archaic Forms of Social Movements in the 19th and 20th Century* (Glencoe, Ill.: Free Press, 1959). Smith also makes this point in *Shooting Cowboys and Indians*, 141–42.

39. Smith, *Shooting Cowboys and Indians*, 58, 134.

40. Ibid., 145–46. A print of *Broncho Billy's Last Hold Up* survives at the MoMA. A print of *Broncho Billy's Heart* survives at the NFTVA.

41. Ibid., 146–47.

42. Ibid., 144.

43. Ibid., 134, 149, 151–52. See Martin Levin, ed., *Five Boyhoods: Howard Lindsay, Harry Golden, Walt Kelly, William K. Zusser, and John Updike* (Garden City, N.Y.: Doubleday, 1962).

44. Anderson's real name was Max Aaronson; his "good badman" character thus offered a model of assimilation that stood in for another form of assimilation that could not be represented or at least publicized.

45. See "Two Great 'Flying A' Releases," *Bio* (1 June 1911), 395. A 35mm viewing print of *The Ranchman's Vengeance* is available at the NFM.

46. A 35mm viewing print of *Broncho Billy's Mexican Wife* (767 feet) is available at the George Eastman House (GEH).

47. The film is especially interesting because it was released during the initial years of the Mexican Revolution, which threatened to involve the United States. For an analysis of a contrasting jingoistic attitude toward Mexicans characteristic of the 101 Ranch Wild West shows, see Reddin, *Wild West Shows*, 168–69.

48. See "Motion Picture Reviews," *B* (20 May 1911), 13.

49. Although the *World*'s reviewer found the film "very interesting," he also objected to scenes like this as "too evidently 'being played' "—"Comments on the Films," *MPW* (26 August 1911), 544. See also "Motion Picture Reviews," *B* (19 August 1911), 15.

50. A 35mm viewing print of *The Poisoned Flume* (972 feet) is available at the NFTVA. Dwan seems to conflate this film with either *The Ranchman's Vengeance* or another later film in his interview with Peter Bogdanovich, in *Allan Dwan: The Last Pioneer* (New York: Praeger, 1971), 20. Bison's *Lucky Bob* (October 1911), whose story is set against the construction of a large dam, is one of the few other westerns to concern itself with the historical development of the West—"Critical Reviews of Independent Films," *NYMT* (1 October 1911), 4.2: 4.

51. Donald Worster, *Rivers of Empire: Water, Aridity, and the Growth of the American West* (New York: Oxford University Press, 1985), 6–7.

52. Worster encapsulates the development of the American West into three stages: incipience (1847–1890s), florescence (1900–1940s), and empire (1940s on)—*Rivers of Empire,* 64.

53. See ibid., 96–111.

54. See, for instance, Richard Slotkin, *Gunfighter Nation: The Myth of the Frontier in Twentieth-Century America* (New York: Atheneum, 1992), 22–24.

55. A 16mm print of *The Driver of the Deadwood Stage* is available at the MoMA. A slightly earlier film, IMP's *Through the Air* (1911), also conflates past and present in its hero's commandeering of a small dirigible to beat a rival in racing to stake a gold claim: a 35mm viewing print (808 feet) is available at the NFTVA.

56. The figure of the dime novel boy reader continued to circulate in one-reel comedies such as Bison's *Avery's Dream* (April 1911), in which a messenger boy falls asleep and dreams that he "rescues all sorts of folks" from "the wildest of Indians [and] the fiercest of bandits"—"Critical Reviews of Independent Films," *NYMT* (9 April 1911), 4.1: 9.

57. Reviewers objected to the "improbability" of this film's story and its conflation of past and present, fact and fiction—see, for instance, "Reviews of Licensed Films," *NYDM* (18 December 1912), 31.

58. Here I have drawn on a 35mm viewing print of *The Cowboy Millionaire* available at the NFM, as well as Verhoeff's analysis of the film in *After the Beginning,* 32–33, 88–89.

59. See "Notes d'Amérique," *CJ* (23 December 1911), 5.

60. See, for instance, the Cosmopolitan Film ads for Bison-101 films in *Bio* (14 March 1912), 752, (28 March 1912), xii, and (6 June 1912), 722. See also the weekly listings of Bison-101 films, released through Paul Hodel, in "Nouveautés ciné-matographiques," *Ciné-Journal,* from April through September, 1912.

61. "Pick of the Programmes," *Bio* (25 April 1912), 289. See also "A First Rate Indian Film," *Bio* (8 August 1912), 437.

62. "Pick of the Programmes," *Bio* (25 April 1912), 291.

63. "Reviews of Film Supply Co. Films," *NYDM* (6 November 1912), 33.

64. *The Man They Scorned* was one of the first films shown at Lynn's Central Square Theatre, when it became an exclusive venue for Kay-Bee and Broncho films in November 1912—see the Central Square ad, *LDI* (30 November 1912), 2. A possible variation on this story occurs in Broncho's *The Greenhorn* (October 1913), where the hero is described as Russian (which usually meant Jewish)—see "Feature Films on the Market," *NYDM* (29 October 1913), 33. Jewish characters rarely showed up in westerns, and those that did were stereotypes, as was the "Hebrew banker" in Selig's *Why the Sheriff Is a Bachelor* (October 1911)—see "Reviews of Licensed Films," *NYDM* (1 November 1911), 29.

65. "Pick of the Programmes," *Bio* (25 April 1912), 289, 291; Louis Reeves Harrison, "The 'Bison-101' Headliners," *MPW* (27 April 1912), 320–22.

66. Although many Indians worked on Ince's Bison-101 westerns, it is worth noting, as Smith writes, that they rarely played anything other than extras and had no creative input; indeed, Ince took a conventionally paternalistic attitude toward them—Smith, *Shooting Cowboys and Indians,* 118–21.

67. See the full-page Paul Hodel ad for the film in *CJ* (6 July 1912), 64.

68. See, for instance, the Bison-101 ads in *MPN* (11 May 1912), 28, and *MPW* (18 May 1912), 588.

69. *"Lieutenant's Last Fight*—Wonderful Military Film," *MPN* (25 May 1912), 24–25; and "Stories of Licensed Films," *MPW* (1 June 1912), 868–69. This analysis is based on an incomplete 35mm viewing print of *The Lieutenant's Last Fight* available at the NFM.

70. The internal quotation, probably from a concluding intertitle (now missing), comes from "Independent Films," *MPW* (1 June 1912), 868.

71. The phrases come from Verhoeff's analysis of this film in *After the Beginning,* 45.

72. Simmon offers an extended analysis of this film in "Pocahontas Meets Custer: *The Invaders,*" in *The Invention of the Western Film,* 55–78. Another variation on this story can be seen in Broncho's *The Burning Brand* (January 1913), in which the son of an army chaplain discovers he is the adopted half-breed son of a chief's daughter (told in flashback); an outcast denied marriage to a colonel's daughter, he is rescued by his tribal ancestors and made their chief, leads them in an attack on the army outpost, and then tries to negotiate a peace and is killed. See "Reviews of Mutual Films," *NYDM* (25 December 1912), 30.

73. The *Mirror's* review of *The Invaders* was curiously muted, chiefly calling attention to several historical inaccuracies, perhaps reflecting the trade weekly's characteristically "masculine" perspective on moving pictures—see "Reviews of Film Supply Co. Films," *NYDM* (27 November 1912), 31.

74. Simmon argues that this story line evokes the defeat of Custer's Seventh Cavalry as well as "Fetterman's massacre," which took place ten years earlier, in 1866; indeed, one of the Indians serving as a consultant and extra for the film, Luther Standing Bear, was eight years old when his father participated in that famous battle against Custer—Simmon, *The Invention of the Western Film,* 64, 69.

75. Harrison, "The Invaders," *MPW* (9 November 1912), 542. This analysis is based on a 35mm viewing print of *The Invaders* (2,741 feet) available at the LoC. Recently this print has been included in the *More Treasures from American Film Archives* DVD (National Film Preservation Foundation, 2004).

76. This perspective, Simmon argues, was similar to that of post–Civil War officers such as General George Crook, who, in *His Autobiography* (1960), described the army's position as "an impossible [one] between put-upon Indians [with whom he empathized] and western business interests who wanted them swept out of the way"—Simmon, *The Invention of the Western Film,* 70.

77. Other two- and three-reels films such as Kalem's *Colleen Bawn* and Vitagraph's *Vanity Fair* had appeared earlier in France, respectively, in October 1911 and early March 1912. Two of D. W. Griffith's first two-reel films were westerns, *A Pueblo Legend* and *The Massacre,* but in France they were not released, respectively, until September and November 1912.

78. John Burke had publicized Buffalo Bill's Wild West precisely in these terms, as "the great epic of American history"—see Burke, "Buffalo Bill's Wild West and Congress of Rough Riders of the World," *Philadelphia Sunday Dispatch,* 12 September 1885, quoted in Reddin, *Wild West Shows,* xiii. Writers such as Owen Wister and Frank Norris also had long argued that the Wild West could provide material for a national epic—see, for instance, Wister, "The Evolution of the Cow-Puncher," *Harper's Monthly* 91 (September 1895), 602–17; and Norris, "The Frontier Gone at Last," *World's Work* 3 (1902), reprinted in Donald Pizer, ed., *The Literary Criticism of Frank Norris* (Austin:

University of Texas Press, 1964), 111. In producing "a sense of history" at the turn of the last century, Verhoeff argues, westerns inevitably "engage in specific discourses of nationalism"—Verhoeff, *After the Beginning*, 100. More specifically, Smith understands Ince's "historical frontier spectacles" as vehicles of "American nationalism"—Smith, *Shooting Cowboys and Indians*, 125.

79. "Moving-Picture Business Abroad," *M* (June 1911), 142. For an insightful analysis of the *picaresque*, derived from this article, in which the connotations of "mastery, distance, and appropriation" make westerns such "a consumable and an exportable vision of 'American life,' " see Verhoeff, *After the Beginning*, 202–3.

80. "Topics of the Week: The Popularity of Western Films," *Bio* (18 August 1910), 4. See also Reddin, *Wild West Shows*, 94.

81. The French had expressed a similar fascination with the Indians of Buffalo Bill's Wild West—see Reddin, *Wild West Shows*, 100. For a succinct analysis of the French conception of American barbarism, see Jody Blake, *Le Tumulte noir: Modernist Art and Popular Entertainment in Jazz Age Paris, 1900–1930* (University Park: Pennsylvania State University Press, 1999). Interestingly, the French not only linked animal vitality and technological power in their view of the United States but subsumed all kinds of different figures—"peaux rouges," "Negroes," cowboys, gauchos—within the category of the "barbaric," especially in their fascination with "exotic" dances—see *Le Tumulte noir*, 53–54.

82. Rosaldo's concept of "imperialist nostalgia" is discussed in Ann Fabian, "History for the Masses: Commercializing the Western Past," in William Cronon, George Miles, and Jay Gitlin, eds., *Under an Open Sky: Rethinking America's Western Past* (New York: Norton, 1992), 232–33.

83. Buffalo Bill's Wild West served as a similar "object lesson in physical force, exercise, and la jeunesse"—see Reddin, *Wild West Shows*, 101. See also *Le Tumulte noir*, 56.

84. For an analysis of the Indian's ideological function in westerns produced prior to the early 1910s, see Abel, *The Red Rooster Scare*, 167–71. This "imperial" vision, Simmon argues, encouraged stories that set "two races, Indian and white, both depicted as equally nomadic, on horses or in wagons, contending for the open space" of the West—Simmon, *The Invention of the Western Film*, 53.

85. In late 1912, the Historical Pageant Film Company released *United States*, the first of several multiple-reel historical subjects—see the General Film Publicity & Sales ad, *NYMT* (27 October 1912), 4.2: 3.

86. For an excellent study of historical pageantry, see David Glassberg, *American Historical Pageantry: The Uses of Tradition in the Twentieth Century* (Chapel Hill: University of North Carolina Press, 1990), especially pp. 4–5. The term "innovative nostalgia" comes from Robert M. Crunden, *Ministers of Reform: The Progressives' Achievement in American Civilization, 1889–1920* (New York: Basic Books, 1982), x, 90. Michael Kammen rightly criticizes Crunden's narrow use of term in *The Mystic Chords of Memory: The Transformation of Tradition in American Culture* (New York: Knopf, 1991), 271.

87. Perhaps not unexpectedly, films that explicitly depicted immigrants and the problems of assimilation were rare during the early 1910s. Exceptions included Solax's *The Making of an American Citizen* (1912), in which a male Russian peasant (in contrast to his wife) has to be taught by force how to behave as an American, and

Kalem's *The Alien* (May 1913), in which an Italian family man and skilled mechanic (wrongly implicated in a ring of opium smugglers) "develops a wholesome respect for the laws of his new country and takes an oath of allegiance to the United States"— see "Licensed Film Stories," *MPW* (3 May 1913), 508–9.

88. The hypothetical spectators of the following sentences are based on data gathered about each city from the 1910 census records, the 1914 *American Newspaper Annual and Directory,* and a survey of local newspapers.

89. Mary Heaton Vorse, "Some Picture Show Audiences," *Outlook* 98 (24 June 1911), 443, 445.

90. "Internationalism and the Picture," *MPW* (17 September 1910), 621.

91. Miriam Bratu Hansen, "Fallen Women, Rising Stars, New Horizons," *Film Quarterly* 54.1 (Fall 2000), 12.

92. "Latest Film Snapshots Local and Worldwide," *CL* (2 March 1913), M11. At the time, Michael Kammen writes, "every conceivable mode of education," including moving pictures, "was viewed as a potential contribution to solving the nation's pressing social problem of extreme heterogeneity"—Kammen, *The Mystic Chords of Memory,* 244.

93. Emilie Altenloh, *Zur Soziologie des Kinos: Die Kino-Unternehmung und die sozialen Schichten ihrer Besucher* (Jena: Eugen Diedrichs, 1914), 11–12, paraphrased in Göktürk, "Moving Images of America in Early German Cinema," 99.

94. A 35mm viewing print of *Sallie's Sure Shot* (971 feet) is available at the NFTVA.

95. A 35mm viewing print of *A Range Romance* (825 feet) is available at the LoC.

96. Verhoeff, *After the Beginning,* 323–24.

97. Although disguise, including cross-dressing, played a significant role in early Civil War films (as chapter 5 will demonstrate), it did not in early westerns, perhaps for historical reasons: "The West . . . was relatively unstructured and allowed a certain freedom [and] most women there did not have to play games to express their adventurous spirit or to move ahead." See Kathleen De Grave, *Swindler, Spy, Rebel: The Confidence Woman in Nineteenth-Century America* (Columbia: University of Missouri Press, 1995), 34.

98. The *World* praised Schaefer for putting "a good deal of imagination into her interpretation of the woman"—see "Comments on the Films," *MPW* (4 May 1912), 425. Somewhat more conventional was Vitagraph's *At the End of the Trail* (June 1912), in which a young Mexican woman sacrifices herself for a white sheriff and is mourned by the white lawmen but not by her villainous father. A 35mm viewing print of *At the End of Trail* is available at the NFM.

99. A 35mm viewing print of *Una of the Sierras* (924 feet) is available at the NFTVA.

100. It may simply be due to chance, but *Una of the Sierra* seems not to have been reviewed in *Moving Picture World* and *New York Dramatic Mirror.* A brief review in the *Morning Telegraph* described the film as an "Eastern" rather than a "Western"—"Important Films of the Week," *NYMT* (17 November 1912), 4.2: 4. The only references I have seen to its exhibition occurred in late November 1912, at the Voyons in Lowell and the Olympia in Lynn.

101. See, for instance, Nancy Tillman Romalov, "Unearthing the Historical Reader, or Reading Girls' Reading," in Larry Sullivan and Lydia Cushman Schurman, eds., *Pioneers, Passionate Ladies, and Private Eyes* (New York: Hawthorne Press, 1996), 87–101.

102. See Wallis, *The Real Wild West*, 4–5, 221–26, 229–31, 307–8. See also Reddin, *Wild West Shows*, 161, 171.

103. See, for instance, "Daring Girl Rider Coming," *DMN* (27 July 1912), 3; and "Summer Amusements," *DMN* (28 July 1912), 12. See also Wallis, *The Real Wild West*, 358.

104. See, for instance, Gertrude Price, "The Great Spirit Took Mona, But in This Girl She Still Lives," *DMN* (6 February 1913), 12; "Western Girl You Love in the 'Movies' Is a Sure Enough Suffrager," *DMN* (11 February 1913), 3; "Runs, Rides, Rows," *DMN* (16 April 1913), 6; and "Everyone Is for Busy Ann 'Calamity' Ann You Know!" *DMN* (29 April 1913), 10.

105. See, for instance, "Nervy as Ever to Act the Most Daring Things Ever Seen on the Stage!—Heroine of Movies," *DMN* (17 November 1912), 7; and "Sometimes the Beautiful Maiden Is REALLY Snatched from the Jaws of Death," *DMN* (13 March 1913), 10.

106. See, for instance, "Girls with Wild West Show to Help Women Gain Equal Suffrage," *TB* (17 August 1912), 7.

107. See "American Films Abroad," *MPW* (4 November 1911), 357.

108. This was also the case with the New York reception of the 101 Ranch Wild West shows at Madison Square Garden in 1914—see Reddin, *Wild West Shows*, 170–72.

109. Gordon Amusement controlled ten theaters in New England as well as the newly built Gordon in Rochester and was then building a large theater in Boston— see "The Evolution of the Motion Picture IX: From the Standpoint of the Exhibitor," *NYDM* (20 August 1913), 31.

110. See the cartoon in Epes Winthrop Sargent, "Advertising for Exhibitors," *MPW* (5 April 1913), 40; and Jas. S. Mcquade, "Why Broncho Billy Left Bear County," *MPW* (27 September 1913), 1371. An incomplete 35mm viewing print of *Why Broncho Billy Left Bear County* (537 feet), also without intertitles, is available at the GEH.

111. "Valuable Consular Reports," *MPW* (9 May 1914), 811.

112. W. Stephen Bush, "No Lowering of Standards," *MPW* (24 January 1914), 389. This kind of claim was repeated in "Facts and Comments," *MPW* (29 August 1914), 1211.

113. See the photo and caption of Gilbert M. Anderson in the *NYMT* (6 July 1913), 4: 3.

114. See "Reviews of Licensed Films," *NYDM* (3 September 1913), 29; and the Essanay ad, *NYDM* (8 October 1913), 35. *The Good-for-Nothing*, Anderson's first four-reel western, did not appear until June 1914—see the Essanay ad, *MPW* (27 June 1914), 1771.

115. "Reviews of Licensed Films," *NYDM* (17 September 1913), 29. A surviving 35mm print of *Episode at Cloudy Canyon* at the NFTVA, apparently complete and with its original title, also has no intertitles. This suggests that Essanay one-reel westerns during this period may merit closer attention for their development of certain conventions of representation and narration—"tell[ing] their story unaided and without confusion"—that soon would become crucial to the "classical Hollywood cinema."

116. See "Selig Releasing Western Thriller," *M* (31 May 1913), 395–96; "Feature Films," *NYDM* (11 June 1913), 27; "Comments on the Films," *MPW* (21 June 1913), 1251; "Reviews of Licensed Films," *NYDM* (3 September 1913), 29; "Tom Mix," *NYMT*

(23 November 1913), 5: 5; and "Feature Films on the Market," *NYDM* (26 November 1913), 32. In late February 1914, even Biograph, now that Griffith had left the company, finally released his two-reel *The Massacre*, which had been produced more than one year earlier and distributed only in Europe—"Feature Films of the Week," *NYDM* (4 March 1914), 34. Gunning offers a fine analysis of the editing in *The Massacre*'s climactic battle scene but does not mention that the film was released long after its production—Gunning, *D. W. Griffith and the Origins of American Narrative Film*, 271–73.

117. George D. Proctor, "What the Coming Season Means to Motion Pictures," *NYMT* (7 September 1913), 5: 1.

118. See, for instance, Hanford C. Judson, "The Big Horn Massacre," *MPW* (13 December 1913), 1261; "Reviews of Feature Films," *NYDM* (24 December 1913), 39; "Feature Films of the Week," *NYDM* (21 January 1914), 32; and "Reviews of Feature Films," *NYDM* (18 February 1914), 42.

119. The only serious study of Fielding, which came to my attention quite late, is Linda Kowall Woal, "Romaine Fielding: The West's Touring Auteur," *Film History* 7. 4 (1995), 401–25.

120. Ibid., 404–5, 407–8. A review of *The Price of Jealousy* described it as "one of the Mexican border plays which the Lubin company have been producing"—"Important Films of the Week," *NYMT* (16 February 1913), 4.2: 4.

121. Woal, "Romaine Fielding," 410. Fielding later also was praised for innovating the practice of having a "detail watcher" (or what would soon become a "script girl") take notes on every scene that was filmed—"Fielding to Employ 'Detail Watcher,' " *NYMT* (14 December 1913), 4.1: 8

122. "Feature Film Reviews," *NYMT* (13 April 1913), 4.2: 2.

123. Woal, "Romaine Fielding," 414–15. The *Morning Telegraph* found this film "beautifully staged" but, for some, "extremely repulsive"—"Important Films of the Week," *NYMT* (2 November 1913), 5: 2. *The Rattlesnake—A Psychical Species* apparently survives, at the LoC—see Simmon, *The Invention of the Western Film*, 34.

124. See, for instance, "An Indian Star," *M* (26 July 1913), 24; and the prominence given the Indian actors in the Thomas H. Ince ad, *NYDM* (24 December 1913), 26. By contrast, other companies such as Selig, Vitagraph, and Bison (Universal), after Darkfeather left the company, tended to have white actors play Indian or Mexican roles—see, for instance, Selig's *The Tie of Blood* (June 1913), Vitagraph's *When the West Was Young* (October 1913), and Bison's *The White Vacquero* (October 1913). Alison Griffiths analyzes this white masquerade, focused on Griffith westerns, in "Playing at Being Indian." This practice also was widespread in historical pageants—see, for instance, Glassberg's analysis of Percy Mackaye's *Pageant of St. Louis*, late May and early June 1914, in *American Historical Pageantry*, 173–94.

125. "Feature Films of the Week," *NYDM* (25 February 1914), 36; and Louis Reeves Harrison, "The Squaw Man," *MPW* (28 February 1914), 1068. Even Fielding accepted this shift, with a feature-length adaptation of *The Eagle's Nest* (December 1914)—see Woal, "Romaine Fielding," 416.

126. James S. McQuade, "The Spoilers," *MPW* (11 April 1914), 186–87; "Strand Theater Opens," *NYDM* (15 April 1914), 31; and W. Stephen Bush, "Opening of the Strand," *MPW* (18 April 1914), 371.

127. It is this period of Hart, Mix, and Ford westerns, which first reached a high point in 1917, rather than the earlier prewar period that most interests George Fenin

and William Everson, in *The Western: From the Silents to the Seventies,* rev. ed. (New York: Grossman, 1973), 74–129. The most recent study of Hart can be found in Smith, "The Aryan," in *Shooting Cowboys and Indians,* 157–85.

128. Louis Reeves Harrison, "Big Changes Taking Place," *MPW* (3 January 1914), 24.

Entr'acte 3: A "Forgotten" Part of the Program

1. Robert C. Allen, "Manhattan Myopia, or, Oh, Iowa!" *Cinema Journal* 35.3 (Spring 1996), 75–103; and Ben Singer, "New York, Just Like I Pictured It . . . ," *Cinema Journal* 35.3 (Spring 1996), 104–28. The occasion of this debate (just one part of a larger argument) was Singer's essay "Manhattan Nickelodeons: New Data on Audiences and Exhibitors," *Cinema Journal* 34.3 (Spring 1995), 5–35.

2. I take up this debate between Singer and Allen more fully in "Reframing the Vaudeville/ Moving Pictures Debate, with Illustrated Songs," in Leonardo Quaresima and Laura Vichi, eds., *The Tenth Muse* (Udine: Forum, 2001), 473–84. Eileen Bowser has made a similar argument that, before the emergence of the feature-length film, most moving picture theaters ran "variety shows," but like Singer and Allen she gives more attention to vaudeville than to illustrated songs—see Bowser, *The Transformation of Cinema,* 20, 191. Both Singer and Allen undoubtedly would welcome this or any other study of changing exhibition formats that moved beyond the boundary limits of their own work on New York City; in fact, Allen calls for just such studies, citing Gregory Waller's on Lexington (Kentucky), Kathryn Fuller's on itinerant showmen such as Cook & Harris (in the Northeast), and his own on various locations in North Carolina—Allen, "Manhattan Myopia, or, Oh, Iowa!" 96–99.

3. For an analysis of the origins, function, and significance of illustrated songs during the nickelodeon period, see Richard Abel, "That Most American of Attractions, the Illustrated Song," in Richard Abel and Rick Altman, eds., *The Sounds of Early Cinema* (Bloomington: Indiana University Press, 2001), 143–55. The "song illustrator" had been a common vaudeville act during the decade prior to the first nickelodeons, especially in "family vaudeville," which involved smaller theaters and shorter programs than found in "high-class" vaudeville.

4. David Hulfish describes the primary duties of one of three operators in a "large exclusive picture theater" as that of projecting "nothing but stereopticon slides, both announcement and song slides"—see Hulfish, *Cyclopedia of Motion-Picture Work* (Chicago: American Technical Society, 1914 [1911]), 26. By late 1912, the slides were assumed to be projected by means of a separate "dissolving stereopticon"—"He's the Guy Who Put the 'Move' in Pictures," *NYMT* (24 November 1912), 4.2: 2. For an excellent analysis of the little-known role played by projectionists during this period, see Timothy Barnard, "The 'Machine Operator': *Deus ex machina* of the Storefront Cinema." *Framework* 43.1 (Spring 2001), 41–75.

5. As Singer in particular notes, it is important to acknowledge the self-interest of each trade journal's position in the struggle for control or dominance within the moving picture industry—Singer, "New York, Just Like I Pictured It . . . ," 114–15.

6. See, for instance, "How the 'Small Time' Advanced," *V* (11 December 1909), 24, 156; and "Loew Enterprises Assume Formidable Proportions," *V* (2 February 1910), 5. See also "Change in Nickel Shows," *N* (11 March 1911), 276; and "A Talk with Mar-

cus Loew," *M* (May 1911), 88–89. The "small-time" or "pop" vaudeville, in which the pictures appeared as an interlude for the live acts, served as the focal point for much of Singer and Allen's debate—see especially Allen, "Manhattan Myopia, or, Oh, Iowa!" 84–89; and Singer, "New York Just as I Pictured It . . . ," 113–22. Allen is especially incisive on how Keith's UBO blacklist of performers in 1909 allowed the Shuberts to finance the booking of quality performers in the small-time vaudeville of Loew, Fox, and Lubin.

7. Robert Grau, "How Moving Picture Makes Theatergoers," *MPN* (28 October 1911), 9. Earlier, Grau had been leery of the "pop" vaudeville strategy advocated by Loew and others—see Grau, "Vaudeville in Moving Picture Theatres," *MPW* (7 May 1910), 726.

8. Henry, "New England Notes," *MPW* (3 December 1910), 1293. See also C. W. Lawford, "Why Vaudeville Was Called Upon," *MPW* (27 August 1910), 455.

9. Allen makes this point in "Manhattan Myopia, or, Oh, Iowa," 86–88; Singer contests this, but relies primarily on city surveys from 1913–15, in "New York, Just as I Pictured It, . . . " 118–20.

10. "Vaudeville in Picture Theaters," *N* (February 1910), 86. See also "Objectionable Vaudeville," *MPW* (19 March 1910), 415. In St. Louis, "cheap vaudeville" was reintroduced in 1911, through the efforts of O. T. Crawford—see James S. McQuade, "Motion Picture Affairs in St. Louis," *MPW* (4 November 1911), 362.

11. Epes W. Sargent, "Vaudeville in the Picture Theatre," *FI* (30 July 1910), 4. See also "Vaudeville Put in Its Place," *MPW* (9 July 1910), 93.

12. J. M. B., "Vaudeville—Music—Uniforms," *MPW* (19 November 1910), 1166.

13. The *News,* for instance, offered this conclusion from an informal survey of "all sorts of theaters": while the majority preferred "some vaudeville . . . it depend[ed] on the vaudeville," for there were scores of houses where the vaudeville was "so absolutely rotten [as to be] beyond endurance"—"The Picture and the Player," *MPN* (18 February 1911), 20. But see also "The Diluted Picture," *MPW* (5 November 1910), 1038; "Vaudeville Worse Than the Moving Picture Shows," *MPW* (24 December 1910), 1473; "Pictures and Vaudeville in New York," *N* (14 January 1911), 42; "Vaudeville," *MPN* (14 October 1911), 6; and "Motion Pictures: 'Spectator's' Comments," *NYDM* (29 November 1911), 24.

14. See, for instance, the range of articles from "The Picture Show Singer," *MPW* (12 December 1908), 475; to " 'Spectator's' Comments," *NYDM* (5 February 1910), 16; and H. F. Hoffman, "The Singer and the Song," *MPW* (4 June 1910), 935. See also "Music in Picture Theaters," *N* (July 1909), 4.

15. "New Denver Theatre," *FI* (11 June 1910), 16; "The Illustrated Song," *MPW* (19 November 1910), 1161. See also "Observations by Our Man about Town," *MPW* (24 December 1910), 1463.

16. *The Bijou Theatre* (Boston, 1910), n.p. This booklet first was mentioned in "Refined Picture Theatre," *NYDM* (8 February 1911), 28. The same point was made later by Mabel B. Ury in "The Evolution of a Picture Show," *M* (February 1912), 58.

17. "The Song," *MPN* (2 December 1911), 28.

18. "To Whom Are We Responsible for the Inferiority of Lantern Slides Used to Illustrate Songs?" *MPN* (16 September 1911), 6.

19. See, for instance, "Song Slide Department," *FI* (18 December 1909), 18–19, and (25 December 1909), 17–18. See also "A Day with the Song Slide Man [DeWitt

C. Wheeler]," *FI* (4 December 1909), 5–6; and "The Rehabilitation of the Lantern Slide," *MPW* (22 January 1910), 83. When *Moving Picture World* incorporated *Film Index* in July 1911, it continued the practice of listing the weekly song slide releases from a half dozen manufacturers. Sometime in 1910, the *News* took up a similar position of advocacy by including brief listings of illustrated songs in a column called "Varieties in Moving Picture Theatres"—see, for instance, "Varieties in Moving Picture Theatres," *MPN* (28 January 1911), 20–21. No copies of the *News* seem to survive prior to January 1911.

20. See, for instance, J. M. B., "Vaudeville—Music—Uniforms," *MPW* (19 November 1910), 1166; "Illustrated Song Slides," *MPN* (28 January 1911), 10; "A Beautiful Song Slide," *N* (25 February 1911), 6; "Illustrated Song Slides," *MPW* (27 May 1911), 1178; "The Song," *MPN* (26 August 1911), 19; and "Vaudeville Again," *M* (June 1911), 117. There were exceptions to this campaign, of course: for instance, W. Stephen Bush asserted at one point that "the illustrated song [was] clearly on the wane," but his chief interest lay in promoting the lecture as the "added attraction" of the future—see Bush, "The Added Attraction," *MPW* (18 November 1911), 533.

21. "Unique Effects in Song Slides," *FI* (6 May 1911), 12–14. See also "History of Slide Making in America," *N* (25 March 1911), 329–30; T. Stanley Curtis, "Lantern Slide Making," *M* (November 1911), 217–20; and "Motion Pictures," *NYDM* (29 November 1911), 24.

22. "A Novel Competition," *MPW* (23 July 1910), 194.

23. Hulfish, *Cyclopedia of Motion-Picture Work,* 11–30.

24. For a survey of moving picture theaters in St. Louis, see James McQuade, "Motion Picture Affairs in St. Louis," *MPW* (4 November 1911), 362–65.

25. See, for instance, "Moving Pictures and Vaudeville," *SLT* (5 January 1910), 11.

26. See, for instance, "Moving Pictures and Vaudeville," *SLT* (27 May 1910), 17.

27. "Moving Pictures and Vaudeville," *SLT* (27 May 1910), 17.

28. Six months later, John Bradlet praised the theaters in the downtown district for adhering to the principle of "only good pictures and no vaudeville and a 10-cent admission"—see "St. Louis," *MPW* (5 November 1910), 1053.

29. Charles Morris, "A Picture Theater in Mission Style," *N* (November 1909), 137–38.

30. "Boston, Mass.," *MPW* (26 November 1910), 1234, (17 December 1910), 1423, and (24 December 1910), 1472.

31. Frank Madison, "Springfield, Ill., Picture Shows," *MPW* (17 December 1910), 1420–21.

32. "Chicago Notes," *MPW* (31 December 1910), 1540; and "The Majestic Theater at Sioux City," *N* (21 January 1911), 71–72.

33. Charles Morris, "The Milwaukee Princess Theater," *N* (1 February 1910), 61–62; and Morris, "Butterfly Theater at Milwaukee," *M* (October 1911), 159–60. For further information on the Butterfly, see "Motion Picture Theatre Construction Department," *MPN* (29 November 1913), 35.

34. Clippings Book for the Nickel Theatre and Bijou Theatre, Providence, 29 March 1910–4 January 1913, Keith-Albee Collection, Special Collections, University of Iowa Library.

35. See Abel, "That Most American of Attractions," 145–46, 149.

36. See the Nickel ads in the *Providence News,* in June 1912—Nickel Theatre and

Bijou Theatre, Providence, 29 March 1910–4 January 1913, Clippings Book, Series IV, Keith-Albee Collection, Special Collections, University of Iowa Library.

37. See, for instance, "Pastime Theatre," *LST* (27 August 1911), 6; the Star Casino ad, *LST* (3 September 1911), 6; and the Opera House ads, *LST* (31 March 1912), 6, and (7 September 1913), 2. The Academy of Music also included illustrated songs with its vaudeville acts and moving pictures—see the Academy of Music ad, *LCC* (28 March 1912), 9.

38. See the Central Square ad, *LDI* (26 March 1912), 2; and "The Critic's Comment," *LDI* (26 November 1912), 11.

39. See the Olympia ad, *LDI* (21 December 1912), 2; and the Comique ad, *LDI* (18 January 1913), 2.

40. The Crystal reintroduced illustrated songs as an advertised act on its programs in the middle of February 1913 and continued to advertise their performance by Ray W. Fay well into the summer months—see the Crystal ads beginning in the *CRR* (16 February 1913), 3.

41. "Advertising the Picture," *MPN* (15 November 1913), 31. In praising the Saxe Theatre in Chicago, the *News* also reprinted the program on a souvenir blotter, where two illustrated songs alternated with three pictures, one of which was a two-reel "exclusive feature"—"Advertising the Picture," *MPN* (29 November 1913), 31.

42. See "Black Cat Theater Opens Tomorrow" and the Chicago Song Slide Exchange ad, *DMN* (30 January 1914), 8.

43. John Rathbun, "Motion Picture Making and Exhibiting," *M* (26 July 1913), 72.

44. See "Song Slides" and the Scot & Van Altena ad, *MPW* (12 April 1913), 190; and the Chicago Song Slide Exchange ad, *MPN* (4 October 1913), 36.

45. See the "Moving Pictures" block ad in the *BT* (5 January 1913), 4: 5. For several weeks, neither the Blue Mouse nor the Picture Garden listed any of their pictures.

46. See the Picture Garden and New Pickwick ads, *BT* (13 April 1913), 3: 5; and the Blue Mouse and Lexington ads, *BT* (27 April 1913), 3: 5. It is possible that "spotlight singing" may not have been accompanied by song slides.

47. See, for instance, the Crystal and Isis ads, *MJ* (13 April 1913), 8: 9.

48. See the Elite and New Park ads, *MT* (4 May 1913), Society: 11.

49. See the Seville ad, *MJ* (30 November 1913), 8: 10; and "Moving Pictures," *MJ* (14 December 1913), 8: 9.

50. See the Empress Company ad, *TNB* (4 January 1914), 4.

51. See the Princess ad, *TB* (4 April 1914), 11.

52. Perhaps the earliest example of a color slide that promoted upcoming moving pictures is one for Broncho Billy, dating from 1912 or 1913. It is part of a large collection of promotional slides, archived in the Literature Department of the Cleveland Public Library, and viewable on the library's Web site.

53. George Rockhill Craw, "Swelling the Box Office Receipts," *MPW* (13 May 1911), 1060. The reference to "monochromatic picture plays" suggests that most films were released in tinted prints, whose uniform color might change only from sequence to sequence.

54. This and other song slides are reproduced in Tom Sweeney, "Set to Music," *Minneapolis Star Tribune Magazine* (4 April 1993), 4–17. They come from the Marnan Collection, owned by Margaret and Nancy Bergh of Minneapolis, who graciously allowed me to do some research in their archive in 1999.

55. These song slide images also are in the Marnan Collection; the quotation comes from "Unique Effects in Song Slides," *FI* (6 May 1911), 13.

56. Early evidence of such hired singers or "pluggers" can be found in "Timely Tattle," *American Musicians and Art Journal* 22.8 (24 April 1906), 14; and "Publishers' Gossip," *American Musicians and Art Journal* 22.11 (12 June 1906), 28. I thank the Berghs for sharing their notes on this little-known trade journal. A late description of this practice occurs in "Hammering Out Tunes in the Popular Song Factory," *CRR* (12 January 1913), 2: 17.

57. "Current Song Hits," *M* (October 1911), 195.

58. Jos. F. Hennegan, "Music and the Picture Show," *B* (3 February 1912), 13. Again, this is a cross-media practice that has enjoyed a revival, much transformed, during the past twenty years in which both television and moving pictures often serve to promote new songs, formerly on audiotapes and now on CDs or Web sites.

59. Ernest J. Luz uses this phrase for music to accompany moving pictures in "Picture Music," *MPN* (26 October 1912), 29.

60. At an early stage in my research, another pattern seemed to emerge that eventually I could not fully substantiate—see Abel, "Reframing the Vaudeville/Moving Picture Debate, with Illustrated Songs," 479. The combination show of moving pictures and vaudeville (with or without illustrated songs) seemed more prominent in the Northeast, whereas that of moving pictures and illustrated songs (with or without added musical performances) seemed more prominent in the Midwest. Initially I thought this difference could be attributed to the fact that high-class vaudeville originated and flourished in the Northeast and that, by contrast, a strong musical tradition developed in the Midwest, as the result of large numbers of German immigrants—for the latter, see Teaford, *Cities of the Heartland*, 82–90.

61. As evidence, see the hundreds of postcards collected in Lauren Rabinovitz's CD-ROM, *Yesterday's Wonderlands*, forthcoming from University of Illinois Press.

62. This is precisely what a "Brooklyn Mother" suggested in "Illustrated Song Slides," *MPN* (28 January 1911), 10. One prominent manufacturer, Henry Ingram, even specialized in making song slides for old popular ballads—see "Editorial: The Tremendous Demand for Song Slides," *MPW* (28 September 1907), 467–68.

Chapter 4: The "Usable Past" of Civil War Films

1. "America's Great Civil War Began Fifty Years Ago Today with the Bombardment of Fort Sumter," "Facts about Greatest Modern War—America's Civil War," J. S. C. Abbott, "The Federal Story," and E. A. Pollard, "The Confederate Story," *DMN* (12 April 1911), 4.

2. See the full-page ad, *CL* (14 April 1912), M8. For a summary analysis of Lossing's history, see Thomas J. Pressly, *Americans Interpret Their Civil War* (New York: Free Press, 1962), 58–59.

3. Jim Cullen, *The Civil War in Popular Culture: A Reusable Past* (Washington, D.C.: Smithsonian Institution, 1995), 182–83.

4. David W. Blight, *Race and Reunion: The Civil War in American Memory* (Cambridge, Mass.: Harvard University Press, 2001), 383–91. Blight is especially prescient in noting that, although many black men built and serviced the camp, no black vet-

erans were invited and that black newspapers "were wary, even resentful, of the celebrations at Gettysburg."

5. Glassberg, *American Historical Pageantry*, 209–11; David Mayer, "Opening a Second Front: The Civil War, the Stage, and D. W. Griffith," in Leonardo Quaresima and Laura Vichi, eds., *The Tenth Muse: Cinema and the Other Arts* (Udine: Forum, 2001), 491–502; and David Mayer, "Swords and Hearts," in Cherchi Usai, *The Griffith Project*, 5: 110–14.

6. See especially C. Vann Woodward, *Origins of the New South, 1877–1913* (Baton Rouge: Louisiana State University Press, 1971). Here again, Herbert Blau's "question of what is commonly remembered and adhered to, or thought of as better forgotten," especially as applied to the construction of community, has resonance—see Blau, *The Audience*, 21.

7. Nina Silber, *The Romance of Reunion: Northerners and the South, 1865–1900* (Chapel Hill: University of North Carolina Press, 1993), 4. The literature on the Lost Cause is extensive, but see, in particular, Blight, *Race and Reunion*, 255–99.

8. James Ford Rhodes, *History of the United States from the Compromise of 1850*, 8 vols. (New York: Harper and Brothers/Macmillan, 1893–1906). See also Pressley, *Americans Interpret Their Civil War*, 166–95; Cullen, *The Civil War in Popular Culture*, 20–23; and Blight, *Race and Reunion*, 357–59. Another influential historian was William Dunning, who, in *Reconstruction, Political and Economic, 1865–1877* (1907), argued that "black incapacity was responsible for the failure of Reconstruction"—Bruce Chatwin, *The Reel Civil War: Mythmaking in American Film* (New York: Knopf, 2001), 30.

9. Kammen, *The Mystic Chords of Memory*, 113, 217.

10. Silber, *The Romance of Reunion*, 5–6, 105–22.

11. Other sources of such spectacle that remain to be examined are large illustrated histories of the war, such as *Leslie's Illustrated Famous Leaders and Battle Scenes of the Civil War* (New York: Frank Leslie, 1896), which included hundreds of woodcut illustrations, many of them allegedly done by artist observers.

12. See also Louis Reeves Harrison's reference to the "distinctive peculiarities in pure New England and Southern strains [of racial stock], and . . . their delightful combination in men and women of the West"—Harrison, "Picturing Americans," *MPW* (14 March 1914), 1360.

13. Dudley Miles, "The Civil War as a Unifier," *Sewanee Review* 21 (January 1913), 188–97.

14. Bowser, *The Transformation of Cinema*, 178.

15. "The Girl Spy," *MPW* (22 May 1909), 672.

16. "A Letter Which Makes Us All Feel Good," *MPW* (28 May 1910), 883.

17. "Observations by Our Man about Town," *MPW* (18 June 1910), 1041.

18. "Critical Reviews of Licensed Films," *NYMT* (2 April 1911), 4.1: 6.

19. Ellen C. Clayton, *Female Warriors. Memorials of Female Valour and Heroism, From the Mythological Ages to the Present Era*, vol. 2 (London, 1879), 121—quoted in Elizabeth Young, *Disarming the Nation: Women's Writing and the American Civil War* (Chicago: University of Chicago Press, 2002), 149.

20. Elizabeth D. Leonard, *All the Daring of the Soldier: Women of the Civil War Armies* (New York: Norton, 1999).

21. Young, *Disarming the Nation*, 1–6, 149–94. For a study of these Civil War women

as less well known versions of "confidence men," see De Grave, *Swindler, Spy, Rebel,* 96–114. Even an excellent historian such as Blight ignores these women and devotes a chapter exclusively to male writers from Albion W. Tourgée and Thomas Nelson Page to Ambrose Bierce—Blight, "The Literature of Reunion and Its Discontents," in *Race and Reunion,* 211–54.

22. *The Girl Spy* seems to have been rereleased as *Adventures of a Girl Spy* (1912), a 35mm viewing print of which (863 feet) is available at the NFTVA. Chatwin briefly mentions, but pays little attention to, Gauntier's "girl spy" films—Chatwin, *The Reel Civil War,* 41.

23. "Reviews of Licensed Films," *NYDM* (4 January 1911), 30. *The Girl Spy before Vicksburg* was one of "two special feature pictures," shown Monday through Wednesday, at the Theatre Comique in Lynn—see the Comique ad, *LDI* (31 December 1910), 2. The father-and-son story of Selig's *The Spy* (January 1911) was more conventional in depicting the war, although the "atmosphere . . . of the old Southern homestead" was praised—see "Reviews of Licensed Films," *NYDM* (1 February 1911), 31.

24. Originating in the Revolutionary War, and based on women such as Mary Ludwig Hays McCauley and Margaret Cochran Corbin, the Molly Pitcher figure was a lower-class woman (often an immigrant) who took up "the task of loading and firing her husband's artillery piece when he falls in battle." "Throughout and well beyond the Civil War," Leonard writes, "the name and imagery of 'Molly Pitcher' offered a popular and precious symbol of extraordinary female bravery"—see Leonard, *All the Daring of the Soldier,* 155–56. "Reviews of Licensed Films," *NYDM* (5 July 1911), 21, and (12 July 1911), 24; "Comments on the Films," *MPW* (22 July 1911), 124; and "Installation of Moving Picture Machines in New York City Public Schools a Matter of Safety and Expense," *MPN* (6 January 1912), 5. *Motography,* however, compared *The Little Soldier of '64* unfavorably with *Railroad Raiders of '62* (June 1912)—see "Reviews of Current Films," *M* (July 1911), 42.

25. "Reviews of Licensed Films," *NYDM* (12 April 1911), 31.

26. A 35mm viewing print of *The Railroad Raiders of '62* (818 feet) is available at the LoC. This film probably was directed by Kenean Buel, who headed the Kalem production unit in Jacksonville, Florida, from the late spring of 1911 through at least 1912—Bowser, *The Transformation of Cinema,* 154.

27. Although Charlie Keil cites *The Railroad Raiders of '62* for its early use of a camera mounted on a train, he does not mention its dramatic use of low-angle framing—see Charlie Keil, *Early American Cinema in Transition* (Madison: University of Wisconsin Press, 2001), 156–60.

28. "Reviews of Licensed Films," *NYDM* (21 June 1911), 31.

29. After several years of wintering in Florida, Kalem finally constructed a permanent studio in Jacksonville—see Bowser, *The Transformation of Cinema,* 152–53.

30. See the Orpheum ad, *CN* (12 November 1911), 15; and "Comments on the Films," *MPW* (5 October 1912), 41. A 35mm viewing print of *The Lost Freight Car* (712 feet) is available at the LoC. An incomplete 16mm viewing print of *The Grit of the Girl Telegrapher* (258 feet) is available at the GEH.

31. Mayer, "Swords and Hearts," 112–13.

32. Young, *Disarming the Nation,* 2.

33. See also Selig's *The Common Enemy* (October 1910), in which "the family on the screen" is equated with "the family of the nation"—Chatwin, *The Reel Civil War,* 55.

34. "Comments on the Films," *MPW* (19 November 1911), 1178. See also Lee Grieveson's analysis of *The Fugitive,* in Cherchi Usai, *The Griffith Project,* 4: 211–14.

35. "Comments on the Films," *MPW* (5 April 1911), 31. See also Pathé American's *The Rival Brothers' Patriotism* (April 1911), where one Northern brother sacrifices himself for another when he learns, from a letter, that the woman he loves has chosen the other brother over him. An incomplete 16mm viewing print of *The Rival Brothers' Patriotism* (371 feet) is available at the LoC.

36. The *Mirror*'s review is quoted in Tom Gunning's excellent analysis of the film, in Cherchi Usai, *The Griffith Project,* 4: 141–46.

37. "Comments on the Films," *MPW* (20 August 1910), 407. In plays such as *Down in Dixie* (1894) and *Colonel Carter of Cartersville* (1891), by contrast, this kind of critique had been directed humorously at "old southern gentlemen"—see Silber, *The Romance of Reunion,* 120–21.

38. This pair of films was singled out in "Two Notable Films," *MPN* (11 February 1911), 14. Besides offering an analysis of these two films, Chatwin provides a useful survey of black characters in Civil War films, as well as others, of the early 1910s—Chatwin, *The Reel Civil War,* 45–46, 79–95.

39. The fervently loyal black servant was a crucial character, for instance, in William Gillette's *Held by the Enemy* (1886) and Townsend's *The Pride of Virginia* (1901)—see Silber, *The Romance of Reunion,* 108. See "Reviews of Licensed Films," *NYDM* (25 January 1911), 30; "Comments on the Films," *MPW* (28 January 1911), 195–96; and Thompson's analyses of the two films in Cherchi Usai, *The Griffith Project,* 4: 246–51. Viewing copies of the 35mm paper prints of both films are available at the LoC.

40. Mayer, "Swords and Hearts," 113.

41. The "lost home" was a central trope in Civil War stage melodramas, often threatened by destruction (whether the property or its inhabitants) "but ultimately regained and restored"—Mayer, "Opening a Second Front," 496.

42. Vachel Lindsay, *The Art of the Moving Picture* (New York: Liveright, 1970 [1915]), 72–73. In fact, Lindsay made the unusual recommendation, for the time, that the film "should be kept in the libraries and the Universities as a standard."

43. "A Remarkable War Picture," *NYDM* (1 November 1911), 27; W. Stephen Bush, "The Battle," *MPW* (4 November 1911), 367; and "Reviews of Licensed Films," *NYDM* (15 November 1911), 28. See also Steven Higgins, "The Battle," in Cherchi Usai, *The Griffith Project,* 5: 139–41. A 16mm viewing print of *The Battle* is available at the GEH.

44. See the Theatre Voyons ads, *LCC* (8 November 1911), 9, and (20 November 1911), 9; the Comique ad, *LDI* (22 November 1911), 2; and "Films Worth Seeing," *CL* (24 December 1911), B7.

45. "Licensed Film Stories," *MPW* (3 February 1912), 416; "Reviews of Licensed Films," *NYDM* (14 February 1912), 27, 30; and "Comments on the Films," *MPW* (17 February 1912), 581.

46. "Reviews of Licensed Films," *NYDM* (12 June 1912), 29. This film also was included in a rhymed advertisement for one day's program at the Haynic Theater in Fairmont, Minnesota, reproduced in Epes Winthrop Sargent, "Advertising for Exhibitors," *MPW* (5 October 1912), 37.

47. "Licensed Film Stories," *MPW* (13 January 1912), 140; "Reviews of Licensed Films," *NYDM* (24 January 1912), 38; and "Comments on the Films," *MPW* (3 February 1912), 392.

48. For a thorough examination of the music Simon arranged or composed for Kalem films, see Herbert Reynolds, "Aural Gratification with Kalem Films: A Case History of Music, Lectures, and Sound Effects, 1907–1917," *Film History* 12.4 (2000), 417–42.

49. "Splendid Kalem Film," *MPW* (2 March 1912), 770–71.

50. Colonial ad, *DMN* (15 March 1912), 10; "At the Theatres," *LT* (19 March 1912), 6; and "Laughs and Tears in Photo-Play Stories of the Week," *CL* (24 March 1912), S6. The Nickel Theatre screening in Lawrence came shortly after the resolution of the city's long, violent textile mill strike.

51. "Offerings at the Lyric," *MJ* (11 March 1912), 4; and the Lyric ad, *MJ* (11 March 1912), 9.

52. "Licensed Film Stories," *MPW* (9 March 1912), 690. That the actress playing this Southern mother could evoke sympathy in Northern audiences is suggested in the *Mirror*'s review of this "strong and virile little drama"—see "Reviews of Licensed Films," *NYDM* (20 March 1912), 29.

53. "Comments on the Films," *MPW* (23 March 1912), 1062.

54. By contrast, Vitagraph released a special "One-Reel Feature for Independence Day," starring Ralph Ince—see "Lincoln's Gettysburg Address," *MPW* (15 June 1912), 1017–18.

55. "Licensed Film Stories," *MPW* (27 July 1912), 366; Louis Reeves Harrison, "The Siege of Petersburg," *MPW* (13 July 1912), 151. Dan Frost is called "poor white trash" in the cast list of characters, which also is given at the beginning of the surviving print.

56. See the large Rex Theatre ads, *YV* (28 July 1912), 16, and (4 August 1912), 15; "What the Showmen Offer in Theaters and Parks," *MJ* (28 July 1912), 8: 8; the Theatre Comique ad, *LDI* (9 November 1912), 2; and "Superior Theater," *CL* (10 November 1912), B5.

57. A 16mm viewing print of *The Siege of Petersburg* (216 feet) is available at the LoC.

58. "The Darling of the C.S.A.," *MPW* (31 August 1912), 884; "Reviews of Licensed Films," *NYDM* (11 September 1912), 30.

59. See the Seville Theatre ad, *MJ* (8 September 1912), 8: 8; the Theatre Voyons ad, *LCC* (13 September 1912), 11; the Odeon ad, *CN* (20 October 1912), 12; and the Orpheum ad, *CN* (20 October 1912), 13.

60. *The Confederate Ironclad* can be found on program 1 of *Treasures from American Film Archives* (DVD, 2000). Scott Simmon suggests that Kalem built the film's story around the availability of this replica—see *Treasures from the American Film Archives: Program Notes* (Washington, D.C.: National Preservation Foundation, 2000), 10.

61. That Rose and Yancey as well as Elinor literally become spectators of this battle accentuates its attraction as climactic spectacle. Martin Marks, "*The Confederate Ironclad* (1912): About the Music," in *Treasures from American Film Archives: Program Notes,* 11. For publicity, see "Advanced Glimpse of Offerings Promised in Local Theaters," *MJ* (6 October 1912), 8: 11. In Cleveland, the Superior theater showed *The Confederate Ironclad* one weekend and followed it two days later with a return booking of *The Siege of Petersburg*—"Superior Theater," *CL* (10 November 1912), B5.

62. The first half of the film included songs suited to the heroine, such as "Good-By Rose" and "Dixie Rose"—see Marks, "*The Confederate Ironclad* (1912)," 11.

63. A 35mm viewing print of *The Informer* (965 feet) is available at the LoC.

64. "Reviews of Licensed Films," *NYDM* (27 November 1912), 28.

65. A reviewer in the *World* found this film "a long advance over *The Battle,* by the same company," and "far more thrilling"—see "Comments on the Films," *MPW* (7 December 1912), 976.

66. "A War Romance in Pictures," *MJ* (14 May 1912), 4.

67. The location of a Kalem production unit in Florida and the Southern victories that marked the initial years of the war, which probably coincided with fiftieth-anniversary commemorations, obviously played some role in the making of "Southern war pictures," but neither sufficiently explains why such films appealed to audiences across the United States.

68. Silber, *The Romance of Reunion,* 6–10; and Young, *Disarming the Nation,* 15.

69. "Doings in Los Angeles," *MPW* (6 July 1912), 35.

70. Louis Reeves Harrison, "Sundered Ties," *MPW* (14 September 1912), 1056–57. See also the laudatory review in "Reviews of Supply Co. Films," *NYDM* (18 September 1912), 32. *Sundered Ties* also was fictionalized in *PM* (October 1912), 25–31. A rare reference to this film's screening, on Saturday, occurs in Anderson's Theatre ad, *BT* (6 October 1912), 4: 4.

71. This language comes not only from Harrison but also from an anonymous reviewer in "Comments on the Films," *MPW* (28 September 1912), 1278.

72. "Independent Film Stories," *MPW* (9 November 1912), 598; and "Comments on the Films," *MPW* (23 November 1912), 769. A sketch of the suggested music and cues for *When Lee Surrenders* is provided in Ernst Luz, "Picture Music," *MPN* (16 November 1912), 17.

73. Apparently unaware of the ideological significance of the "romance of reunion," Chatwin comes close to belittling the marriage of Southern women to Northern men in these films—Chatwin, *The Reel Civil War,* 62.

74. "Comments on the Films," *MPW* (21 December 1912), 1186; and "Independent Film Stories," *MPW* (21 December 1912), 1232. Kay-Bee's *The Sharpshooter* (February 1913) deploys a kind of divine intervention, in the form of lightning, which blinds a villainous Union sharpshooter who already has killed the hero's younger brother and now is about to shoot the hero (Charles Ray) returning from prison to meet the heroine—"Comments on the Films," *MPW* (15 February 1913), 681; and "Independent Film Stories," *MPW* (15 February 1913), 716.

75. "Feature Films on the Market," *NYDM* (26 March 1913), 25; "Independent Film Stories," *MPW* (29 March 1913), 1364; and "Comments on the Films," *MPW* (5 April 1913), 50.

76. Chatwin briefly discusses these "girl spies" as related to the "wild women" in dime novels and Buffalo Bill's Wild West—Chatwin, *The Reel Civil War,* 67–68.

77. For information on Belle Boyd and Pauline Cushman, see Leonard, *All the Daring of the Soldier,* 25–35, 57–62.

78. "History and Thrills," *NYDM* (12 March 1913), 28. See also Jas. S. McQuade, "Pauline Cushman, the Federal Spy," *MPW* (22 March 1913), 1201–2; and "Feature Films on the Market," *NYDM* (2 April 1913), 25. This Civil War film was featured at the March 31 opening of the New Grand Central in downtown St. Louis—Jas. S. McQuade, "Chicago Letter," *MPW* (19 April 1913), 265.

79. "Historical Incident in Two Reel Feature," *M* (15 March 1913), 185–86.

80. While Keil's analysis of this film's first reel seems spot on—it is constructed to

highlight these unusual overhead shots of spying—his analysis of the second reel fails to take into account the historical knowledge that most audiences would have supplied as a context for what now can seem elliptical and confusing in Boyd's actions. See Keil, *Early American Cinema in Transition,* 191–95.

81. "Important Films of the Week," *NYMT* (23 February 1913), 4.2: 2; and H. C. Judson, "A Daughter of the Confederacy," *MPW* (1 March 1913), 892–93.

82. Revivals of *Shenandoah* were especially cheered during the 1898 Spanish-American War—see Silber, *The Romance of Reunion,* 180. Kalem adapted the play as a three-reel feature for release in July 1913—George Blaisdell, "Shenandoah," *MPW* (28 June 1913), 1339–40; and "Feature Films on the Market," *NYDM* (2 July 1913), 28.

83. "Independent Film Stories," *MPW* (7 December 1912), 1018; and "Comments on the Films," *MPW* (14 December 1912), 1082.

84. "Reviews of Mutual Films," *NYDM* (1 January 1913), 33.

85. "Reviews of Mutual Films," *NYDM* (22 January 1913), 33. See also Bowser, *The Transformation of Cinema,* 179.

86. "Independent Film Stories," *MPW* (22 February 1913), 812.

87. NYMP ad, "*MPN* (26 October 1912), 2; and "Independent Film Stories," *MPW* (9 November 1912), 598. Several months later, Universal-Bison worked a variation on this story in *The Battle of Bull Run* (March 1913), where a sister (played by Grace Cunard) and brother serve as Northern spies; after both the brother and her Confederate lover are killed on the battlefield, the sister has a vision of the two (roundly criticized in the trade press) and collapses and dies, heartbroken—see "H. C. Judson, "The Battle of Bull Run," *MPW* (15 March 1913), 1107; and "Reviews of Feature Films," *NYDM* (19 March 1913), 29.

88. Louis Reeves Harrison, "Two Strong 'Kay-Bee' Subjects," *MPW* (23 November 1912), 754.

89. "Independent Film Stories," *MPW* (22 March 1913), 1252; "Feature Films on the Market," *NYDM* (26 March 1913), 25; and "Comments on the Films," *MPW* (5 April 1913), 49. The *Morning Telegraph* hailed *The Light in the Window* as "one of the best Civil War stories told recently"—"Feature Film Reviews," *NYMT* (30 March 1913), 4.2: 2. By contrast, Broncho's *A War Time Mother's Sacrifice* (July 1913) ends with a Southern mother, whose son has shot himself in the garret of their home (after being duped and falsely accused by Northern spies), placing his body "among the dead on the battlefield that he may be found with the appearance of an honorable end"—"Feature Films on the Market," *NYDM* (30 July 1913), 28.

90. "Feature Films on the Market," *NYDM* (14 May 1913), 28.

91. "Feature Films on the Market," *NYDM* (16 July 1913), 28.

92. Louis Reeves Harrison, "The Pride of the South," *MPW* (15 March 1913), 1086.

93. A 35mm viewing print of most of the final reel of *The Pride of the South* (755 feet) is available at the LoC.

94. "Mutual Films," *NYDM* (5 March 1913), 33; and "Important Films of the Week," *NYMT* (9 March 1913), 4.2: 4.

95. "Comments on the Films," *MPW* (3 May 1913), 489.

96. "Feature Films on the Market," *NYDM* (2 April 1913), 25.

97. "Feature Films of the Week," *NYDM* (19 November 1913), 33. By contrast, in Kalem's earlier one-reel *Prisoners of War* (March 1913), a congressman's daughter, upon learning the real story of an old Union veteran (indebted for his life to a South-

ern friend, he lets him escape execution as a spy), persuades her father to argue successfully on his behalf for a pension—see "Licensed Film Stories," *MPW* (15 March 1913), 1126; and "Comments on the Films," *MPW* (5 April 1913), 47.

98. "Comments on the Films," *MPW* (19 April 1913), 282; and "Independent Film Stories," *MPW* (26 April 1913), 420.

99. "Feature Films on the Market," *NYDM* (7 May 1913), 28; and "Comments on the Films," *MPW* (17 May 1913), 705.

100. George Blaisdell, "In Slavery Days," *MPW* (10 May 1913), 600.

101. "Independent Film Stories," *MPW* (29 March 1913), 1366; "Feature Films on the Market," *NYDM* (2 April 1913), 25; and "Comments on the Films," *MPW* (5 April 1913), 50.

102. A 35mm viewing print of *With Lee in Virginia* (1,899 feet) is available at the GEH.

103. Compare the pathos of this film's ending, which still relies on a degree of sentimental nostalgia, with the rare condemnation of black lynching (at least, that spurred on by misinterpretation) in Majestic's one-reel *The Night Riders* (April 1913)—see "Comments in the Films," *MPW* (12 April 1913), 166.

104. See the ads for *The Battle of Gettysburg* in *MPW* (3 May 1913), 448–49, (7 June 1913), 1061, and (12 July 1912), 113; and in *NYMT* (11 May 1913), 4.2: 2. Many newspapers celebrated this anniversary—see, for instance, the "Gettysburg Section" of the *Minneapolis Sunday Journal*'s Pictorial Magazine (29 June 1913).

105. "Reviews of Universal Films," *NYDM* (15 January 1913), 57. See also "Comments on the Films," *MPW* (25 January 1913), 365.

106. A 35mm viewing print of the third reel of *Sheridan's Ride* (990 feet) is available at the LoC.

107. "Feature Film Reviews," *NYMT* (18 May 1913), 4.2: 2; and "Feature Films," *NYDM* (11 June 1913), 27. Chatwin certainly accepts the *Mirror*'s praise, attributing the film's success to both Ince and scriptwriter C. Gardner Sullivan; unfortunately, he also offers scarcely any documentation—Chatwin, *The Reel Civil War,* 48–49.

108. An incomplete 35mm viewing print of this film, retitled *The Fifth Anniversary of the Battle of Gettysburg* (816 feet) is available at the LoC.

109. "Reviews of Universal Films," *NYDM* (6 August 1913), 31.

110. For an analysis of the "Anglo-Saxonism" that served to unite North and South, see Silber, *The Romance of Reunion,* 172–82.

111. "Patriotic Confederate Veterans," *Independent* 52 (5 July 1900), 1629—quoted in Silber, *The Romance of Reunion,* 180. An editorial cartoon in the *Chicago Inter-Ocean* (30 May 1898) epitomized this spirit of reconciliation, with a pair of Union and Confederate soldiers standing on a pedestal on which is carved the word "Loyalty"—reproduced in Blight, *Race and Reunion,* 351. One of the more popular songs during the Spanish-American War was C. H. Addison's "The Blue and Gray Together," the song sheet cover for which is reproduced in Silber, *The Romance of Reunion,* 184. The song may have been based on Frances Miles Finch's popular poem "The Blue and the Gray," published in the *Atlantic Monthly* (1867)—see Blight, *Race and Reunion,* 84–85.

112. Miles, "The Civil War as a Unifier," 194–95; and "Doings at Los Angeles," *MPW* (10 May 1913), 582. The films set in the Philippines were to be directed by Francis Ford; those set in Cuba, by Harry McRae.

113. "Independent Film Stories," *MPW* (17 May 1913), 736.

114. "Comments on the Films," *MPW* (31 May 1913), 921.

115. "Comments on the Films," *MPW* (14 June 1913), 1138.

116. "Comments on the Films," *MPW* (28 June 1913), 1361.

117. "The G.A.R. made a practice of acquiring and presenting American flags to public schools and colleges" between 1885 and 1915—see Kammen, *The Mystic Chords of Memory*, 204.

118. "Reviews of Mutual Films," *NYDM* (1 January 1913), 33.

119. Louis Reeves Harrison, "Historical Photoplays," *MPW* (17 May 1913), 680.

120. Henry, "Correspondence: New England," *MPW* (26 October 1912), 357.

121. " 'Sheridan's Ride' Seen by Local Exhibitors," *CL* (26 January 1913), W8. See also the Universal ad on the same page.

122. "Week's Events in Pictureland," *CL* (9 February 1913), W4. See also the Corona and Mall ads and "Many Big Features in Week's Programs," *CL* (26 January 1913), W8.

123. " 'Sheridan's Ride' Seen by Local Exhibitors," W8.

124. See, for instance, the Family ad, *DMN* (27 January 1913), 6; and the Empress ad in *TNB* (29 January 1913), 13.

125. "Correspondence," *MPW* (14 June 1913), 1151.

126. "Correspondence," *MPW* (26 July 1913), 439.

127. See Chase's ad, *WS* (1 June 1913), 23; the Providence Opera House ads, *PT* (11 June 1913), 5, and (13 June 1913), 5; and the Alhambra ads, *CN* (29 June 1913), 12, and (3 July 1913), 3. The film returned to Washington one weekend in late October—see the Garden ad, *WS* (26 October 1913), 2: 3.

128. See the Crystal ads and "Moving Pictures," *MJ* (3 November 1912), 8, and (10 November 1912), 8.

129. See, for instance, the large Central Square ad, *LDI* (23 November 1912), 2.

130. The Lynn post of the Civil War veterans group, the GAR, "was one of the largest and most active in the country"—see Melder, *Life and Times in Shoe City*, 7.

131. Universal-Bison films were distributed through Victor Film Service; Broncho and Kay-Bee films, by Mutual through Lake Shore Film Supply.

132. "Best Features at Local League Theaters," *CL* (23 February 1913), M11.

133. "Big Features Are Shown This Week," *CL* (16 March 1913), M10; "Features of Week at Local Houses," *CL* (11 May 1913), C4; "Here's Where to Find the Best Shows," *CL* (25 May 1913), C4; and "Special July 4 Feature Films at All Houses," *CL* (29 June 1913), C4.

134. "You'll Be Sorry If You Miss Them," *CL* (2 February 1913), B4.

135. "Latest Film Snapshots Local and Worldwide," *CL* (2 March 1913), M11.

136. Anna Everett, *Returning the Gaze: A Genealogy of Black Film Criticism, 1909–1949* (Durham, N.C.: Duke University Press, 2001).

137. This 1914 survey information is reproduced in Rev. J. J. Phelan, *Motion Pictures as a Phase of Commercialized Amusement in Toledo, Ohio* (Toledo: Little Book, 1919), 55–56. This important document is reproduced in *Film History* 13.3 (2001).

138. Foster, *Vaudeville and Motion Picture Shows*, 26–27.

139. For a fuller analysis of the probable audience at the Pawtucket Star, see Abel, "Patchwork Maps of Movie-Going, 1911–1913."

140. Tony Horwitz, *Confederates in the Attic: Dispatches from the Unfinished Civil War* (New York: Pantheon, 1998), 389. The phrase that Horwitz quotes from Robert Penn

Warren probably comes from *The Legacy of the Civil War,* 1961. For a specific sense of how moving pictures could function as "lessons" for "newly naturalized citizens," see DeLysle F. Cass, "Higher Education of the Motion Picture," *M* (August 1912), 97–101.

141. "Comments on the Films," *MPW* (25 January 1913), 365.

142. "Feature Films of the Week," *NYDM* (12 November 1913), 33.

143. Kathy Peiss, *Cheap Amusements: Working Women and Leisure in Turn-of-the-Century New York* (Philadelphia: Temple University Press, 1986); and Nan Enstad, *Ladies of Leisure, Girls of Adventure: Working Women, Popular Culture, and Labor Politics at the Turn of the Twentieth Century* (New York: Columbia University Press, 1999).

144. Enstad, *Ladies of Leisure, Girls of Adventure,* 2.

145. Clara E. Laughlin, "The Girl Who Earns $6 a Week," *The Work-a-Day Girl* (New York: Fleming H. Revell, 1913), 127–55.

146. Bowser, *The Transformation of Cinema,* 179.

147. "Feature Films of the Week," *NYDM* (4 January 1914), 32. See also Bowser, *The Transformation of Cinema,* 180.

148. "Feature Films of the Week," *NYDM* (18 January 1914), 36.

Entr'acte 4: Another "Forgotten" Part of the Program

1. See the reproduction of this survey information in J. J. Phelan, *Motion Pictures as a Phase of Commercialized Amusement in Toledo, Ohio* (Toledo: Little Book Press, 1919), 49–56, reprinted in *Film History* 13.3 (2001), 251–53.

2. Mary Heaton Vorse, "Some Picture Show Audiences," *Outlook* 98 (24 June 1911), 447–48.

3. See the 17 May 1910 letter from C. Leyman to George Kleine, in the George Kleine Collection, Box 24: Gaumont folder, Manuscript Division, Library of Congress, Washington, D.C.

4. The 1994 Amsterdam Workshop, for instance, transfixed invited participants with a half dozen programs of early nonfiction films selected from the Nederlands Filmmuseum; those returning the following year found even more in the Amsterdam Workshop programs devoted to color in silent cinema. A 1998 workshop on early travel films has led to a DVD, *Exotic Europe: Journeys into Early Cinema* (Nederlands Filmmuseum, 2000). And anyone who has traveled to the annual Giornate del cinema muto knows that early nonfiction films consistently are among the "revelations" or "discoveries" of its weeklong, morn-to-midnight screenings. Two other new books on early nonfiction should be mentioned: Alison Griffiths, *Wondrous Differences: Cinema, Anthropology, and Turn-of-the-Century Visual Culture* (New York: Columbia University Press, 2003); and Jennifer Peterson, *World Pictures: Travelogue Films and the Lure of the Exotic* (Durham, N.C.: Duke University Press, 2005).

5. For an all-too-brief appraisal of nonfiction during the nickelodeon period, see Abel, *The Red Rooster Scare,* 131–32.

6. See the announcement in *MPW* (9 April 1910), 545. A copy of this catalog can be found in the George Kleine Collection, Manuscript Division, Library of Congress, Washington, D.C.

7. Quoted from the "author's preface" in "The New Kleine Catalog," *FI* (16 April 1910), 6.

8. "The New Kleine Catalog," 6.

9. "Correspondence: Selecting a Show," *MPW* (23 April 1910), 652. See also "Industrial Films," *MPW* (30 April 1910), 688.

10. "What Pathé Is Doing," *MPW* (24 June 1911), 1434–35.

11. "Current Educational Releases," *M* (October 1911), 156–57. See also E. V. Morrison's report on the proliferation of nonfiction films in "The Status of the Moving Picture Business," *B* (3 February 1912), 8.

12. See, for instance, E. B. Lockwood, "Travelogues and Topicals," *M* (June 1912), 257. Compare the first two columns, which specifically highlight Gaumont and Pathé films—*M* (October 1911), 188–89, and (November 1911), 231–32—with two of the last, which highlight Edison, Lubin, and Selig films—*M* (May 1912), 222–23, and (17 August 1912), 139–40.

13. See the Voyons ad, *LST* (29 May 1910), 8; "Theatrical Notes," *DMRL* (5 June 1910), 6; "What Is Going on at Local Theatres," *BP* (3 September 1911), 28; and the Tremont Temple ad, *BA* (4 November 1911), 14.

14. See "At Leading Theaters," *CL* (7 January 1912), B7, (21 January 1912), S6, (18 February 1912), B6, and (31 March 1912), S8; and the Colonial ad, *CL* (5 June 1912), M5.

15. See the Premier ad, *BA* (26 January 1912), 16; the Scenic Theatre ads, *LST* (28 January 1912), 6, and (4 February 1912), 6; and the Voyons ad, *LST* (11 February 1912), 3.

16. See "New York Fires in Moving Pictures Today," *YV* (9 April 1911), 15; the Grand ad, *YV* (23 April 1911), 16; "At Leading Theaters," *CL* (14 January 1912), S6; the Home ad, *CL* (21 January 1912), S6; and the Voyons ad, *LST* (21 January 1912), 6.

17. See the Comique and Olympia ads, *LDI* (26 October 1912), 2; and Saxe's Lyric ad, *MJ* (27 October 1912), 8:11.

18. See the Odeon ad, *CN* (10 September 1911), 4, and (24 December 1911), 15; and the Central Square ads, *LDI* (2 December 1911), 2, and (22 June 1912), 2.

19. See the rare Roma ad, *YV* (22 October 1911), 16; the Mall ad, *CL* (26 November 1911), S5; the Voyons ad, *LST* (26 November 1911), 5; the Grand ad, *CN* (10 December 1911), n.p.; and "Turkish War Now Seen in the Films," *BA* (17 December 1911), E6. Another set of films on the "Balkan War" circulated widely a year later in the same cities (and in two Cleveland theaters that advertised in the labor weekly)— see the Central Square ad, *LDI* (13 November 1912), 2, and the Comique and Olympia ads, *LDI* (14 December 1912), 2; the Voyons ad, *LCC* (28 November 1912), 7; the Doan ad, *CL* (3 December 1912), B7; the Grand and Auditorium ads, *CN* (8 December 1912), 16, 17; and "Big Holiday Films at Local Theaters," *CL* (22 December 1912), S5.

20. R.P. Stoddard, "Films All Should See," *CL* (19 November 1911), B7.

21. "At the Leading Theaters," *CL* (17 December 1911), S7.

22. "At the Leading Theaters," *CL* (31 December 1911), B7, (21 January 1912), S6, and (4 February 1912), S6. Some manufacturers also saw how film could help make their production processes more efficient—see "Factory Efficiency Studied by Films," *M* (1 February 1913), 71–73.

23. YMCA ad, *LDI* (7 October 1911), 2. The YMCA became an important distributor and exhibitor of nonfiction film—see John Collier, "Motion Pictures and YMCA Work," *M* (21 December 1912), 493–95. This was less true of the YWCA, but see "Y.W.C.A. Using Pictures," *N* (4 February 1911), 130.

24. See "At the Leading Theaters," *CL* (14 January 1912), S5, and (31 March 1912), S8; the Grand ad, *CN* (31 March 1912), 17; "The Week in Moving Pictures," *YV* (30 June 1912), 16; and "At the Theatres," *LCC* (26 August 1912), 5.

25. See the Lyric ads, *MJ* (17 December 1911), 8:11, (3 March 1912), 8:9, and (9 July 1912), 4.

26. For an excellent introduction to the early travel film, see Jennifer Lynn Peterson, "Travelogues and Early Nonfiction Film," in Keil and Stamp, *American Cinema's Transitional Era*, 191-213.

27. See the Voyons ads, *LCC* (5 December 1910), 5, and (26 February 1911), 6; and the Scenic ads, *LST* (6 August 1911), 7, and (17 March 1912), 6.

28. See the Comique ads, *LDI* (16 September 1911), 2, and (12 March 1912), 2; "The Critic's Comment," *LDI* (3 February 1912), 14; and the Central Square ads, *LDI* (20 April 1912), 2, and (8 June 1912), 2.

29. "At the Photo Plays," *TNB* (9 March 1912), 3.

30. Pathé-Frères first experimented with a French newsreel as early as 1908 and was releasing a weekly version, *Pathé Journal*, throughout Europe by 1910. Raymond Fielding gives some attention to the emergence of *Pathé Weekly* but cites only one venue for its first year of exhibition, the Keith-Albee and Orpheum vaudeville circuits—see Fielding, *The American Newsreel, 1911-1967* (Norman: University of Oklahoma Press, 1972), 75.

31. See the Pathé-Frères ad, *MPW* (29 July 1911), 179; and the Colonial ad, *DMRL* (23 April 1912), 2.

32. See "The Pathé Weekly," *MPW* (23 September 1911), 871; and "The Pathé Weekly," *B* (2 September 1911), 14.

33. See the Voyons ad, *LST* (27 August 1911), 6.

34. See the Orpheum ads, *DMT* (9 September 1911), 2, and the *DMRL* (17 September 1911), Magazine Section: 7. Previously, the Orpheum simply had listed the "kinodrome" service or its "late-up-to-date photoplays."

35. See the Comique ad, *LDI* (23 September 1911), 2; "The Week in Moving Pictures," *YV* (1 October 1911), 19; and "Great Variety in Orpheum Bill for This Week," *CN* (8 October 1911), 18.

36. "At the Photo Plays," *TNB* (30 January 1912), 7, and (10 February 1912), 7.

37. In early 1910, Pathé launched a national advertising campaign in several Sunday newspapers (in Chicago, Cleveland, Detroit, and Baltimore), reminding moviegoers of the "quality" that its "Rooster brand" had long guaranteed. The first of these ads appeared in the *CT* (6 February 1910), 2: 6, and in the *Chicago Record-Herald* (6 February 1910), 7: 3. Succeeding ads promoted comedy, tragedy, travel pictures, educational pictures, juvenile pictures, and historical pictures. See also "Pathé Pointers," *FI* (26 March 1910), 6; and "Novel Advertising Campaign," *NYDM* (26 March 1910), 20.

38. "Boosting Pathé Film," *CL* (28 January 1912), W8.

39. See the Pathé Weekly ads, *CL* (28 January 1912), W8, (4 February 1912), S6, (11 February 1912), S6, and (18 February 1912), B6.

40. See the Pathé Weekly ad, *CR* (18 February 1912), 19.

41. Lillian Conlon, "Newspaper vs. Newspicture," *MPSM* (March 1912), 90-93.

42. See the Gaumont Weekly ads, *CL* (11 February 1912), S6, (18 February 1912), B6, and (25 February 1912), S6. See also "New Weekly a Hit," *CL* (25 February 1912), S6.

43. See "At the Photo Plays," *TNB* (24 February 1912), 3, and (23 March 1912), 7; "At the Leading Theaters," *CL* (10 March 1912), S6; "Park Features Today," *YV* (7 April 1912), 21; and the Grand ad, *CN* (12 May 1912), 14.

44. See "At the Photo Plays," *TNB* (9 November 1912), 8; the Grand ad, *CN* (22 December 1912), 20; the Unique/Mutual ad, *DMN* (26 January 1913), 6; and the Central Square ad, *LDI* (11 January 1913), 2.

45. See also the Mutual ad, *NYMT* (22 December 1912), 4.2: 3.

46. Film Man, "Comments and Suggestions," *NYDM* (30 October 1912), 25.

47. See, for instance, the Family and Colonial ads, *DMRL* (19 April 1912), 5, and (23 April 1912), 2. Indeed, in September 1912, the Colonial promoted *Pathé Weekly* even more than the Berchel Theatre did its special weeklong road show engagement of *Queen Elizabeth*—see the Berchel ad, *DMRL* (15 September 1912), Magazine Section: 7; and the Colonial ad, *DMT* (19 September 1912), 3.

48. See, for instance, the Pathé-Frères ad, *MPW* (7 October 1911), insert. *Pathé Weekly* often concluded with a Paris fashion show, a "feature" that "proved especially attractive" and whose "possibilities . . . as a business getter for the theater manager [could] hardly be overestimated"—see "The Pathé Weekly," *MPW* (23 September 1911), 871. The significance of Paris fashion shows, developed by major American department stores around 1905, cannot be underestimated—see, for instance, William Leach, *Land of Desire: Merchants, Power, and the Rise of a New American Culture* (New York: Pantheon, 1993), 95–104.

49. See the Crescent ad, *CL* (14 April 1912), S6; and the Mall ad, *CL* (26 May 1912), S6. Two years later, the *Chicago Herald* and *Saint Louis Times* launched their own weekly newsreel for distribution, respectively, to forty and thirty picture theaters in those cities—see the *Chicago Herald Movies* ads in the *Chicago Herald* (26 June 1914), 2, and (27 June 1914), 18, and "Exhibitors News," *MPW* (27 June 1914), 1850.

50. "Texas Moving Picture Weekly to Start July 1," *New York Morning Telegraph* (15 June 1913), 4.2: 2.

51. See the Pathé Weekly ad, *MPW* (21 June 1913), 1220–21; and "Two Pathé Weeklies," *CL* (22 June 1913), C4.

52. See, for instance, the Coliseum ad, *DMRL* (3 July 1910), 7; the Family ad, *DMRL* (8 August 1910), 5; the People's ad, *CRR* (22 September 1910), 3; "Theaters Will Report Kilbane-Attell Fight," *CL* (18 February 1912), B6; the Mall and Princess ads, *CL* (17 March 1912), S6; the Clark ad, *CL* (24 March 1912), S6; "Benefit T.M.A. Canton Lodge No. 129," *CR* (24 March 1912), 18; and the Grand ad, *YV* (31 March 1912), 21.

53. Dan Streible, "Race and the Reception of Jack Johnson Fight Films," in Daniel Bernardi, ed., *The Birth of Whiteness: Race and the Emergence of U.S. Cinema* (New Brunswick, N.J.: Rutgers University Press, 1996), 170–200. See also Lee Grieveson, *Policing Cinema: Movies and Censorship in Early Twentieth-Century America* (Berkeley and Los Angeles: University of California Press, 2004), 121–50. In Des Moines, where the *Johnson-Jeffries Fight* was not shown in regular picture theaters, a newspaper story claimed that Vitagraph was leasing such fight pictures only in "stag" theaters—see "Fight Films to 'Stags,' " *DMN* (11 July 1910), 8; and the Colonial ad, *DMN* (17 July 1910), 6. By contrast, in Canton, the film was shown for three days at the Meyers Lake amusement park, and "ladies especially" were invited—see the Meyers Lake ad, *CN* (20 September 1910), 6.

54. See the Orpheum ad, *TNB* (10 August 1912), 9; and "Cops Bang the Lid on Two Local Theaters," *TNB* (14 August 1912), 2.

55. See the Colonial ad, *DMRL* (11 August 1910), 5; and the Voyons ad, *LST* (23 October 1910), 4.

56. See the Grand ad, *DMN* (15 January 1911), 4; and Foster's ad, *DMN* (26 February 1911), 6.

57. See "At the Leader Chain Houses This Week," *CL* (26 November 1911), S5; the Park ad, *YV* (10 December 1911), 21; and "At the Leading Theaters," *CL* (17 December 1911), S7. *The Fall Round-Up* also was featured several months later in Des Moines—see the Family ad, *DMRL* (17 April 1912), 7.

58. See "At the Leading Theaters," *CL* (25 February 1912), S6; the Comique and Olympia ads, *LDI* (4 March 1912), 2; "At the Leading Theaters," *CL* (17 March 1912), S6; and the Home ad, *CL* (24 March 1912), S6.

59. See, for instance, the Gordon Park ad, *CL* (17 November 1912), B5; and the Princess ad, *CL* (1 December 1912), B5.

60. This excludes, of course, women's suffrage films such as *Votes for Women* (1912) and worker or labor union films, which are discussed extensively in, respectively, Stamp, *Movie-Struck Girls,* 168–94; and Steven J. Ross, *Working-Class Hollywood: Silent Film and the Shaping of Class in America* (Princeton, N.J.: Princeton University Press, 1998), 56–111.

61. See the Colonial ad, *DMN* (18 February 1911), 3. One year later, the film also appeared one Sunday evening at the Belasco in Washington—see the Belasco ad, *WS* (25 February 1912), 2: 3.

62. Charles Musser and Carol Nelson, *High-Class Moving Pictures: Lyman H. Howe and the Forgotten Era of Traveling Exhibition, 1880–1920* (Princeton, N.J.: Princeton University Press, 1991), 215–17.

63. For an informative summary of Howe's exhibitions in selected cities, see Musser and Nelson, *High-Class Moving Pictures,* 295–99.

64. See the Colonial ads, *CL* (7 May 1911), C5, and (28 May 1911), M7; the Grand ads, *YV* (3 September 1911), 16, (31 March 1912), 21, (8 September 1912), 18, and (30 March 1913), 12.

65. See the Colonial ads, *CL* (2 June 1912), M3, (9 June 1912), M3, and (16 June 1912), W6.

66. The *Durbar in Kinemacolor* proved quite popular in several eastern metropolises: in Philadelphia, it ran for three months; in Boston, for nearly five—Musser and Nelson, *High-Class Moving Pictures,* 217–19, 229–32. Yet in Pawtucket, during a three-day run at the Star (28–30 March 1912), it did only moderately well; but its audience was largely working-class, and 60 percent of the receipts went to Kinemacolor—see the Star Theatre cash books (9 December 1911–18 October 1913), Box 10, Keith-Albee Collection, Special Collections, University of Iowa Library.

67. "Gaumont Gets South Pole Pictures," *B* (23 March 1912), 47.

68. "At the Photo Plays," *TNB* (15 June 1912), 7.

69. See the Olympic ad, *CRR* (25 June 1912), 3; and the Palace ad, *CRR* (14 July 1912), 3.

70. See the Cook Theater ad, *RH* (22 September 1912), 25.

71. See the Dreamland ad, *LDI* (1 March 1913), 2; Belasco ads, *WS* (11 May 1913), 2: 3, (18 May 1913), 2: 3, (8 June 1913), 2: 3, and (22 June 1913), 2: 3; Cort ad, *SFC*

(14 September 1913), 18; Auditorium ad, *TNB* (1 November 1913), 4; and Savoy ads, *SFC* (2 November 1913), 18, and (30 November 1913), 18. Ponting's own tour was promoted by special news releases and syndicated newspaper pieces such as, respectively, "Antarctic Pictures of Scott Expedition Shown," *NYMT* (15 June 1913), 4.2: 2; and Gertrude Price, " 'Farthest South' Movie Men Bring Back Pictures of Awful Ice and Snow Where Scott Perished," *DMN* (16 June 1913), 2. See also "Moving Pictures of Capt. Scott's Dash to the South Pole at the Lyric Theatre Wonderfully Interesting," *MPN* (7 June 1913), 11.

72. See the Columbia ad, *TNB* (17 February 1912), 2; "Marvelous Arctic Film," *B* (4 May 1912), 10; "Carnegie Museum Expedition of 1911," *MPW* (20 April 1912), 216; and "Special Feature Review," *NYDM* (29 May 1912), 27. A rival version appeared later that year—see the Beverly B. Dobbs Original Alaska-Siberia Motion Pictures ad, *NYMT* (27 October 1912), 4.2: 5.

73. See "At the Mall," *CL* (25 August 1912), W5; and the Grand ad, *YV* (22 September 1912), 18. Among those technical problems were poor photographic quality, badly handled exhibition, and Kleinschmidt's own nervous, barely audible voice—Musser and Nelson, *High-Class Moving Pictures*, 233.

74. "The Paul Rainey African Pictures," *MPW* (20 April 1912), 214–15.

75. "Reviews of Special Feature Subjects," *NYDM* (24 April 1912), 27; and "Rainey Pictures' Remarkable Run," *NYDM* (21 August 1912), 25. By September, there were five "companies" touring the film around the country—see the William Harris ad, *NYDM* (25 September 1912), back cover. See also Musser and Nelson, *High-Class Moving Pictures*, 230–32.

76. See the Shubert ads, *RDC* (6 October 1912), 22, and (1 December 1912), 23; "A Trapped Hyena, Paul J. Rainey's African Hunting Pictures: Metropolitan," *MJ* (20 October 1912), 8: 8; the Providence Opera House ads, *PT* (23 October 1912), 5, and (26 October 1912), 3; the Valentine ads, *TB* (16 November 1912), 7, and (26 April 1913), 22; the B. of L. E. Auditorium ad, *CL* (22 December 1912), M5; and the Berchel ad, *DMN* (1 March 1913), 3.

77. See "Darkest African Motion Pictures," *LE* (14 February 1913), 16; the Colonial ad, *LE* (17 February 1913), 6; and the Grand Opera House ad, *Sioux City Tribune* (29 March 1913), 5.

78. "Zukor to Handle New Kearton African Animal Pictures," *NYMT* (25 May 1913), 4.2: 3; and "Cherry Kearton Animal Pictures," *MPW* (14 June 1913), 1140. Former president Roosevelt had introduced Kearton's animal pictures when they were first shown at the Playhouse in New York City—"Roosevelt Introduces Kearton's Animal Films," *NYMT* (23 February 1913), 4.2: 1.

79. For an excellent study of turn-of-the-century mass magazines, see Richard Ohmann, *Selling Culture: Magazines, Markets, and Class at the Turn of the Century* (London: Verso, 1996).

80. G. Brown Goode is quoted in Robert Rydell, *All the World's a Fair* (Chicago: University of Chicago Press, 1984), 44–45. See also Tom Gunning, "The World as Object Lesson: Cinema Audiences, Visual Culture, and the St. Louis World's Fair," *Film History* 6.4 (1994), 422–44.

81. This contests the general notion, expressed even by Musser and Peterson, that nonfiction served as a pause, a moment of recovery, easing the transition from one story film to another in the program—see Daan Hertogs and Nico de Klerk, eds., *Non-*

fiction from the Teens (Amsterdam: Nederlands Filmmuseum, 1994), 29; and Peterson, "Travelogues and Early Nonfiction Film," 197–98.

82. Pathé-Frères promoted this "guarantee" in its trade press ads, but it also received encouragement from "Reviews of Notable Films," *MPW* (12 August 1911), 359–60; and "The Pathé Weekly," *MPW* (23 September 1911), 871.

Chapter 5: The "Usable Present" of Thrillers

1. "Foreign Films in the American Market," *NYDM* (12 February 1913), 29.

2. Bowser, *The Transformation of Cinema*, 50.

3. These phrases come from W. Stephen Bush, "Problems in Pictures," *MPW* (16 December 1911), 877; and C. H. Claudy, "Modern Melodrama," *MPW* (13 January 1912), 112.

4. See " 'Spectator's' Comments," *NYDM* (6 December 1911), 28, and (10 January 1912), 28.

5. See "The Dangers of the Foreign Market," *MPW* (16 December 1911), 877–78; and " 'Spectator's' Comments," *NYDM* (10 January 1912), 28.

6. Tom Gunning, "Tracing the Individual Body: Photography, Detectives, and Early Cinema," in Leo Charney and Vanessa Schwartz, eds., *Cinema and the Invention of Modern Life* (Berkeley and Los Angeles: University of California Press, 1995), 20.

7. Carol Armbruster, "French Pulp Fiction in Turn-of-the-Century America" (panel on France and America: Exchanges and Rivalries in the Modern Era, Society of French Historical Studies Conference, University of North Carolina, 10 March 2001).

8. Abel, *The Red Rooster Scare*, 87–104, 118–40.

9. "Moving Picture News and Reviews," *V* (18 April 1908), 13. See also Lucy France Pierce, "The Nickelodeon," *World Today* (October 1908), reprinted in Gerald Mast, ed., *The Movies in Our Midst: Documents in the Cultural History of Film in America* (Chicago: University of Chicago Press, 1982), 56.

10. See, for instance, "The Melodrama," *NYDM* (1 June 1907), 14; and "Public Taste in Pictures as Viewed by M. E. Feckles," *Show World* (7 September 1907), 9. Carl Laemmle summed up this difference quite succinctly: "Let's cater more to the happy side of life. There's enough of the seamy side without exposing it to further view." See "Moving Picture Industry Great," *Show World* (29 June 1907), 29.

11. Abel, *The Red Rooster Scare*, 91–94, 101.

12. Ibid., 138–39.

13. See, for instance, "Music and Picture," *MPW* (31 December 1910), 1518–19.

14. "The Qualitative Picture," *MPW* (25 June 1910), 1089–90.

15. See specifically "Variety's Own Picture Reviews," *V* (5 March 1910), 13. *Variety's* attack also was explicitly anti-Semitic because *Ouchard's* characters were clearly Jewish. The film also "met with strong objection" from customers in New Orleans—see the 14 March 1910 letter from Imported Film & Supply Co. to the Selig Company, Selig Collection, Folder 459, Margaret Herrick Library, AMPAS.

16. Thomas Bedding, "Baltimore and the Picture," *MPW* (20 August 1910), 399.

17. See " 'World' Crusade a Fizzle," *NYDM* (5 October 1910), 29.

18. See, for instance, J. C. Hemmet, "Leaping Lioness Cheated of Prey by Bare 40 Inches," *CL* (29 October 1911), C8. This story clearly served to build expectations for

Paul J. Rainey's African Hunt, released several months later. See also "Lassoing Lions with 'Buffalo Jones,' " *NYMT* (5 June 1910), M: 7. Selig, of course, already had profited from such films as *Roosevelt in Africa* (1910).

19. "Captain Kate," *MPW* (8 July 1911), 1569–70. A 16mm viewing print of *Captain Kate* is available at the LoC. I thank Jennifer Bean for drawing my attention to this film. For a review of the previous animal picture, *Back to the Primitive,* see "A Remarkable Film," *MPW* (20 May 1911), 1115.

20. "Magical Changes at the Lyric," *MJ* (19 September 1911), 12.

21. Selig advertised *Lost in the Jungle* for at least a month before its release in late October—see, for instance, the Selig ad, *NYDM* (27 September 1911), 30.

22. "*Lost in the Jungle* (Selig)," *MPW* (14 October 1911), 109; and "Reviews of Licensed Films," *NYDM* (1 November 1911), 30–31.

23. See the Voyons ad, *LCC* (30 October 1911), 4; the Olympia ad, *LDI* (18 November 1911), 2; and "Great Picture Held Over at the Orpheum," *CN* (26 November 1911), 16.

24. See the ad for "Blindfolded" in *TB* (25 February 1911), 15; Allan Stephens, "A Guest of the City," *NYMT* (14 August 1910), 2: 3; and Charles Francis Bourke, "The Prima Donna's Diamonds: A Pinkerton Detective Fact Story," *NYMT* (24 November 1912), 2: 3. For a brief but insightful analysis of Nick Carter and *Tip Top Weekly,* see Denning, *Mechanic Accents,* 204–6.

25. Examples include "New Method of Scientific Apprehension of Criminals Carries Bertillon's System of Identification a Step Further," *CL* (17 September 1911), C2; "Running Down the Forger—the 'Silent' Criminal," *NYMT* (19 November 1911), M: 5; and Richard G. Conover, "Does Science Aid the Criminal or the Crime Detector?" *CL* (3 December 1911), C7.

26. "Reviews of Licensed Films," *NYDM* (1 February 1911), 31.

27. "Reviews of Licensed Films," *NYDM* (12 April 1911), 34.

28. Gunning, "Tracing the Individual Body," 20.

29. "Reviews of Independent Films," *NYDM* (8 November 1911), 32.

30. See the Majestic ad in *SPN* (5 November 1911), 15. *King the Detective* also appeared at the Hart, in Toledo—see the Hart ad in *TNB* (8 November 1911), 15.

31. "Reviews of Licensed Films," *NYDM* (20 December 1911), 34; and "Films Worth Seeing," *CL* (24 December 1911), B7. *The Battle* was praised in this very same column.

32. C. H. Claudy, "Modern Melodrama," *MPW* (13 January 1912), 112. This criticism of *In the Grip of Alcohol* immediately followed Claudy's "Hurrah" for *The Battle.*

33. The quotation actually comes from a review of the second film in the *Zigomar* series—see "*Zigomar contre Nick Carter,*" *CJ* (9 March 1912), 57. For an analysis of this and the other two Zigomar films, see Abel, *The Ciné Goes to Town,* 358–60, 366–67.

34. "Reviews of Notable Films," *MPW* (14 October 1911), 108. *Zigomar* also was the first French film to be fictionalized in *PM* (February 1912), 56–57.

35. See the Feature & Educational Film ad, *CL* (3 December 1911), S5; "Zigomar a Great Success," *CL* (17 December 1911), S7; "At the Leading Theaters," *CL* (7 January 1912), B7, (14 January 1912), S5, and (21 January 1911), S6; and the Knickerbocker ad, *CL* (7 April 1912), S8. See also the Éclair ad, *B* (9 December 1911), 99.

36. "Another Branch Office for the F. & E. Company," *NYMT* (7 January 1912), 4.2: 1.

37. See the Rex ad, *YV* (31 December 1911), 16; and the Park ad, *YV* (7 January 1912), 17.

38. See the Crown ad in *TNB* (27 January 1912), 9; the Auditorium ad in *CN* (25 February 1912), 15; and the Elite ad in *DMN* (18 April 1912), 7.

39. For an analysis of *Zigomar*, see Abel, *The Ciné Goes to Town*, 358–59.

40. Wallace Irwin, "Colonel Crowe of Cripple Creek: A Word for Moving Picture Shows," *Chicago Daily News* (2 December 1911), 7. See also such stories on criminal French women as "Never Trust a Woman," *NYMT* (1 October 1911), M: 8; and "Beauty Who Charmed King and Commoner," *NYMT* (8 October 1911), M: 8.

41. See the F & E Film ad in *NYMT* (10 December 1911), 4.2: 4.

42. W. Stephen Bush, "Do Longer Films Make Better Shows," *MPW* (28 October 1911), 275.

43. Jas. S. McQuade, "Kings of the Forest," *MPW* (28 September 1912), 1254–56; and "Reviews of Licensed Films," *NYDM* (20 November 1912), 32. An incomplete 35mm viewing print of *Kings of the Forest* (1,370 feet) is available at the NFTVA.

44. See the Orpheum ad, *CN* (22 November 1912), 6.

45. See "Genuine African Jungle," *CL* (10 November 1912), B5; and "Doings in Los Angeles," *MPW* (7 December 1912), 969. A rare surviving one-sheet publicizing *Kings of the Forest* can be found in the Selig Collection, Margaret Herrick Library, AMPAS.

46. In late 1913, Selig listed eight films that demonstrated its "originality in devising and producing plays in jungleland"—see the Selig ad, *MPN* (22 November 1913), 57.

47. "Feature Film Reviews," *NYMT* (1 June 1913), 4.2: 2.

48. See, for instance, the Grand Opera ad in *CN* (11 June 1913), 6.

49. James S. McQuade, "Alone in the Jungle," *MPW* (7 June 1913), 1006. See also Jas. S. McQuade, "The Terrors of the Jungle," *MPW* (8 November 1913), 590. A rare surviving press sheet offers six different "cuts" for exhibitors to use in publicizing *Alone in the Jungle*—Selig Collection, Margaret Herrick Library, AMPAS.

50. "Special Film Releases," *NYMT* (19 January 1913), 4.2: 3; "The Wizard of the Jungle," *MPW* (5 April 1913), 55; and "Feature Film Reviews," *NYMT* (17 August 1913), 4.2: 2. Some newspapers carried a full page "fictionalization" of at least one of these films—see, for instance, "The Wizard of the Jungle," *CN* (1 June 1913), 13.

51. See the Gaumont ad, *MPN* (4 May 1912), 3; and "Reviews of Supply Co. Films," *NYDM* (10 July 1912), 32.

52. See the Gaumont ad, *MPN* (31 August 1912), 5; "*In the Land of the Lions*," *MPW* (21 September 1912), 1164; and the Columbia Theatre ads, *CRR* (31 October 1912), 3, and (3 November 1912), 3. Some theaters also promoted this film for its color—see the Garden ad, *WS* (29 September 1912), 2:7.

53. See the General Film ad, *MPW* (16 November 1912), 682; the Knickerbocker ad, *CL* (17 November 1912), M5; as well as various theater listings in the *Leader* throughout December.

54. "Supply Co. Films," *NYDM* (29 January 1913), 38.

55. See "*The Margrave's Daughter*," *MPW* (9 March 1912), 875–76; W. Stephen Bush, "*The Margrave's Daughter*," *MPW* (30 March 1912), 1156; and Virginia West, "*The Margrave's Daughter*," *MPN* (27 April 1912), 12–13.

56. "Blanche Walsh a Success," *NYDM* (24 July 1912), 27.

57. For an analysis of these detective film series, see Abel, *The Ciné Goes to Town*, 195–98, 354–58.

58. "Reviews of Licensed Films," *NYDM* (10 July 1912), 31.

59. "Important Films of the Week," *NYMT* (27 April 1913), 4.2: 4; and "Reviews of Licensed Films," *NYDM* (7 May 1913), 35. An earlier title was "The Adventure of the Counterfeit Bills"—see "Important Films of the Week," *NYMT* (5 January 1913), 4.2: 5.

60. "Important Films of the Week," *NYMT* (27 October 1912), 4.2: 5.

61. "Important Films of the Week," *NYMT* (17 November 1912), 4.2: 4; and "Feature Film Reviews," *NYMT* (4 May 1913), 4.2: 2. Another detective film, *Wanted by the Police*, also purportedly used a dictograph to apprehend criminals—see the Mittenthal Film ad, *NYMT* (1 June 1913), 4.2: 2.

62. See "Baggott Appears in Mystery Play," *CL* (28 December 1913), S10; and the Seville ad, *MJ* (28 December 1913), 8: 10. See also "Reviews of Feature Films," *NYDM* (14 January 1914), 72. Others in the series included *The Detective in Formula 879* (February 1914) and *King the Detective in the Marine Mystery* (March 1914).

63. Selig also invested briefly in the format, with "The Man in the Street" series (August 1913)—see the Selig ad, *NYMT* (17 August 1913), 4.2: 3; and "Important Films of the Week," *NYMT* (31 August 1913), 4.2: 6. Other companies dabbled in detective films: an example would be Lubin's *Violet Dare, Detective* (June 1913)—see "Important Films of the Week," *NYMT* (15 June 1913), 4.2: 4.

64. "Edison-McClure," *MPW* (29 June 1912), 1212.

65. Stamp, *Movie-Struck Girls*, 137–39. Stamp offers a particularly incisive analysis of episode 8, comparing the film print and published story versions.

66. "Edison Detective Series Popular," *M* (12 July 1913), 17; "Featured as 'Kate Kirby,' " *M* (26 July 1913), 58; and "Important Films of the Week," *NYMT* (20 July 1913), 4.2: 3.

67. "Important Films of the Week," *NYMT* (27 July 1913), 4.2: 3; and "Reviews of Licensed Films," *NYDM* (30 July 1913), 29.

68. "Famous Players Engage J. Searle Dawley," *MPN* (7 June 1913), 19.

69. See "Edison to Begin New Series," *M* (1 November 1913), 326; and the Edison ad, *NYMT* (2 November 1913), 5: 4.

70. See the Edison ad, *M* (15 November 1913), 9; and "Reviews of Licensed Films," *NYDM* (10 December 1913), 43.

71. See also the Edison ads in *M* (10 January 1914), 8, and in *NYDM* (4 February 1914), 41. Other titles included *The Mystery of the Dover Express* (December 1913) and *The Mystery of the Talking Wire* (January 1914).

72. See, for instance, "Film Synopses," *B* (23 March 1912), 95; the Atlas ad, *B* (30 March 1912), 59; and the Street & Smith "warning" ad, *B* (25 May 1912), 62.

73. "Feature Photo-Play Has Lieut. Petrosino Picture Coming," *NYMT* (17 November 1912), 4.2: 2; and the Feature Photoplay ad, *NYMT* (17 November 1912), 4.2: 3. At the same time, this company advertised a series based on the Frank Merriwell character in *Tip Top Weekly*, but they either were never released or quickly disappeared, perhaps because of copyright difficulties—see the Feature Photoplay ad, *NYMT* (24 November 1912), 4.2: 3.

74. See the Mall ad, *CL* (8 December 1912), B7; the Feature Photoplay ad, *NYMT*

(22 December 1912), 4.2: 2; and "Police Raids at Cleveland," *MPW* (21 December 1912), 1192. *Moving Picture World*, for instance, never printed a review of the film, and Feature Photoplay publicly exposed this in an ad, *NYMT* (22 December 1912), 4.2: 2.

75. See the Colonial ad, *TB* (18 December 1912), 4; the Dreamland ad, *LDI* (4 January 1913), 2; and the Colonial ad, *DMN* (10 April 1913), 8. For an astute analysis of how early American films represented "Italian types" within a shifting racialist discourse, see Giorgio Bertellini, "Black Hands and White Hearts: Italian Immigrants as 'Urban Racial Types' in Early American Film Culture," *Urban History* 31.3 (2004), 374–98.

76. See the Kalem ad, *NYDM* (26 February 1913), 32; and "Detective Burns in Vivid Kalem Drama," *NYDM* (19 March 1913), 29. Some newspapers also carried special stories devoted to Burns—see, for instance, "Great Cases of Detective Burns," *DFP* (6 April 1913), Features: 8.

77. "Kalem Sued by General Film over Burns Picture," *NYMT* (6 April 1913), 4.2: 1. See the Saxe's Lyric ad, *MJ* (6 April 1913), 9; and the Olympia ad, *LDI* (7 April 1913), 2. One of the few references after that is to a Sunday screening at a small theater in Toledo—see the Diamond ad, *TB* (31 May 1913), 8.

78. George Blaisdell, "An Hour before Dawn," *MPW* (25 October 1913), 360; "Reviews of Feature Films," *NYDM* (26 November 1913), 33; and George Blaisdell, "The Port of Doom," *MPW* (29 November 1913), 989.

79. Royal L. Baker, "Crime-Impelling Moving Pictures Are Now Obsolete," *NYMT* (10 March 1912), 4.2: 1.

80. See, for instance, "Auto Bandits Terrorize Paris, Rivaling the Exploits of Most Notorious Westerners," *DMN* (13 April 1912), 4; and "The Phantom Bandits: Paris, Ever the Home of the Unusual, Furnishes the World Its Very First Automobile Ghost Story," *SFC* (21 April 1912), Magazine Section, 2.

81. Maurice Le Blanc, "Bonnot, Tiger Bandit," *CL* (12 May 1912), C1–2.

82. "The Auto Cracksman Loots—Sometimes Slays—And Is Off Like a Flash," *New York Sunday Tribune* (3 September 1911), 2: 1.

83. See "Penitentiary Pictures," *B* (15 June 1912), 10; the America's Features Film ad, *B* (15 June 1912), back cover; "Convict Life Stirring Picture," *B* (13 July 1912), 10; and the Orpheum ad, *CN* (5 January 1913), 12.

84. See the New York Film ads, *NYMT* (7 July 1912), 4.2: 4, (14 July 1912), 4.2: 3, and (21 July 1912), 4.2: 3; and *MPW* (13 July 1912), 167. *Lights and Shadows of Chinatown or The Yellow Peril* was produced by Continental Kunstfilm of Berlin. Another minor distributor, General Film Publicity and Sales, handled the three-reel *In a Woman's Grip or The Black Cat*, produced by Vitascope in Berlin—see the General Film Publicity and Sales ad, *NYMT* (22 September 1912), 4: 9

85. For an analysis of several of these Éclair films, see Abel, *The Ciné Goes to Town*, 359–61, 363–65.

86. See the Universal Features ads in *NYMT* (12 May 1912), 4.2: 2, (26 May 1912), 4.2: 5, and (15 June 1912), 52; *B* (3 June 1912), 54; and *MPN* (15 June 1912), 48.

87. See "Auto Bandits of Paris (Éclair Feature)," *NYDM* (19 June 1912), 24; and "Sensational Auto Bandits Film," *NYDM* (19 June 1912), 25.

88. "Redemption," *MPW* (20 April 1912), 221–22.

89. In Philadelphia, *The Auto Bandits of Paris* "had a most popular run in local the-

aters" and continued to draw large crowds as late as March 1913—see "Correspondence: Philadelphia," *MPW* (5 April 1913), 67.

90. See the Colonial ads, *TNB* (7 June 1912), 5, and (14 September 1912), 2; "At the Photo Plays," *TNB* (11 November 1912), 2, (21 November 1912), 5, and (7 December 1912), 8.

91. See the Palace ad, *CRR* (4 July 1912), 3; and "Correspondence: Louisville," *MPW* (26 October 1912), 358.

92. See the Central Square Theatre ads, *LDI*, from 3 August 1912 to 21 September 1912.

93. See the Princess ads, *CL* (18 August 1912), W5, and (25 August 1912), W5; the Alpha ads, *CG* (27 July 1912), 2, (19 August 1912), 3, (14 September 1912), 3, (21 September 1912), 2, (19 October 1912), 3, and (2 November 1912), 3; and the Norwood ad, *CL* (17 November 1912), B5. The Princess was one of only two downtown theaters to advertise in the city's labor weekly—see the Princess ad, *CC* (18 January 1913), 2. In Flint, Michigan, a city with a rapidly growing working-class population due to the new auto industry, the Jewel Theater also featured Éclair thrillers on weekends or holidays—see the Jewel ads, *Flint Journal* (23 November 1912), 9, (27 November 1912), 2, and (18 January 1913), 9.

94. W. Stephen Bush, "Advertising and Criticizing," *MPW* (23 November 1912), 750; and Bush, "Avoid Crime and Carrion," *MPW* (4 January 1913), 24–25.

95. "The Movies," *DMN* (3 December 1912), 10.

96. See, for instance, Louis Reeves Harrison, "Gar-El-Hama," *MPW* (2 November 1912), 436.

97. "States' Rights pictures are usually purchased on the strength of one or more exciting scenes," said Gaumont's advertising manager, as if acknowledging the company's commitment to sensational melodramas—see John B. Clymer, "What an Advertising Manager Ought to Know," *MPN* (28 December 1912), 16. Gaumont also provocatively ran ads that imitated the multiple story heads in sensational newspapers—see, for instance, the Gaumont ads in *NYMT* (19 January 1913), 4.2: 4, (26 January 1913), 4.2: 5, and (2 February 1913), 4.2: 4. The company allegedly also rejected a scheme for getting rid of "undesirables" by each week inserting the photograph of a "wanted" bank robber in the *Gaumont Weekly* so as to "make it impossible for the said crook to live in the United States"—see "Gaumont Receives Unusual Proposition from Detective Agency," *MPN* (15 February 1913), 31. For an analysis of these Gaumont films, see Abel, *The Ciné Goes to Town*, 351–54, 368–70.

98. "In the Grip of the Vampire," *MPN* (21 December 1912), 13; "In the Grip of the Vampire," *MPW* (31 December 1912), 1308; and "Supply Co. Films," *NYDM* (1 January 1913), 33.

99. The French company itself called attention to this innovation, at least in films of three or more reels—see "The House of Gaumont," *M* (9 August 1913), 107.

100. "Comments on the Films," *MPW* (11 January 1913), 160; and "The White Gloved Band," *MPW* (18 January 1913), 266.

101. "Feature Films on the Market," *NYDM* (9 April 1913), 28.

102. See the Princess ads for largely French crime thrillers in *YV*, from (19 January 1913), 20, to (23 March 1913), 24.

103. See the small Airdome ads, *CN* (9 July 1913), 3, and (31 July 1913), 3.

104. Louis Reeves Harrison, "The Fascinating Criminal," *MPW* (26 April 1913),

356. For his scathing attack on "rotten realism," see Harrison, "Red-Light Films," *MPW* (11 October 1913), 133. Rarely were American films mentioned in such attacks: an exception was *The Wages of Sin*, excoriated as "a disgusting film," in "Ex-Cathedra," *MPN* (31 May 1913), 7.

105. Hugh Hoffman, "The Rajah's Casket," *MPW* (17 May 1913), 686.

106. See, for instance, "Feature Film Reviews," *NYMT* (2 March 1913), 4.2: 2; and "Reviews of Feature Films," *NYDM* (5 March 1913), 31. Unlike the French crime thrillers, *Tigris* also was adapted by Virginia West as the weekly short story published in *MPN* (8 March 1913), 17–19.

107. For an analysis of the five *Fantomas* films, see Abel, *The Ciné Goes to Town*, 370–80.

108. See the Gaumont ads, *NYDM* (2 July 1913), 34; and *MPW* (12 July 1913), 119.

109. See the Gaumont ad, *NYDM* (2 July 1913), 119.

110. The *Morning Telegraph*, for instance, did not include *Fantomas* in its "Feature Film Reviews" and briefly summarized the plot—"Important Films of the Week," *NYMT* (22 June 1913), 4.2: 3. In reviewing Essanay's *The Forbidden Way*, the *Mirror* mentioned the current popularity of "crook plays," most of them merely "fair" or "indifferent"—see "Feature Films on the Market," *NYDM* (16 July 1913), 28.

111. "Feature Films on the Market," *NYDM* (25 June 1913), 25.

112. "*Fantomas*," *MPW* (26 July 1913), 438; and Bush, "*Fantomas, or the Man in Black*," *MPW* (8 November 1913), 594.

113. Frank E. Woods, "Pictures Divided into Three Grades," *NYDM* (9 July 1913), 25.

114. Hanford C. Judson, "*Fantomas III*," *MPW* (22 December 1913), 1531.

115. See "Feature Films at Local Playhouses," *CL* (31 August 1913), C4.

116. See the Orpheum ads, *CN* (16 October 1913), 3, and (11 December 1913), 12.

117. See the Orpheum ad, *YV* (7 December 1913), 58.

118. See the Hart ad, *TUL* (23 January 1914), 2: 11.

119. "At the Theatres," *LCC* (5 March 1914), 4.

120. "Feature Films on the Market," *NYDM* (11 March 1914), 34.

121. See the Gaumont ad, *MPN* (18 July 1914), 72.

122. The best study of the debate over "white slave" films can be found in Stamp, *Movie-Struck Girls*, 41–101. It should be noted that the circulation and reception of German sensational melodramas in 1913–14 remain to be examined. After New York Film lost its contract with Continental Kunstfilm, Apex Film apparently became the principal distributor of such films as *Red Powder*—see the Henry Schultz ad, *MPN* (11 January 1913), 16; Hugh Hoffman, "Red Powder," *MPW* (13 September 1913), 1157; and the Apex Film ad, *MPW* (20 September 1913), 1305.

123. "Feature Films Reviews," *MPN* (22 November 1913), 34; and George Blaisdell, "Traffic in Souls," *MPW* (22 November 1913), 849.

124. "Feature Films on the Market," *NYDM* (19 November 1913), 33.

125. " 'Traffic in Souls' a Moral Play; Censors Have Indorsed It," *M* (29 November 1913), 397–98.

126. Stamp, *Movie-Struck Girls*, 52–53.

127. See the Colonial ad, *CL* (14 December 1913), S10; "Traffic in Souls Here This Week," *CL* (14 December 1913), S11; and "Cleveland Enjoys 'Traffic in Souls,' " *CL*

(21 December 1913), S10. In February, the film also played for four days to "big crowds" at the Grand Opera House in Youngstown—see "Traffic in Souls" and the Grand Opera House ad, *YV* (1 February 1914), 56.

128. See the Auditorium ads, *TB* (13 December 1913), 30, and (27 December 1913), 18; and the Shubert ad, *RH* (14 December 1913), 21.

129. See the Globe ads, *BJ* (27 December 1913), 4, and (21 February 1914), 4.

130. See the New Jewel ad, *LST* (15 March 1914), 5; and the Merrick Square ad, *LST* (5 April 1914), 5.

131. See the Metropolitan ads, *SPN* (1 February 19134), 7; and *MJ* (8 March 1914), 9.

132. See the Berchel ad, *DMRL* (17 May 1914), 6.

133. See, for instance, Ben Brewster, "*Traffic in Souls:* An Experiment in Feature-Length Narrative Construction," *Cinema Journal* 31.1 (Fall 1991), 37–56; Staiger, *Bad Women,* 116–46; Stamp, *Movie-Struck Girls,* 70–82; and Kristen Whissel, "Regulating Mobility: Technology, Modernity, and Feature-Length Narration in *Traffic in Souls,*" *camera obscura* 49 (2002), 1–29. The most recent study analyzes *Traffic in Souls* and *The Inside of the White Slave Trade* (also 1913) as "test cases around which intense debates about the social functioning of cinema circulated"—Grieveson, *Policing Cinema,* 151–91.

134. The scenario writer for both *The Rise of Officer 174* and *Traffic in Souls* was Walter McNamara—Grieveson, *Policing Cinema,* 157.

135. Gertrude Price, "Nervy as Ever to Act the Most Daring Things Ever Seen on the Stage!—Heroine of Movies," *DMN* (17 November 1912), 7.

136. The first episode, *The Unwelcome Throne,* premiered in ten theaters in Chicago on Monday, 29 December 1913—see the *Chicago Tribune* letter to the Selig Company, 19 December 1913, Selig Collection, folder 10, Margaret Herrick Library, AMPAS. Thereafter, the serial began its first run, for instance, in Youngstown on Fridays and Saturdays, in Des Moines on Tuesdays, in Canton on Wednesdays and Thursdays, in Cleveland on Sundays, and in Cedar Rapids on Fridays—see "*The Adventures of Kathlyn,*" *YV* (4 January 1914), 56; "The Movies," *DMN* (11 January 1914), 6; the Grand Opera House ad, *CN* (14 January 1914), 8; the Penn Square ad, *CL* (25 January 1914), S12; and the Palace ad, *CRR* (30 January 1914), 2.

137. These installments were written by Harold McGrath. A reproduction of the full-page ad published in the *Chicago Tribune* (4 January 1914) appeared in *MPW* (24 January 1914), 426. See, for instance, the Sunday Magazine Section, *YV* (4 January 1914), 8. That this was an "innovative" campaign that involved nearly fifty newspapers comes from "Innovation," *M* (24 January 1914), 54; and "Selig Resources for 'Kathlyn' Series," *MPN* (31 January 1914), 20.

138. Bowser, *The Transformation of Cinema,* 186. In her chapter on genre films, Bowser does not take up crime films in relation to detective films—another indication of their "foreignness" that has persisted in histories of early American cinema.

139. "Feature Film Reviews," *NYMT* (2 November 1913), 5: 3; and James S. McQuade, "Thor, Lord of the Jungle," *MPW* (6 December 1913), 1126.

140. "Selig Plans Animal Series and Publicity for Miss Williams," *NYMT* (31 August 1913), 5: 1.

141. See "*The Adventures of Kathlyn,*" *YV* (4 January 1914), 56; and James Q. McQuade, "*The Adventures of Kathlyn,*" *MPW* (17 January 1914), 266.

142. McQuade, *"The Adventures of Kathlyn,"* 266.

143. See "Personality—Box Office Magnet," *NYDM* (14 January 1914), 52; and "Feature Films of the Week," *NYDM* (21 January 1914), n.p.

144. "Kathlyn, the Popular Queen," *NYDM* (21 January 1914), 31; and " 'Kathlyn' Causes Much Comment," *NYMT* (25 January 1914), 5: 2. In the meantime, Gaumont had received praise for one of its last animal pictures, *The Lion Hunters*—see "Feature Films," *NYDM* (8 October 1913), 30.

145. " 'Kathlyn' a Big Success," *NYDM* (28 January 1914), 30; and Jas. S McQuade, "Chicago Letter," *MPW* (28 February 1914), 1092.

146. See the full-page ad for *The Adventures of Kathlyn, MJ* (4 January 1914), 1: 14.

147. See the *Kathlyn* ads in the *DFP* (3 January 1914), 6, and (10 January 1914), 7.

148. "Selig Features Big Attractions," *BJ* (7 February 1914), 5; "Correspondence: Cincinnati," *MPW* (16 May 1914), 994.

149. Barbara Wilinsky, "Flirting with Kathlyn: Creating the Mass Audience," in David Desser and Garth S. Jowett, eds., *Hollywood Goes Shopping* (Minneapolis: University of Minnesota Press, 2000), 34–56. See also a clipping, "Selig to Undertake Wide Exploitation of Great Animal Pictures," from the *Waterloo Reporter* (6 September 1913)—Selig Collection, Folder 13, Margaret Herrick Library, AMPAS.

150. Lauren Rabinovitz, "Temptations of Pleasure: Nickelodeons, Amusement Parks, and the Sights of Female Sexuality," *camera obscura* 23 (May 1990), 73. See also Rabinovitz's account of the *Tribune*'s attack on Chicago nickelodeons in 1907, in *For the Love of Pleasure*, 122–28.

151. Wilinsky, "Flirting with Kathlyn," 34, 41, 44.

152. Jas. S. McQuade, "Chicago Letter, " *MPW* (14 March 1914), 1388; and "Movies All the Rage," *BJ* (28 March 1914), 7.

153. For an insightful analysis of serial queen melodramas and of the heroine as an American middle-class figure of the active New Woman, see Singer, *Melodrama and Modernity*, 221–62.

154. " 'Our Mutual Girl' Shortly to Appear as a Great Serial Feature," *NYMT* (16 November 1913), 5: 1; "Mutual Starts Things," *MPW* (13 December 1913), 1260; and "First 'Mutual Girl,' " *NYDM* (24 December 1913), 35.

155. See, for instance, the Mutual Film ad, *NYDM* (11 February 1914), 32.

156. See the Eclectic Film ad, *MPW* (21 March 1914), 1546–47; and "Feature Films of the Week," *NYDM* (1 April 1914), 42.

157. See the Eclectic ad, *MPW* (28 March 1914), 1701.

158. See Hanford C. Judson, "The Perils of Pauline," *MPW* (4 April 1914), 38.

159. Besides the previous ads, see the Eclectic ad, *NYDM* (8 April 1914), 26.

160. See "Motion Picture Theaters of Detroit and Suburbs Where Pathé Frères Pictures Can Be Seen," *Detroit News* (22 March 1914), Financial Section: 8; and "Correspondence," *MPW* (25 April 1914), 544, and (2 May 1914), 698.

161. See the Eclectic ad, *MPW* (11 July 1914), 67.

162. See the Universal ad, *MPW* (4 April 1914), 4–5; "Universal Syndicate Series," *MPW* (4 April 1914), 47; and "Reviews of Feature Films," *NYDM* (8 April 1914), 40. Earlier that year, Cunard also starred in *Female Raffles* or *My Lady Raffles*, a short-lived detective series released by Universal.

163. See, for instance, the *Lucille Love* ads, *CL* (5 April 1914), M5, and (10 April 1914), 7; and "Lucille Love, The Girl of Mystery," *CL* (12 April 1914), N4.

164. The sentence comes from a review of Éclair's *The Ingrate,* one of the few French melodrama thrillers judged "acceptable" by late 1913—see "Feature Films," *NYDM* (8 October 1913), 34.

165. "Feature Films on the Market," *NYDM* (15 October 1913), 32. See also "*Protea,*" *MPW* (11 October 1913), 137.

166. *Protea* was advertised prominently in all the cities whose newspapers I have researched; in fact, in Cleveland, it first appeared at a large suburban theater before moving to the downtown Orpheum—see the Knickerbocker ads, *CL* (23 November 1913), S10, S11; and the Orpheum ad, *CL* (7 December 1913), S12. For the Flint testimonial, see the World Special Films ad, *NYMT* (30 November 1913), 5: 3.

167. Robert E. Welsh, "Where American Films Are Strangers," *NYDM* (14 January 1914), 51. Arthur Lang was referring specifically to the "fifty-three hundred" theaters in Latin America, but the demand seemed just as high in Europe.

Entr'acte 5: Trash Twins

1. "The Moving Picture and the Public Press," *MPW* (6 May 1911), 1006.

2. "Views of the Reviewer," *NYDM* (9 October 1912), 25.

3. See, for instance, "Moving Picture Sections," *M* (5 April 1913), 219.

4. See, for instance, "Facts and Comments," *MPW* (27 December 1913), 1519; and "Exhibitors Hear That Newspaper Advertising Pays," *CL* (22 February 1914), S12. The latter summarized a speech by E. E. Simmons, manager of the downtown Dreamland, to a weekly meeting of the League of Motion Picture Exhibitors in Cleveland.

5. The quote comes from "Why Newspapers?" *Editor and Publisher* (6 May 1911), 17. For an excellent argument about the significance of the newspaper's representation and promotion of moving pictures for a city's population, see Paul Moore's dissertation, "A Rendezvous for Particular People: Showmanship, Regulation, and Promotion of Early Film-Going in Toronto" (York University, 2004).

6. Jan Olsson, "Pressing Inroads: Metaspectators and the Nickelodeon Culture," in John Fullerton, ed., *Screen Culture: History and Textuality* (Eastleigh: John Libbey, 2004), 115–16. Except in the case of specific references, the *New York Morning Telegraph,* the "theater and turf" newspaper, is excluded from this discussion because its Sunday section devoted to "motion pictures and photoplays" (which began publication as early as January 1910 and reached four or five pages by 1912) served as perhaps the most widely circulated trade journal in the industry—by 1913, it was being sold as a separate eight-page supplement.

7. See, for instance, the Voyons ad, *LCC* (1 September 1910), 7; the Colonial ad, *DMN* (8 September 1910), 7; the Odeon ad, *CN* (15 October 1910), 6; and the Comique and Olympia ads, *LDI* (12 December 1910), 2.

8. Owned by the German-American Press Association, the *Times* had a circulation of 75,000 by 1914, far lower than the *Globe-Democrat, Post-Dispatch,* or *Republic*—*American Newspaper Annual and Directory* (Philadelphia: N. W. Ayer & Son, 1914), 526–29.

9. "St. Louis's High-Class Moving-Picture Theatres," *SLR* (6 February 1910), 2: 1; and "Leading Moving Picture and Vaudeville Houses," *SLR* (15 October 1911), 7: 1. See also the reprinting of this first ad page in *MPW* (19 February 1910), 290.

10. Motion Picture Theaters ad, *MJ* (23 October 1910), 8: 2, and (14 May 1911), 8: 2.

11. See, for instance, the "Moving Pictures" columns, *BS* (6 October 1912), 4: 4, and (27 April 1913), 3: 5.

12. "Moving Picture Theatres," *RH* (10 November 1912), 22. This column lasted little more than two months, but it was replaced the following spring by a weekly column of news and gossip, sometimes focused on a single film.

13. "Lovers of the Photo Plays You Will Be Interested," *TNB* (28 January 1913), 1; and "Moving Pictures and Where to See Them," *TNB* (28 January 1913), 13.

14. "News and Doings in the Motion Picture World," *BJ* (6 September 1913), 4.

15. "The Moving Picture and the Press," *MPW* (6 May 1911), 1006. Selig's publicity material can be found in several folders in the Margaret Herrick Library, AMPAS.

16. Gene Morgan, "Moving Pictures and Makers," *CT* (19 November 1911), 2: 2: 5; Reel Observer, "In the Moving Picture World," *CT* (3 December 1911), 2: 2: 5.

17. Stories about Selig and Essanay, for instance, constitute more than half of the "In the Moving Picture World" column, in *CT* (4 April 1912), 10: 4.

18. "Film Criticism in the Lay Press," *MPW* (20 May 1911), 1113. See also " 'Spectator's' Comments," *NYDM* (28 February 1912), 28.

19. Notice of the *Republic*'s column of reviews appeared in "Motion Pictures and the Press," *NYDM* (7 June 1911), 29.

20. "Film Criticism by the St. Louis Republic," *NYMT* (8 October 1911), 4: 2.

21. "Week in Moving Picture Theaters," *YV* (3 September 1911), 17.

22. " A Glimpse at the Menus in the Local Theaters," *MJ* (17 September 1911), 4: 9; and "The New Grand Draws a Throng," *MJ* (19 September 1911), 12. Rothapfel's own photo accompanied a story on the transformation of the Lyric into a moving picture theater—"The Lyric's Reopening," *MJ* (10 September 1911), 5: 8.

23. "The Critic's Comment," *LDI* (22 January 1912), 5.

24. "At the Photo Plays," *TNB* (8 November 1911), 15, and (20 January 1912), 9.

25. "At the Photo Plays," *TNB* (3 February 1912), 7, (14 August 1912), 8, and (7 December 1912), 8.

26. "The Movies," *DMN* (20 November 1912), 7.

27. "The Movies," *DMN* (3 December 1912), 10.

28. *Moving Picture World* briefly reported on this innovation but inaccurately described the page from November 5—"Cleveland Exhibitors on the Job," *MPW* (25 November 1911), 632. The first "Photo-Plays and Players" page appeared in *CL* (3 December 1911), S5.

29. The *Leader* congratulated itself by summarizing an article by William Lord Wright in *Motion Picture News*—see " 'Bill' Wright Writes about Movie Pages," *CL* (7 December 1913), S12.

30. "At the Motion Picture Plays," *BA* (17 March 1912), City Life: 4, (24 March 1912), City Life: 4, and (31 March 1912), City Life: 6.

31. The Film Man, "Comments and Suggestions," *NYDM* (1 January 1913), 25.

32. "At the Moving Picture Playhouses," *DMRL* (9 February 1913), 7.

33. "Motion Pictures," *MT* (16 March 1913), Society: 10.

34. "Toledo to Be Picture Play Authority of Middle West," *TB* (17 May 1913), 7.

35. "Prominent Picture Plays and Picture Play Personalities," *TB* (11 June 1913), 7.

36. "News and Doings in the Motion Picture World," *BJ* (6 September 1913), 4. The subtitle of the banner read, "The Best Motion Pictures in Greater Boston and Where to Find Them."

37. *Photoplay Magazine,* which began appearing monthly in late 1911, also published "photoplay stories," but those were drawn almost exclusively from the Independents.

38. See, for instance, "The Wife's Story [Essanay]," *CT* (12 November 1911), Features: 7. The same story format can be found later in the *Pittsburgh Press,* but in the comics section—see, for instance, "The Lost Son [Lubin]," *PP* (2 March 1913), C6.

39. Other examples include "The Inner Mind" (Selig), *CT* (3 December 1911), 7: 7; and "The First Man—A Newspaper Romance" (Essanay), *CT* (10 December 1911), 7: 7.

40. See the American Film ad, *MPW* (16 March 1912), 980–81. The earliest of these, "Where Broadway Meets the Mountains," appeared in the *DMN* (27 January 1912), 3.

41. These stories included Kalem's *Back to the Kitchen* and Edison's *Charlie's Reform,* appearing in the *Boston Evening Traveler* (24 February 1912), 10A, and (30 March 1912), 10A, respectively.

42. *Motography* pointedly honored Selig and the *Chicago Tribune* for changing the attitude of newspapers and magazines to moving pictures—see "An Innovation," *M* (24 January 1914), 54; and "A Change of Heart," *M* (21 February 1914), 128.

43. "Today's Best Moving Picture Story," *CL* (7 February 1914), 4; and the large ad for the stories in the *CL* (17 February 1914), 7. These stories could be found in such other papers as the *Chicago Tribune* and *Toledo Blade*—see "Today's Best Moving Picture Story," *CT* (5 February 1914), 5; and "Here's the Best Moving Picture Story," *TB* (14 February 1914), 8. The *Tribune* also initiated a biweekly half page of major picture theater ads—see "Special Programs for Today, Sunday, Monday and Tuesday at High-Class Moving Picture Theaters," *CT* (14 February 1914), 7.

44. As an example, see the stories from Edison, Keystone, Thanhouser, and Essanay in "Today's Best Moving Picture Stories," *CL* (18 February 1914), 4. Whether newspapers were being paid to print these film stories or manufacturers were using them to gain "free publicity" remains unclear—see "Free Film Publicity," *Editor and Publisher and Journalist* (13 June 1914), 1097.

45. See the large Famous Players ad, *BJ* (21 March 1914), 7; "The Pride of Jericho," *BJ* (23 March 1914), 7; and "Exhibitors News," *MPW* (30 May 1914), 1278. See also the Pathé ad, *NYDM* (18 February 1914), 28.

46. "Splendid Picture Publicity," *MPW* (11 November 1911), 473.

47. In the *St. Paul Pioneer Press,* the Haskin series ran from 10 October to 21 October 1911 (with the exception of Sunday, 15 October).

48. See, for instance, "The Movies," *DMN* (11 November 1912), 2.

49. "Daily News Reporter Writes from Great California Studios Where They Make Your Wild West Pictures," *DMN* (1 February 1913), 6. According to the 1914 Los Angeles city directory, Price was living in the area by 1913—e-mail communication from Jan Olsson, 24 March 2002. For a more thorough analysis of Price's work, see Abel, "Fan Discourse in the Heartland," forthcoming in a special issue of *Film History,* edited by Amelie Hastie and Shelley Stamp.

50. Price's columns appeared in a half dozen Scripps-McRae newspapers (besides the *Des Moines News*) that I have researched: *Toledo News-Bee, Cleveland Press, Pittsburgh Press, Detroit Times,* and *St. Paul News.* For further information on the Scripps-McRae chain and the United Press Association, see Roy W. Howard, "The United Press As-

sociation," *Editor and Publisher and Journalist* (26 April 1913), 98; and especially Gerald Baldesty, *E. W. Scripps and the Business of Newspapers* (Urbana: University of Illinois Press, 1999).

51. Jas. S. McQuade, "Chicago Letter," *MPW* (19 April 1913), 265.

52. Arthur Leslie ad, *NYMT* (13 December 1914), 7. See also the Arthur Leslie ad, *NYMT* (13 September 1914), 2.

53. Syndicated Publishing Co. ad, *MPN* (8 November 1913), 8.

54. See, for instance, Esther Hoffmann, " 'Drowning Is Pleasant!' " *DMN* (25 July 1914), 1.

55. In fact, Mae Tinee was featured as the week's "movie star" in "The Frame of Public Favor," *CT* (3 January 1915), 8: 7. Frances Peck (aka Mae Tinee) was a friend of Louella Parsons—Samantha Barbas, *The First Lady of Hollywood: A Biography of Louella Parsons* (Berkeley and Los Angeles: University of California Press, 2005), 4.

56. "News of the Movies" first appeared in the *DMT* (12 August 1915), 4, and Day finally began signing the column in the *DMT* (23 February 1916), 4, 5—it was then that the column became a permanent part of the daily "theatrical" page. Day, whose real name was Dorothy Gottlieb, went on to head the public relations department for A. H. Blank's circuit of cinemas in the 1920s and for Central States Theater Corporation from 1933 to 1950—see *Variety Obituaries*, vol. 6, *1964–1968* (New York: Garland, 1988), n.p.

57. Philip Mindil, "Publicity for the Pictures," *MPW* (11 July 1914), 217. See also F. J. Beecroft, "Publicity Men I Have Met," *NYDM* (14 January 1914), 48.

58. This was the case specifically with the *Washington Star*, which was printing "the programs of a large number of moving picture theaters in its amusement columns" almost daily—"Exhibitors News," *MPW* (13 June 1914), 1574. As early as 1911, the newspaper industry itself had concluded that "now . . . women [were] the principal patrons" of Sunday newspapers as a whole—"Sunday Paper for Women," *Editor and Publisher* (29 April 1911), 35.

59. "Cash Prizes for Dramatic Reviews of Moving Picture Shows," *TB* (18 February 1911), 1.

60. See, for instance, "Osgar Cleverly Saves a Historic Film by His Presence of Mind," *DMN* (4 May 1913), 13; "A Heroic Wild West Film That Turned Out a Disappointment," *DMN* (5 May 1913), 6; and "Osgar Pirates the Death Scene in 'Queen Elizabeth,' " *DMN* (14 May 1913), 6.

61. "Many Nickels Make Mr. Movieman a Statler Swell. Yes. REELLY," *CL* (19 January 1913), M1.

62. "Watching the 'Movie' Man Show Films" and "Here Are the Men Who Show You Moving Pictures in Lynn!" *LDI* (8 November 1913), 14.

63. This series ran in the *Canton News* from 15 January 1914 through 22 March 1914. An even earlier, full-page "moral reform" article, "Show Children the World" (through moving pictures), appeared in the *CN* (5 November 1911), 13.

64. Julien T. Baber, "Efficient Publicity Work," *MPW* (30 May 1914), 1270.

Chapter 6: "The Power of Personality in Pictures"

1. See, for instance, Gertrude Price, "Stunning Mary Pickford—Only 19 Now—Quits $10,000 'Movies' Career to Shake Her Golden Locks as a Belasco Star," *TNB* (4 January 1913), 4; and *DMN* (9 January 1913), 7.

2. Advertising & Specialty Company ad, *NYMT* (26 January 1913), 4.2: 4. See, for instance, the Grand Opera ad, which used Pickford's name to promote *The New York Hat, CN* (15 January 1913), 4.

3. The crucial study is Richard deCordova, *Picture Personalities: The Emergence of the Star System in America* (Urbana: University of Illinois Press, 1990); but see also Janet Staiger, "Seeing Stars," *Velvet Light Trap* 20 (Summer 1983), 10–14; Bowser, *The Transformation of Cinema*, 106–19; and Fuller, *At the Picture Show*, 115–49. I briefly build on these studies in *The Red Rooster Scare*, 147–50.

4. See especially deCordova, *Picture Personalities*, 85–92. The most recent study, which focuses on the middle and late 1910s, is Shelley Stamp, " 'It's a Long Way to Filmland': Starlets, Screen Hopefuls, and Extras in Early Hollywood," in Keil and Stamp, *American Cinema's Transitional Era*, 332–51.

5. Warren Susman, " 'Personality' and the Making of Twentieth-Century Culture," in *Culture as History: The Transformation of American Society in the Twentieth Century* (New York: Pantheon, 1973), 281–83.

6. "On the Screen," *MPW* (5 February 1910), 167.

7. The Kalem Stock Company photo also was printed in *MPW* (15 January 1910), 50.

8. For a more thorough analysis of Laemmle's publicity campaign, see deCordova, *Picture Personalities*, 56–61.

9. The *New York Dramatic Mirror* first awarded this title to Vitagraph's Florence Turner, according to Bowser, a bit later, in June 1910—see Bowser, *The Transformation of Cinema*, 113.

10. "Popular Film Star to Visit Here; Signed Photos for Times Readers," *SLT* (22 March 1910), 4; "Moving Picture Star Will Arrive Friday at 5:25 P.M.," *SLT* (24 March 1910), 3; "Moving Picture Star Who Will Reach St. Louis Today," *SLT* (25 March 1910), 13; "Moving Picture Star Who Is Greeted by Thousands on Entering St. Louis," *SLT* (26 March 1910), 3; and " 'Silent Star' Delighted with Reception Here," *SLT* (28 March 1910), 4.

11. The first of these photos appeared in *SLT* (29 March 1910), 13; the last, in *SLT* (22 April 1910), 15.

12. "Vitagraph Notes," *MPW* (2 April 1910), 515; "A Vitagraph Night for the Vitagraph Girl," *FI* (23 April 1910), 3; "The Vitagraph Girl," *NYDM* (23 April 1910), 20; and "Vitagraph Girl Feted," *MPW* (23 April 1910), 644. The sheet music cover for this "waltz song" was reproduced in *Film Index*. Turner's appearances began in Brooklyn, not far from where the Vitagraph studio was located.

13. "The Kalem Girl," *FI* (7 May 1910), 3. For the publicity campaign involving Marion Leonard, see deCordova, *Picture Personalities*, 67–69.

14. "Feature Picture Actor," *NYMT* (20 November 1910), 4.1: 4.

15. Bowser, *The Transformation of Cinema*, 114.

16. Lux Graphicus [Bedding], "On the Screen," *MPW* (8 October 1910), 807.

17. "Notes," *NYMT* (5 March 1911), 4.1: 5.

18. "Vitagraph Notes," *NYMT* (8 January 1911), 4: 6.

19. The first of these star photos was of the "Vitagraph Players," *NYMT* (26 February 1911), 4: 4. By September, the *Morning Telegraph* was reproducing single star photos—see "A Pathé Beauty and Artiste: Octavia Handworth," *NYMT* (3 September 1911), 4: 2.

20. "Picture Personalities," *MPW* (3 December 1910), 1281, (17 December 1910), 1402, and (18 February 1911), 351. See also the photo story about "Miss Mary Pickford," *MPW* (24 December 1910), 1462.

21. "Player on the Screen," *FI* (1 April 1911), 9.

22. Riley & Halliday ad, *NYMT* (5 November 1911), 4.2: 5. At least one such slide (in color), promoting Broncho Billy, survives in a special collection at the Cleveland Public Library. This particular slide still was available from General Film's Poster Department in early 1914—see the General Film ad, *MPW* (31 January 1914), 563. See also the American Film ad, *M* (14 June 1913), 5.

23. *NYDM* (6 December 1911), front cover.

24. See especially Kathryn Fuller, "Motion Picture Story Magazine and the Gendered Construction of the Movie Fan," in *At the Picture Show,* 133–49.

25. The March 1911 issue (the earliest I have seen) included photos of Lottie Briscoe, Maurice Costello, Florence Lawrence, Alice Joyce, Charles Kent, Florence Turner, and Clara Williams—tantalizingly free of any link to the manufacturers. The "Gallery of Picture Players" expanded to a dozen pages in the June 1911 issue.

26. "The Value of Stars," *N* (25 March 1911), 322.

27. Susman, " 'Personality' and the Making of Twentieth-Century Culture," 277. One of those that Susman references is Funk and Wagnalls's *Mental Efficiency Series* (1915).

28. Ibid., 271–80.

29. Mary Whiton Calkins, *An Introduction to Psychology* (New York, 1902), quoted in Glenn, *Female Spectacle,* 93. Glenn provides an excellent overview of this early twentieth-century concept of personality in "The Strong Personality," 74–95.

30. Susman, " 'Personality' and the Making of Twentieth-Century Culture," 277.

31. "Personality a Force in Pictures," *NYDM* (15 January 1913), 44. For an influential study of the concept of authenticity during this period, see Miles Orvell, *The Real Thing: Imitation and Authenticity in American Culture* (Chapel Hill: University of North Carolina Press, 1989).

32. The monthly was sold at newsstands and moving picture theaters as well as to subscribers—"The Motion Picture Story Magazine," *MPSM* (May 1911), inside front cover.

33. "Answers to Inquiries," *MPSM* (August 1911), 144–46.

34. *Photoplay Magazine* initially was far less successful than *Motion Picture Story Magazine* and nearly ceased publication by 1915—Fuller, *At the Picture Show,* 159. In its special issue on moving pictures (3 February 1912), *Billboard* belatedly reproduced photos of individual players, grouped in blocks according to manufacturer.

35. "Novel Advertising for Exhibitors," *NYMT* (19 November 1911), 4.2: 5. Newspaper stories using this material appeared even earlier—see "Popular Actor in Princess Plays," *YV* (15 October 1911), 14; "This Man's Photo Seen Every Day by 300,000," *CN* (5 November 1911), 15.

36. "Santa Claus' Stationary Portraits of Moving Picture Stars," *CL* (24 December 1911), Copperplate Pictorial Section, 3.

37. In Youngstown, "Bullets" Anderson was so popular that, from the fall of 1911 through early 1912, one downtown theater could use his name and photo to promote Essanay westerns as headliners on its Sunday programs; the same thing happened slightly later at a downtown theater in Canton. See, for instance, the Princess ads, *YV*

(22 October 1911), 17, and (17 December 1911), 24; the Orpheum ad, *CN* (28 April 1912), 14; and "Orpheum Theater," *CN* (9 June 1912), 12.

38. See the announcement in *NYMT* (24 September 1911), 4: 6.

39. "Florence E. Turner Wins First Prize in Popularity Contest," *NYMT* (17 December 1911), 8: 1.

40. Ibid.

41. "Popular Player Contest," *MPSM* (January 1912), 133.

42. "Popular Player Contest," *MPSM* (June 1912), 139. These were "honorific prizes" because "the first fifty on the list [would] receive a handsome engraving," while the top five vote-getters would receive five sets of books.

43. "Popular Player Contest," *MPSM* (June 1912), 146.

44. "The Photoplay Matinee Girl," *FI* (3 June 1911), 11–12. The shifting interest of the "matinee girl" from the theater to motion pictures also was noted in "Improvement in Motion Pictures," *B* (4 January 1912), 1. The *Film Index* article even mentions *Motion Picture Story Magazine* in conjunction with this new female fan. During its first five years, the "Answers to Inquiries" column in *Motion Picture Story Magazine* reveals, according to Fuller, that the magazine's readership was 60 percent female and 40 percent male—Fuller, *At the Picture Show,* 140.

45. "Chats with the Players," *MPSM* (February 1912), 135–38.

46. Bowser, *The Transformation of Cinema,* 117.

47. Vitagraph ads, *MPSM* (March 1912), 151, and (June 1912), 161. See also the reproduction of more than a dozen postcards in Q. David Bowers, "Souvenir Postcards and the Development of the Star System, 1912–1914," *Film History* 3.1 (1989), 39–45.

48. See the "Portraits of Popular Picture Players" ad, *MPSM* (May 1912), 159; and the "12 Beautiful Colored Portraits of Motion Picture Players Free" ad, *MPSM* (July 1912), 149.

49. Linder was the only European star to receive more than 1,000 votes, but placed seventy-ninth overall in the *Motion Picture Story Magazine* contest.

50. "At the Leading Theaters," *CL* (21 January 1912), S6; "Jimmie," *MPSM* (May 1911), 6; and "Jimmy, of the Gaumont Co.," *B* (11 November 1911), 15. Gaumont was the only foreign company to have photos of its actors included in *Motion Picture Story Magazine*'s "Gallery of Picture Players" or to have scenes from its travel films appear elsewhere in the magazine.

51. One exception was the "wonderful Henri Krauss," featured in *The Hunchback* (*Notre Dame de Paris*)—see the Dreamland ad, *LDI* (15 February 1913), 2. Even before the many newspaper reports on the Bonnot gang (see chapter 5), some papers continued to circulate stories about sensational French crimes, especially ones committed by women—see, for instance, "Never Trust a Woman," *NYMT* (1 October 1911), Magazine Section, 8; and "Beauty Who Charmed King and Commoner, Blackmailer Who Made the Gay Dogs Pay, Is Held as Thief," *NYMT* (8 October 1911), Magazine Section, 8. This anti-French discourse probably was one reason that French-language newspapers such as *L'Etoile* in Lowell (aimed at middle-class readers) hardly ever had stories or even ads promoting French sensational melodrama films.

52. Very briefly, Gaumont also seemed about to promote Yvette Andreyor—see the photographs in *B* (8 June 1912), 11, and in *MPSM* (September 1912), 13—and Suzanne Grandais—see the photograph in *PM* (February 1913), 8. The only other

French "picture personality" to be singled out was Stacia Napierkowska, in a production photo of Pathé-Frères' *The Anonymous Letter* that appeared on the front cover of *MPSM* (May 1912).

53. "At the Photo Plays," *TNB* (20 April 1912), 2, and (20 June 1912), 10. Nielsen's first films may also have circulated in duped prints: in Youngstown, the Park listed her as a "New York favorite and one of the prettiest actresses on stage" in the cast of *Wine, Woman and Song*, "a fascinating story of American life"—see the Park ad, *YV* (7 April 1912), 21.

54. Central Square Theatre ad, *LDI* (31 August 1912), 2.

55. "At the Photo Plays," *TNB* (14 October 1912), 13. In *Moving Picture World*, the Toledo firm distributing Nielsen's films was Tournament Film Exchange; in the Empress ad, it was called U.S. Feature Film Company.

56. Ada Barrett, "A Plea for the Photoplay," *MPSM* ((July 1911), 115.

57. Here, I would suggest reversing Bowser's argument that "the coming of the feature film influenced the building of the star system"—see Bowser, *The Transformation of Cinema*, 118.

58. See the Victor Film Service ad, *CL* (1 December 1912), B5.

59. See the back cover ad for Helen Gardner Picture Players, *NYDM* (5 June 1912), and the front cover of *NYDM* (24 July 1912).

60. "Florence Lawrence Famous Picture Star," *NYDM* (31 July 1912), 13; " 'The Man with a Hundred Faces,' Interview with John Bunny," *NYDM* (11 September 1912), 25; and "Florence Turner Talks about Acting," *NYDM* (30 October 1912), 28.

61. See the front covers of *NYDM* (2 October 1912), (13 November 1912), and (6 December 1912). For an astute analysis of the mail-order monthly *Ladies World*, especially in relation to the more middle-class monthly *Ladies Home Journal*, see Ellen Gruber Garvey, "Rewriting Mrs. Consumer: Class, Gender, and Consumption," in *The Adman in the Parlor: Magazines and the Gendering of Consumer Culture, 1880s to 1910s* (New York: Oxford University Press, 1996), 135–65.

62. Contest announcement, *NYMT* (18 August 1912), 4.2: 1. The rules governing this contest were byzantine. Although coupons were published each day of the week from August through December, Monday and Saturday coupons counted ten votes each; Tuesday, Thursday, and Friday, five votes each; Wednesday, three votes; and Sunday, only one vote—"Rules Governing Popularity Voting Contest," *NYMT* (3 September 1912), 2.

63. "Martha Russell Voted the Most Popular Moving Picture Player," *NYMT* (29 December 1912), 4.2: 1.

64. The figure for August (10,765), however, places him far lower, closer to Costello (8,109) and Anderson (6,685).

65. "Prize Puzzle Contest," *MPSM* (September 1912), 111–12.

66. "A Tale of the French Settlers," *MPSM* (December 1912), 129.

67. This contest was announced in a large ad in *DMN* (10 February 1913), 3; the winners were listed in a similar ad in *DMN* (17 February 1913), 7. The theaters were both licensed and independent; three were located downtown; one was on the prosperous west side of the city; another was on the less prosperous east side.

68. "Likes Pictures, But Loves Stage More," *NYDM* (26 February 1913), 29; "Actor's Views of Exhibitors," *NYDM* (12 March 1913), 35; and "Unspoiled by Fame Is Mary Pickford," *NYDM* (19 March 1913), 28.

69. Mabel Condon, "Sans Grease Paint and Wig," *M* (12 October 1912), 287–88, (26 October 1912), 325–26, (23 November 1912), 403–4, (21 December 1912), 481, and (15 February 1913), 111–12. A photo of Broncho Billy, "the world's most popular photoplay star," also appeared on the back cover of *Motography* (26 July 1913).

70. "Motography's Gallery of Picture Players," *M* (5 April 1913), 235, and (19 April 1913), 279.

71. Estelle Kegler, "The Charm of Wistfulness," *PM* (August 1913), 34–35.

72. Bowser, *The Transformation of Cinema*, 117–18. A review of Selig's *One of Nature's Noblemen*, for instance, mentions "the cast as given in the advance notice of the film"—see "Critical Reviews of Licensed Films," *NYMT* (4 June 1911), 4: 7.

73. See, for instance, the Orpheum ads, *CN* (21 April 1912), 15, (12 May 1912), 14, and (26 May 1912), 14; and the Odeon ad, *CN* (5 May 1912), 14.

74. See, for instance, the Odeon ads, *CN* (13 October 1912), 12, and (20 October 1912), 12.

75. Odeon ad, *CN* (22 December 1912), 21.

76. Advertising & Specialty ad, *NYMT* (26 January 1913), 4.2: 4.

77. In early 1913, *Motion Picture Story Magazine* boasted of having "nearly a million readers"—"The Musings of a Photoplay Philosopher," *MPSM* (January 1913), 121. The combined readership of the Scripps-McRae newspapers and their affiliates likely was at least several million, although it would be difficult to estimate the number that read Price's syndicated stories.

78. Gertrude Price, "Dolores Cassinelli of Essanay," *DMN* (12 November 1912), 8; Gertrude Price, "King Baggot Detests Sentimental Stuff; Longs to Be Regular Dyed-in-the-Wool Rip Roarin' Jake," *DMN* (7 December 1912), 2; Gertrude Price, "Mary Fuller? Why, Of Course, You've Met Mary! And Such a Deep-Dyed Pessimist Is This Slip-of-a-Girl Who Likes Witches, Old People and Poor Folks Most," *DMN* (28 December 1912), 4; Gertrude Price, "Funniest, Fattest Man in the Movies Is John Bunny Who Plays 'Mr. Pickwick,' " *DMN* (29 December 1912), 4; "The Airman's Hoodoo Is What Mabel of the Movies Calls Her Pretty Self," *DMN* (4 March 1913), 7; and " 'Dimples' Costello Writes Name on Thousands of Pictures for Dear Public," *DMN* (11 April 1913), 12.

79. Gertrude Price, "Everybody Writes to Pretty Helen, Starlet of the Flying A," *DMN* (23 February 1913), 4; Price, "This Boy Acts, Travels, Studies; But Success Has Not Spoiled Him," *DMN* (2 June 1913), 2; and Price, " 'Movie Industry Is Great New Field for 'Natural' Actors, Girls and Boys," *DMN* (8 October 1913), 6. W. Stephen Bush later would "pay a well-deserved tribute" to child actors in a column that first appeared as "The Screen Children's Gallery," *MPW* (28 February 1914), 1066.

80. Aunt Gertie, "A Little Personality about a Great Big Man [Thomas Edison]," *DMN* (3 June 1913), 3.

81. "The Dustman, as Told by Aunt Gertie," *DMN* (9 June 1913), 5; and "The Little Mermaid, as Told by Aunt Gertie," *DMN* (26 June 1913), 7.

82. Aunt Gertie, "Just Think—This Real Princess Loves to Go to the Movies," *DMN* (25 May 1913), 3.

83. "He's the Matinee Idol of the Movies," *TNB* (11 December 1912), 2; "Movie Stars Who Play Leads in Western Dramas at Unique Theater," *DMN* (12 December 1912), 7; Price, "The Great Spirit Took Mona, But in This Girl She Still Lives," *DMN* (6 February 1913), 12; Price, "Would You Guess That This Cowboy Is a New York

Actor?" *DMN* (15 February 1913), 2; and Price, "Picturesque Indian Maid Is Fearless-Ambitious-Clever!" *DMN* (27 April 1913), 4. See also the article on Louise Lester and her "Flying A" western series: "Everyone Is for Busy Ann, 'Calamity' Ann You Know!" *DMN* (29 April 1913), 10.

84. "Runs, Rides, Rows," *DMN* (16 April 1913), 6.

85. Early in 1912, American chose the *News* as one of fifty dailies across the country in which to publish "'Flying A' stories" so that people would subsequently "want to see them." Although only three stories ever appeared, they suggest that "Flying A" films circulated and may have been popular in Des Moines, despite the fact that no theater ever advertised them. See the American Film ad in *MPW* (16 March 1912), 980–81; and the first story, "The Grub Stake Mortgage—A Moving Picture Short Story of Western Life," *DMN* (17 January 1912), 10.

86. See, for instance, "Here They Are! Snapshots from 'Wounded Knee,' Where Our 'Movie' Experts Are," *DMN* (23 October 1913), 4; and Price, "Indian Braves Adopt Heap Big 'Movie' Man and Call Him 'Wanbli Wiscasa,'" *DMN* (2 November 1913), 4. For information in the trade press on this film's production, see Charles J. Ver Halen, "Bringing the Old West Back," *MPN* (22 November 1913), 19–20.

87. James McQuade, "Chicago Letter," *MPW* (7 February 1914), 660, and (14 March 1914), 1388–89; and "'Buffalo Bill' Picture Shown," *MPW* (14 March 1914), 1370. For a good discussion of this film's production, distribution, and exhibition, as well as its difference from Cody's previous enterprises, see Joy S. Kasson, *Buffalo Bill's Wild West: Celebrity, Memory, and Popular History* (New York: Hill and Wang, 2000), 257–63.

88. Gertrude Price, "'Miss Billie Unafraid,'—Torn by a Tiger but Nervy as Ever to Act the Most Daring Things Even Seen on the Stage!—Heroine of Movies," *DMN* (17 November 1912), 7; Price, "Stunning Mary Pickford," 7; "Movie Queen Is Alice Joyce," *DMN* (1 March 1913), 1; and "Live with Flowers and Grow Beautiful, Says Girl," *DMN* (29 November 1913), 5.

89. "Bored by World, Actress Goes to 'Movies' to Get Thrills!" *DMN* (17 March 1913), 8.

90. "She Reads Balzac, Likes Baseball, and Is Pretty," *DMN* (9 April 1913), 4.

91. "Face Is Fortune of Tallest Picture Player Who Sheds Real Tears for Sake of Art," *DMN* (25 March 1913), 4.

92. Gertrude Price, "No One Will Ride Pinto but Dainty, Daring Clara," *DMN* (27 March 1913), 6.

93. "No Thrill to Her to Be 'Killed' 365 Times a Year," *DMN* (24 December 1913), 8.

94. See, for instance, "Daring Girl Rider Coming," *DMN* (27 July 1912), 3; and "Summer Amusements," *DMN* (28 July 1912), 12.

95. Gertrude Price, "Charming Little Woman Runs 'Movie' Business by Herself, and Makes Big Success," *DMN* (9 February 1913), 2; "Lucky Thirteen Word Proves to be a New Money Making Position," *DMN* (15 May 1913), 8; and Gertrude Price, "Sad Endings Are All Right, Says This Woman Director," *DMN* (27 September 1913), 5.

96. Gerald Baldasty, *E. W. Scripps and the Business of Newspapers* (Urbana: University of Illinois Press, 1999).

97. E. W. Scripps to Robert F. Paine, 26 February 1906—cited in Baldasty, *E. W. Scripps and the Business of Newspapers,* 147.

98. Quotation from Minutes of Conference Between E. W. Scripps, E. B. Scripps, and George Putnam, 17 August 1902—cited in Baldasty, *E. W. Scripps and the Business of Newspapers,* 104.

99. The *News* was especially interested in the Socialist Party's political triumph in Milwaukee, Wisconsin—see, for instance, Dorothy Dale, "The Rule of the Socialists in Milwaukee and What They Are Doing," *DMN* (21 July 1910), 4.

100. R. F. Paine to W. D. Wasson, 27 January 1906—cited in Baldasty, *E. W. Scripps and the Business of Newspapers,* 141.

101. Baldasty, *E. W. Scripps and the Business of Newspapers,* 143.

102. John Brigham, *History of Des Moines and Polk County, Iowa* I (Chicago: S. J. Clarke, 1911), 558.

103. See, for instance, "Des Moines Women Found in All Fields of Labor," *DMN* (7 July 1907), 9; and "Women Are Rapidly Taking the Jobs That Belong to Men," *DMN* (6 October 1907), Sunday Supplement, 3. According to these articles, 1,200 women ran machines in the garment, hosiery, and glove factories, another 1,200 "girls and women" worked as store clerks, perhaps close to that number were employed in insurance offices and allied printing companies, and hundreds more were working as stenographers (or typewriters, as they were then often called) in other businesses and government offices or as nurses in hospitals. Years later, the *News* was still promoting this "special attention," but now with a featured "Women's Page"—see the front-page ad in *DMN* (24 June 1914), 1.

104. "At the Moving Picture Playhouses," *DMRL* (9 February 1913), 7; and "News of Photoplays and Photoplayers," *DMRL* (13 April 1913), 7.

105. The *Cleveland Leader* several times reported favorably on the continuing protest in the trade press against using "movies" because "it harms the business"—"Photo-Plays and Players," *CL* (10 December 1911), S5; "Protest Against Use of Name, 'Movie'," *CL* (20 October 1912), S5. See also " 'Spectator's' Comments," *NYDM* (15 May 1912), 25; and Epes Winthrop Sargent, "Advertising for Exhibitors," *MPW* (31 August 1912), 872. For an excellent analysis of this nomenclature debate over moving pictures, see Waller, "Photodramas and Photoplays, Stage and Screen, 1909–1915," 575–85.

106. Most explicitly in drama critic Walter Pritchard Eaton's "The Menace of the Movies," *American Magazine* 86 (September 1913), 60. But see also J. Esenwein, J. Berg, and A. Leeds, *Writing the Photoplay: A Complete Manual of Instruction in the Nature, Writing and Marketing of the Moving-Picture Play* (Springfield, Mass.: Home Correspondence School, 1913).

107. Gertrude Price, "Here's a Story for Kiddies; 10-Year Old Movie Star Draws $100 a Week," *DMN* (30 December 1912), 1.

108. " 'Most Engaged Girl' in All America Is Miss Adrienne Kroell; She's Proposed to Nearly Every Day—And by a Different Man!" *DMN* (14 November 1912), 12.

109. See the Edison ad, *NYMT* (25 January 1914), 5: 2; and "Important Films of the Week," *NYMT* (1 February 194), 5: 5. Although unheralded, Price was one of many women working as prominent journalists at the time, a dozen of which were featured in a series written by A. C. Hasselbarth, "Women Writers of American Press," in *Editor and Publisher and Journalist,* between October 1913 and May 1914.

110. For especially relevant studies of the cultural figure of the New Woman, see Lois Rudnick, "The New Woman," in Adele Heller and Lois Rudnick, eds., *1915: The*

Cultural Moment (New Brunswick, N.J.: Rutgers University Press, 1991), 69–81; Susan Glenn, "Introduction," in *Female Spectacle: The Theatrical Roots of Modern Feminism* (Cambridge, Mass.: Harvard University Press, 2000), 1–8; and Singer, *Melodrama and Modernity*, 241–53.

111. See "Suffragettes See Parade Picture," *DMN* (25 June 1912), 5; and *"Votes for Women* in Picture Play," *DMN* (27 June 1912), 5. For more information on and an analysis of *Votes for Women*, see Stamp, *Movie-Struck Girls*, 175–79. The *Cleveland Leader* also was a strong advocate of women's suffrage; moreover, it often heralded the New Woman in articles on athletic figures, such as "A Modern Race of Amazons," *CL* (6 August 191), C1; in full-page ads for the Ohio Woman Suffrage Party, such as "Her Job," *CL* (1 September 1912), M4; and in stories such as "The Stick-Up Girl: A True Story of an Uncaught Outlaw," *CL* (16 March 1913), Feature Section, 1.

112. Gertrude Price, "A Day with General Jones and Her Army of 'Hikers' on Their Way to the Capitol," *DMN* (23 February 1913), 3.

113. "Western Girl You Love in the 'Movies' Is a Sure Enough Suffrager," *DMN* (11 February 1913), 3. The "cowgirls" of the 101 Ranch Wild West show also were linked with the suffrage movement—see "Girls with Wild West Show to Help Women Gain Equal Suffrage," *TB* (17 August 1912), 7.

114. Gertrude Price, "Only Movie Players Live in this Town," *TNB* (6 January 1914), 13.

115. Gertrude Price, "Sees the Movies as Great New Field for Women Folk," *TNB* (30 March 1914), 14. The article includes a head shot of Price herself, as one of those "women folk." Only a month later did *Motion Picture Story Magazine* publish a long article on professional women working as scenario editors in the industry, including Marguerite Bertsch (Vitagraph), Louella Parsons (Essanay, Chicago), Josephine Rector (Essanay, Niles), and several "graduates of Beta Breuil's 'scenario class' " at Vitagraph—Edwin M. La Roche, "A New Profession for Women," *MPSM* (May 1914), 83–88.

116. Parsons is quoted in Rosalind Rosenberg, *Beyond Separate Spheres: Intellectual Roots of Modern Feminism* (New Haven, Conn.: Yale University Press, 1982), 172. I myself have taken the quotation from Glenn, *Female Spectacle*, 5.

117. See the Victoria ad, *RH* (24 January 1913), 6; "Actor Enjoys Work in Motion Picture Talks," *NYMT* (9 March 1913), 4.2: 8; the Cameraphone ad, *CL* (9 March 1913), M5; and "Actor Bushman at Cameraphone Today," *CL* (16 March 1913), M10.

118. See the 31 May 1913 and 7 June 1913 Treasurer's Statements, Pawtucket Theater Cash Books, 1911–1913—Keith-Albee Collection, Special Collections, University of Iowa Library. The reported receipts of $268.80 were higher than Saturday's ($199.95), usually the best day of the week; the previous Friday's receipts had been $78.55, and the following Friday's, $60.10. The fee for the Kid's appearance was $60.

119. The Film Man, "Comment and Suggestion," *NYDM* (30 April 1913), 25; "Personality—Box-Office Magnet," *NYDM* (14 January 1914), 52.

120. "Here Is an Easy Way to See Pictures Free," *CL* (15 December 1912), S5; and "Who Will Get Free Tickets This Week?" *CL* (22 December 1912), S5.

121. See, for instance, "If You Would See Photo-Plays Free, Send in Answers to These Puzzles," *CL* (19 January 1913), M5; and "Get Acquainted with Scenes and Players; To Know Them Means Free Theater Tickets," *CL* (23 February 1913), M11.

122. "Photoplay Magazine's Great Popularity Contest," *PM* (July 1913), 61. Mutual

also promoted its "Stars of the Film World" in a full-page ad in *PM* (September 1913), 121.

123. "Popular Player Contest," *MPSM* (March 1913), 141, and (April 1913), 117–18. A more reliable subscription figure probably was 215,000—see "Class and Trade Publications," in *American Newspaper Annual and Directory* (Philadelphia: N. W. Ayer & Son, 1914), 1230.

124. "Popular Player Contest," *MPSM* (June 1913), 113, and (October 1913), 109, 112. Explaining Fielding's popularity in 1913 demands further research. In 1914, the magazine sponsored a "Great Artist Contest," and the top four winners included one young newcomer: Earle Williams (487,295 votes), Clara Kimball Young (442,340), Mary Pickford (437,670), and Warren Kerrigan (435,355)—"Who Are the Greatest Photoplay Artists," *MPSM* (January 1914), 174–75; and "The Great Artist Contest," *MPSM* (October 1914), 128.

125. "Ladies' World Contest," *MPW* (3 January 1914), 56; and "Bushman Wins Big Contest," *MPW* (23 May 1910), 1120–21.

126. Initially each coupon clipped from the monthly, filled out, and mailed counted ten votes, but in "the closing weeks . . . each coupon sent in counted fifty votes"—"Bushman Wins Big Contest," 1120. Even with this complicated system, the *World* estimated that perhaps half of *Ladies World*'s 1 million readers sent in coupons. Costello was very popular outside the United States, for instance, winning a contest held by *Pictures and Picture Goers* in London—see "Costello Wins Contests Abroad," *MPW* (27 June 1914), 1837.

127. "Exhibitors News: St. Louis," *MPW* (4 April 1914), 94.

128. "Exhibitors News: St. Louis," *MPW* (9 May 1914), 842, and (13 June 1914), 1556. According to the latter column, "The *St. Louis Globe-Democrat* devoted a whole page of its Sunday magazine on May 17 to photographs and histories of the men and women of St. Louis who have made a mark on the moving picture stage."

129. Jennifer Bean, "Technologies of Early Stardom and the Extraordinary Body," in Jennifer Bean and Diane Negra, eds., *A Feminist Reader in Early Cinema* (Durham, N.C.: Duke University Press, 2002), 412. This essay is reprinted, with slight revisions, from *camera obscura* 48 (2001), 9–56.

130. James M. McQuade, "Photoplayer Who Flirts with Fate," *FI* (3 June 1911), 11. See also "Trip in Hydroplane Climax of Thrills for Kathlyn Williams," *NYMT* (6 October 1912), 4.2: 2. Later stories on the filming of Selig's *The Adventures of Kathlyn* often celebrated Williams's courage in working with wild animals—see "Lions Can't Scare This Young Lady," *NYMT* (21 December 1913), 5: 1.

131. "Serious Mishap of Picture Actress," *MPW* (9 December 1911), 823; "Essanay Leading Woman a Real Heroine," *MPW* (16 December 1911), 894; and "Heroic Edna Fisher," *NYDM* (20 December 1911), 29.

132. Louis Reeves Harrison, "The 'Bison-101' Headliners," *MPW* (27 April 1912), 321.

133. Kalem titled its 1915 film series with Joyce simply *The Alice Joyce Series*.

134. Bean, "Technologies of Early Stardom and the Extraordinary Body," 34.

135. Susan Glenn makes the case for an earlier parallel development in the theater by focusing on figures such as Bernhardt, Eva Tanguey, and Marie Dressler: "By opening a space for female performers to become *both* spectacles *and* personalities, the popular theater promoted the development of the first self-consciously 'modern'

expression of new womanhood."—see Glenn, *Female Spectacle*, 7. The crucial distinction with female movie performers was their engagement in action, thrills, and danger.

136. See, for instance, Esther Hoffmann, " 'Drowning Is Pleasant!' " *DMN* (25 July 1914), 1.

137. Jan Olsson's research reveals that Price apparently accepted a permanent position at the *Los Angeles Record* (a Scripps-McRae newspaper), eventually serving as editor of the paper's "Women's Page" and later as its "Club" editor. She remained a member of the *Record*'s staff into the early 1930s. E-mail communication from Jan Olsson, 24 March 2002.

138. Although never a fan of the western, W. Stephen Bush did admit that, in the early 1910s, it once "was thought to be the foundation and hope of the motion picture [but] it came to its destined end where the 'freak' feature will shortly follow it."—see Bush, "No Lowering of Standards," *MPW* (24 January 1914), 389. See also an article on the U.S. consul reports in England, claiming that cowboy and Indian pictures no longer were popular in Europe—"Valuable Consular Reports," *MPW* (9 May 1914), 811.

139. Esther Hoffmann, "Most Beautiful Blond in World in Movieland," *DMN* (6 September 1914), 5; and "The Little Movie Star Is Good Friend of Princess of Portugal," *DMN* (9 September 1914), 5. The epithet for Gish came from David Belasco. Hoffman's stories soon began to appear under the title "Who's Who on the Films"—see *DMN* (19 October 1914), 7.

140. "Mutual Starts Things," *MPW* (13 December 1913), 1260.

141. See, for instance, "Mutual Girl Series," *MPW* (27 December 1913), 1525; and the Mutual ad, *NYMT* (1 February 1914), 5: 3.

142. See especially Singer, *Melodrama and Modernity*, 223–25.

143. "Movie Girl in Social Whirl Is Artist-Horsewoman-Wit," *DMN* (8 April 1913), 4.

144. "Every Movie Fan Knows This Face," *DMN* (10 July 1914), 1.

145. See, for instance, the Billie Burke column that ran almost daily in the *Des Moines News*, from June through at least September 1912. For one week in October 1912, the *Boston Globe* ran a series signed by Madame Sarah Bernhardt—see the announcement in *BG* (6 October 1912), 51. See also Lily Langtry, "Beauty, Youth and the Joy of Living," *NYMT* (27 October 1912), 2: 8; and "Lillian Russell Seen in Kinemacolor Beauty Talk," *NYMT* (9 March 1913), 4.2: 1.

146. Idah M'Glone Gibson, "Would You Have a Pleasing Personality?" *DMN* (10 July 1914), 5.

147. Idah M'Glone Gibson, "The Eyes Reveal What You Are," *DMN* (15 July 1914), 5; and Gibson, "Beverly Bayne Dispels Beauty Beliefs," *DMN* (16 July 1914), 5.

148. Gibson, "Would You Have a Pleasing Personality?" 5.

149. William Lord Wright, "Dame Fashion and the Movies," *MPSM* (September 1914), 107–10.

150. "Exhibitors News: Washington, D.C.," *MPW* (13 June 1914), 1574.

151. George Blaisdell, " 'Little Mary' and Her Correspondents," *MPW* (11 July 1914), 280. According to Blaisdell, " 'America's Sweetheart' [was] the striking title applied to her by Exhibitor [Sid] Grauman of San Francisco."

BIBLIOGRAPHY

Abel, Richard. *The Ciné Goes to Town: French Cinema, 1896–1914.* Berkeley and Los Angeles: University of California Press, 1994.

———. *The Red Rooster Scare: Making Cinema American, 1900–1910.* Berkeley: University of California Press, 1999.

Abel, Richard, and Rick Altman, eds. *The Sounds of Early Cinema.* Bloomington: Indiana University Press, 2001.

Alexander, Charles C. *Here Lies the Country: Nationalism and the Arts in Twentieth-Century America.* Bloomington: Indiana University Press, 1980.

Allen, Robert C. "Manhattan Myopia, or, Oh, Iowa!" *Cinema Journal* 35.3 (Spring 1996), 75–103.

Altman, Rick. *Film/Genre.* London: British Film Institute, 1999.

———. *Silent Film Sound.* New York: Columbia University Press, 2004.

Anderson, Benedict. *Imagined Communities: Reflections on the Origin and Spread of Nationalism.* Rev. ed. London: Verso, 1991.

Anderson, Robert. "The Motion Picture Patents Company: A Re-evaluation." In Tino Balio, ed., *The American Film Industry,* 133–52. 2nd ed. Madison: University of Wisconsin Press, 1985.

Appleby, Joyce, Lynn Hunt, and Margaret Jacob. *Telling the Truth about History.* New York: Norton, 1994.

Baldasty, Gerald. *E. W. Scripps and the Business of Newspapers.* Urbana: University of Illinois Press, 1999.

Barnard, Timothy. "The 'Machine Operator': *Deus ex machina* of the Storefront Cinema." *Framework* 43.1 (Spring 2001): 41–75.

Bean, Jennifer. "Technologies of Early Stardom and the Extraordinary Body." In Jennifer Bean and Diane Negra, eds., *A Feminist Reader in Early Cinema,* 404–43. Durham, N.C.: Duke University Press, 2002.

Bernardi, Daniel, ed. *The Birth of Whiteness: Race and the Emergence of U.S. Cinema.* New Brunswick, N.J.: Rutgers University Press, 1996.

Bertellini, Giorgio. "Black Hands and White Hearts: Italian Immigrants as 'Urban

Racial Types' in Early American Film Culture." *Urban History* 31.3 (2004), 374–398.

Billington, Ray Allen. *Land of Savagery, Land of Promise: The European Imagery of the American Frontier in the Nineteenth Century.* New York: Norton, 1981.

Blake, Jody. *Le tumulte noir: Modernist Art and Popular Entertainment in Jazz Age Paris, 1900–1930.* University Park: Pennsylvania State University Press, 1999.

Blau, Herbert. *The Audience.* Baltimore: Johns Hopkins University Press, 1990.

Blight, David W. *Race and Reunion: The Civil War in American Memory.* Cambridge, Mass.: Harvard University Press, 2001.

Blom, Ivo. *Jean Desmet and the Early Dutch Film Trade.* Amsterdam: Amsterdam University Press, 2003.

Bogdanovich, Peter. *Allan Dwan: The Last Pioneer.* New York: Praeger, 1971.

Bowser, Eileen. *The Transformation of Cinema, 1907–1915.* New York: Scribner's, 1991.

Brewster, Ben. "*Traffic in Souls:* An Experiment in Feature-Length Narrative Construction." *Cinema Journal* 31.1 (Fall 1991), 37–56.

Brownlow, Kevin. *The War, the West, and the Wilderness.* New York: Knopf, 1978.

Buscombe, Edward, and Roberta Pearson, eds. *Back in the Saddle Again: New Essays on the Western.* London: British Film Institute, 1998.

Butsch, Richard. *The Making of American Audiences: From Stage to Television, 1850-1990.* Cambridge: Cambridge University Press, 2000.

Charney, Leo, and Vanessa Schwartz, eds. *Cinema and the Invention of Modern Life.* Berkeley: University of California Press, 1995.

Chatwin, Bruce. *The Reel Civil War: Mythmaking in American Film.* New York: Knopf, 2001.

Cherchi Usai, Paolo, ed. *The Griffith Project.* Vols. 4–7. London: British Film Institute, 2000–2003.

Cooper, Mark Garrett. *Love Rules: Silent Hollywood and the Rise of the Managerial Class.* Minneapolis: University of Minnesota Press, 2003.

Cronon, William, George Miles, and Jay Gitlin, eds. *Under an Open Sky: Rethinking America's Western Past.* New York: Norton, 1992.

Cullen, Jim. *The Civil War in Popular Culture: A Reusable Past.* Washington, D.C.: Smithsonian Institute, 1995.

Czitrom, Daniel J. *Media and the American Mind: From Morse to McLuan.* Chapel Hill: University of North Carolina Press, 1982.

De Grave, Kathleen. *Swindler, Spy, Rebel: The Confidence Woman in Nineteenth-Century America.* Columbia: University of Missouri Press, 1995.

deCordova, Richard. *Picture Personalities: The Emergence of the Star System in America.* Urbana: University of Illinois Press, 1990.

Denning, Michael. *Mechanic Accents: Dime Novels and Working-Class Culture in America.* 2nd ed. London: Verso, 1998.

Enro, Arthur L., Jr., ed. *Cotton Was King: A History of Lowell, Massachusetts.* Lowell: New Hampshire Publishing, 1976.

Enstad, Nan. *Ladies of Leisure, Girls of Adventure: Working Women, Popular Culture, and Labor Politics at the Turn of the Twentieth Century.* New York: Columbia University Press, 1999.

Everson, William K. *A Pictorial History of the Western Film.* New York: Citadel, 1969.

Fuller, Kathryn. *At the Picture Show: Small-Town Audiences and the Creation of Movie Fan Culture.* Washington, D.C.: Smithsonian Institution, 1996.

Garvey, Ellen Gruber. *The Adman in the Parlor: Magazines and the Gendering of Consumer Culture, 1880s to 1910s.* New York: Oxford University Press, 1996.

Glaab, Charles N., and Morgan J. Barclay. *Toledo: Gateway to the Great Lakes.* Tulsa, Okla.: Continental Heritage Press, 1982.

Glassberg, David. *American Historical Pageantry: The Uses of Tradition in the Twentieth Century.* Chapel Hill: University of North Carolina Press, 1990.

Gleason, Philip. "American Identity and Americanization." In Stephen Thernstrom, ed., *Harvard Encyclopedia of American Ethnic Groups,* 38–47. Cambridge, Mass.: Harvard University Press, 1980.

Glenn, Susan. *Daughters of the Shtetl: Life and Labor in the Immigrant Population.* Ithaca, N.Y.: Cornell University Press, 1990.

———. *Female Spectacle: The Theatrical Roots of Modern Feminism.* Cambridge, Mass.: Harvard University Press, 2000.

Gomery, Douglas. *Shared Pleasures: A History of Movie Presentation in the United States.* Madison: University of Wisconsin Press, 1992.

Grieveson, Lee. *Policing Cinema: Movies and Censorship in Early Twentieth-Century America.* Berkeley: University of California Press, 2004.

Griffiths, Alison. "Playing at Being Indian: Spectatorship and the Early Western." *Journal of Popular Film and Television* 29.3 (Fall 2001), 100–111.

———. *Wondrous Differences: Cinema, Anthropology, and Turn-of-the-Century Visual Culture.* New York: Columbia University Press, 2003.

Gunning, Tom. *D. W. Griffith and the Origins of American Narrative Film: The Early Years at Biograph.* Urbana: University of Illinois Press, 1991.

Hansen, Miriam. *Babel and Babylon: Spectatorship in American Silent Film.* Cambridge, Mass.: Harvard University Press, 1991.

Hansen, Miriam Bratu, "The Mass Production of the Senses: Classical Cinema as Vernacular Modernism." In Christine Gledhill and Linda Williams, eds., *Re-inventing Film Studies,* 332–50. London: Arnold, 2000.

Havig, Alan. "The Commercial Amusement Audience in Early 20th-Century American Cities." *Journal of American Culture* 5.1 (1982), 1–19.

Heinze, Andrew R. *Adapting to Abundance: Jewish Immigrants, Mass Consumption, and the Search for American Identity.* New York: Columbia University Press, 1990.

Hertogs, Daan, and Nico de Klerk, eds. *Nonfiction from the Teens.* Amsterdam, Nederlands Filmmuseum, 1994.

Higgins, Steven. "I film di Thomas H. Ince." *Griffithiana* 18–21 (October 1984), 155–94.

Higson, Andrew. "The Concept of National Cinema." *Screen* 30.4 (1989), 36–46.

———. "The Limiting Imagination of National Cinema." In Mette Hjort and Scott MacKenzie, eds., *Cinema and Nation,* 63–74. London: Routledge, 2000.

Hobsbawm, Eric J. *Social Bandits and Primitive Rebels: Studies in Archaic Forms of Social Movements in the 19th and 20th Century.* Glencoe, Ill.: Free Press, 1959.

Hobsbawm, Eric J., and Terence Ranger, eds. *The Invention of Tradition.* Cambridge: Cambridge University Press, 1983.

Holmquist, June Drenning. *They Chose Minnesota: A Survey of the State's Ethnic Groups.* St. Paul: Minnesota Historical Society, 1981.

Horwitz, Tony. *Confederates in the Attic: Dispatches from the Unfinished Civil War.* New York: Pantheon, 1998.

Hulfish, David. *Cyclopedia of Motion-Picture Work.* Chicago: American Technical Society, 1914 [1911].

Ignatiev, Noel. *How the Irish Became White.* New York: Routledge, 1995.

Jacobson, Matthew Frye. *Special Sorrows: The Diasporic Imagination of Irish, Polish, and Jewish Immigrants in the United States.* Cambridge, Mass.: Harvard University Press, 1995.

————. *Whiteness of a Different Color: European Immigrants and the Alchemy of Race.* Cambridge, Mass.: Harvard University Press, 1998.

Kammen, Michael. *The Mystic Chords of Memory: The Transformation of Tradition in American Culture.* New York: Knopf, 1991.

Kasson, Joy S. *Buffalo Bill's Wild West: Celebrity, Memory, and Popular History.* New York: Hill and Wang, 2000.

Keil, Charlie. *Early American Cinema in Transition.* Madison: University of Wisconsin Press, 2001.

Keil, Charlie, and Shelley Stamp, eds. *American Cinema's Transitional Era: Audiences, Institutions, Practices.* Berkeley and Los Angeles: University of California Press, 2004.

Kiehn, David. *Broncho Billy and the Essanay Company.* Berkeley, Calif.: Farwell Books, 2003.

Koszarski, Richard. *Fort Lee: The Film Town.* Rome: John Libbey, 2004.

Kusmer, Kenneth. *A Ghetto Takes Shape: Black Cleveland, 1870–1930.* Urbana: University of Illinois Press, 1976.

Lacassin, Francis. "The Éclair Company and European Popular Literature from 1907 to 1919." *Griffithiana* 47 (May 1993), 61–87.

Lamphere, Louise. *From Working Daughters to Working Mothers: Immigrant Women in a New England Industrial Community.* Ithaca, N.Y.: Cornell University Press, 1987.

Leach, William. *Land of Desire: Merchants, Power, and the Rise of a New American Culture.* New York: Pantheon, 1993.

Leonard, Elizabeth D. *All the Daring of the Soldier: Women of the Civil War Armies.* New York: Norton, 1999.

Melder, Keith. *Life and Times in Shoe City: The Shoe Workers of Lynn.* Salem, Mass.: Essex Institute, 1979.

Musser, Charles, and Carol Nelson. *High-Class Moving Pictures: Lyman H. Howe and the Forgotten Era of Traveling Exhibition, 1880–1920.* Princeton, N.J.: Princeton University Press, 1991.

Ohmann, Richard. *Selling Culture: Magazines, Markets, and Class at the Turn of the Century.* London: Verso, 1996.

Olsson, Jan. "Pressing Inroads: Metaspectators and the Nickelodeon Culture." In John Fullerton, ed., *Screen Culture: History and Textuality,* 113–35. Eastleigh: John Libbey, 2004.

Orvell, Miles. *The Real Thing: Imitation and Authenticity in American Culture.* Chapel Hill: University of North Carolina Press, 1989.

Peiss, Kathy. *Cheap Amusements: Working Women and Leisure in Turn-of-the-Century New York.* Philadelphia: Temple University Press, 1986.

Peterson, Jennifer. *World Pictures: Travelogue Films and the Lure of the Exotic.* Durham, N.C.: Duke University Press, 2005.

Portes, Jacques. *Fascination and Misgivings: The United States in French Opinion, 1870–1914.* Trans. Elborg Forster. Cambridge: Cambridge University Press, 2000.

Pressly, Thomas J. *Americans Interpret Their Civil War.* New York: Free Press, 1962.

Quinn, Michael. "Distribution, the Transient Audience, and the Transition to the Feature Film." *Cinema Journal* 40.2 (Winter 2001), 35–56.

Rabinovitz, Lauren. *For the Love of Pleasure: Women, Movies, and Pleasure in Turn-of-the-Century Chicago.* New Brunswick, N.J.: Rutgers University Press, 1998.

Reddin, Paul. *Wild West Shows.* Urbana: University of Illinois Press, 1999.

Reynolds, Herbert. "Aural Gratification with Kalem Films: A Case History of Music, Lectures, and Sound Effects, 1907–1917." *Film History* 12.4 (2000), 417–42.

Rosenzweig, Roy. *Eight Hours for What We Will: Workers and Leisure in an Industrial City, 1870–1920.* Cambridge: Cambridge University Press, 1983.

Ross, Steven J. *Working-Class Hollywood: Silent Film and the Shaping of Class in America.* Princeton, N.J.: Princeton University Press, 1998.

Rudnick, Lois. "The New Woman." In Adele Heller and Lois Rudnick, eds., *1915: The Cultural Moment,* 69–81. New Brunswick, N.J.: Rutgers University Press, 1991.

Rydell, Robert. *All the World's a Fair.* Chicago: University of Chicago Press, 1984.

Saxton, Alexander. *The Rise and Fall of the White Republic: Class, Politics, and Mass Culture in Nineteenth-Century America.* London: Verso, 1990.

Silber, Nina. *The Romance of Reunion: Northerners and the South, 1865–1900.* Chapel Hill: University of North Carolina Press, 1993.

Simmon, Scott. *The Invention of the Western Film: A Cultural History of the Genre's First Half-Century.* Cambridge: Cambridge University Press, 2003.

Singer, Ben. "Manhattan Nickelodeons: New Data on Audiences and Exhibitors." *Cinema Journal* 34.3 (Spring 1995), 5–35.

———. *Melodrama and Modernity: Early Sensational Cinema and Its Contexts.* New York: Columbia University Pres, 2000.

———. "New York, Just Like I Pictured It. . . . " *Cinema Journal* 35.3 (Spring 1996), 104–28.

Slotkin, Richard. *Gunfighter Nation: The Myth of the Frontier in Twentieth-Century America.* New York: Atheneum, 1992.

Smith, Andrew Brodie. *Shooting Cowboys and Indians: Silent Western Films, American Culture, and the Birth of Hollywood.* Boulder: University of Colorado Press, 2003.

Staiger, Janet. *Bad Women: Regulating Sexuality in Early American Cinema.* Minneapolis: University of Minnesota Press, 1995.

———. "Combination and Litigation: Structures of US Film Distribution, 1891–1917." *Cinema Journal* 23.2 (Winter 1984), 41–72.

———. "Seeing Stars." *Velvet Light Trap* 20 (Summer 1983), 10–14.

Stamp, Shelley. *Movie-Struck Girls: Women and Motion Picture Culture after the Nickelodeon.* Princeton, N.J.: Princeton University Press, 2000.

Stokes, Melvyn, and Richard Maltby, eds. *American Movie Audiences: From the Turn of the Century to the Early Sound Era.* London: British Film Institute, 1999.

Streeby, Shelley. *American Sensations: Class, Empire, and the Production of Popular Culture.* Berkeley: University of California Press, 2002.

Sullivan, Larry, and Lydia Cushman Schurman, eds. *Pioneers, Passionate Ladies, and Private Eyes.* New York: Hawthorne Press, 1996.

Susman, Warren. *Culture as History: The Transformation of American Society in the Twentieth Century.* New York: Pantheon, 1973.

Teaford, J. C. *Cities of the Heartland: The Rise and Fall of the Industrial Midwest.* Bloomington: Indiana University Press, 1993.

Thirteenth Census of the United States, III: Population Reports by States. Washington, D.C.: Government Printing Office, 1913.

Thompson, Kristin. *Exporting Entertainment: America in the World Film Market, 1907–1934.* London: British Film Institute, 1985.

Trachtenberg, Alan. *The Incorporation of America: Culture and Society in the Gilded Age.* New York: Hill and Wang, 1982.

Truettner, William. *The West as America.* Washington, D.C.: Smithsonian Institution, 1991.

Turconi, David, and Paolo Cherchi Usai, eds. *Vitagraph Co. of America: Il cinema prima di Hollywood.* Pordenone: Edizioni Studio Tesi, 1987.

Valentine, Maggie. *The Show Starts on the Sidewalk: An Architectural History of the Movie Theatre.* New Haven, Conn.: Yale University Press, 1994.

Van Tassel, David D., ed. *The Encyclopedia of Cleveland History.* Bloomington: Indiana University Press, 1996.

Verhoeff, Nanna. *After the Beginning: Westerns before 1915.* Utrecht: University of Utrecht, 2002.

Waller, Gregory. *Main Street Amusements: Movies and Commercial Entertainment in a Southern City, 1896–1930.* Washington, D.C.: Smithsonian Institution, 1995.

———, ed. *Moviegoing in America: A Sourcebook in the History of Film Exhibition.* London: Blackwell, 2002.

———. "Photodramas and Photoplays, Stage and Screen, 1909–1915." In Leonardo Quaresima and Laura Vicki, eds., *The Tenth Muse: Cinema and the Other Arts,* 575–85. Udine: Forum, 2001.

Wallis, Michael. *The Real Wild West: The 101 Ranch and the Creation of the American West.* New York: St. Martin's Press, 1999.

West, Elliott, and Paula Petrik, eds. *Small Worlds: Children and Adolescents in America, 1850–1950.* Lawrence: University Press of Kansas, 1992.

Whissel, Kristen. "Regulating Mobility: Technology, Modernity, and Feature-Length Narration in *Traffic in Souls.*" *camera obscura* 49 (2002), 1–29.

Wilinsky, Barbara. "Flirting with Kathlyn: Creating the Mass Audience." In David Desser and Garth S. Jowett, eds., *Hollywood Goes Shopping,* 34–56. Minneapolis: University of Minnesota Press, 2000.

Woal, Linda Kowall. "Romaine Fielding: The West's Touring Auteur." *Film History* 74 (1995), 401–25.

Worster, Donald. *Rivers of Empire: Water, Aridity, and the Growth of the American West.* New York: Oxford University Press, 1985.

Young, Elizabeth. *Disarming the Nation: Women's Writing and the American Civil War.* Chicago: University of Chicago Press, 2002.

INDEX

Text: 10/12 Baskerville
Display: Baskerville
Compositor: Binghamton Valley Composition, LLC
Printer and binder: Maple-Vail Manufacturing Group